THOMAS DANIEL YOUNG, *General Editor*

EDMUND WILSON

A Bibliography

Fugitive Bibliographies

ROBERT PENN WARREN

ALLEN TATE

EDMUND
Wilson

A BIBLIOGRAPHY

Compiled by Richard David Ramsey

David Lewis   New York

For Mr. and Mrs. Richard Dean Ramsey

Copyright © 1971 by David Lewis, Inc.

Library of Congress Catalog card number: 72-132842
SBN number: 912012-03-X
Manufactured in the United States of America
by Haddon Craftsmen, Inc.

Designed by Edward Aho.

First Printing.

CONTENTS

CONTENTS

PREFACE

Despite Edmund Wilson's reputation as a distinguished critic and his many contributions to a variety of genres, no one has attempted to compile a comprehensive list of his writings and the most important commentary about them. This bibliography, which proposes to fill this need, is indebted to numerous checklists, the most significant of which are the following: Warner Berthoff, *Edmund Wilson*, No. 67 in University of Minnesota Pamphlets on American Writers (Minneapolis: University of Minnesota Press, 1968), pp. 46-47; Charles P[aul] Frank, *Edmund Wilson*, No. 152 in Twayne's United States Authors Series, ser. ed. Sylvia E. Bowman (New York: Twayne Publishers, 1970), pp. 197-204; William J. Lewis, "Edmund Wilson: A Bibliography," *Bulletin of Bibliography*, XXV (May 1958), 145-149, 151; Arthur Mizener, "Edmund Wilson: A Checklist," *Princeton University Library Chronicle*, V, No. 2 (February 1944), 62-78; Sherman Paul, *Edmund Wilson: A Study of Literary Vocation in Our Time* (Urbana: University of Illinois Press, 1965), pp. 222-224; and the "Edmund Wilson" item in *Bibliography Supplement*, ed. Richard M. Ludwig, supplement to Vol. III of *Literary History of the United States*, ed. Robert E. Spiller *et al.* (New York: Macmillan Company, 1959), pp. 238-239.

This bibliography is divided into twelve sections:

Section I is a chronological list of books written or edited by Wilson. Contents of each book are listed; contents of subsequent editions are listed only when they differ from the original. Every attempt has been made to obtain comprehensive listings, although some omissions may have occurred because of the lack of complete publication records. In Section I signed reviews of Wilson's books are listed alphabetically by the reviewers' surnames; unsigned reviews are then listed alphabetically by name of the publication in which the review appeared. Section II is an alphabetical list of Wilson's essays and short descriptive and expository prose sketches. The reprintings of each essay are given in chronological order. Although I have indicated some of the more substantial alterations which Wilson made in certain essays, his customary practice of revising between subsequent reprintings has precluded describing all such changes. The contents of an essay not reprinted in one of Wilson's books are given with the entry in Section II.

Book Reviews (Section III) by Wilson are listed alphabetically according to author or editor of the work reviewed. Plays and dialogues, stories, and poems are cited in the same manner as essays. The first part of Section VII is a list of translations of Wilson's works arranged alphabetically by language and, under each language, chronologically by date of publication; the second part gives an alphabetical list of Wilson's translations into English. The four parts of Miscellanea (Section VIII) are General Miscellanea, Editorial Comment by Wilson, Periodicals Edited by Wilson, and Drawings by Wilson. Locations of manuscript collections are given alphabetically in Section IX. The correspondence (Section X) is divided into three parts: Letters by Wilson, Letters to Wilson, and Letters about Wilson; only published letters are cited. Section XI is an alphabetical list of biographical and critical items about Wilson, with descriptive annotations. Theses and dissertations are listed alphabetically in Section XII.

This bibliography is intended to be complete through March 1970. To minimize errors, virtually every item has been examined. Though some articles were printed anonymously, a diligent effort was made to verify the authorship of all items. Brackets ([ ]) have been placed around any title supplied from another printing or from the first line of the material. The abbreviation *EW* is used in place of the full name *Edmund Wilson* in citations.

Although space does not permit naming the hundreds of people who have helped in the compilation of this work, I should like to express my appreciation to Mr. Edmund Wilson; Miss Marilyn Craig, Mrs. Lois V. Greist, and Mrs. Deane D. Stevens of the Joint University Libraries, Nashville, Tennessee; Miss Fairba Russell of the East Dallas Christian School, Dallas, Texas; Mr. Donald Gallup, curator of the Beinecke Rare Book and Manuscript Library, New Haven, Connecticut; Miss Margaret Nicholson and Mr. John Peck of Farrar, Straus and Giroux; Mr. Robert H. Land, chief of the General Reference and Bibliography Division, Library of Congress; Signore Emanuele Casamassima, director of the Biblioteca Nazionale Centrale, Florence, Italy; and Mr. John P. Baker of the New York Public Library. The Sparks Memorial Fellowship Fund of Phi Kappa Phi gave me financial assistance during much of the research.

DAVID RAMSEY

Nashville, Tennessee
July 1, 1970

I / BOOKS

A. Books by Wilson

The Evil Eye: A Comedy in Two Acts (play). Princeton, New Jersey: Property of Princeton University Triangle Club, 1915. "For the Use of Cast Candidates Exclusively," this is a 26-page booklet noncirculating in the Rare Book Collection, Princeton University Library. The lyrics for this musical comedy presented by the Princeton University Triangle Club were written by F. Scott Fitzgerald.

The Undertaker's Garland (essay, poems, and story), by John Peale Bishop and EW. New York: Alfred A. Knopf, 1922.

> *Contents* (by EW)
>   "Preface" (essay)
>   "The Death of the Last Centaur" (poem)
>   "The Funeral of a Romantic Poet" (poem)
>   "The Death of an Efficiency Expert" (poem)
>   "The Death of a Soldier" (story)
>   "Emily in Hades" (story)
>   "Epilogue" (poem)

Signed Reviews

Benet, William Rose. *Literary Review of the New York Evening Post,* III, No. 8 ["Fall Book Number"] (28 October 1922), section 3, p. 145.

Holden, Raymond. *New Republic,* XXXIII (14 February 1923), 329.

Morris, Lloyd. *Literary Digest International Book Review,* I, No. 1 (December 1922), 88-89.

Pure, Simon. *Bookman,* LVI (January 1923), 609.

Rascoe, Burton. *Vanity Fair,* XIX, No. 3 (November 1922), 25, 108.

Seldes, Gilbert. *Dial,* LXXIII (November 1922), 574-578.

Unsigned Reviews
Bookman, LVI (December 1922), 511.
New York Times Book Review, 28 January 1923, p. 2.

Discordant Encounters: Plays and Dialogues. New York: Albert and Charles Boni, 1926.

Contents

"The Poet's Return: Mr. Paul Rosenfeld and Mr. Matthew Josephson"

"The Delegate from Great Neck: Mr. Van Wyck Brooks and Mr. Scott Fitzgerald"

"Mrs. Alving and Œdipus: A Professor of Fifty and a Journalist of Twenty-five"

"In the Galapagos: Mr. William Beebe and a Marine Iguana"

"Cronkhite's Clocks: A Pantomime with Captions (for a score by Leo Ornstein)"

"The Crime in the Whistler Room"

Signed Reviews
Aiken, Conrad. *World* (New York), 3 April 1927, p. 13m.

Deutsch, Babette. *New York Herald Tribune Books,* III, No. 23 (20 February 1927), 17.

Fadiman, Clifton P. *Literary Review,* VII, No. 32 (16 April 1927), 4.

H., S. *Boston Transcript,* 16 March 1927, part 3, p. 4, col. 7.

Unsigned Reviews
Dial, LXXXII (May 1927), 433.
Independent, CXIX (30 July 1927), 117.
Saturday Review of Literature, III (2 April 1927), 700.
Theatre Arts Monthly, XI (December 1927), 960.

I Thought of Daisy (novel). New York: Charles Scribner's Sons, 1929.

Signed Reviews
Chamberlain, John. *New York Times Book Review,* 18 August 1929, p. 9.

Dawson, Margaret Cheney. *New York Herald Tribune Books,* V, No. 49 (25 August 1929), 5.

Dodd, Lee Wilson. *Saturday Review of Literature,* VI (23 November 1929), 439.

Meade, Norah. *Nation,* CXXX (1 January 1930), 20.

Segal, David I. See in Items about Wilson.

Tasker, J. Dana. *Outlook and Independent,* CLII (28 August 1929), 710-711.

Unsigned Review
Springfield Republican, 15 September 1929, p. 7e.

I Thought of Daisy. London: W. H. Allen, 1952. Reissue.

Unsigned Reviews
Times (London), 8 March 1952, p. 4, col. 6.
Times Literary Supplement, 7 March 1952, p. 169.

I Thought of Daisy. New York: Ballantine Books, 1953. Paperback reissue.

Contents
> This and the following reissue contain the novel preceded by "Foreword, 1953."

Signed Reviews
Aldridge, John W. See in Items about Wilson.

Crane, Milton. *Saturday Review of Literature,* XXXVI, No. 20 (16 May 1953), 16, 41.

I Thought of Daisy. New York: Farrar, Straus and Young, 1953. Hardback reissue of Ballantine Books printing.

Signed Reviews
Aldridge, John W. See in Items about Wilson.

Crane, Milton. *Saturday Review of Literature,* XXXVI, No. 20 (16 May 1953), 16, 41.

I Thought of Daisy, No. 1876 in Penguin Books. Harmondsworth, Middlesex, England: Penguin Books, 1963. Reissue without "Foreword, 1953."

Signed Review
Ricks, Christopher. *New Statesman,* LXV (8 February 1963), 208.

I Thought of Daisy, No. NS28 in Avon Books. New York: Avon Books, 1968. Reissue.

Galahad [and] *I Thought of Daisy* (story and novel), rev. ed. of *I Thought of Daisy*. New York: Farrar, Straus and Giroux, 1967.

Contents
  "Galahad" (story)
  "I Thought of Daisy" (novel)

Signed Reviews
Davis, Robert Gorham. *New York Times Book Review*, 9 July 1967, pp. 1, 43.
Hicks, Granville. *Saturday Review*, L (1 July 1967), 17-18.
Jackson, Paul R. *Books Today* (*Chicago Sunday Tribune*), IV (9 July 1967), 1.
Jones, Frank N. *Library Journal*, CXII (15 June 1967), 2437.
Kauffman, Stanley. *New Republic*, CLVI (17 June 1967), 27.
Lask, Thomas. *New York Times*, 21 June 1967, p. 45.
Levensohn, Alan. *Christian Science Monitor*, LIX (6 July 1967), 13.
Shapiro, Karl. *Book Week*, IV (25 June 1967), 5.
Thompson, John. *New York Review of Books*, IX (28 September 1967), 8, 10, 12.

Unsigned Reviews
Kirkus Service, XXXV (15 May 1967), 637.
Publishers' Weekly, CXCI (17 April 1967), 52.
Time: The Weekly Newsmagazine, LXXXIX (23 June 1967), 98.

Galahad [and] *I Thought of Daisy*, rev. ed. of *I Thought of Daisy*, No. N319 in Noonday Books. New York: Farrar, Straus and Giroux, 1967. Paperback reissue.

Galahad [and] *I Thought of Daisy*, rev. ed. of *I Thought of Daisy*. Toronto: Ambassador Books, 1967. Reissue.

Galahad [and] *I Thought of Daisy*, rev. ed. of *I Thought of Daisy*, No. N319 in Noonday Books. Toronto: Ambassador Books, 1967. Paperback reissue.

Poets, Farewell! (poems and essays). New York: Charles Scribner's Sons, 1929.

Contents

    I. ["When all the young were dying"]
    II. ["Poets, farewell!—farewell, gay pastorals!"]
    III. ["Here where your blue bay's hook is half begun"]
    IV. ["—And you who faint at either's hard expense"]
    V. ["Dim screens obscure the dawn"]

Signed Reviews

Dodd, Lee Wilson. *Yale Review*, XIX (Winter 1930), 389-391.

McHugh, Vincent. *New York Evening Post*, 16 November 1929, p. 12m, cols. 7-8.

Walton, Eda Lou. *Nation*, CXXX (2 April 1930), 399.

Z[abel], M[orton] D[auwen]. *Poetry: A Magazine of Verse*, XXXV (January 1930), 222-226.

Unsigned Review

New York Times Book Review, 1 December 1929, p. 45.

Axel's Castle: A Study in the Imaginative Literature of 1870-1930 (essays). New York: Charles Scribner's Sons, 1931. Reprinted in 1932, 1934, 1935, 1936, 1939, 1940, 1942.

Contents

    Dedicatory epistle to Christian Gauss
    "Symbolism"
    "W. B. Yeats"
    "Paul Valery"
    "T. S. Eliot"
    "Marcel Proust"
    "James Joyce"
    "Gertrude Stein"
    "Axel and Rimbaud"
    "Appendix I" (general miscellanea)
      "Three Versions of a Passage from James Joyce's New Novel"
    "Appendix II" (translation by Wilson)
      "Memoirs of Dadaism by Tristan Tzara"

Signed Reviews

Brown, E. K. *International Journal of Ethics*, XLII (January 1932), 249. See also same author in Items about Wilson.

Chevalier, H[aakon] M[aurice]. *University of California Chronicle*, XXXIII (October 1931), 478-482.

C[oates], R. M. *New Yorker*, VII, No. 3 (7 March 1931), 86, 88.

Delatte, F. *Revue de l'Université de Bruxelles*, XXXIX (October-November 1933), 123-128.

Dupee, Frederick. *Symposium: A Critical Review*, II (April 1931), 264-267.

Hansen, Harry. *World* (New York), 9 February 1931, p. 9.

———. *Harper's Magazine*, CLXII (April 1931), "Among the New Books," pages not numbered.

Hazlitt, Henry. *Nation*, CXXXII (4 March 1931), 245-246.

Hicks, Granville. *Forum and Century: The Magazine of Controversy*, LXXXV (April 1931), viii, x, xii.

Josephson, Matthew. See same author, "Essays on Modern Masters," in Items about Wilson.

Mattheissen, F. O. See in Items about Wilson.

Munson, Gorham. *Atlantic Monthly*, CXLVIII (August 1931), "The Atlantic Bookshelf," p. 12.

O'Brien, Justin. *Commonweal*, XIII (29 April 1931), 721-722.

Rascoe, Burton. *New York Herald Tribune Books*, VII (1 March 1931), 7.

R[obbins], F[rances] L[amont]. *Outlook and Independent*, CLVII (18 February 1931), 267.

Smith, Bernard. *Modern Monthly*, VI, No. 1 (Winter 1931), 100-104.

Tate, Allen. *Hound & Horn*, IV (July-September 1931), 619-624.

Troy, William. *New York Times Book Review*, 22 February 1931, p. 2.

Unsigned Reviews

Among Our Books (Carnegie Library of Pittsburgh), XXXVI, No. 4 (April 1931), 36.

Booklist, XXVII (April 1931), 357.

Boston Evening Transcript, 18 March 1931, part 3, p. 3, col. 5.

Open Shelf (Cleveland Public Library), No. 9-10 (September 1931), p. 121.

Springfield Republican, 14 February 1931, p. 8.

Axel's Castle: A Study in the Imaginative Literature of 1870-1930. London: Charles Scribner's Sons, 1931. Reissue. Reprinted in 1932, 1934, 1935, 1936, 1939, 1940, 1942, 1950.

Signed Reviews
Collins, H. P. *Criterion: A Literary Review*, X (July 1931), 745-747.
Dobrée, Bonamy. *Spectator*, CXLVI (18 April 1931), 641-642.
Murphy, Gwendolyn. *Discovery: A Monthly Popular Journal of Knowledge* (London), XVII (August 1936), 248-249.

Axel's Castle: A Study in the Imaginative Literature of 1870-1930. New York: Charles Scribner's Sons, 1948, 1950. Reissue.

Axel's Castle: A Study in the Imaginative Literature of 1870-1930, Student's Ed. New York: Charles Scribner's Sons, 1958. Paperback reissue.

Axel's Castle: A Study in the Imaginative Literature of 1870-1930, No. SL12 in Scribner Library. New York: Charles Scribner's Sons, 1959. Paperback reissue.

Axel's Castle: A Study in the Imaginative Literature of 1870-1930, Student's Ed. London: Charles Scribner's Sons, 1959. Paperback reissue.

Axel's Castle: A Study in the Imaginative Literature of 1870-1930, in Scribner Library. New York: Charles Scribner's Sons, 1960. Paperback reissue.

Axel's Castle: A Study in the Imaginative Literature of 1870-1930, No. 539L in Fontana Library. London and Glasgow: William Collins Sons and Company, 1961. Reissue.

Signed Reviews
Kermode, Frank. See same author, "Edmund Wilson and Mario Praz," in Items about Wilson.
Raymond, John. *Punch*, CCLIV (3 April 1968), 508.

Unsigned Reviews
Times (London), 21 October 1967, p. 22, cols. 2-3.
Times Literary Supplement, 5 May 1961, p. 280.

The American Jitters: A Year of the Slump (essays). New York: Charles Scribner's Sons, 1932.

Contents
"Dwight Morrow in New Jersey"
"Political Headquarters"
"Foster and Fish"
"Aladdin's Lecture Palace"
"The Bank of United States"
"The Metropolitan"
"Communists and Cops"
"Detroit Motors"
"Red Cross and County Agent"
"Senator and Engineer"
" 'Still—': Meditations of a Progressive"
"A Bad Day in Brooklyn"
"The First of May"
"Two Protests"
"Frank Keeney's Coal Diggers"
"Tennessee Agrarians"
"The Freight-Car Case"
"The Enchanted Forest"
"Indian Corn Dance"
"The Fourth of July"
"Hoover Dam"
"The City of Our Lady the Queen of the Angels"
"Eisenstein in Hollywood"
"The Jumping-Off Place"
"The Independent Farmer"
"Lawrence, Mass."
"The Best People"
"The Case of the Author"
"A Man in the Street"

Signed Reviews
Barnes, Harry Elmer. *American Journal of Sociology,* XXXVIII (September 1932), 307-308.
C., T. *Commonweal,* XVI (29 June 1932), 248.
Chamberlain, John. *New York Times Book Review,* 17 April 1932, p. 10.
Stolberg, Benjamin. *New York Herald Tribune Books,* VIII (17 April 1932), 7.
Warner, Arthur. *Nation,* CXXXV (6 July 1932), 17.
Whipple, Leon. *Survey,* LXVIII (1 July 1932), 312.

Unsigned Reviews

Among Our Books (Carnegie Library of Pittsburgh), XXXVII, No. 8 (October 1932), 59.

Boston Evening Transcript, 30 April 1932, "Book Section," p. 2, cols. 5-6.

Springfield Republican, 16 April 1932, p. 10.

Devil Take the Hindmost [British title for *The American Jitters*]: *A Year of the Slump.* London: Charles Scribner's Sons, 1932. Reissue with different title.

Signed Reviews

Agar, Herbert. *New Statesman and Nation,* N.S. IV (6 August 1932), 160.

Common, Jack. *Adelphi* (London), N.S. (3rd ser.) V, No. 1 (October 1932), 72-73.

Culver, Donald. *Scrutiny,* I (September 1932), 196-199.

Fluegge, Karl W. *Zeitschrift für Sozialforschung,* II, No. 3 (November 1933), 476.

Unsigned Reviews

Spectator, CXLIX (6 August 1932), 188.

Times Literary Supplement, 2 June 1932, p. 400.

The American Jitters: A Year of the Slump, in Essay Index Reprint Series. Freeport, New York: Books for Libraries Press, 1968. Reissue.

The American Jitters: A Year of the Slump. See also "The Earthquake: October, 1930-October, 1931" in Essays.

Travels in Two Democracies (dialogues, essays, and story). New York: Harcourt, Brace and Company, 1936.

Contents

"Prologue" (dialogue)
   "The Man in the Mirror"
"U. S. A., November, 1932-May, 1934" (primarily essays)
   I. "Election Night" (essay)
   II. "Hull-House in 1932" (essay)
   III. "Illinois Household" (dialogue)
   IV. "A Great Dream Come True" (essay)
   V. "Inaugural Parade" (essay)
   VI. "Shaw at the Metropolitan" (essay)
   VII. "Sunshine Charley" (essay)
   VIII. "The Old Stone House" (essay)

IX. "The Second Battle of Oriskany" (essay)
X. "Saving the Right People and Their Butlers" (essay)
XI. "What to Do Till the Doctor Comes: From the Diary of a Drinker-Out" (essay)
XII. "Miss Barrows and Doctor Wirt" (essay)
XIII. "Japanese Cherry Blossoms" (essay)
"Flashback: Lieutenant Franklin" (story)
"Lieutenant Franklin"

"U.S.S.R., May-October, 1935" (essays)
I. "Old England"
II. "London to Leningrad"
III. "Leningrad Theaters"
IV. "On the Margin of Moscow"
["First Days in Moscow"]
["Letters in the Soviet Union"]
["Stalin as Ikon"]
["Russian Idyls"] (includes EW's translation of the Russian popular song ["Ekh, sharabán, da sharabán"])
["Russian Paradoxes"] (fragment of essay)
V. "Volga Idyll"
VI. "Odessa: Counter-Idyll" (includes EW's translation of S. Marshak's poem "Stripes and Whiskers")
VII. "Final Reflections"
"Epilogue"
"The Traveler"

Signed Reviews

Brickell, Herschell. *Review of Reviews*, XCIV (July 1936), 12.

Cowley, Malcolm. See same author, "Flight from the Masses" and "Postscript to a Paragraph," in Items about Wilson.

Duffus, R. L. *New York Times Book Review*, 14 June 1936, pp. 3, 20.

Feld, Rose C. *New York Herald Tribune Books*, XII (7 June 1936), 6.

Hazlit, Henry. *Yale Review*, XXVI (Autumn 1936), 187-189.

Hindus, Maurice. *Saturday Review of Literature*, XIV (6 June 1936), 7.

Marshall, Margaret. *Nation*, CXLII (24 June 1936), 816-817.

Mason, H. A. *Scrutiny*, V (March 1937), 456-458.

Parrish, Wayne W. *Churchman,* CL (August 1936), 17.
Pass, Sylvia. *Christian Century,* LIII (2 September 1936), 1165-1166.
Rodman, Selden. *Common Sense,* V, No. 7 (July, 1936), 25-26.
S., L. A. *Christian Science Monitor,* XXVIII (15 July 1936), 10.
Schnell, Jonathan. *Forum and Century,* XCVI (September 1936), vii.
Thompson, Frederic. *Commonweal,* XXIV (31 July 1936), 351.
Thompson, Ralph. *New York Times,* 29 May 1936, p. 17.

Unsigned Reviews
Booklist, XXXII (July 1936), 317.
Catholic World, CXLIII (September 1936), 765.
Christian Science Monitor, XXVIII (15 July 1936), 10.
Current History, XLIV (July 1936), 127-128.
Springfield Republican, 11 June 1936, p. 12.
Time: The Weekly Newsmagazine, XXVII (1 June 1936), 68.

Travels in Two Democracies. Toronto: George McLeod (distributor), 1936. Reissue.

This Room and This Gin and These Sandwiches: Three Plays. New York: New Republic, 1937.

Contents
    "The Crime in the Whistler Room"
    "A Winter in Beech Street"
    "Beppo and Beth"

Signed Reviews
B., W. R. *Saturday Review of Literature,* XVI (24 July 1937), 20.
Burke, Kenneth. *Nation,* CXLV (31 July 1937), 133-134.
Eaton, Walter Prichard. *New York Herald Tribune Books,* XIV (19 September 1937), p. 25.

Unsigned Review
Theatre Arts Monthly, XXI (October 1937), 825.

The Triple Thinkers: Ten Essays on Literature. New York: Harcourt, Brace and Company, 1938.

Contents

"Mr. More and the Mithraic Bull"
"Is Verse a Dying Technique?"
"In Honor of Pushkin"
   I. " 'Evgeni Onegin' "
   II. " 'The Bronze Horseman' " (includes EW's translation of
      Pushkin's "The Bronze Horseman: A Petersburg Tale")

"A. E. Housman: The Voice, Sent Forth, Can Never Be Re-
called"
"Flaubert's Politics"
"The Ambiguity of Henry James"
"John Jay Chapman: The Mute and the Open Strings"
"The Satire of Samuel Butler"
"Bernard Shaw at Eighty"
"Marxism and Literature"

Signed Reviews

Blackmur, R. P. *Virginia Quarterly Review*, XIV (Summer 1938), 446-450.

Boyd, Ernest. *Saturday Review of Literature*, XVII (26
March 1938), 10.

Conolly, Francis X. *Commonweal*, XXVII (15 April 1938),
695-696.

Dupee, F. W. *Partisan Review*, IV, No. 6 (May 1938),
48-51.

Freeman, Joseph. *New Masses*, XXVII (12 April 1938),
"Literary Section," pp. 73-79.

Goodale, Ralph Hinsdale. *Christian Century*, LV (1 June
1938), 695-696.

Guerard, Albert. *New York Herald Tribune Books*, XIV
(27 March 1938), 2.

Jack, Peter Munro. *New York Times Book Review*, 20
March 1938, p. 2.

McCarty, Norma. See in Items about Wilson.

Matthiessen, F. O. *New Republic*, XCIV (6 April 1938),
279-280.

R[eynolds], H[orace]. *Christian Science Monitor*, XXX (28
March 1938), 16.

Riley, Lester Leake. *Churchman,* CLII (15 May 1938), 26-27.

R[odman], S[elden]. *Common Sense,* VII, No. 5 (May 1938), 26-27.

Strauss, Harold. *Yale Review,* XXVII (Summer 1938), 816-819.

Wilson, T[ed] C. See in Items about Wilson.

Zabel, Morton Dauwen. *Nation,* CXLVI (21 May 1938), 590-592.

Unsigned Reviews
Booklist, XXXIV (1 April 1938), 286.

Pratt Institute Quarterly Booklist, Ser. V, No. 108 (Winter 1939), 24.

Time: The Weekly Newsmagazine, XXI (21 March 1938), 75.

Wisconsin Library Bulletin, XXXIV (May 1938), 110.

The Triple Thinkers: Ten Essays on Literature. Toronto: George McLeod (distributor), 1938. Reissue.

Signed Review
Brown, E. K. See in Items about Wilson.

The Triple Thinkers: Ten Essays on Literature. London: Oxford University Press, 1938. Reissue.

Signed Reviews
Chapman, Frank. *Criterion: A Literary Review,* XVIII (January 1939), 350-352.

Evans, B. Ifor. *Year's Work in English Studies,* XIX (1938), 11-12.

Rickword, Edgell. *Spectator,* CLXI (11 November 1938), 819-820.

Stonier, G. W. *New Statesman and Nation,* XVI (22 October 1938), 652, 654.

Unsigned Review
Times Literary Supplement, 12 November 1938, p. 729.

The Triple Thinkers: Twelve Essays on Literary Subjects, Rev. and Enl. Ed. of *The Triple Thinkers: Ten Essays on Literature.* New York: Oxford University Press, 1948.

Contents
"Foreword"
"Mr. More and the Mithraic Bull"
"Is Verse a Dying Technique?"
"In Honor of Pushkin"
    I. " 'Evgeni Onegin' "
    II. " 'The Bronze Horseman' " (includes EW's translation of
        Pushkin's "The Bronze Horseman: A Petersburg Tale")
"A. E. Housman: The Voice, Sent Forth, Can Never Be Re-
    called"
"The Politics of Flaubert"
"The Ambiguity of Henry James"
"John Jay Chapman"
"Bernard Shaw at Eighty"
"Marxism and Literature"
"Morose Ben Jonson"
" 'Mr. Rolfe' "
"The Historical Interpretation of Literature"

Signed Reviews
Farrelly, John. *New Republic,* CXIX (22 November 1948),
  24-25.
Redman, Ben Ray. *Saturday Review of Literature,* XXXII
  (29 January 1949), 30.
Whicher, George F. *New York Herald Tribune Weekly
Book Review,* XXV (2 January 1949), 5.

Unsigned Review
New Yorker, XXIV, No. 49 (29 January 1949), 64.

The Triple Thinkers: Twelve Essays on Literary Subjects,
Rev. and Enl. Ed. of *The Triple Thinkers: Ten Essays on
Literature.* London: John Lehmann, 1952. Reissue.

Signed Review
Thompson, F. Y. *Year's Work in English Studies,* XXXIII
  (1952), 15.

Unsigned Review
Times Literary Supplement, 9 May 1952, pp. 313, 318.

The Triple Thinkers: Twelve Essays on Literary Subjects,
Rev. and Enl. Ed. of *The Triple Thinkers: Ten Essays on
Literature,* No. A550 in Pelican Books. Harmondsworth,
Middlesex, England: Penguin Books, 1962. Reissue.

The Triple Thinkers: Twelve Essays on Literary Subjects,
Rev. and Enl. Ed. of *The Triple Thinkers: Ten Essays on
Literature.* New York: Oxford University Press, 1963. Re-
issue with corrections.

The Triple Thinkers: Twelve Essays on Literary Subjects,
Rev. and Enl. Ed. of *The Triple Thinkers: Ten Essays on
Literature,* No. GB96 in Galaxy Books. New York: Oxford
University Press, 1963. Reissue.

The Triple Thinkers: Twelve Essays on Literary Subjects,
Rev. and Enl. Ed. of *The Triple Thinkers: Ten Essays on
Literature.* Toronto: Oxford University Press, 1963. Re-
issue.

The Triple Thinkers: Twelve Essays on Literary Subjects,
Rev. and Enl. Ed. of *The Triple Thinkers: Ten Essays on
Literature,* No. GB96 in Galaxy Books. Toronto: Oxford
University Press, 1963. Reissue.

*To the Finland Station: A Study in the Writing and Acting
of History* (essays). New York: Harcourt, Brace and Company, 1940.

Contents

I.
1. "Michelet Discovers Vico"
2. "Michelet and the Middle Ages"
3. "Michelet and the Revolution"
4. "Michelet Tries to Live His History"
5. "Michelet Between Nationalism and Socialism"
6. "Decline of the Revolutionary Tradition: Renan"
7. "Decline of the Revolutionary Tradition: Taine"
8. "Decline of the Revolutionary Tradition: Anatole France"

II.
1. "Origins of Socialism: Babeuf's Defense"
2. "Origins of Socialism: Saint-Simon's Hierarchy"
3. "Origins of Socialism: The Communities of Fourier and
   Owen"
4. "Origins of Socialism: Enfantin and the American Socialists"
5. "Karl Marx: Prometheus and Lucifer"
6. "Karl Marx Decides to Change the World"
7. "Friedrich Engels: The Young Man from Manchester"
8. "The Partnership of Marx and Engels"
9. "Marx and Engels: Grinding the Lens"

10. "Marx and Engels Take a Hand at Making History"
11. "The Myth of the Dialectic"
12. "Marx and Engels Go Back to Writing History"
13. "Historical Actors: Lassalle"
14. "Historical Actors: Bakúnin"
15. "Karl Marx: Poet of Commodities and Dictator of the Proletariat"
16. "Karl Marx Dies at His Desk"

   III.
1. "Lenin: The Brothers Ulyánov"
2. "Lenin: The Great Headmaster"
3. "Trotsky: The Young Eagle"
4. "Trotsky Identifies History with Himself"
5. "Lenin Identifies Himself with History"
6. "Lenin at the Finland Station"

"Appendices" (general miscellanea)
   "Appendix A" (play)
      "Karl Marx: A Prolet-Play"
   "Appendix B" (essay)
      "Marx on the Differential Calculus"
   "Appendix C" (translation by Wilson)
      "Engels to Marx, February 13, 1851"
   "Appendix D" (essay)
      "Herr Vogt and His Modern Successors"
"Index"

Signed Reviews

Auden, W. H. *Common Sense,* IX, No. 11 (November 1940), 22-23.

Cleveland, C. O. *Commonweal,* XXXIII (25 October 1940), 32-33.

Cowley, Malcolm. See same author, "From the Finland Station," in Items about Wilson.

Fadiman, Clifton. *New Yorker,* XVI, No. 33 (28 September 1940), 60-61.

Florinsky, Michael T. *New York Times Book Review,* 6 October 1940, pp. 5, 18.

Gannett, Lewis. *Boston Evening Transcript,* 28 September 1940, part 5, p. 3, cols. 1-2.

Garrison, W. E. *Christian Century,* LVII (4 December 1940), 1514.

Hacker, Louis. *Saturday Review of Literature,* XXII (5 October 1940), 11-12.

Hook, Sidney. *New York Herald Tribune Books*, XVII (29 September 1940), 5.

Jones, Howard Mumford. *Yale Review*, XXX (Winter 1941), 393-395

McC., H. *More Books: The Bulletin of the Boston Public Library*, XV (November 1940), 382.

Niebuhr, Reinhold. *Nation*, CLI (28 September 1940), 274-276.

Thompson, Wallace F. *Churchman*, CLIV (1 December 1940), 18.

Unsigned Reviews

Atlantic Monthly, CLXVI (December 1940), "The Atlantic Bookshelf," pages not numbered.

Time: The Weekly Newsmagazine, XXXVI, No. 16 (14 October 1940), 116, 118.

To the Finland Station: A Study in the Writing and Acting of History. Toronto: McLeod (distributor), 1940. Reissue.

Signed Review

Brown, E. K. See in Items about Wilson.

To the Finland Station: A Study in the Writing and Acting of History. London: M. Secker and Warburg, 1940. Reissue.

To the Finland Station: A Study in the Writing and Acting of History. London: M. Secker and Warburg, 1941. Reissue.

Signed Review

Brogan, D. W. *Spectator*, CLXVII (15 August 1941), 159.

Unsigned Review

Times Literary Supplement, 30 August 1941, p. 414.

To the Finland Station: A Study in the Writing and Acting of History, "New Edition." London: M. Secker and Warburg, 1942. Reissue.

To the Finland Station: A Study in the Writing and Acting of History. Garden City, New York: Doubleday, 1947. Reissue.

To the Finland Station: A Study in the Writing and Acting of History, No. A6 in Anchor Books. Garden City, New York: Doubleday and Company, 1953.

Contents
> Same as previous issues, but with substitution of "Summary as of 1940" (essay) for "Appendices."

To the Finland Station: A Study in the Writing and Acting of History, No. A6 in Anchor Books. Garden City, New York: Doubleday & Company, 1955. Reissue.

To the Finland Station: A Study in the Writing and Acting of History, No. A6 in Doubleday Anchor Books. London: Mayflower Publishing Company, 1958. Reissue.

To the Finland Station: A Study in the Writing and Acting of History. Gloucester, Massachusetts: Peter Smith, 1959. Clothbound reissue of the Anchor Books reprinting.

To the Finland Station: A Study in the Writing and Acting of History, No. 469L in Fontana Library. London: William Collins Sons, 1960. Reissue. Out of print in 1970. Same contents as Anchor Books reissues.

Unsigned Reviews
Observer, 16 October 1966, p. 22.
Times Literary Supplement, 4 November 1960, p. 710.

The Boys in the Back Room: Notes on California Novelists (essays), autographed ed. San Francisco: Colt Press, 1941.

Contents
> "The Playwright in Paradise: A Legend of the Beverly Hills" (poem)
> "James M. Cain"
> "John O'Hara"
> "William Saroyan"
> "Hans Otto Storm"
> "John Steinbeck"
> "Facing the Pacific"
> "Postscript"

The Boys in the Back Room: Notes on California Novelists, 1st trade ed. San Francisco: Colt Press, 1941. Reissue.

Signed Reviews

Brown, E. K. See in Items about Wilson.

Curtiss, Mina. *Nation,* CLIII (2 August 1941), 96-97.

Fadiman, Clifton. *New Yorker,* XVII, No. 21 (5 July 1941), 53-54.

Ferguson, Otis. *New Republic,* CV (7 July 1941), 26-27.

Rugoff, Milton. *New York Herald Tribune Books,* XVII (3 August 1941), 14.

Stauffer, Donald A. *Virginia Quarterly Review,* XVIII (Spring 1942), 293-299.

Unsigned Reviews

Booklist, XXXVIII (September 1941), 7.

The Boys in the Back Room: Notes on California Novelists. See also "The Boys in the Back Room" in Essays.

The Wound and the Bow: Seven Studies in Literature (essays). [Boston]: Houghton Mifflin Company (Cambridge, Massachusetts: Riverside Press), 1941.

Contents

"Dickens: The Two Scrooges"
  ["Dickens and the Marshalsea Prison"]
  ["Dickens: The Two Scrooges"]
  ["The Mystery of Edwin Drood"]
"The Kipling that Nobody Read"
"Uncomfortable Casanova"
"Justice to Edith Wharton"
"Hemingway: Gauge of Morale"
"The Dream of H. C. Earwicker"
"Philoctetes: The Wound and the Bow"

Signed Reviews

Colum, Mary M. *American Mercury,* LIII (November 1941), 627-629.

Daiches, David. *New Republic,* CV (25 August 1941), 257-258.

De Vane, William C. *Yale Review,* XXXI (Winter 1942), 384-387.

D[owning], E[leanor]. *Catholic World,* CLIV (January 1942), 500-501.

Garnett, Emily. *Library Journal,* LVI (1 July 1941), 520.

Hankiss, Jean. *Erasmvs: Specvlvm scientiarvm*, I, No. 11-12 (1 July 1947), cols. 601-603.

Jack, Peter Munro. *New York Times Book Review*, 24 August 1941, pp. 5, 26.

Jones, Howard Mumford. See in Items about Wilson.

Kazin, Alfred. *New York Herald Tribune Books*, XVIII (31 August 1941), 2.

McC., H. *More Books: The Bulletin of the Boston Public Library*, XVI (September 1941), 331.

Stauffer, Donald A. *Virginia Quarterly Review*, XVIII (Spring 1942), 293-299.

Wagenknecht, Edward. *Modern Language Quarterly*, III (March 1942), 161-164.

Wright, Cuthbert. *Commonweal*, XXIV (5 September 1941), 475.

Zabel, Morton Dauwen. See in Items about Wilson.

Unsigned Reviews

Booklist, XXXVIII (September 1941), 7.

New Yorker, XVII, No. 28 (23 August 1941), 68.

Open Shelf (Cleveland Public Library), No. 7-9 (July 1941), p. 16.

Pratt Institute Quarterly Booklist, Ser. VI, No. 6 (December 1941), p. 17.

Time: The Weekly Newsmagazine, XXXVIII (18 August 1941), 74-75.

The Wound and the Bow: Seven Studies in Literature. Toronto: Thomas Allen, 1941. Reissue.

Signed Review

Brown, E. K. See in Items about Wilson.

The Wound and the Bow: Seven Studies in Literature. London: M. Secker and Warburg, 1942. Reissue.

Signed Reviews

Leavis, F. R. *Scrutiny*, XI (Summer 1942), 72-73.

Stonier, G. W. *New Statesman and Nation*, XXIII (18 April 1942), 259-260.

Turner, W. J. *Spectator*, CLXVIII (17 April 1942), 380, 382.

Unsigned Reviews
Times Literary Supplement, 23 May 1942, p. 259.
Times Literary Supplement, 23 May 1942, p. 260.

The Wound and the Bow: Seven Studies in Literature. New York: Oxford University Press, 1947. Reissue with corrections.

Signed Reviews
Fiedler, Leslie. *New Leader,* XXX, No. 50 (13 December 1947), 15.
Wanning, Andrews. *Furioso,* III, No. 3 (Spring 1948), 76-79.

The Wound and the Bow: Seven Studies in Literature. Toronto: Oxford University Press, 1947. Reissue.

The Wound and the Bow: Seven Studies in Literature. London: W. H. Allen, 1952. Reissue of Oxford 1947 printing.

Unsigned Review
Times Literary Supplement, 19 December 1952, p. 840.

The Wound and the Bow: Seven Studies in Literature. New York: Oxford University Press, 1959. Reissue of 1947 printing.

The Wound and the Bow: Seven Studies in Literature. "Revised Edition," No. UP36 in University Paperbacks. London: Methuen and Company, 1961. Reissue with corrections.

The Wound and the Bow: Seven Studies in Literature, Rev. Ed., No. GB136 in Galaxy Books. New York: Oxford University Press, 1965. Reissue with corrections.

Note-Books of Night (poems, essays, and story), autographed ed. San Francisco: Colt Press, 1942.

Contents
  "Night in May" (poem)
  "Bishop Praxed's Apology or The Art of Thinking in Poetry or A Gospel of Falsity for an Age of Doubt" (poem)
  "A House of the Eighties" (poem)
  "The Extrovert of Walden Pond: To Betty Spencer" (poem)
  "Disloyal Lines to an Alumnus" (poem)
  "Riverton" (poem)

"The Voice: On a Friend in a Sanitarium" (poem)

["This blue world with its high wide sky of islands!"] (poem)

["Poured full of thin gold sun, September—houses white and bare"] (poem)

"Provincetown, 1936" (poem)

"The Dark Room" (poem)

"Nightmare" (poem)

["Dawns, dawns, that split with light"] (poem)

["After writing"] (poem)

"Home to Town: Two Highballs" (poems)

   "First Highball"

   "Second Highball"

"Response of the Gentle Scholars" (poem)

["These funny muffled woods; the rusted stream"] (poem)

["The crows of March are barking in the wood"] (poem)

["The days and nights—pressure and relief"] (poem)

"Birth and Death of Summer" (poem)

"November Ride" (poem)

"Chorus of Stalin's Yes-Men" (poem)

"Some Americans Still in Spain to Some Stalinists Still in America" (poem)

["My dear, you burn with bright green eyes"] (poem)

["The grass brown, the bushes dry"] (poem)

"The Omelet of A. MacLeish" (poem)

"The Good Neighbor" (poem)

"The Woman, the War Veteran and the Bear" (poem)

"Lesbia in Hell" (poem)

"Return from Louisiana" (essay)

"The Three Limperary Cripples: Musings between sleeping and waking, and immediately after reading Joyce, by the literary editor of a liberal weekly" (story)

"Word-Fetishism or Sick in Four Languages at Odessa" (essay)

"The Moon in a Dream" (essay)

"Variations on a Landscape" (essay)

"At Laurelwood" (essay)

Note-Books of Night, 1st trade ed. San Francisco: Colt Press, 1942. Reissue.

Signed Reviews

Bogan, Louise. *New Yorker*, XVIII, No. 47 (9 January 1943), 50-51.

Chamberlain, John. *New York Times*, 26 January 1943, p. 17.

Colum, Mary M. *New York Times Book Review*, 29 November 1942, pp. 12, 50.

Drew, Elizabeth. *New York Herald-Tribune Books*, XIX (6 December 1942), 50.

Humphries, Rolfe. *New Republic*, CVIII (4 January 1943), 26-27.

Warren, Robert Penn. *Nation*, CLV (5 December 1942), 625.

Unsigned Review
Time: The Weekly Newsmagazine, XLI (4 January 1943), 92.

Note-Books of Night, "First English Edition." London: Secker and Warburg, 1945. Reissue.

Unsigned Review
Times Literary Supplement, 21 July 1945, p. 347.

Note-Books of Night. London: Secker and Warburg, 1945. Reissue.

Memoirs of Hecate County (stories). Garden City, New York: Doubleday and Company, 1946.

Contents
1. "The Man Who Shot Snapping Turtles"
2. "Ellen Terhune"
3. "Glimpses of Wilbur Flick"
4. "The Princes with the Golden Hair"
5. "The Milhollands and Their Damned Soul"
6. "Mr. and Mrs. Blackburn at Home"

Signed Reviews
Bates, Ralph. *New York Times Book Review*, 31 March 1946, pp. 7, 16.

Cowley, Malcolm. *New Republic*, CXIV (25 March 1946), 418-419.

Kazin, Alfred. See same author, "Le Misanthrope," in Items about Wilson.

Match, Richard. *New York Herald Tribune Weekly Book Review*, XXII (10 March 1946), 3.

Peterson, Virgilia. *Commonweal*, XLIII (12 April 1946), 660.

Poore, Charles. *New York Times*, 7 March 1946, p. 23.

Smith, Harrison. *Saturday Review of Literature,* XXIX, No. 12 (23 March 1946), 22.

Trilling, Diana. *Nation,* CLXII (30 March 1946), 379-381.

Unsigned Reviews

Newsweek, XXVII, No. 10 (11 March 1946), 96, 98.

Virginia Kirkus Bookshop Service, Inc. Bulletin, XIV (15 January 1946), 21.

United States Quarterly Book List, II (September 1946), 183-184.

Time: The Weekly Newsmagazine, XLVII (25 March 1946), 102.

Memoirs of Hecate County. Toronto: McClelland, 1946. Reissue.

Signed Review

Trott, Elizabeth. *Canadian Forum,* XXVI (October 1946), 163.

Memoirs of Hecate County, Vol. 157 in Zephyr Books. Stockholm and London: Continental Book Company, 1947. Reissue.

Memoirs of Hecate County. London: W. H. Allen, 1951. Reissue.

Signed Review

Pritchett, V. S. *New Statesman and Nation,* XLI (30 June 1951), 752.

Unsigned Review

Times Literary Supplement, 1 June 1951, p. 337.

Memoirs of Hecate County, "New Ed." London: W. H. Allen, 1958. Reissue.

Memoirs of Hecate County, New Ed. New York: L. C. Page, 1959. Reissue with changes warranting a new copyright.

Signed Reviews

Janeway, Elizabeth. *New York Times Book Review,* 3 January 1960, p. 5.

Wain, John. See same author, "Edmund Wilson: The Critic as Novelist," in Items about Wilson.

Memoirs of Hecate County, New Ed. Toronto: Ambassador Books, 1959. Reissue.

Memoirs of Hecate County, Panther Ed. London: Panther Books, Hamilton & Company, 1960. Reissue.

Memoirs of Hecate County, New Ed., No. T2004 in Signet Books. New York: New American Library, 1961. Reissue.

Memoirs of Hecate County, New Ed., No. T2004 in Signet Books. New York: New American Library of World Literature, 1962. Reissue.

Memoirs of Hecate County, Panther Ed. London: Panther Books, 1963. Reissue.

Memoirs of Hecate County, Panther Ed. London: Panther Books, 1964. Reissue.

Memoirs of Hecate County, New Ed., No. N270 in Noonday Books. New York: Noonday Press, 1965. Reissue.

Signed Review
Kermode, Frank. *Book Week,* II (30 May 1965), 12-13.

Memoirs of Hecate County, New Ed. Rexdale, Ontario: Ambassador Books, 1966. Paperback reissue.

Memoirs of Hecate County, New Ed., No. U7060 in Ballantine Books. New York: Ballantine Books, 1967. Reissue.

Europe Without Baedeker: Sketches Among the Ruins of Italy, Greece, & England (essays). Garden City, New York: Doubleday and Company, 1947.

Contents
["Preface to the First Edition"]
"Notes on London at the End of the War"
"Roman Diary: Arrival—a Visit to Santayana"
"Roman Diary: Sketches for a New Piranesi"
"Two Survivors: Malraux and Silone"
"Through the Abruzzi with Mattie and Harriet"
"Roman Diary: Russian Exiles"
"Roman Diary: British Officials"
"London in Midsummer"
"Rome in Midsummer"
"Notes on Liberated Milan"

"Greek Diary: Notes on Liberated Athens"
"Greek Diary: A Trip to Delphi—Notes on the British in Greece"
"Greek Diary: Communists, Socialists and Royalists"
"Greek Diary: Views of Bull-Headed Crete"
"Stopover in Naples"
"Homecoming—Final Reflections"
"Appendices"
  "Appendix A"
  "Appendix B"
  "Appendix C"

Signed Reviews

Chiaromonte, Nicola. *Partisan Review,* XV (February 1948), 245-249.

Fremantle, Anne. *Commonweal,* XLVIII (16 January 1948), 354-355.

Goodman, Anne L. *New Republic,* CXVII (24 November 1947), 26-27.

Hart, H. W. *Library Journal,* LXXII (15 October 1947), 1469.

Haydn, Hiram. *New York Herald Tribune Weekly Book Review,* XXIV (9 November 1947), 6.

H[ogan], W[illiam]. *This World (San Francisco Chronicle),* XI, No. 30 (30 November 1947), 31.

Mowrer, Edgar. *Saturday Review of Literature,* XXX (25 October 1947), 15-16.

Sheean, Vincent. *New York Times Book Review,* 19 October 1947), pp. 3, 41.

Spender, Stephen. *Nation,* CLCXV (29 November 1947), 592-595.

Unsigned Reviews

Booklist, XLIV (1 December 1947), 132.

Bulletin from Virginia Kirkus' Bookshop Service, XV (1 September 1947), 490.

Times Literary Supplement, 3 January 1948, p. 10.

Europe Without Baedeker: Sketches Among the Ruins of Italy, Greece, & England. Toronto: McClelland, 1947. Reissue.

Europe Without Baedeker: Sketches Among the Ruins of Italy, Greece & England. London: Secker and Warburg, 1948. Reissue.

Signed Review
Pritchett, V. S. *New Statesman and Nation*, XXXVII (19 February 1949), 183.

Europe Without Baedeker: Sketches Among the Ruins of Italy, Greece and England, together with Notes from a European Diary: 1963-1964, 1st rev. ed. of *Europe Without Baedeker: Sketches Among the Ruins of Italy, Greece, & England.* New York: Farrar, Straus and Giroux, 1966.

Contents
　　"Preface to the First Edition"
　　"Preface to the Second Edition"
　　"Notes on London at the End of the War"
　　"Roman Diary: Arrival; A Visit to Santayana"
　　"Roman Diary: Sketches for a New Piranesi"
　　"Two Survivors: Malraux and Silone"
　　"Through the Abruzzi with Mattie and Harriet"
　　"Roman Diary: Russian Exiles"
　　"Roman Diary: British Officials"
　　"London in Midsummer"
　　"Rome in Midsummer"
　　"Notes on Liberated Milan"
　　"Greek Diary: Notes on Liberated Athens"
　　"Greek Diary: A Trip to Delphi; Notes on the British in Greece"
　　"Greek Diary: Communists, Socialists and Royalists"
　　"Greek Diary: Views of Bull-Headed Crete"
　　"Stopover in Naples"
　　"Homecoming; Final Reflections"
　　"Appendices"
　　　　"Appendix A"
　　　　"Appendix B"
　　　　"Appendix C"
　　"Notes from a European Diary: 1963-1964"
　　　　1. "Paris"
　　　　2. "Rome"
　　　　3. "Budapest"

Signed Reviews
Barkham, John. *World Journal Tribune* (New York), I (4 October 1966), 15.
Dupee, F. W. *New York Review of Books*, VII (17 November 1966), 3-5.
Gambee, Ruth R. *Library Journal*, XCI (July 1966), 3425-3426.

Kitching, Jessie. *Publishers' Weekly*, CLXXXIX (27 June 1966), 97.

Nossiter, Bernard D. *Book Week*, IV (11 September 1966), 3, 12.

Pritchett, V. S. See in Items about Wilson.

Unsigned Reviews
Booklist and Subscription Books Bulletin, LXIII (15 November 1966), 366.
Choice, IV (June 1967), 412.
Virginia Kirkus Service, XXXIV (15 May 1966), 530.
Publishers' Weekly, CXCIII (5 February 1968), 69.

Europe Without Baedeker: Sketches Among the Ruins of Italy, Greece and England, together with Notes from a European Diary: 1963-1964, 1st rev. ed. of *Europe Without Baedeker: Sketches Among the Ruins of Italy, Greece, & England*, No. N311 in Noonday Books. New York: Noonday Press, 1966. Paperback reissue.

Europe Without Baedeker: Sketches Among the Ruins of Italy, Greece and England, together with Notes from a European Diary: 1963-1964, 1st rev. ed. of *Europe Without Baedeker: Sketches Among the Ruins of Italy, Greece, & England*. Toronto: Ambassador Books, 1966. Reissue.

Europe Without Baedeker: Sketches Among the Ruins of Italy, Greece and England, together with Notes from a European Diary: 1963-1964, 1st rev. ed. of *Europe Without Baedeker: Sketches Among the Ruins of Italy, Greece, & England*, No. N311 in Noonday Books. Toronto: Ambassador Books, 1966. Paperback reissue.

Europe Without Baedeker: Sketches Among the Ruins of Italy, Greece and England, together with Notes from a European Diary: 1963-1964, 1st rev. ed. of *Europe Without Baedeker: Sketches Among the Ruins of Italy, Greece, & England*. London: Rupert Hart-Davis, 1967. Reissue.

Signed Reviews
Jacobson, Dan. *Listener*, LXXVIII (28 September 1967), 400.

Pritchett, V. S. *New Statesman,* LXXIV (22 September 1967), 357-358.

Unsigned Reviews
Times (London), 21 September 1967, p. 7, col. 4.
Times Literary Supplement, 7 December 1967, p. 1184.

Europe Without Baedeker: Sketches Among the Ruins of Italy, Greece and England, together with Notes from a European Diary: 1963-1964, 1st rev. ed. of *Europe Without Baedeker: Sketches Among the Ruins of Italy, Greece, & England.* New York: Farrar, Straus and Giroux, 1968. Reissue.

Europe Without Baedeker: Sketches Among the Ruins of Italy, Greece and England, together with Notes from a European Diary: 1963-1964, 1st rev. ed. of *Europe Without Baedeker: Sketches Among the Ruins of Italy, Greece, & England,* No. N311 in Noonday Paperbacks. New York: Farrar, Straus and Giroux, 1968. Reissue.

The Triple Thinkers: Twelve Essays on Literary Subjects (1948). See *The Triple Thinkers: Ten Essays on Literature* (1938).

The Little Blue Light: A Play in Three Acts. New York: Farrar, Straus and Company, 1950. Twice printed before publication.

Signed Reviews
Atkinson, Brooks. See in Items about Wilson.
Butcher, Fanny. *Chicago Sunday Tribune,* 28 May 1950, p. 3.
Clurman, Harold. *New Republic,* CXXIII (18 September 1950), 21-22.
Eaton, Walter Prichard. *New York Herald Tribune Book Review,* XXVII (26 November 1950), 27.
Fergusson, Francis. *New York Times Book Review,* 25 June 1950, p. 14.
Freedley, George. *Library Journal,* LXXV (July 1950), 1192.
Newman, James R. *New Republic,* CXXIII (21 August 1950), 21-22.

Nichols, Luther. *This World* (*San Francisco Chronicle*), XIV, No. 8 (25 June 1950), 20.

[Whittemore, Reed]. *Furioso*, V, No. 4 (Fall 1950) [mistakenly printed as No. 3 (Summer 1950)], 71-72.

Unsigned Reviews
Atlantic Monthly, CLXXXVI (August 1950), 86.
Booklist, XLVII (1 September 1950), 10.
Bulletin from Virginia Kirkus' Bookshop Service, XVIII (15 April 1950), 252.
Newsweek, XXXV, No. 22 (29 May 1950), 85.

The Little Blue Light: A Play in Three Acts. Toronto: Clarke, Irwin and Company (distributor), 1950. Reissue.

The Little Blue Light: A Play in Three Acts. London: Victor Gollancz, 1951. Reissue.

Unsigned Review
Times Literary Supplement, 20 April 1951, p. 249.

The Little Blue Light: A Play in Three Acts. Toronto: Clarke, Irwin and Company (distributor), 1951. Reissue.

The Little Blue Light: A Play in Three Acts. See also "The Little Blue Light: A Play in Three Acts" in Plays and Dialogues.

Classics and Commercials: A Literary Chronicle of the Forties (essays). New York: Farrar, Straus and Company, 1950.

Contents
"Archibald MacLeish and the Word"
"Van Wyck Brooks's Second Phase"
"The Boys in the Back Room"
    1. "James M. Cain"
    2. "John O'Hara"
    3. "William Saroyan"
    4. "Hans Otto Storm"
    5. "John Steinbeck"
    6. "Facing the Pacific"
    7. "Postscript"
"Max Eastman in 1941"
"T. K. Whipple"
"The Antrobuses and the Earwickers"
"Alexander Woollcott of the Phalanx"
"The Poetry of Angelica Balabanoff"

"Mr. Joseph E. Davies as a Stylist"
"Thoughts on Being Bibliographed"
"Through the Embassy Window: Harold Nicolson"
"Kay Boyle and the *Saturday Evening Post*"
"The Life and Times of John Barrymore"
" 'Never Apologize, Never Explain': The Art of Evelyn Waugh"
"John Mulholland and the Art of Illusion"
"What Became of Louis Bromfield"
"J. Dover Wilson on Falstaff"
"A Toast and a Tear for Dorothy Parker"
"A Treatise on Tales of Horror"
"A Guide to *Finnegans Wake*"
"A Novel by Salvador Dali"
"A Long Talk about Jane Austen"
" 'You Can't Do This to Me!' Shrilled Celia"
"Aldous Huxley in the World Beyond Time"
"Vladimir Nabokov on Gogol"
"Katherine Anne Porter"
"A Picture to Hang in the Library: Brooks's Age of Irving"
"Why Do People Read Detective Stories?"
"Bernard Shaw on the Training of a Statesman"
"Reëxamining Dr. Johnson"
"Leonid Leonov: The Sophistication of a Formula"
"Who Cares Who Killed Roger Ackroyd?"
" 'Mr. Holmes, They Were the Footprints of a Gigantic Hound!' "
"Glenway Wescott's War Work"
"A Cry from the Unquiet Grave"
    ["Connolly's 'Unquiet Grave;' Thurber's 'White Deer' "]
    ["Lesser Books by Brilliant Writers"]
"Tales of the Marvellous and the Ridiculous"
"Thackeray's Letters: A Victorian Document"
"Splendors and Miseries of Evelyn Waugh"
"George Saintsbury's Centenary"
"Ambushing a Best-Seller"
"The Apotheosis of Somerset Maugham"
"William Saroyan and His Darling Old Providence"
"Oscar Wilde: 'One Must Always Seek What Is Most Tragic' "
"George Grosz in the United States"
"An Old Friend of the Family: Thackeray"
"Gilbert Without Sullivan"
"George Saintsbury: Gourmet and Glutton"
"Books of Etiquette and Emily Post"
"A Dissenting Opinion on Kafka"
"Jean-Paul Sartre: The Novelist and the Existentialist"
"The Musical Glasses of Peacock"
"Edith Wharton: A Memoir by an English Friend"

"The Sanctity of Baudelaire"
"Van Wyck Brooks on the Civil War Period"
"An Analysis of Max Beerbohm"
"The Original of Tolstoy's Natasha"
" 'The Most Unhappy Man on Earth' "
"William Faulkner's Reply to the Civil-Rights Program"
"In Memory of Octave Mirbeau"
"A Revival of Ronald Firbank"
"Paul Rosenfeld: Three Phases"
"Index"

Signed Reviews

Arvin, Newton. *New York Times Book Review,* 19 November 1950, p. 6.

Barrett, William. *Saturday Review of Literature,* XXXIV (27 January 1951), 12-13.

Eulau, Heinz. *Antioch Review,* X (December 1950), 546-549.

Freedley, George. *Library Journal,* LXXV (1 October 1950), 1659.

Honig, Edwin. See in Items about Wilson.

Howe, Irving. *Partisan Review,* XVIII (January-February 1951), 124-128.

Hughes, Serge. *Commonweal,* LIII (2 March 1951), 523-524.

Krim, Seymour. See in Items about Wilson.

Miller, Perry. See in Items about Wilson.

Mizener, Arthur. *New Republic,* CXXIV (19 February 1951), 20-21.

Parrott, L. M. *Theater Arts,* XXXV (February 1951), 92.

Rolo, Charles J. See in Items about Wilson.

Rugoff, Milton. *New York Herald Tribune Book Review,* XXVII (26 November 1950), 8.

Snell, George. *This World (San Francisco Chronicle),* XIV, No. 43 (25 February 1951), 20.

Unsigned Reviews

Bulletin from Virginia Kirkus' Bookshop Service, XVIII (1 August 1950), 458.

Time: The Weekly Newsmagazine, LVI (20 November 1950), 110.

Classics and Commercials: A Literary Chronicle of the Forties.
Toronto: Clarke, Irwin and Company (distributor), 1950.
Reissue.

Classics and Commercials: A Literary Chronicle of the Forties.
London: W. H. Allen, 1951. Reissue.

Signed Reviews
Farrelly, John. See in Items about Wilson.
Loiseau, J. *Études anglaises,* V (August 1952), 273-274.
Pritchett, V. S. *New Statesmen and Nation,* XLIII (12 Jan-
uary 1952), 41-42.

Unsigned Reviews
Times Literary Supplement, 5 January 1951, p. 6.
Times Literary Supplement, 14 December 1951, p. 811.

Classics and Commercials: A Literary Chronicle of the Forties.
Toronto: Clarke, Irwin and Company (distributor), 1951.
Reissue.

Classics and Commercials: A Literary Chronicle of the Forties,
No. V218 in Vintage Books. New York: Random House,
1962. Paperback reissue.

Classics and Commercials: A Literary Chronicle of the Forties,
No. V218 in Vintage Books. Toronto: Random House of
Canada, 1962. Paperback reissue.

Classics and Commercials: A Literary Chronicle of the Forties.
London: W. H. Allen, 1966. Reissue.

Classics and Commercials: A Literary Chronicle of the Forties.
New York: [Book-of-the-Month Club, 1966]. The Book-of-
the-Month Club distributed copies made from Farrar, Straus
and Company plates with Farrar, Straus and Company appearing as publisher on title page. Reissue.

Classics and Commercials: A Literary Chronicle of the Forties,
No. N327 in Noonday Books. New York: Noonday Press,
1967. Paperback reissue.

Classics and Commercials: A Literary Chronicle of the Forties,
No. N327 in Noonday Books. Toronto: Ambassador Books,
1967. Paperback reissue.

The White Sand (poem). [Boston: Thomas Todd (printer)],
10 December 1950. Only 12 copies were printed of this
10-page pamphlet. See also "The White Sand" in Poems.

*Three Reliques of Ancient Western Poetry Collected by Ed-
mund Wilson from the Ruins of the Twentieth Century*
(poems). [Boston: Thomas Todd (printer), 1951]. Paperback, 13 pp.

Contents
  "The Mass in the Parking Lot"
  "Reversals, or *Plus ça change*"
  "Cardinal Merry Del Val"

*Three Reliques of Ancient Western Poetry Collected by Ed-
mund Wilson from the Ruins of the Twentieth Century.*
No publisher, *ca.* 1960. Paperback reissue.

*Three Reliques of Ancient Western Poetry Collected by Ed-
mund Wilson from the Ruins of the Twentieth Century.*
[New York: Gotham Book Mart, 1964]. Paperback reissue.

*Three Reliques of Ancient Western Poetry Collected by Ed-
mund Wilson from the Ruins of the Twentieth Century.*
See also "Three Reliques of Ancient Western Poetry" in
Poems.

*The Shores of Light: A Literary Chronicle of the Twenties
and Thirties* (essays). New York: Farrar, Straus and
Young, 1952.

Contents
  "Foreword"
  "Prologue, 1952: Christian Gauss as a Teacher of Literature"
  "F. Scott Fitzgerald"
  "Mr. E. A. Robinson's Moonlight"
  "Two Novels of Willa Cather"
    I. *"One of Ours"*
    II. *"A Lost Lady"*
  "Ezra Pound's Patchwork"
  "Wallace Stevens and E. E. Cummings"
  "Byron in the Twenties"
    I. "The New Byron Letters"
    II. "Byron and His Biographers"
  "Late Violets from the Nineties"
  "Greenwich Village in the Early Twenties" (stories)
    I. "The Road to Greenwich Village"
    II. *"Fire-Alarm"*

"Sherwood Anderson's *Many Marriages*"
"Ring Lardner's American Characters"
"Eugene O'Neill and the Naturalists"
    I. "Eugene O'Neill as Prose-Writer"
    II. "All God's Chillun and Others"
"The New American Comedy"
"A Vortex in the Nineties: Stephen Crane"
"Emergence of Ernest Hemingway" (includes the essay "Mr. Hemingway's Dry Points" and three letters by Hemingway to EW)
"Imaginary Dialogues" (dialogues)
    I. "The Poet's Return: Mr. Paul Rosenfeld and Mr. Matthew Josephson"
    II. "The Delegate from Great Neck: Mr. F. Scott Fitzgerald and Mr. Van Wyck Brooks"
"Gilbert Seldes and the Popular Arts"
    I. *"The Seven Lively Arts* (1924)"
    II. *"The Great Audience* (1950)"
"Houdini"
"Poe at Home and Abroad"
"The Tennessee Poets"
    I. "A Water-Colorist"
    II. *"Fugitives"*
"The Muses Out of Work"
"Upton Sinclair's *Mammonart*"
"The Pilgrimage of Henry James"
"The All-Star Literary Vaudeville"
"The Critics: A Conversation"
"Pope and Tennyson"
"A Letter to Elinor Wylie"
"Firbank and Beckford"
"A Preface to Persius: Maudlin Meditations in a Speakeasy"
"Burlesque Shows"
    I. "The National Winter Garden"
    II. *"Peaches—A Humdinger"*
"E. E. Cummings's *Him*"
"A Great Magician"
"Mencken's Democratic Man"
"Woodrow Wilson at Princeton"
"American Heroes: Frémont and Frick"
"The Sportsman's Tragedy"
"A Poet of the Pacific"
"Art Young"
"Greenwich Village at the End of the Twenties" (general miscellanea)
    I. "15 Beech Street" (story)
    II. "Hans Stengel" (essay)

"The Critic Who Does Not Exist"
"A Weekend at Ellerslie"
"Thornton Wilder"
"The Death of Elinor Wylie"
"Burton Rascoe"
"Signs of Life: *Lady Chatterley's Lover*"
"Dostoevsky Abroad"
"Citizen of the Union"
"Virginia Woolf and the American Language"
"Dos Passos and the Social Revolution"
"T. S. Eliot and the Church of England"
"Dahlberg, Dos Passos and Wilder"
"Notes on Babbitt and More"
"Sophocles, Babbitt and Freud"
" 'H. C.' "
"The Nietzschean Line"
"The Literary Consequences of the Crash"
"The Economic Interpretation of Wilder"
"Schnitzler and Philip Barry"
"Joseph de Maistre"
"An Appeal to Progressives"
"The Literary Class War"
"C. L. Dodgson: The Poet Logician"
"Lytton Strachey"
"The Satire of Samuel Butler"
"André Malraux"
"Gertrude Stein Old and Young"
    I. "27, rue de Fleurus"
    II. *"Things As They Are"*
"Mr. Wilder in the Middle West"
"The Literary Worker's Polonius: A Brief Guide for Authors and
    Editors"
"The Classics on the Soviet Stage"
"Letter to the Russians about Hemingway" (includes EW's trans-
    lation of "Ot redaktsii")
"Talking United States"
"American Critics, Left and Right"
    I. "Communist Criticism"
    II. "Bernard De Voto"
"It's Terrible! It's Ghastly! It Stinks!"
"The Oxford Boys Becalmed"
"Prize-Winning Blank Verse"
" 'Give That Beat Again' "
"Dream Poetry"
" 'Cousin Swift, You Will Never Be a Poet' "
"Peggy Bacon: Poet with Pictures"
"Twilight of the Expatriates" (includes a letter by Henry Miller)

"The Pleasures of Literature: By a Book Lover"
"Cold Water on Bakunin"
"Shut Up That Russian Novel"
"Marxism at the End of the Thirties"
"Epilogue, 1952: Edna St. Vincent Millay" (includes the poems
    "Provincetown" and ["Shut out the Square!"] and a letter by
    EW to Millay)
"Index"

Signed Reviews

Butcher, Fanny. *Chicago Sunday Tribune*, 26 October
    1952, Part 4, p. 4.

Carrier, Warren. *Western Review*, XVII (Summer 1953),
    329-334.

Carver, Wayne. *Western Humanities Review*, VII, No. 1
    (Winter 1952-1953), 77-79.

Chase, Richard. *Partisan Review*, XX (January-February
    1953), 112-114.

Cowley, Malcolm. See same author, "Edmund Wilson's
    Specimen Days," in Items about Wilson.

Getlein, Frank. *Commonweal*, LVII (12 December 1952),
    262.

Gregory, Horace. *New York Herald Tribune Book Review*,
    XXIX (26 October 1952), 1, 29.

Honig, Edwin. See in Items about Wilson.

Kazin, Alfred. See same author, "The Critic and the Age,"
    in Items about Wilson.

Parrish, Stephen Maxfield. *Virginia Quarterly Review*,
    XXIX (Winter 1953), 155-160.

Phillips, William. See same author, "The Wholeness of
    Literature: Edmund Wilson's Essays," in Items about
    Wilson.

Poore, Charles. *New York Times Book Review*, 26 Octo-
    ber 1952, p. 1.

Prescott, Orville. *New York Times*, 24 October 1952, p. 21.

Rolo, Charles J. *Atlantic Monthly*, CXC (December 1952),
    98.

Ruhm, Herbert. *This World* (*San Francisco Chronicle*),
    XVI, No. 28 (9 November 1952), 16.

Scott, W. T. *Saturday Review*, XXXV, No. 46 (15 No-
    vember 1952), 25.

Unsigned Reviews
Booklist, XLIX (1 December 1952), 122.
Bookmark (New York State Library), XII, No. 3 (December 1952), 55.
New York Herald Tribune Book Review, XXIX (2 November 1952), 2.
Newsweek, XL, No. 17 (27 October 1952), 117-118.

The Shores of Light: A Literary Chronicle of the Twenties and Thirties. London: W. H. Allen and Company, 1952. Reissue.

Signed Reviews
Allen, Walter. *New Statesman and Nation*, XLV (7 March 1953), 268.
Evans, B. Ifor. *Adelphi*, N.S. (3rd ser.) XXIX (Second Quarter, 1953), 194-199.
Loiseau, J. *Études anglaises*, VI (November 1953), 368.

Unsigned Reviews
Listener, XLIX, No. 1246 (15 January 1953), iii.
Times Literary Supplement, 12 December 1952, p. 811.

The Shores of Light: A Literary Chronicle of the Twenties and Thirties, "First Vintage edition," No. 181 in Vintage Books. New York: Random House, 1961. Paperback reissue.

The Shores of Light: A Literary Chronicle of the Twenties and Thirties. New York: Farrar, Straus and Giroux, 1965. Reissue.

The Shores of Light: A Literary Chronicle of the Twenties and Thirties. London: W. H. Allen, 1966. Reissue.

The Shores of Light: A Literary Chronicle of the Twenties and Thirties. New York: [Book-of-the-Month Club, 1966]. The Book-of-the-Month Club distributed copies made from Farrar, Straus and Giroux plates with Farrar, Straus and Giroux appearing as publisher on title page. Reissue.

The Shores of Light: A Literary Chronicle of the Twenties and Thirties, No. N326 in Noonday Books. New York: Noonday Press, 1967. Paperback reissue.

Unsigned Review
Publishers' Weekly, CXCII (3 July 1967), 62.

The Shores of Light: A Literary Chronicle of the Twenties and Thirties, No. N326 in Noonday Books. Toronto: Ambassador Books, 1967. Paperback reissue.

Wilson's Christmas Stocking: Fun for Young and Old (poems). [Boston: Thomas Todd (printer), 1953.]

Contents
  "Scurrilous Clerihews"
    "The Paradox of Thornton Wilder"
    "Enemies of Promise"
    "The Art of Education"
    "John Dos Passos, Esqre"
    "e. e. cummings, esquirrel"
    "The Tates"
    "The Whites"
    "The Walkers"
    "Metternich's Great Admirer"
  "Anagrams on Eminent Authors"
  "Relaxed Crossword Puzzles"
  "Easy Exercises in the Use of Difficult Words"
    "September Landscape"
    "Nursery Vignette"
    "Peter Florescent, Peter Marcescent; Peter Dehiscent, Peter Resipiscent"
    "Scène de Boudoir"
    "Lakeside"
    "Heraldic Battle"
    "Palace Dusk"
  "Brief Comments on Mistaken Meanings"
    "Junk"
    "A Dream for Daniel Updike"
    "Words Across the Channel"
    "Le Bluff"
    "The Purist's Complaint"
  "Memories of the Poetry of the Nineties, Written Down While Waiting for Long-Distance Calls"
    I. "Sonnet"
    II. "Drafts for a Quatrain"
  "Miniature Dialogues"
    ["Said Mario Praz to Mario Pei"]
    ["Said Gaylord Hauser to Gathorne-Hardy"]
  "Colloquy between Oneida and Lewis Counties, New York"
  "Something for my Russian Friends"

"Le Violon d'Ingres de Sirine"
"Fun in the Balkans"
"An Incident of the Occupation"
"Something for my Jewish Friends"
"Something about the Author"
["A message you'll expect, my friends"]

Five Plays. London: W. H. Allen, 1954.

Contents
"Preface" (essay)
"Cyprian's Prayer"
"The Crime in the Whistler Room"
"This Room and This Gin and These Sandwiches"
"Beppo and Beth"
"The Little Blue Light"

Signed Reviews
B., M. *Spectator,* CXCII (9 April 1954), 446.
R., J. *Manchester Guardian,* 30 April 1954, p. 4.

Unsigned Review
Times Literary Supplement, 23 April 1954, p. 261.

Five Plays. New York: Farrar, Straus and Young, 1954. Reissue.

Signed Reviews
Cosman, Max. *Theatre Arts,* XXXIX, No. 8 (August 1955), 13.
Fergusson, Francis. *New York Times Book Review,* 15 August 1954, pp. 4, 15.
Krutch, Joseph Wood. *New York Herald Tribune Book Review,* XXXI (22 August 1954), 6.

Unsigned Review
New Yorker, XXX, No. 18 (19 June 1954), 104.

Five Plays. New York: Farrar, Straus and Giroux, 1969. Reissue reprinted by offset method from 1954 printing.

Eight Essays, No. A37 in Anchor Books. Garden City, New York: Doubleday, 1954.

Contents
"Dickens: The Two Scrooges"
["Dickens and the Marshalsea Prison"]

["Dickens: The Two Scrooges"]
["The Mystery of Edwin Drood"]
"Hemingway: Gauge of Morale"
"A. E. Housman: The voice, sent forth, can never be recalled"
"Bernard Shaw at Eighty"
"The Vogue of the Marquis de Sade"
"Abraham Lincoln: The Union as Religious Mysticism"
"The Pre-Presidential T. R."
"The Holmes-Laski Correspondence"

The Scrolls from the Dead Sea (essays). New York: Oxford University Press, 1955.

Contents
  "The Metropolitan Samuel"
  "The Essene Order"
  "The Monastery"
  "The Teacher of Righteousness"
  "What Would Renan Have Said?"
  "General Yadin"

Signed Reviews

Albright, William F. *New York Herald Tribune Book Review,* XXXII (16 October 1955), 3.

Breaden, Richard P. *Library Journal,* LXXX (1 November 1955), 2520.

Burrows, Millar. *Journal of Biblical Literature,* LXXV, Part 2 (June 1956), 148-149.

Butz, Robert C. *This World (San Francisco Chronicle),* XIX, No. 27 (30 October 1955), 19.

Cross, Frank M., Jr. See in Items about Wilson.

Fitzmyer, Joseph A. *Commentary,* LXIII (9 December 1955), 260-261.

Fritsch, Charles T. *Review of Religion* (Columbia University), XXI (November 1956), 52-54.

Gill, Theodore A. *Christian Century,* LXXII (26 October 1955), 1240-1241.

Harrison, Joseph G. *Christian Science Monitor,* 8 December 1955, p. 9.

Howlett, Duncan. See in Items about Wilson.

Peters, Edward H. *Catholic World,* CLXXXII (December 1955), 238.

Philbrick, Richard. *Chicago Sunday Tribune,* 6 November 1955, Part 4, p. 18.

Poore, Charles. *New York Times,* 13 October 1955, p. 29.

Reed, William L. *Archaeology,* IX, No. 1 (March 1956), 71.

Rolo, Charles J. *Atlantic Monthly,* CXCVI (December 1955), 92, 94.

V[aux], [Le P.] R[oland Guérin] d[e]. *Revue biblique* (Paris), LXIII (juillet 1956), 472-473.

Unsigned Reviews
Booklist, LII (15 December 1955), 155.
Bulletin from Virginia Kirkus' Service, XXIII (1 September 1955), 698-699.
Saturday Review, XXXIX, No. 9 (3 March 1956), 30.
Time: The Weekly Newsmagazine, LXVI (7 November 1955), 132.

The Scrolls from the Dead Sea. Toronto: Oxford University Press, 1955. Reissue.

The Scrolls from the Dead Sea. London: W. H. Allen, 1955. Reissue.

Signed Reviews
Collins, L. John. *Theology,* LIX (April 1956), 162-164.
Hooke, S. H. *Journal of the Royal Central Asian Society,* XLIII, Part 3 and 4 (July-October 1956), 279.
Martin, Kingsley. *New Statesman and Nation,* L (26 November 1955), 709.
Montefiore, Hugh. *Spectator,* CXCV (9 December 1955), 809-810, 812. See also same author in Items about Wilson.
Rowley, H. H. *Manchester Guardian,* 25 November 1955, p. 14.

Unsigned Reviews
Times (London), 22 December 1955, p. 9, cols. 2-3.
Times Literary Supplement, 30 March 1956, "Religious Books Section," p. iv.

The Scrolls from the Dead Sea. London: George Allen and Unwin, 1955. Reissue.

The Scrolls from the Dead Sea. New York: Oxford University Press, 1956. Reissue.

Signed Review
Cantera, Francisco. *Arbor: Revista general di investigación y cultura* (Madrid), XXXVI (enero 1957), 132-133.

The Scrolls from the Dead Sea. London: W. H. Allen, 1956. Reissue.

The Scrolls from the Dead Sea, "amplified and revised" ed., No. 160 in Fontana Books. London and Glasgow: Collins, 1957. Paperback reissue with slight amplification and revision. Reprinted in 1958 and 1960.

The Scrolls from the Dead Sea, No. M69 in Meridian Books. New York: Meridian Books, 1959. Reissue.

Signed Review
Bernini, G[iuseppe P]. *Gregorianum: Comentarii de re theologica et philosophica editi a professoribus Pontificiae Universitatis Gregorianae,* XLI, No. 2 (1960), 325-326.

The Scrolls from the Dead Sea. See also *The Dead Sea Scrolls 1947-1969* (1969) in Books by Wilson and "The Scrolls from the Dead Sea" in Essays.

A Christmas Delirium (poems). [Boston: Thomas Todd (printer), 1955]. Paperback.

Contents
    "The Children's Hour"
    "From the Geckese"
    "Imaginary Dialogues"
        " 'Within the Rim' "
        "Two New England Girls"
        "Peterhof"
        "At the Algonquin"
        "A Ghost of Old Baltimore"
        "An Old Faith for New Needs"
        "27, Rue de Fleurus"
        "The Rabbi Turned Away in Disdain"
    ["History as a Crystalline Sea-Anemone"]

"The Pickerel Pond: A Double Pastoral"
["Gimme the gimmick, Gustave!"]
["He consulted a typical timing guide"] (story)
["Looking out on the high chalkbound cliffs"] (story)
"The Rats of Rutland Grange: A Christmas Story" (poem)
"Superrat" (drawing)

Red, Black, Blond and Olive: Studies in Four Civilizations: Zuñi, Haiti, Soviet Russia, Israel (essays). New York: Oxford University Press, 1956.

Contents
"Zuñi (1947)"
  "The Pueblo"
  "The Anthropologists"
  "Shálako"
  "Navaho Interlude"
  "Shálako Continued"
  "Departure"
"Haiti (1949)"
  "Cotton Blossom Express"
  "Miami"
  "Two West Indian Authors"
  "King Christophe's Citadel"
  "Color Politics"
  "Marbial"
  "Haitian Literature"
  "Voodoo Converts"
  "Pastor McConnell"
  "Port-au-Prince"
"Soviet Russia (1935)"
  I. "Old England"
  II. "London to Leningrad"
  III. "Leningrad Theaters"
  IV. "On the Margin of Moscow"
      ["First Days in Moscow"]
      ["Letters in the Soviet Union"]
      ["Stalin as Ikon"]
      ["Russian Idyls"] (includes EW's translation of the Russian popular song ["Ekh, sharabán, da sharabán"])
      ["Russian Paradoxes"] (fragment of essay)
  V. "Volga Idyll"
  VI. "Odessa: Counter-Idyll" (contains EW's translation of S. Marshak's poem "Whiskers and Stripes")
  VII. "Final Reflections"
"Israel (1954)"

I. "On First Reading Genesis"
II. "Éretz Yisraél"
    "Samaritan Passover"
    "The Guardians of the City"
    "The Fiction of S. Y. Agnon"
    "Theocracy"
    "Tanách"
    "Jerusalem the Golden"
    "Degániya"
    "Éretz Yisraél"
"Postscript"

Signed Reviews

Butz, Robert C. *This World (San Francisco Chronicle)*, XIX, No. 51 (15 April 1956), 21.

Duffus, R. L. *New York Times Book Review*, 1 April 1956, p. 7.

Graves, Robert. See in Items about Wilson.

Harrison, Joseph G. *Christian Science Monitor*, 22 March 1956, p. 7.

Redman, Ben Ray. *Chicago Sunday Tribune*, 25 March 1956, p. 3.

Robinson, C. A., Jr. *Saturday Review*, XXXIX, No. 12 (24 March 1956), 17.

Rolo, Charles J. *Atlantic Monthly*, CXCVII (May 1956), 84-85.

Weales, Gerald. *Commonweal*, LXIV (20 April 1956), 77-78.

Unsigned Reviews

Booklist and Subscription Books Bulletin, LII (1 May 1956), 360.

Bookmark (New York State Library), XV (April 1956), 160.

Red, Black, Blond and Olive: Studies in Four Civilizations: Zuñi, Haiti, Soviet Russia, Israel. London: W. H. Allen, 1956. Reissue.

Signed Reviews

C[unliffe], M[arcus] F. *Manchester Guardian*, 6 July 1956, p. 6.

Pritchett, V. S. *New Statesman and Nation,* LI (16 July 1956), 693-694.

Quennell, Peter. *Spectator,* CXCVII (6 July 1956), 23-24.

Unsigned Review
Times Literary Supplement, 28 September 1956, p. 566.

A Literary Chronicle: 1920-1950 (essays), No. A85 in Anchor Books. Garden City, New York: Doubleday & Company, 1956.

Contents

"Prologue, 1952: Christian Gauss as a Teacher of Literature"
"F. Scott Fitzgerald"
"Ring Lardner's American Characters"
"Emergence of Ernest Hemingway" (includes the essay "Mr. Hemingway's Dry Points" and three letters by Hemingway to EW)
"Gilbert Seldes and the Popular Arts"
   I. *"The Seven Lively Arts* (1924)"
   II. *"The Great Audience* (1950)"
"Poe at Home and Abroad"
"The All-Star Literary Vaudeville"
"Mencken's Democratic Man"
"The Sportsman's Tragedy"
"Thornton Wilder"
"The Death of Elinor Wylie"
"Signs of Life: *Lady Chatterley's Lover*"
"Dostoevsky Abroad"
"Citizen of the Union"
"Dos Passos and the Social Revolution"
"T. S. Eliot and the Church of England"
"Dahlberg, Dos Passos and Wilder"
"Notes on Babbitt and More"
"The Nietzschean Line"
"Lytton Strachey"
"André Malraux"
"The Literary Worker's Polonius: A Brief Guide for Authors and Editors"
"Letter to the Russians about Hemingway" (includes EW's translation of "Ot redaktsii")
"It's Terrible! It's Ghastly! It Stinks!"
"Twilight of the Expatriates" (includes a letter by Henry Miller)
"The Boys in the Back Room"
   1. "James M. Cain"
   2. "John O'Hara"

    3. "William Saroyan"
    4. "Hans Otto Storm"
    5. "John Steinbeck"
    6. "Facing the Pacific"
    "Postscript"
"Alexander Woollcott of the Phalanx"
"Mr. Joseph E. Davies as a Stylist"
"The Life and Times of John Barrymore"
" 'Never Apologize, Never Explain': The Art of Evelyn Waugh"
"What Became of Louis Bromfield"
"J. Dover Wilson on Falstaff"
"A Toast and a Tear for Dorothy Parker"
"A Treatise on Tales of Horror"
"A Guide to *Finnegans Wake*"
"A Long Talk about Jane Austen"
" 'You Can't Do This to Me!' Shrilled Celia"
"Katherine Anne Porter"
"A Picture to Hang in the Library: Brooks's Age of Irving"
"Why Do People Read Detective Stories?"
"Reexamining Dr. Johnson"
"Leonid Leonov: The Sophistication of a Formula"
"Who Cares Who Killed Roger Ackroyd?"
" 'Mr. Holmes, They Were the Footprints of a Gigantic Hound!' "
"Splendors and Miseries of Evelyn Waugh"
"George Saintsbury's Centenary"
"Ambushing a Best-Seller"
"Oscar Wilde: 'One Must Always Seek What Is Most Tragic' "
"Books of Etiquette and Emily Post"
"A Dissenting Opinion on Kafka"
"Jean-Paul Sartre: The Novelist and the Existentialist"
"The Musical Glasses of Peacock"
"The Original of Tolstoy's Natasha"
"William Falkner's Reply to the Civil-Rights Program"
"Index"

A Literary Chronicle: 1920-1950. Gloucester, Massachusetts: Peter Smith, 1961. Reissue.

A Piece of My Mind: Reflections at Sixty (essays). New York: Farrar, Straus and Cudahy, 1956.

  Contents
    "Religion"
      ["Religion is the cult of a god"]
      "Notes on the Churches"
    "The United States"
      ["Types of American Presidents"]
      "Americanism"

"War"
   ["The question of American expansion"]
   "Confession of a Non-Fighter"
"Europe"
"Russia"
   ["The fine photographs by Cartier-Bresson"]
   "A Later Bulletin"
"The Jews" (general miscellanea)
   ["Notes on Gentile Pro-Semitism: New England's 'Good
      Jews' "] (essay)
   "The Messiah at the Seder" (story)
"Education"
   "Reflections on the Teaching of Latin"
   "The Need for Judaic Studies"
   "The Problem of English"
"Science" (dialogue)
   "In the Galapagos"
"Sex"
"The Author at Sixty"

Signed Reviews

Arvin, Newton. *New York Times Book Review,* 18 November 1956, p. 4.

Cosman, Max. *Arizona Quarterly,* XIII (Summer 1957), 186-187.

Edel, Leon. *New Republic,* CXXXV (17 December 1956), 25-26.

Geismar, Maxwell. *Nation,* CLXXXIII (8 December 1956), 502-504.

Krutch, Joseph Wood. *Saturday Review,* XXXIX (17 November 1956), 22.

McDonnell, Thomas P. *Catholic World,* CLXXXV (May 1957), 128-131.

Maddocks, Melvin. *Christian Science Monitor,* 15 November 1956, p. 17.

Redman, Ben Ray. *Chicago Sunday Tribune,* 25 November 1956, p. 6.

Rolo, Charles J. *Atlantic Monthly,* CXCVIII (November 1956), 103-105.

Rugoff, Milton. *New York Herald Tribune Book Review,* XXXIII (11 November 1956), 5.

Walbridge, Earle F. *Library Journal,* LXXXI (1 November 1956), 2583.

Unsigned Reviews

Booklist and Subscription Books Bulletin, LIII (1 January 1957), 221.

Bookmark (New York State Library), XVI (December 1956), 61.

Bulletin from Virginia Kirkus Service, XXIV (1 September 1956), 665-666.

New Yorker, XXXII, No. 39 (17 November 1956), 242.

Newsweek, XLVIII, No. 20 (12 November 1956), 134, 136-137.

Open Shelf (Cleveland Public Library), No. 7-12 (December 1956), p. 2.

A Piece of My Mind: Reflections at Sixty. Toronto: Ambassador Books, 1956. Reissue.

A Piece of My Mind: Reflections at Sixty. London: W. H. Allen, 1957. Reissue.

Signed Review
Allen, Walter. *New Statesman,* LIII (23 March 1957), **388.**

Unsigned Reviews
Times (London), 14 March 1957, p. 13, col. 2.
Times Literary Supplement, 19 April 1957, p. 240.

A Piece of My Mind: Reflections at Sixty, No. A143 in Anchor Books. Garden City, New York: Doubleday, 1958. Paperback reissue.

A Piece of My Mind: Reflections at Sixty, No. A143 in Anchor Books. Toronto: Doubleday Canada, 1958. Paperback reissue.

A Piece of My Mind: Reflections at Sixty, ed. with notes in Japanese by Keiichi Harada. Tokyo: Shohakusha, 1966. An edition with English text and copyright 1966 on Japanese notes.

The American Earthquake: A Documentary of the Twenties and Thirties (essays), in Anchor Books. Garden City, New York: Doubleday & Company, 1958.

Contents

"Stravinsky"
"The Problem of the Higher Jazz"
"Moscow, Athens and Paris"
  " 'Lysistrata' "
  "Opera Comique"
"Thoughts on Leaving New York for New Orleans"
"All God's Chillun" (stories)
  "A Cotton-Mill Owner"
  "A Steamboat Captain"
  "A New Orleanian"
"The Old Conviviality and the New: New Orleans"
"Return from Louisiana"
"After the Game: Princeton and Yale Ten Years Ago"
  (story)
"Reunion" (story)
"The Men from Rumpelmayer's" (story)
"Judd Gray and Mrs. Snyder" (essay)
"The Age of Pericles: An Expressionist Play" (dialogue)

II. "The Earthquake: October 1930-October 1931"
"Dwight Morrow in New Jersey"
"Political Headquarters"
"Foster and Fish"
"Aladdin's Lecture Palace"
"The Bank of United States"
"The Metropolitan Opera House"
"Communists and Cops"
"Detroit Motors"
"Red Cross and County Agent"
"Senator and Engineer"
" 'Still'—: Meditations of a Progressive"
"A Bad Day in Brooklyn"
"May First: The Empire State Building; Life on the Passaic River"
"Two Protests"
"Frank Keeney's Coal Diggers"
"Tennessee Agrarians"
"The Scottsboro Freight-Car Case"
"The Enchanted Forest"
"Indian Corn Dance"
"Fourth of July Celebration"
"Hoover Dam"
"The City of Our Lady the Queen of the Angels"
"Eisenstein in Hollywood"
"The Jumping-Off Place"
"Back East: October Again: A Strike in Lawrence, Mass."
"Mr. and Mrs. X"
"A Man in the Street"

III. "Dawn of the New Deal: 1932-1934"
   "Election Night"
   "Hull-House in 1932"
   "Illinois Household" (dialogue)
   "A Great Dream Come True"
   "Washington: Inaugural Parade"
   "Sunshine Charley"
   "Bernard Shaw at the Metropolitan"
   "The Old Stone House"
   "The Second Battle of Oriskany"
   "Saving the Right People and Their Butlers"
   "What to Do Till the Doctor Comes: From the Diary of a
      Drinker-Out" (story)
   "Washington: Glimpses of the New Deal"
      1. "Japanese Cherry Blossoms"
      2. "The Old Brick and Marble Shell"
      3. "Miss Barrows and Dr. Wirt"
      4. "Reinstating the Red Man"
      5. "The Delegates from Duquesne"
      6. "Madam Secretary"
      7. "The Zero Hour"
   "Postscripts of 1957"

Signed Reviews

Hogan, William. *This World* (*San Francisco Chronicle*),
   XXI, No. 42 (9 February 1958), 22.

Johnson, Gerald W. *New York Herald Tribune Book Review*, XXXIV (9 March 1958), 4.

Kazin, Alfred. See same author, "The Historian as Reporter:
   Edmund Wilson and the 1930's," in Items about Wilson.

Krutch, Joseph Wood. *Saturday Review*, XLI (22 February 1958), 23.

Maddocks, Melvin. *Christian Science Monitor*, 13 February 1958, p. 11.

Mercer, Blaine. *Social Education*, XXIII (February 1959), 92.

Schlesinger, Arthur M., Jr. *New York Times Book Review*, 9 February 1958, p. 3.

Wagenknecht, Edmund. *Chicago Sunday Tribune*, 9 February 1958, Part 4 ("The Magazine of Books"), p. 3, col. 5.

Walbridge, E. F. *Library Journal*, LXXXIII (1 March 1958), 762.

Wyllie, Irvin G. *Virginia Quarterly Review*, XXXIV (Autumn 1958), 644-647.

Unsigned Reviews
Bookmark (New York State Library), XVII (March 1958), 143.
New Yorker, XXXIV, No. 20 (5 July 1958), 62-63.
Newsweek, LI, No. 6 (10 February 1958), 110-111.
Virginia Kirkus Service, XXV (1 December 1957), 886.

The American Earthquake: A Documentary of the Twenties and Thirties, in Anchor Books. Toronto: Doubleday Canada, 1958. Reissue.

The American Earthquake: A Documentary of the Twenties and Thirties, in Anchor Books. London: W. H. Allen, 1958. Reissue.

Signed Reviews
Brogan, D. W. *Manchester Guardian*, 22 April 1958, p. 6.
Forster, E. M. *Listener*, LIX (22 May 1958), 865.
Le Breton, M. *Études anglaises*, XI (October-December 1958), 373.
O'Donnell, Donat [pseud. for Cruise O'Brien, Conor]. *Spectator*, CC (25 April 1958), 536-537.
Pritchett, V. S. *New Statesman*, LV (26 April 1958), 541-542.

Unsigned Reviews
Times (London), 24 April 1958, p. 13, col. 3.
Times Literary Supplement, 25 April 1958, p. 226.

The American Earthquake: A Documentary of the Twenties and Thirties. Garden City, New York: Doubleday, 1964. Reissue.

Signed Review
Garraty, J. A. *New York Times Book Review*, 12 April 1964, p. 45.

The American Earthquake: A Documentary of the Twenties and Thirties. Toronto: Doubleday Canada, 1964. Reissue.

*The American Earthquake: A Documentary of the Twenties
and Thirties.* Gloucester, Massachusetts: Peter Smith, 1964.
The Anchor Books printing rebound.

Apologies to the Iroquois (essays), with a study of "The Mohawks in High Steel" by Joseph Mitchell. New York: Farrar, Straus and Cudahy, 1960.

> *Contents* (by EW)
> "Standing Arrow"
> "Onondaga"
> "St. Regis"
> "The Tuscaroras"
> "The Seneca Republic"
> "Seneca New Year's Ceremonies"
> "The Six Nations Reserve"
> "Growth and Causes of Iroquois Resurgence"
> "The Little Water Ceremony"

Signed Reviews

Ash, Lee. *Library Journal,* LXXXV (1 January 1960), 117-
118.

Auden, W. H. *Mid-Century,* No. 9 (February 1960), pp.
2-11.

B., A. R. *Springfield Republican,* 20 March 1960, p. 4d.

Chamberlain, John. *Wall Street Journal,* CLV, No. 60 (28
March 1960), 10, col. 6.

Gannett, Lewis. *New York Herald Tribune Book Review,*
XXXVI (13 March 1960), 1.

Graf, Robert J., Jr. *Chicago Sunday Tribune,* 3 April 1960,
Part 4 ("The Magazine of Books"), p. 3, col. 5.

Hendrick, Kimmis. *Christian Science Monitor,* 18 April
1960, p. 9.

Hepworth, Janice Creveling. *Western Humanities Review,*
XV (Winter 1961), 86-87.

Hess, John L. See in Items about Wilson.

Highet, Gilbert. *Book-of-the-Month-Club News,* March
1960, p. 7.

Hutchens, John K. *New York Herald Tribune,* 11 March
1960, p. 13, cols. 6-8.

La Farge, Oliver. *New York Times Book Review,* 20 March
1960, p. 7.

Manfred, Frederick. *Saturday Review*, XLIII (4 June 1960), 31.

Moses, Robert. See in Items about Wilson.

Poore, Charles. *New York Times*, 12 March 1960, p. 19.

Walls, Jim. *This World (San Francisco Chronicle)*, XXIII, No. 47 (13 March 1960), 18.

Unsigned Reviews

Booklist and Subscription Books Bulletin, LVI (15 April 1960), 507.

Bookmark (New York State Library), XIX (February 1960), 119.

Virginia Kirkus Service, XXVII (1 December 1959), 908.

Virginia Quarterly Review, XXXVI (Summer 1960), xc.

Apologies to the Iroquois, with a study of "The Mohawks in High Steel" by Joseph Mitchell. Toronto: Ambassador Books, 1960. Reissue.

Apologies to the Iroquois, with a study of "The Mohawks in High Steel" by Joseph Mitchell. London: W. H. Allen, 1960. Reissue.

Signed Reviews

Brogan, D[ennis] W[illiam]. *Guardian* (Manchester), 27 May 1960, p. 8.

O'Donnell, Donat. See Cruise O'Brien, Conor ("Serpents"), in Items about Wilson.

Price, R. G. G. *Punch*, CCXXXVIII (15 June 1960), 855.

Pritchett, V. S. *New Statesman*, LIX (21 May 1960), 759-760.

Reeves, James. *Time and Tide*, XLI (25 June 1960), 741.

Sigal, Clancy. *Listener*, LXIV (14 July 1960), 69.

Wilson, Angus. *Encounter*, XV, No. 2 (August 1960), 82-83.

Unsigned Reviews

Times (London), 19 May 1960, p. 17, col. 3.

Times Literary Supplement, 3 June 1960, p. 347.

Apologies to the Iroquois, with a study of "The Mohawks in High Steel" by Joseph Mitchell, No. V313 in Vintage Books. New York: Random House, 1966. Reissue.

Signed Review
Bannon, Barbara A. *Publishers' Weekly,* CLXXXIX (10 January 1966), 90.

Apologies to the Iroquois, with a study of "The Mohawks in High Steel" by Joseph Mitchell, No. V313 in Vintage Books. Toronto: Random House, 1966. Reissue.

Apologies to the Iroquois, with a study of "The Mohawks in High Steel" by Joseph Mitchell. New York: Farrar, Straus and Giroux, 1970. Reissue.

Apologies to the Iroquois. See also "Apologies to the Iroquois" in **Essays.**

Night Thoughts (poems). New York: Farrar, Straus and Cudahy, 1961.

Contents
"1917-1919"
  "Southampton"
  "Epitaphs"
    I. "American Soldiers"
    II. "American Officers and Soldiers Who Committed Suicide"
    III. "A Young German"
    IV. "A Hospital Nurse"
  "New Ode to a Nightingale"
  "Chaumont"
  "The New Patriotism"
"Europe"
  "To a Painter Going Abroad"
  "Stucco and Stone: To John Peale Bishop"
  "The Lido"
  "Boboli Gardens"
"Lesbia"
  "Lesbia in Hell"
  ["Shut out the square!"]
  "Infection"
  "A Young Girl Indicted for Murder"
  "The Dark Room"
  "Nightmare"
  "Provincetown"
"New Jersey and New York"
  "Highballs: To John Amen"
  "A Train Out of the Terminal"
  "To an Actress"

"American Masterpieces: To Stark Young"
"Copper and White"
"Prose of the Twenties" (essays)
"Jersey Coast"
    I. "A Train's Whistle"
    II. "Swimming"
    III. "The Summer Hotel"
"Oneida County Fair"
"Translations"
  "Death Warrant"
  "Dedication for a Book"
  "The Night Attack"
"Poets, Farewell!: 1929"
  ["When all the young were dying"]
  ["Here where your blue bay's book is half begun"]
  ["—And you who faint at either's hard expense"]
  ["Dim screens obscure the dawn"]
"Parody, Satire and Nonsense"
  "Nocturne: Impromptu to a Lady"
  "Quintilian"
  "The Extravert [sic] of Walden Pond"
  "Tannhäuser"
  "The Omelet of A. MacLeish"
  "Bishop Praxed's Apology: or The Art of Thinking in Poetry
    or A Gospel of Falsity for an Age of Doubt"
  "Disloyal Lines to an Alumnus"
  "The Playwright in Paradise: A Legend of the Beverly Hills"
"Elegies and Wakeful Nights"
  "Night in May"
  "Riverton"
  "A House of the Eighties"
  "The Voice: On a Friend in a Sanitarium"
  ["This blue world with its high wide sky of islands!"]
  ["Poured full of thin gold sun, September—houses white and
    bare"]
  "Provincetown, 1936"
  ["Dawns, dawns, that split with light"]
  ["After writing"]
  ["The crows of March are barking in the wood"]
  "Home to Town: Two Highballs"
    "First Highball"
    "Second Highball"
  "The Woman, the War Veteran and the Bear"
  ["My dear, you burn with bright green eyes"]
  "On Editing Scott Fitzgerald's Papers"
"Stamford"
  ["These funny muffled woods; the rusted stream"]

["The days and nights—pressure and relief"]
"Birth and Death of Summer"
"The Good Neighbor"
"November Ride"
["The grass brown, the bushes dry"]
"Prose of the Thirties" (essays)
   "Word-Fetishism or Sick in Four Languages in Odessa"
   "The Moon in a Dream"
   "Variations on a Landscape"
   "At Laurelwood: 1939"
"Three Reliques of Ancient Western Poetry Collected from the Ruins of the Twentieth Century, 1951"
   "The Mass in the Parking Lot"
   "Reversals, or *Plus ça change*"
   "Cardinal Merry Del Val"
"A Christmas Stocking: Fun for Young and Old, 1953"
   "Scurrilous Clerihews"
      "The Paradox of Thornton Wilder"
      "Enemies of Promise"
      "The Art of Education"
      "John Dos Passos, Esqre"
      "e. e. cummings, esquirrel"
      "The Tates"
      "The Whites"
      "The Walkers"
      "Metternich's Great Admirer"
   "Anagrams on Eminent Authors"
   "Relaxed Crossword Puzzles"
   "Easy Exercises in the Use of Difficult Words"
      "September Landscape"
      "Nursery Vignette"
      "Peter Florescent, Peter Marcescent; Peter Dehiscent, Peter Resipiscent"
      "Scène de Boudoir"
      "Lakeside"
      "Heraldic Battle"
      "Palace Dusk"
   "Brief Comments on Mistaken Meanings"
      "Junk"
      "A Dream for Daniel Updike"
      "Words across the Channel"
      "Le Bluff"
      "The Purist's Complaint"
   "Memories of the Poetry of the Nineties, Written Down While Waiting for Long-Distance Calls"
     I. "Sonnet"
     II. "Drafts for a Quatrain"

"Miniature Dialogues"
  ["Said Mario Praz to Mario Pei"]
  ["Said Gayelord Hauser to Gathorne-Hardy"]
  "Colloquy between Oneida and Lewis Counties, New York"
"Something for my Russian Friends"
  "Le Violon d'Ingres de Sirine"
  "Fun in the Balkans"
  "An Incident of the Occupation"
"Something for my Jewish Friends"
"Something about the Author"
  ["A message you'll expect, my friends"]
"A Christmas Delirium, 1955"
  "The Children's Hour"
  "From the Geckese"
  "Imaginary Dialogues"
    " 'Within the Rim' "
    "Two New England Girls"
    "Peterhof"
    "At the Algonquin"
    "A Ghost of Old Baltimore"
    "An Old Faith for New Needs"
    "27, rue de Fleurus"
    "The Rabbi Turned Away in Disdain"
  ["History as a Crystalline Sea-Anemone"]
  "The Pickerel Pond: A Double Pastoral"
  ["Gimme the gimmick, Gustave!"]
  ["He consulted a typical timing guide"] (story)
  ["Looking out on the high chalkbound cliffs"] (story)
  "The Rats of Rutland Grange: A Christmas Story" (poem)
  "Superrat" (drawing)
"The White Sand: 1950" (poem)
"A Note on the Elegiac Meter" (essay)

Signed Reviews

Adams, Phoebe. *Atlantic Monthly*, CCVIII (December 1961), 115.

Cloyne, George. *New York Herald Tribune Books*, XXXVIII (24 December 1961), 7.

Hogan, William. *San Francisco Chronicle*, 11 December 1961, p. 35.

Hutchens, John K. *New York Herald Tribune*, 27 December 1961, p. 19.

Robie, Burton A. *Library Journal*, LXXXVI (15 November 1961), 3957.

Swenson, May. *Poetry*, CII (May 1963), 118-125.

Wain, John. *New York Times Book Review,* 10 December 1961, pp. 4, 52.

Unsigned Reviews

Booklist and Subscription Books Bulletin, LVIII (1 January 1962), 274.

Bookmark (New York State Library), XXI (June 1962), 258.

Bulletin from Virginia Kirkus' Service, XXIX, No. 19 (1 October 1961), 946.

New Yorker, XXXVII, No. 49 (20 January 1962), 118, 120.

Newsweek, LVIII (4 December 1961), 90-91.

Time: The Weekly Newsmagazine, LXXVIII (8 December 1961), 102.

Night Thoughts. Toronto: Ambassador Books, 1962. Reissue.

Night Thoughts. London: W. H. Allen, 1962. Reissue.

Signed Reviews

Enright, D. J. *New Statesman,* LXIII (22 June 1962), 901-902.

Sinclair, Andrew. *Guardian* (Manchester), 18 May 1962, p. 10.

Unsigned Reviews

Library Review (Glasgow), XVIII, No. 134 (Autumn 1962), 564.

Times (London), 17 May 1962, p. 16, col. 3.

Times Literary Supplement, 20 July 1962, p. 526.

Times Weekly Review, 24 May 1962, p. 11.

Night Thoughts, No. N253 in Noonday Paperbacks. New York: Noonday Press, 1964. Paperback reissue.

Patriotic Gore: Studies in the Literature of the American Civil War (essays). New York: Oxford University Press, 1962.

Contents
    "Introduction"
    "Harriet Beecher Stowe"
    "Calvin Stowe; Francis Grierson; *The Battle Hymn of the Republic;* The Union as Religious Mysticism"
    "Abraham Lincoln"

"Northern Soldiers: Ulysses S. Grant"
"Northern Soldiers: William T. Sherman"
"Northerners in the South: Frederick L. Olmsted, John T. Trow-
bridge"
"Northerners in the South: Charlotte Forten and Colonel Hig-
ginson"
"Three Confederate Ladies: Kate Stone, Sarah Morgan, Mary
Chesnut"
"Southern Soldiers: Richard Taylor, John S. Mosby, Robert E.
Lee"
["Tales of Soldiers and Civilians"]
["John Singleton Mosby, 'The Gray Ghost' "]
"Diversity of Opinion in the South: William J. Grayson, George
Fitzhugh, Hilton [sic] R. Helper"
"Alexander H. Stephens"
"The Myth of the Old South; Sidney Lanier; The Poetry of the
Civil War; Sut Lovingood"
"Novelists of the Post-War South: Albion W. Tourgée, George W.
Cable, Kate Chopin, Thomas Nelson Page"
"Ambrose Bierce on the Owl Creek Bridge"
"The Chastening of American Prose Style; John W. De Forest"
"Justice Oliver Wendell Holmes"
"Index" (by Frances S. Radley)

Signed Reviews

Aaron, Daniel. See same author, "Edmund Wilson's War,"
in Items about Wilson.

Angle, Paul M. *Chicago Sunday Tribune Magazine of
Books*, CXXI (29 April 1962), 5.

————. *South Atlantic Quarterly*, LXI (Autumn 1962),
567-568.

Atkinson, Brooks. *New York Times*, 27 April 1962, p. 32.

Barrett, William. *Atlantic Monthly*, CCIX (May 1962),
120, 122.

Bewley, Marius. See same author "Northern Saints and
Southern Nights," in Items about Wilson.

Botsford, Keith. See in Items about Wilson.

Caldwell, Russell R. *Personalist*, XLIV (Summer 1963),
413.

Catton, Bruce. *American Heritage*, XIII (August 1962),
109-110.

Commager, Henry Steele. *New York Times Book Review*,
29 April 1962, pp. 1, 24.

Corrington, John W. *Georgia Review,* XVII (Spring 1963), 93-95.

Current, Richard N. *Progressive,* XXVI (October 1962), 45-46.

Dabney, Lewis M. See in Items about Wilson.

Darrell, Margery. *Book-of-the-Month-Club News,* May 1962, p. 6.

Davis, Joe Lee. *American Quarterly,* XIV (Winter 1962), 633-634.

Donald, David. *New York Herald Tribune Books,* XXXVIII (29 April 1962), 4, 15.

Dowdey, Clifford. *Virginia Quarterly Review,* XXXVIII (Summer 1962), 528-532.

Eisenschimi, Otto. *Chicago Jewish Forum,* XXI, No. 2 (Winter 1962-1963), 167.

Fatout, Paul. *Mississippi Valley Historical Review,* XLVII (September 1962), 341.

Foster, Charles H. *New England Quarterly,* XXXV (December 1962), 524-527.

Gerard, David. *Civil War Times Illustrated,* I, No. 2 (May 1962), 33-35.

Granger, Bruce Ingham. *Books Abroad,* XXXVII (Spring 1963), 204-205.

Gregory, Charles. *New-York Historical Society Quarterly,* XLVII (October 1963), 468-469.

Hardwick, Elisabeth. *Harper's Magazine,* CCXXV (July 1962), 86, 88.

Harwell, Richard. *Civil War History,* IX (March 1963), 100-101.

Haselden, Kyle. *Christian Century,* LXXIX (18 July 1962), 889-890.

Hesseltime, William B. *History News,* XIX (November 1963), 16-17.

Hicks, Granville. *Saturday Review,* XLV (28 April 1962), 16.

Hogan, William. *San Francisco Chronicle,* 27 April 1962, p. 39.

Howe, Irving. See same author, "Edmund Wilson and the Sea Slugs," in Items about Wilson.

Hutchens, John K. *New York Herald Tribune,* 30 April 1962, p. 21, cols. 4-6.

Kazin, Alfred. *Holiday,* XXXVIII, No. 6 (December 1965), 163.

———. *Reporter,* XXVI, No. 11 (24 May 1962), 43-46.

Kovács, József. *Helikon: Világirodalmi figyelo* (Budapest: Institute of Literary History of the Hungarian Academy of Sciences), X, No. 2-3 (1964), 352-353.

L, S. G. *Midcontinent American Studies Journal,* IV (Spring 1963), 73.

Lerner, Arthur. *Phylon,* XXIII (Fall 1962), 308-309.

Littlejohn, David. See in Items about Wilson.

Lynn, Kenneth S. *New Republic,* CXLVI (25 June 1962), 21-24.

McCarthy, Charles W. *Army,* XIII (December 1962), 87.

Miller, Perry. *Christian Science Monitor,* 26 April 1962, p. 5.

[Nordell, Roderick]. *Christian Science Monitor,* 29 November 1962, p. 5b.

Podhoretz, Norman. See same author, "Mr. Wilson and the Kingdom of Heaven," in Items about Wilson.

Poore, Charles. *New York Times,* 26 April 1962, p. 31.

Raleigh, John Henry. *Partisan Review,* XXIX (Summer 1962), 425-436.

Rubin, Louis D., Jr. See in Items about Wilson.

Shepard, Odell. *Nation,* CXCIV (19 May 1962), 447-448.

Simpson, Lewis P. *Journal of Southern History,* XXVIII (November 1962), 486-488.

Slaughter, Frank G. *Florida Historical Quarterly,* XLI (January 1963), 290-291.

Smith, Thelma E. *Library Journal,* LXXXVII (1 June 1962), 2141.

Thorp, Willard. *American Literature,* XXXIV (January 1963), 574-575.

Tomlinson, Charles. *Poetry,* CII (August 1963), 341-345.

Vinocur, Jacob. *Western Humanities Review,* XVII (Autumn 1963), 364-365.

Warren, Robert Penn. *Commentary,* XXXIV (August 1962), 151-158.

Weeks, Ramona. *New Mexico Quarterly,* XXXII (Spring-Summer 1962), 76-77.

Woodward, C. Vann. *American Scholar,* XXXI (Autumn 1962), 638, 640, 642.

Unsigned Reviews

Booklist and Subscription Books Bulletin, LVIII (1 June 1962), 676-677.

Bulletin from Virginia Kirkus' Service, XXX (1 April 1962), 347.

Georgia Historical Quarterly, XLVI (September 1962), 326-327.

Newsweek, LIX (30 April 1962), 100-101.

Time: The Weekly Newsmagazine, LXXIX (4 May 1962), 93.

Patriotic Gore: Studies in the Literature of the American Civil War, No. GB160 in Galaxy Books. New York: Oxford University Press, 1962. Paperback reissue.

Patriotic Gore: Studies in the Literature of the American Civil War. Toronto: Oxford University Press, 1962. Reissue.

Signed Reviews

Brown, Craig. *Canadian Forum,* XLII (October 1962), 160-161.

Fehrenbacher, Don E. *Canadian Historical Review,* XLIV (March 1963), 56.

Patriotic Gore: Studies in the Literature of the American Civil War. London: André Deutsch, 1962. Reissue.

Signed Reviews

Conquest, Robert. *Listener,* LXVIII (12 July 1962), 69.

Cruise O'Brien, Conor. *New Statesman,* LXIII (22 June 1962), 899-900.

Cunliffe, Marcus. *Spectator,* CCVIII (22 June 1962), 829-830.

Gray, Simon. See in Items about Wilson.

Green, Martin. *History Today,* XII (November 1962), 807.

Sinclair, Andrew. *Guardian* (Manchester), 22 June 1962, p. 6.

Unsigned Reviews

Economist, CCIV (28 August 1962), 623.

Times (London), 2 August 1962, p. 13, cols. 1-2.

Times Literary Supplement, 20 July 1962, p. 526.

Patriotic Gore: Studies in the Literature of the American Civil War, No. GB160 in Galaxy Books. New York: Oxford University Press, 1966. Paperback reissue with corrections.

Patriotic Gore: Studies in the Literature of the American Civil War. Don Mills, Ontario: Oxford University Press, 1966. Paperback reissue.

The Cold War and the Income Tax: A Protest (essays). New York: Farrar, Straus and Company, 1963.

> *Contents*
> "A Bad Case of Tax Delinquency"
> "The Delinquent in the Hands of the IRS"
> "Everybody Is Under Suspicion"
> "What Rip Van Winkle Woke Up To"
> "Bureaucratic Theology: The Tax Jungle"
> "The Point of View of a Former Socialist"
> "What Our Money Is Going For"
> "What About American Literature?"
> "How Can We Account for Ourselves?"
> "The Artificial Cholera Epidemic"
> "The Soft Sell for CBR"
> "How Free Is the Free World?"
> "The Case of Major Eatherly"
> "The Strategy of Tax Refusal"

Signed Reviews

Bazelon, David T. *Commentary,* XXXVIII (August 1964), 67-68.

Davis, Saville R. *Christian Science Monitor,* 23 November 1963, p. 9.

Demott, Benjamin. *Harper's Magazine,* CCXXVII (December 1963), 110.

Dos Passos, John. *National Review,* XVI (28 January 1964), 71-74.

Epstein, Jason. *New York Review of Books,* I, No. 7 (28 November 1963), 9-11.

Gilman, Richard. *New Republic,* CXLIX (30 November 1963), 25-27.

Johnson, Gerald W. *New York Times Book Review,* 10 November 1963, p. 3.

Leães, Luiz, Gastão. *Supplemento literário* (in Saturday daily ed. of *O estado de S. Paulo*), Year XI, No. 516 (18 February 1967), p. 6.

Peretz, Martin. *Nation,* CXCII (30 November 1963), 371-372.

Poore, Charles. *New York Times,* 5 November 1963, p. 29.

Ransom, Harry Howe. *Saturday Review,* XLVII (11 January 1964), 60.

Sheed, Wilfrid. See in Items about Wilson.

Vidal, Gore. *Book Week* (*New York Herald Tribune*), I (3 November 1963), 3.

Weales, Gerard. *Reporter,* XXIX (5 December 1963), 63-64.

Woy, James B. *Library Journal,* LXXXVIII (15 November 1963), 4387-4388.

Unsigned Reviews
Newsweek, LXII (21 October 1963), 121-122.

Time: The Weekly Newsmagazine, LXXXII, No. 23 (6 December 1963), 124, 127.

Virginia Quarterly Review, XL (Winter 1964), xxxv.

The Cold War and the Income Tax: A Protest. Toronto: Ambassador Books, 1963. Reissue.

The Cold War and the Income Tax: A Protest. London: W. H. Allen, 1964. Reissue.

Signed Review
Cruise O'Brien, Conor. See same author, "Critic into Prophet," in Items about Wilson.

Unsigned Reviews
Times (London), 19 March 1964, p. 17, col. 3.

Times Literary Supplement, 9 April 1964, p. 283.

The Cold War and the Income Tax: A Protest, No. P2475 in Signet Books. New York: New American Library of World Literature, 1964.

O Canada: An American's Notes on Canadian Culture (essays). New York: Farrar, Straus and Giroux, 1965.

Contents

> ["My introduction to the cultural life of Canada"]
> "Morley Callaghan of Toronto"
> ["O Canada: An American's Notes on Canadian Culture"]

Signed Reviews

Anderson, Quentin. *New Republic*, CLII (29 May 1965), 26-28.

Barrett, William. *Atlantic Monthly*, CCXV (May 1965), 149-150.

Compton, Neil. *Commentary*, XL (August 1965), 75-76.

Davies, Robertson. *New York Times Book Review*, 16 May 1965, p. 30.

Elson, Robert T. *Saturday Review*, XLVIII (29 May 1965), 37.

Fuller, Edmund. *Wall Street Journal*, XLV (10 June 1965), 16.

Godsell, Geoffrey. *Christian Science Monitor*, 11 May 1965, p. [9].

Moore, Brian. *Book Week*, II (9 May 1965), 4.

Muggeridge, Malcolm. *Esquire*, LXIII, No. 5 (May 1965), 44-46.

Ossman, Albert J., Jr. *Social Education*, XXIX (October 1965), 400-401.

Poore, Charles. *New York Times*, CXIV (13 May 1965), 35.

Ready, William. *Library Journal*, XC (15 May 1965), 2264-2265.

Richler, Mordecai. *New York Review of Books*, V (30 September 1965), 6, 8-9.

Santoni, Ronald E. *Progressive*, XXX (March 1966), 40-41.

Woodcock, George. *Commonweal*, LXXXIII (3 December 1965), 290.

———. *New Leader*, XLVIII, No. 10 (10 May 1965), 17-18.

Unsigned Reviews

Best Sellers, XXV (15 May 1965), 88.

Booklist and Subscription Books Bulletin, LXI (1 June 1965), 947.

Choice, II (November 1965), 571.

Virginia Kirkus Service, Inc., XXXIII (15 March 1965), 349.

Virginia Quarterly Review, XLI (Autumn 1965), cxl-cxli.

O Canada: An American's Notes on Canadian Culture. Toronto: Ambassador Books, 1965. Reissue.

Signed Reviews

Cook, Ramsay. *Canadian Forum,* XLV (August 1965), 114-115.

Grosskurth, Phyllis. *Tamarack Review,* No. 37 (Autumn 1965), pp. 106-109.

O Canada: An American's Notes on Canadian Culture, No. N301 in Noonday Books. New York: Noonday Press, 1966. Reissue.

Unsigned Review

Saturday Review, XLIX, No. 51 (17 December 1966), 38.

O Canada: An American's Notes on Canadian Culture. London: Rupert Hart-Davis, 1967. Reissue.

Signed Reviews

Burgess, Anthony. *Spectator,* CCXIX (4 August 1967), 133-134.

Jacobson, Dan. *Listener,* LXXVIII (28 September 1967), 400.

Levine, Norman. *Manchester Guardian Weekly,* XCVII (17 August 1967), 11.

Peter, John. *Observer,* 23 July 1967, p. 21.

Pritchett, V. S. *New Statesman,* LXXIV (22 September 1967), 357-358.

Unsigned Reviews

Punch, CCLIII (23 August 1967), 291.

Times Literary Supplement, 31 August 1967, p. 780.

O Canada: An American's Notes on Canadian Culture. See also "O Canada: An American's Notes on Canadian Culture" in Essays.

The Bit Between My Teeth: A Literary Chronicle of 1950-1965 (essays). New York: Farrar, Straus and Giroux, 1965.

Contents

"The Genie of the Via Giulia"
"Index"

Signed Reviews

Crews, Frederick C. *New York Review of Books,* V, No. 8 (25 November 1965), 4-5.

Fadiman, Clifton. *Holiday,* XXXIX (January 1966), 109-111.

Fremont-Smith, Elliot. *New York Times,* 17 December 1965, p. 37, cols. 1-3.

Fuller, Edmund. *Wall Street Journal,* XLVI (23 February 1966), 16.

Gilman, Richard. See in Items about Wilson.

Handlin, Oscar. *Atlantic,* CCXVI (December 1965), 148.

Hicks, Granville. *Saturday Review,* XLVIII, No. 47 (20 November 1965), 35-36.

Jacobson, Dan. *Commentary,* XLI (May 1966), 92, 94-95.

Kramer, Hilton. *New Leader,* XLVIII (6 December 1965), 3-4.

Levensohn, Alan. *Christian Science Monitor,* XLVIII (6 January 1966), 11.

Lewis, R. W. B. *New York Times Book Review,* 12 December 1965, pp. 1, 43-45.

McGlinchee, Claire. *America,* CXIV (22 January 1966), 152, 154.

Muggeridge, Malcolm. *Esquire,* LXV (April 1966), 86.

Pickrel, Paul. *Harper's Magazine,* CCXXXII (January 1966), 95-96.

Poirier, Richard. *Book Week (New York Herald Tribune),* III (19 December 1965), 2-3, 11.

Pryce-Jones, Alan. *New York Herald Tribune,* 30 November 1965, p. 23, cols. 5-7.

Unsigned Reviews

American Literature, XXXVIII (May 1966), 273.

Booklist and Subscription Books Bulletin, LXII (15 December 1965), 393.

Choice, III (March 1966), 30.

Christian Century, LXXXII (1 December 1965), 1484.

Newsweek, LXVI (29 November 1965), 101-102.

Newsweek, LXVI (27 December 1965), 72.

Virginia Kirkus Service, XXXIII (15 September 1965), 1027.

The Bit Between My Teeth: A Literary Chronicle of 1950-1965, No. N328 in Noonday Books. New York: Noonday Press, 1965. Paperback reissue.

The Bit Between My Teeth: A Literary Chronicle of 1950-1965. Toronto: Ambassador Books, 1965. Reissue.

The Bit Between My Teeth: A Literary Chronicle of 1950-1965. London: W. H. Allen, 1966. Reissue.

Signed Reviews
Amis, Kingsley. *New Statesman,* LXXI (14 January 1966), 51-52.

Burgess, Anthony. *Spectator,* CCXVI (14 January 1966), 47-48.

Cunliffe, Marcus. *Manchester Guardian Weekly,* XCIV (20 January 1966), 10.

Furbank, P. N. *Listener,* LXXV (27 January 1966), 142.

Gross, John. *Observer,* 9 January 1966, p. 25.

Symons, Julian. *London Magazine,* N.S. VI (April 1966), 100-103.

Willy, Margaret, and J. M. Redmond. *Year's Work in English Studies,* XLVI (1965), 316-317.

Unsigned Reviews
Economist, CCXVIII (5 February 1966), 520.

Times (London), 13 January 1966, p. 13, col. 3.

Times Literary Supplement, 17 February 1966, p. 124.

The Bit Between My Teeth: A Literary Chronicle of 1950-1965. New York: Farrar, Straus and Giroux, 1966. Reissue.

The Bit Between My Teeth: A Literary Chronicle of 1950-1965. Toronto: Ambassador Books, 1966. Reissue.

The Bit Between My Teeth: A Literary Chronicle of 1950-1965. New York: [Book-of-the-Month Club], 1966. The Book-of-the-Month Club distributed copies made from Farrar, Straus and Giroux plates with Farrar, Straus and Giroux appearing as publisher on title page. Reissue.

The Bit Between My Teeth: A Literary Chronicle of 1950-1965, No. N328 in Noonday Books. New York: Noonday Press, 1967. Paperback reissue.

The Bit Between My Teeth: A Literary Chronicle of 1950-1965, No. N328 in Noonday Books. Toronto: Ambassador Books, 1967. Paperback reissue.

Europe Without Baedeker: Sketches Among the Ruins of Italy, Greece and England, together with Notes from a European Diary: 1963-1964 (1966). See *Europe Without Baedeker: Sketches Among the Ruins of Italy, Greece, & England* (1947).

Holiday Greetings 1966 (poems). [Boston: Thomas Todd (printer), 1966].

Contents
"Merry Monsters"
"Something for My Italian Friends"
"Something for My Hungarian Friends"
"Fabulous Word Squares"
"Homecoming"

Galahad [and] I Thought of Daisy (1967). See *I Thought of Daisy* (1929).

A Prelude: Landscapes, Characters and Conversations from the Earlier Years of My Life (essays). New York: Farrar, Straus and Giroux, 1967.

Contents
"First Trip to Europe, 1908"
"Family"
"School and College Friends"
"Princeton, 1912-1916" (includes the poems "Colloquial [off him, it, etc.]," "Huysmans at Chartres," and "The Dark Hour (Swift in His Last Days)")
"Plattsburgh, Summer of 1916"
"New York, 1916-1917" (includes the poems "Colloquial [berry (jewel)]," "Princeton," and "Princeton, 1917")
"The Army, 1917-1919" (includes the poems "September, 1917," "The Trains," and "Princeton, April, 1917"; the story "The Death of a Soldier"; the poems "[More lament for the world left behind.]," ["One thing I know that saves me much remorse"], and "Treves, December, 1918"; the story "Lieutenant

Franklin"; and the poems "Colloquial [Oftentimes: most of the doctors]" and "Army")

Signed Reviews

Davis, Robert Gorham. *New York Times Book Review*, 9 July 1967, pp. 1, 43.

Hicks, Granville. *Saturday Review*, L, No. 26 (1 July 1967), 17-18.

Jackson, Paul R. *Books Today* (*Chicago Sunday Tribune*), IV (9 July 1967), 1.

Jones, Frank N. *Library Journal*, CXII (1 June 1967), 2151.

Kauffman, Stanley. *New Republic*, CLVI (17 June 1967), 27.

Kazin, Alfred. See same author, "Edmund Wilson: His Life and Books," in Items about Wilson.

Lask, Thomas. *New York Times*, 21 June 1967, p. 45.

Levensohn, Alan. *Christian Science Monitor*, LIX (6 July 1967), 13.

Maloff, Saul. *Newsweek*, LXIX (26 June 1967), 75.

Shapiro, Karl. *Book Week*, IV (25 June 1967), 5.

Solotaroff, Theodore. *Life*, LXII (23 June 1967), 10.

Thompson, John. *New York Review of Books*, IX, No. 5 (28 September 1967), 8, 10, 12.

Turnbull, Andrew. *Harper's Magazine*, CCXXXV (September 1967), 120-123.

Unsigned Reviews

Booklist and Subscription Books Bulletin, LXIII (15 July 1967), 1177.

Choice, V (June 1968), 488.

Kirkus Service, XXXV (1 May 1967), 594.

National Observer, VI (26 June 1967), 19.

Publisher's Weekly, CXCI (12 June 1967), 56.

Time: The Weekly Newsmagazine, LXXXIX (23 June 1967), 98.

Virginia Quarterly Review, XLIV (Winter 1968), xxviii.

A Prelude: Landscapes, Characters and Conversations from the Earlier Years of My Life. Toronto: Ambassador Books, 1967. Reissue.

A Prelude: Landscapes, Characters and Conversations from the Earlier Years of My Life. London: W. H. Allen, 1967. Reissue.

Signed Reviews

Burgess, Anthony. *Spectator,* CCXIX (29 September 1967), 363-365.

Jacobson, Dan. *Listener,* LXXVIII (28 September 1967), 400.

Pritchett, V. S. *New Statesman,* LXXIV (22 September 1967), 357-358.

Richler, Mordecai. *Manchester Guardian Weekly,* XCVII (21 September 1967), 11.

Toynbee, Philip. *Observer,* 10 September 1967, p. 23.

Unsigned Reviews

Times (London), 21 September 1967, p. 7, cols. 3-4.

Times Literary Supplement, 7 December 1967, p. 1184.

A Prelude: Landscape, Characters and Conversations from the Earlier Years of My Life. See also "A Prelude" in Essays.

The Fruits of the MLA (essay), in New York Review Books. New York: New York Review, 1968.

Contents

["The Fruits of the MLA"] (includes a letter by EW to Jason Epstein; a postscript to the essay includes letters about EW by Paul Baender [partially reprinted], William H. Y. Hackett [partially reprinted], and Theodore Besterman)

The Duke of Palermo and Other Plays With an Open Letter to Mike Nichols. New York: Farrar, Straus and Giroux, 1969.

Contents

"The Lamentable Tragedy of the Duke of Palermo"
"Dr. McGrath"
"Osbert's Career, or The Poet's Progress"
"Open Letter to Mike Nichols" (essay)

Signed Reviews

Bermel, Albert. *Nation,* CCIX (25 August 1969), 156-157.

Buck, Richard M. *Library Journal,* XCIV (15 March 1969), 1157.

Jackson, Katherine Gauss. *Harper's Magazine,* CCXXXVIII, No. 1426 (March 1969), 109.

Lewis, R. W. B. *New York Times Book Review,* 2 March 1969, pp. 4, 46-48.

Unsigned Review
Choice, VI (November 1969), 1244.

The Duke of Palermo and Other Plays With an Open Letter to Mike Nichols. W. H. Allen of London has imported 500 sheets printed by Farrar, Straus and Giroux.

The Dead Sea Scrolls 1947-1969 (essays). New York: Oxford University Press, 1969.

Contents
    "The Scrolls from the Dead Sea, 1955"
        I. "The Metropolitan Samuel"
        II. "The Essene Order"
        III. "The Monastery"
        IV. "The Teacher of Righteousness"
        V. "What Would Renan Have Said?"
        VI. "General Yadin"
    "1955-1967"
      "Introduction"
        I. "Polemics"
        II. "The Genesis Apocryphon"
        III. "The Psalms"
        IV. "The Nahum Pesher"
        V. "John Allegro"
        VI. "The Copper Scrolls"
        VII. "The Texts"
        VIII. "The Testimonia"
        IX. "The Epistle to the Hebrews"
        X. "Masada"
        XI. "Dubious Documents"
    " 'On the Eve,' 1967"
        I. "Tattoo"
        II. "Palestinians"
        III. "The Two Jerusalems"
          ["The Scorpion"]
        IV. "The New National Israel Museum"
        V. "Conversations with Yadin and Flusser"
        VI. "Departure"
    "The June War and the Temple Scroll"
    "General Reflections"

"Appendix" (an exchange of letters between EW and "Your Reviewer")

"Index"

Signed Reviews

Bratton, Fred Gladstone. *Saturday Review,* LII, No. 34 (23 August 1969), 43.

Finley, M. I. *Book World,* III, No. 38 (21 September 1969), 5.

Neusner, Jacob. *National Review,* XXI (21 October 1969), 1070-1071.

Stanley, David. *America,* CXXI (6 December 1969), 566.

Vande Kieft, Ruth M. *Nation,* CCIX (29 September 1969), 321-322.

Unsigned Reviews

Best Sellers: The Semi-Monthly Book Review, XXIX (1 August 1969), 174.

Christian Century, LXXXVI (23 July 1969), 996.

The Dead Sea Scrolls 1947-1969. London: W. H. Allen, 1969. Reissue.

Signed Review

Pritchett, V. S. *New Statesman,* LXXIX (2 January 1970), 17.

The Dead Sea Scrolls 1947-1969. See also *The Scrolls from the Dead Sea* (1955).

Upstate: Records and Recollections of Northern New York (essays). New York: Farrar, Straus and Giroux, 1971. A regional history of upstate New York with a diary notebook. The opening chapters describe the region and EW's forebears; and the succeeding chapters, usually one to a year, tell of EW's activities in Talcottville, New York, during the summers from 1950 to 1970. Portions will appear in *New Yorker,* XLVII, prior to book publication in 1971.

B.   Books Edited by Wilson

The Last Tycoon: An Unfinished Novel by F. Scott Fitzgerald together with The Great Gatsby and Selected Stories, by F. Scott Fitzgerald, ed. EW. New York: Charles Scribner's Sons, 1941.

Contents (by EW)
  "Foreword"
Signed Reviews
Adams, J. Donald. *New York Times Book Review,* 9 November 1941, p. 1.
Benét, Stephen Vincent. *Saturday Review of Literature,* XXIV (6 December 1941), 10.
Conklin, Robert J. *Springfield Sunday Union and Republican,* 2 November 1941, p. 7e.
Fadiman, Clifton. *New Yorker,* XVII, No. 40 (15 November 1941), 107-108.
Litell, Robert. *Yale Review,* XXXI (Winter 1942), vi.
Marshall, Margaret. *Nation,* CLIII (8 November 1941), 457.
Rugoff, Milton. *New York Herald Tribune Books,* XVIII (26 October 1941), 18.
Weeks, Edward. *Atlantic Monthly,* CLXIX (January 1942), "The Atlantic Bookshelf," pages not numbered.

Unsigned Reviews
Booklist, XXXVIII (15 December 1941), 130.
Time: The Weekly Newsmagazine, XXXVIII (3 November 1941), 95-96.

The Last Tycoon: An Unfinished Novel, by F. Scott Fitzgerald, ed. EW. London: Grey Walls Press, 1949. Reissue.

Signed Review
Snow, C. P. *Sunday Times* (London), No. 6589 (31 July 1949), p. 3, col. 5.

The Last Tycoon: An Unfinished Novel, by F. Scott Fitzgerald, ed. EW, Part III of *Three Novels,* in Modern Standard Authors Series. New York: Charles Scribner's Sons, 1953. Reissue.

The Last Tycoon: An Unfinished Novel, by F. Scott Fitzgerald, ed. EW, Part III of *Three Novels of F. Scott Fitzgerald,* in Modern Standard Authors Series. New York: Charles Scribner's Sons, 1956. Reissue.

The Last Tycoon: An Unfinished Novel, by F. Scott Fitzgerald, ed. EW. New York: Charles Scribner's Sons, 1958. Reissue.

The Last Tycoon: An Unfinished Novel, by F. Scott Fitzgerald, ed. EW, Part III of *Three Novels,* in Scribner Library. New York: Charles Scribner's Sons, 1970. Paperback reissue.

The Last Tycoon: An Unfinished Novel, by F. Scott Fitzgerald, ed. EW, No. SL242 in Scribner Library. New York: Charles Scribner's Sons, 1970. Paperback reissue.

The Shock of Recognition: The Development of Literature in the United States Recorded by the Men Who Made It (essays), ed. EW. Garden City, New York: Doubleday, Doran and Company, 1943.

Contents (by EW)
"Foreword"
"Introduction" (to Lowell on Poe)
"Introduction" (to Lowell's "A Fable for Critics")
"Introduction" (to Poe)
"Introduction" (to Melville on Hawthorne)
"Introduction" (to Emerson and Lowell on Thoreau)
"Introduction" (to Emerson and Whitman)
"Introduction" (to Bayard Taylor)
"Introduction" (to the Poe Memorial)
"Introduction" (to Henry James on Hawthorne)
"Introduction" (to Henry James on Howells)
"Introduction" (to Twain on Cooper)
"Introduction" (to John Jay Chapman on Emerson)
"Introduction" (to H. G. Wells on Stephen Crane)
"Introduction" (to Howells on Twain)
"Introduction" (to Henry Adams on George Cabot Lodge)
"Introduction" (to T. S. Eliot on Henry James)
"Introduction" (to George Santayana on William James and Josiah Royce)
"Introduction" (to D. H. Lawrence)
"Introduction" (to Amy Lowell)
"Introduction" (to H. L. Mencken)
"Introduction" (to John Dos Passos on E. E. Cummings)
"Introduction" (to Sherwood Anderson)

Signed Reviews
Aaron, Daniel. *New England Quarterly,* XVI (September 1943), 523-524.
Arvin, Newton. *Nation,* CLVII (17 July 1943), 73-74.
B., E. M. *Springfield Republican,* 21 August 1943, p. 6.

Clark, John Abbott. *Commonweal,* XXXVIII (6 August 1943), 400-401.

Derleth, August. *Chicago Sun Book Week,* II, No. 37 (11 July 1943), 5.

Jones, Howard Mumford. *Saturday Review of Literature,* XXVI, No. 22 (10 July 1943), 11.

Mayberry, George. *New Republic,* CVIII (14 June 1943), 802-803.

Schorer, Mark. *Virginia Quarterly Review,* XIX (Summer 1943), 457-464.

Schwartz, Delmore. *Partisan Review,* X (September-October 1943), 439-442.

Thorp, Willard. *Sewanee Review,* LII (April-June 1944), 302-303.

Warren, Robert Penn. *New York Times Book Review,* 13 June 1943, pp. 5, 18.

Wells, Henry W. *College English,* VI (December 1944), 179-180.

Willis, Katherine Tappert. *Library Journal,* LXVIII (15 April 1943), 327.

Unsigned Reviews
Booklist, XL (September 1943), 7-8.
New Yorker, XIX, No. 17 (12 June 1943), 79.

The Shock of Recognition: The Development of Literature in the United States Recorded by the Men Who Made It, ed. EW. Toronto: McClelland, 1943. Reissue.

The Shock of Recognition: The Development of Literature in the United States Recorded by the Men Who Made It, ed. EW, 2nd Ed. New York: Farrar, Straus and Cudahy, 1955. Reissue with additions and corrections.

Signed Reviews
Cunliffe, Marcus. *Year's Work in English Studies,* XXXVII (1956), 241-242.

Hogan, William. *San Francisco Chronicle,* 26 December 1955, p. 17.

Hutchens, John K. *New York Herald Tribune Book Review,* XXXII (18 December 1955), 2.

The Shock of Recognition: The Development of Literature in the United States Recorded by the Men Who Made It, ed. EW, 2nd Ed. London: W. H. Allen, 1956. Reissue.

Signed Reviews
Cunliffe, Marcus. *Year's Work in English Studies,* XXXVII (1956), 241-242.
Moore, Geoffrey. *Manchester Guardian,* 17 April 1956, p. 4.
Pritchett, V. S. *New Statesman and Nation,* LI (5 May 1956), 486-487.

Unsigned Reviews
Times (London), 12 April 1956, p. 13, cols. 4-5.
Times Literary Supplement, 13 April 1956, p. 220.

The Shock of Recognition: The Development of Literature in the United States Recorded by the Men Who Made It, ed. EW, 2 vols. (Vol. I, *The Nineteenth Century,* pp. 1-658, Lowell on Poe through John Jay Chapman on Emerson; Vol. II, *The Twentieth Century,* pp. 659-1290, H. G. Wells on Stephen Crane through Sherwood Anderson's letters to Van Wyck Brooks), Nos. 17-18 in Universal Library. New York: Grossett and Dunlap, 1957. Paperback reissue.

The Shock of Recognition: The Development of Literature in the United States Recorded by the Men Who Made It, ed. EW, No. G83 in Modern Library. New York: Modern Library, 1961. Reissue.

The Crack-Up: With Other Uncollected Pieces, Note-Books and Unpublished Letters Together with Letters to Fitzgerald from Gertrude Stein, Edith Wharton, T. S. Eliot, Thomas Wolfe and John Dos Passos And Essays and Poems by Paul Rosenfeld, Glenway Wescott, John Dos Passos, John Peale Bishop and Edmund Wilson (poems etc.), by F. Scott Fitzgerald *et al.,* ed. EW. New York: New Directions, James Laughlin, 1945.

Contents (by EW)
"Dedication" (poem)

Signed Reviews

Cowley, Malcolm. *New Yorker*, XXI, No. 20 (30 June 1945), 53-54, 57-58.

Jackson, Charles. *Saturday Review of Literature*, XXVIII (14 July 1945), 9-10.

Kelley, H. Gilbert. *Library Journal*, LXX (15 March 1945), 264.

Krutch, Joseph Wood. *New York Herald Tribune Weekly Book Review*, XXI (12 August 1945), 1-2.

Mayberry, George. *New Republic*, CXIII (16 July 1945), 82-83.

O'Hara, John. *New York Times Book Review*, 8 July 1945, p. 3.

Piper, D. H. *Interim*, I (1945), 39-43.

Powers, J. F. *Commonweal*, XLII (10 August 1945), 408-410.

Schorer, Mark. *Yale Review*, XXXV (Autumn 1945), 187-188.

Spectorsky, A. C. *Chicago Sun Book Week*, II (8 July 1945), 1.

Trilling, Lionel. *Nation*, CLXI (25 August 1945), 182-184.

Wanning, Andrews. *Partisan Review*, XII (Fall 1945), 545-551.

Unsigned Reviews

Booklist, XLII (September 1945), 16.

Time: The Weekly Newsmagazine, XLVI (16 July 1945), 90-91.

United States Quarterly Book List, I (September 1945), 15.

The Crack-Up: With Other Uncollected Pieces, Note-Books and Unpublished Letters Together with Letters to Fitzgerald from Gertrude Stein, Edith Wharton, T. S. Eliot, Thomas Wolfe and John Dos Passos And Essays and Poems by Paul Rosenfeld, Glenway Wescott, John Dos Passos, John Peale Bishop and Edmund Wilson, by F. Scott Fitzgerald *et al.*, ed. EW. London: Grey Walls, Falcon Press, 1947. Reissue.

Signed Review

Symons, Julian. *Sunday Times* (London), No. 6491 (7 September 1947), p. 3, col. 6.

Unsigned Reviews

Times Literary Supplement, 27 September 1947, p. 498.
Times Literary Supplement, 29 November 1947, p. 612.
Times Literary Supplement, 20 January 1950, p. 40.

The Crack-Up: With Other Uncollected Pieces, Note-Books and Unpublished Letters Together with Letters to Fitzgerald from Gertrude Stein, Edith Wharton, T. S. Eliot, Thomas Wolfe and John Dos Passos And Essays and Poems by Paul Rosenfeld, Glenway Wescott, John Dos Passos, John Peale Bishop and Edmund Wilson, by F. Scott Fitzgerald *et al.,* ed. EW, No. 54 in New Directions Paperbooks. New York: New Directions, James Laughlin, 1956. Paperback reissue.

The Collected Essays of John Peale Bishop, by John Peale Bishop, ed. EW. New York: Charles Scribner's Sons, 1948.

Contents (by EW)
"Introduction"
See also "Obscurity: Observations and Aphorisms" in General Miscellanea.

Signed Reviews

Fitts, Dudley. *New York Times Book Review,* 10 October 1948, pp. 26-27.

Kennedy, Leo. *Chicago Daily Sun-Times,* 4 October 1948, p. 29, cols. 1-2.

Mercier, Vivian. *Commonweal,* XLIX (17 December 1948), 262.

Meyer, Gerard Previn. *Saturday Review of Literature,* XXXI, No. 40 (2 October 1948), 24.

Unsigned Reviews

Booklist, XLV (15 October 1948), 63.

Bulletin from Virginia Kirkus' Bookshop Service, XVI (1 February 1948), 78.

New Yorker, XXIV, No. 34 (16 October 1948), 134-135.

The Collected Essays of John Peale Bishop, by John Peale Bishop, ed. EW. London: Charles Scribner's Sons, 1948. Reissue.

The Collected Essays of John Peale Bishop, by John Peale Bishop, ed. EW. Toronto: S. J. R. Saunders, 1948. Reissue.

Peasants and Other Stories, by Anton Pavlovich Chekhov, comp. EW, in Anchor Books. Garden City, New York: Doubleday and Company, 1956.

> *Contents* (by EW)
> "Preface" (essay)
> "Peasants" (partially translated by EW).

Peasants and Other Stories, by Anton Pavlovich Chekhov, comp. EW, in Anchor Books. Toronto: Doubleday Canada, 1956. Reissue.

The Nineteenth Century (1957). See *The Shock of Recognition* (1943).

The Twentieth Century (1957). See *The Shock of Recognition* (1943).

II / ESSAYS

"A. E. Housman: The Voice, Sent Forth, Can Never Be Recalled," *New Republic*, XCII (29 September 1937), 206-210;

    Triple Thinkers: Ten Essays, pp. 83-99, and *Triple Thinkers: Twelve Essays*, pp. 60-71;

    A Century of the Essay: British and American, ed. David Daiches (New York: Harcourt, Brace and Company, 1951), pp. 398-412.

    Reprinted as "A. E. Housman: The voice, sent forth, can never be recalled" in *Eight Essays*, pp. 115-128.

    Reprinted as "A. E. Housman" in *A. E. Housman: A Collection of Critical Essays*, ed. Christopher Ricks, No. S-TC-83 in Spectrum Books, Twentieth Century Views, ser. ed. Maynard Mack (Englewood Cliffs, New Jersey: Prentice-Hall, 1968), pp. 14-25.

"A. N. Whitehead and Bertrand Russell," *New Republic*, XLV (30 December 1925), 161-162.

"A. N. Whitehead: Physicist and Prophet," *New Republic*, LI (15 June 1927), 91-96.

"Abraham Lincoln." See "Abraham Lincoln: The Union as Religious Mysticism."

"Abraham Lincoln: The Union as Religious Mysticism," *New*

Yorker, XXIX, No. 4 (14 March 1953), 116, 119-126, 129-136;

Perspectives USA, No. 4 (Summer 1953), pp. 161-174;

Perspectives (British ed. of *Perspectives USA*), No. 4 (Summer 1953), pp. 161-174;

Eight Essays, pp. 181-202.

Reprinted with much additional material as "Abraham Lincoln" in *Patriotic Gore,* pp. 99-130 (esp. pp. 99-106, 119-130).

"The Aesthetic Upheaval in France: The Influence of Jazz in Paris and Americanization of French Literature and Art," *Vanity Fair,* XVII, No. 6 (February 1922), 49, 100.

"After the Play," *New Republic,* XXVI (9 March 1921), 47-48. Review of Arthur Hopkins' production of *Macbeth.*

"After the Play," *New Republic,* XXVI (6 April 1921), 162. Review of John Drinkwater's play *Mary Stuart.*

"After the Play," *New Republic,* XXVI (4 May 1921), 299. Review of Franz Molnar's play *Liliom.*

"Aladdin's Lecture Palace," *New Republic,* LXVII (10 June 1931), 90-92;

American Jitters, pp. 27-32;

American Earthquake, pp. 196-200.

"The Albums of Edward Gorey," *New Yorker,* XXXV, No. 45 (26 December 1959), 60, 62, 65-66;

Bit Between My Teeth, pp. 479-484.

"Aldous Huxley in the World Beyond Time," *New Yorker,* XX, No. 29 (2 September 1944), 64-66;

Classics and Commercials, pp. 209-214.

"Alexander H. Stephens," *Patriotic Gore,* pp. 380-437.

"Alexander Woollcott of the Phalanx." See "Woollcott and Fourier."

"Alice Lloyd and Farfariello," *New Republic,* XLIV (21 October 1925), 230;

American Earthquake, pp. 36-39.

"All God's Chillun and Others," *New Republic,* XXXIX (28 May 1924), 22;

Shores of Light, pp. 101-104.
See also "The All-Star Literary Vaudeville" and "Two
Young Men and An Old One."

"The All-Star Literary Vaudeville," *New Republic,* XLVII
(30 June 1926), 158-163;
American Criticism, 1926, ed. William A. Drake (New
York: Harcourt, Brace and Company, 1926), pp. 337-
358;
Shores of Light, pp. 229-247;
Literary Chronicle: 1920-1950, pp. 76-92.

"Ambiguity in 'The Turn of the Screw.'" See "The Ambiguity of Henry James."

"The Ambiguity of Henry James," *Hound and Horn,* VII,
No. 3 (April-May 1934), 385-406;
Triple Thinkers: Ten Essays, pp. 122-164;
*American Harvest: Twenty Years of Creative Writing in
the United States,* ed. Allen Tate and John Peale Bishop
(New York: L. B. Fisher, 1942), pp. 257-290;
*The Question of Henry James: A Collection of Critical
Essays,* ed. F[rederick] W[ilcox] Dupee (New York:
Henry Holt and Company, 1945), pp. 160-190.
Reprinted with a 1948 postscript in *Triple Thinkers: Twelve
Essays,* pp. 88-132; and *Criticism: The Foundations of
Modern Literary Judgment,* ed. Mark Schorer, Josephine
Miles, and Gordon Mackenzie (New York: Harcourt,
Brace and Company, 1948), pp. 147-162.
Reprinted with 1948 and 1959 postscripts in *A Casebook
on Henry James's "The Turn of the Screw,"* ed. Gerald
Willen, in Crowell Literary Casebooks, ser. ed. William
Van O'Connor (New York: Thomas Y. Crowell Com-
pany, 1959, 1960), pp. 115-153; and *Psychoanalysis and
American Fiction,* ed. Irving Malin, No. D162 in Dutton
Paperbacks (New York: E. P. Dutton & Company,
1965), pp. 143-186.
The version appearing in *Triple Thinkers: Ten Essays* par-
tially reprinted as "Ambiguity in 'The Turn of the
Screw'" in *Five Kinds of Writing: Selections from Brit-
ish and American Authors, Old and New,* ed. Theodore

Morrison and the staff of English A at Harvard University (Boston: Little, Brown and Company, 1941), pp. 292-298.

"Ambrose Bierce on the Owl Creek Bridge," *New Yorker,* XXVII, No. 43 (8 December 1951), 159-160, 163-164, 166, 168, 170. Reprinted in a much revised form and without review of Paul Fatout's *Ambrose Bierce: The Devil's Advocate* in *Patriotic Gore,* pp. 617-634.

"Ambushing a Best-Seller: 'The Turquoise,'" *New Yorker,* XXII, No. 1 (16 February 1946), 85-88. Reprinted with a 1950 short postscript as "Ambushing a Best-Seller" in *Classics and Commercials,* pp. 311-318; *Literary Chronicle: 1920-1950,* pp. 363-369; and *Story, Poem, Essay: A University Reader,* ed. Benjamin B[eard] Hoover and Donald S. Taylor (New York: Henry Holt and Company, 1957), pp. 533-537.

" 'Les Américains Chez Nous': A Review of the Much Talked of Play," *Vanity Fair,* XIV, No. 3 (May 1920), 59, 104.

"American Ballads and Their Collectors," *New Republic,* XLVII (30 June 1926), 168-170.

"An American Caligari." See " 'The Greater Movie Season.' "

"American Comedy," *New Republic,* XXXIX (18 June 1924), 103. Reprinted as "The New American Comedy" in *Shores of Light,* pp. 105-108.

"The American Court," *New Republic,* LII (24 August 1927), 19-20.

"An American Critic on Lytton Strachey," *New Statesman and Nation,* IV (24 September 1932), 344-345.

"American Critics, Left and Right." See "Complaints."

"American Heroes," *New Republic,* LIV (4 April 1928), 223-226. Reprinted as "American Heroes: Frémont and Frick" in *Shores of Light,* pp. 325-338.

"American Jazz Ballet" (printed without title in article entitled "The Doom of Lulu"), *New Republic,* XLIII (27 May 1925), 21. Reprinted with title in sequence entitled

"On and Off Broadway" in section called "The Follies: 1923-1928" in *American Earthquake,* pp. 66-68.

"American Writing: 1941." See ["The second two decades of the century"]. See also *New Republic* in Periodicals Edited by Wilson.

"Americanism," *Piece of My Mind,* pp. 32-36.

"An Analysis of Max Beerbohm," *New Yorker,* XXIV, No. 10 (1 May 1948), 80, 83-86;
Classics and Commercials, pp. 431-441.

"The Anarchists of Taste: Who First Broke the Rules of Harmony, in the Modern World?," *Vanity Fair,* XV, No. 3 (November 1920), 65, 110.

"Anatole France," *New Republic,* LXXII (7 September 1932), 90-92.

"Anatole France's Successor," *New Republic,* LIII (21 December 1927), 141-142.

"André Malraux," *New Republic,* LXXV (9 August 1933), 346-347;
Adelphi (London), N.S. (3rd ser.) VIII, No. 6 (September 1934), 395-399.
Reprinted with a letter from Malraux in *Shores of Light,* pp. 566-574; and *Literary Chronicle: 1920-1950,* pp. 171-178.
Reprinted with the letter from Malraux and a translation of the letter into English in *Malraux: A Collection of Critical Essays,* ed. R. W. B. Lewis, in Spectrum Books, Twentieth Century Views, ser. ed. Maynard Mack (Englewood Cliffs, New Jersey: Prentice-Hall, 1964), pp. 25-30.

"André Malraux: The Museum Without Walls." See "High Discourse on the Arts: André Malraux and Arnold Schoenberg."

"Animals at the Circus" (printed without title in article entitled "The Theatre"), *Dial,* LXXV (July 1923), 101-102.
Reprinted with title in sequence entitled "On and Off

Broadway" in section called "The Follies: 1923-1928" in *American Earthquake,* pp. 57-58.

"An Anthology of the Literary Season," *New Republic,* XLVII (2 June 1926), 62-63.

"The Anthropologists" (printed without title in article entitled "A Reporter in New Mexico: Shalako"), New *Yorker,* XXV, No. 7 (9 April 1949), 68-69. Reprinted with title in a much revised and enlarged form in section entitled "Zuñi (1947)" in *Red, Black, Blond and Olive,* pp. 15-23.

"Anti-Literature," *New Republic,* XLVIII (13 October 1926), 219-220.

"The Antrobuses and the Earwickers," *Nation,* CLVI (30 January 1943), 167-168;
Classics and Commercials, pp. 81-86.

"Apologies to the Iroquois," *New Yorker,* XXXV, No. 35 (17 October 1959), 49-52, 54, 57, 59-60, 62, 64, 66-68, 70-72, 77-79, 81-82, 84, 86-88, 91-92, 94-98, 103-107, 109-114; No. 36 (24 October 1959), 48-50, 52, 54, 57, 59-60, 62, 64, 69-70, 72, 74, 76, 81-84; No. 37 (31 October 1959), 50-52, 54, 56, 59-60, 62, 65-66, 68, 71, 74-78, 81, 83, 86-88, 93-97, 100-104, 109-116; No. 38 (7 November 1959), 96, 98, 101-102, 104, 106, 108, 111-112, 114, 116, 118, 123-124, 126, 128, 130, 133-134, 136-140, 143-150; *Apologies to the Iroquois,* pp. 37-310.

"The Apotheosis of Somerset Maugham." See "Somerset Maugham and an Antidote."

"An Appeal for James Joyce," *New Republic,* CIII (9 December 1940), 797.

"An Appeal to Progressives," *New Republic,* LXV (14 January 1931), 234-238. Reprinted with a postscript in *Shores of Light,* pp. 518-533. Reprinted with postscript and editor's headnote in *The Western World in the Twentieth Century: A Source Book from the Contemporary Civilization Program in Columbia College, Columbia University,* ed. Bernard Wishy (New York: Columbia University Press, 1961), pp. 300-308.

"Appendices," *Europe Without Baedeker,* pp. 421-427, and 1st rev. ed., pp. 350-356.

"Appendix" (by EW and "Your Reviewer"), *Dead Sea Scrolls 1947-1969,* pp. 293-308. See also "Your Reviewer" (*Listener*) in Letters about Wilson.

"Appendix A" (by EW and W. Hanks), *Europe Without Baedeker,* pp. 421-423, and 1st rev. ed., pp. 350-352. See also Hanks, W., in Letters to Wilson.

"Appendix B" (by EW and Captain Francis Noel-Baker, M.P.), *Europe Without Baedeker,* pp. 424-425, and 1st rev. ed., pp. 353-354.

"Appendix B," *To the Finland Station.* See "Marx on the Differential Calculus."

"Appendix C," *Europe Without Baedeker,* pp. 426-427, and 1st rev. ed., pp. 355-356. Includes a poem by an unnamed poet.

"Appendix D." See "Herr Vogt and His Modern Successors."

"Archibald MacLeish and 'the Word,'" *New Republic,* CIII (1 July 1940), 30-32. Reprinted as "Archibald MacLeish and the Word" in *Classics and Commercials,* pp. 3-9.

"Are Artists People?: Some Answers to the New Masses Questionaire" (by EW *et al.,* with EW's replies signed), *New Masses,* III, No. 1 (January 1927), 5-9.

"The Army, 1917-1919," *New Yorker,* XLIII, No. 12 (13 May 1967), 54-56, 58, 61-62, 64, 67-68, 70, 73-76, 78, 80, 85-86, 88, 91-93, 95, 98, 101-102, 104, 109-114, 116, 119-122, 125-128, 131-136, 138, 140-154, 157. Reprinted with inclusion of the poems "Colloquial [Oftentimes: most of the doctors]" and "Army" in *Prelude,* pp. 171-278.

"Art, the Proletariat and Marx," *New Republic,* LXXVI (23 August 1933), 41-45;
Adelphi (London), N.S. (3rd ser.) VII, No. 1 (October 1933), 1-4; No. 2 (November 1933), 112-117.

"Art Young," *New Republic,* LVII (9 January 1929), 217-218;
Shores of Light, pp. 351-356.

"The Artificial Cholera Epidemic," *Cold War and the Income Tax*, pp. 73-82.

"Arvin's Longfellow and New York State's Geology," *New Yorker*, XXXIX, No. 5 (23 March 1963), 174-181. Reprinted without review of *Geologic Map of New York* as "Newton's Arvin's Longfellow" in *Bit Between My Teeth*, pp. 551-560.

"As I Saw Leningrad" (printed with pictures), *Travel*, LXVII (May 1936), 20-23, 60-61. Reprinted without pictures as "Leningrad Theaters" in *Travels in Two Democracies*, pp. 162-178. Reprinted without pictures and with additional material in brackets as "Leningrad Theaters" in *Red, Black, Blond and Olive*, pp. 166-188. First three paragraphs of version appearing in *Red, Black, Blond and Olive* reprinted as "Impressions of Leningrad" in *The Great Travelers: A Collection of Firsthand Narratives of Wayfarers, Wanderers and Explorers in All Parts of the World from 450 B.C. to the Present*, ed. Milton [Allan] Rugoff, Vol. II (New York: Simon and Schuster, 1960), pp. 650-651.

"At Laurelwood: 1939." See "A New Jersey Childhood: 'These Men Must Do Their Duty.'"

"The Author at Sixty," *Piece of My Mind*, pp. 209-235.

"Axël and Rimbaud" (printed with headnote by EW), *New Republic*, LXII (26 February 1930), 34-40; concluded as "Axël and Rimbaud: III," *New Republic*, LXII (5 March 1930), 69-73. Reprinted without headnote in *Axel's Castle*, pp. 257-298.

"Axel's Castle" (essay). See "A Short View of Proust."

"Back East: October Again: A Strike in Lawrence, Mass." See "Lawrence, Mass."

"A Bad Case of Tax Delinquency," *Cold War and the Income Tax*, pp. 3-9.

"A Bad Day in Brooklyn," *New Republic*, LXVI (22 April 1931), 263-266;
American Jitters, pp. 121-132;
American Earthquake, pp. 281-291.

"The Ballets of Jean Cocteau: Theatrical Innovations of the 'Enfant Terrible' of French Art," *Vanity Fair*, XVIII, No. 1 (March 1922), 48, 94.

"The Bank of the United States: II. At City Hall," *New Republic*, LXV (28 January 1931), 290-291. Reprinted as "The Bank of United States" in *American Jitters*, pp. 32-36; and *American Earthquake*, pp. 201-204.

"Bankrupt Britons and Voyaging Romantics," *New Yorker*, XXVI, No. 8 (15 April 1950), 128-130. Reprinted without review of W. H. Auden's *The Enchafèd Flood, or the Romantic Iconography of the Sea* as "Emergence of Angus Wilson" in *Bit Between My Teeth*, pp. 270-273.

"Bees, Wasps and Bombers." See "The Intelligence of Bees, Wasps, Butterflies, and Bombing Planes."

"Bernard DeVoto," *New Republic*, LXXXIX (3 February 1937), 405-408. Reprinted as "Bernard De Voto" in *Shores of Light*, pp. 650-661.

"Bernard Shaw." See "Critics of the Middle Class."

"Bernard Shaw at Eighty," *Atlantic Monthly*, CLXI (February 1938), 198-215;
  Triple Thinkers: Ten Essays, pp. 220-265, and *Triple Thinkers: Twelve Essays*, pp. 165-196;
  George Bernard Shaw: A Critical Survey, ed. Louis Kronenberger (Cleveland and New York: World Publishing Company, 1953), pp. 126-152;
  Eight Essays, pp. 129-166.

"Bernard Shaw at the Metropolitan." See "Shaw in the Metropolitan."

"Bernard Shaw on the Training of a Statesman," *New Yorker*, XX, No. 37 (28 October 1944), 68, 70, 73;
  Classics and Commercials, pp. 238-243.

"Bernard Shaw Since the War," *New Republic*, XL (27 August 1924), 380-381.

"Bernard Shaw Still Speaking," *New Yorker*, XXVII, No. 16 (2 June 1951), 101-102, 104-105. Reprinted as "The Last

Phase of Bernard Shaw" in *Bit Between My Teeth*, pp. 34-40.

"Bert Savoy and Eddie Cantor of the Follies." See "The Theatre" (August 1923).

"The Best People," *Scribner's Magazine*, XCI (March 1932), 153-157;
American Jitters, pp. 284-297.
  Reprinted with editor's headnote in *Contemporary Opinion*, ed. Kendall B[enard] Taft, John Francis McDermott, and Dana O. Jensen (Boston: Houghton Mifflin Company [Cambridge, Massachusetts: Riverside Press], 1933), pp. 112-123.
  Reprinted with another editor's headnote in *Types of Prose Writing*, ed. Clark H[arris] Slover and De Witt T[almadge] Starnes (Boston: Houghton Mifflin Company [Cambridge, Massachusetts: Riverside Press], 1933), pp. 371-380.
  Reprinted as "Mr. and Mrs. X" in *American Earthquake*, pp. 432-440.

"La Boheme," *New Republic*, LXV (4 February 1931), 322. Reprinted as "The Metropolitan" in *American Jitters*, pp. 36-37. Reprinted as "The Metropolitan Opera House" in *American Earthquake*, p. 205.

"Book-Galleries and Book-Shops," *New Republic*, XLVII (4 August 1926), 310-311. Reprinted as "Book Galleries and Book Shops" in *American Earthquake*, pp. 80-83.

"Book Review of Fugitives, An Anthology of Verse." See "The Tennessee Poets" (essays).

"Books and Things," *New Republic*, XXVI (20 April 1921), 240-241.

"Books of Etiquette and Emily Post," *New Yorker*, XXIII, No. 22 (19 July 1947), 58, 60, 63-64, 66;
Classics and Commercials, pp. 372-382;
Literary Chronicle: 1920-1950, pp. 380-389.

"Boswell and Others," *New Republic*, XLIII (1 July 1925), 153-154.

"The Boys in the Back Room," printed in entirety as the book *Boys in the Back Room*. Reprinted with omissions in *Classics and Commercials*, pp. 19-56; and *Literary Chronicle: 1920-1950*, pp. 216-249.

"The Boys in the Back Room: James M. Cain and John O'Hara," *New Republic*, CIII (11 November 1940), 665-666.

Contents
["James M. Cain"]
["John O'Hara"]

"The Boys in the Back Room: William Saroyan," *New Republic*, CIII (18 November 1940), 697-698. Reprinted as "William Saroyan" in *Boys in the Back Room*, pp. 23-32; *Classics and Commercials*, pp. 26-31; and *Literary Chronicle: 1920-1950*, pp. 222-227.

"Broadway," *New Republic*, L (2 March 1927), 45. Reprinted as " 'Broadway' " in *American Earthquake*, pp. 86-88.

"Broadway in August," *New Republic*, XLVIII (1 September 1926), 44-45. Reprinted in slightly abridged form in *American Earthquake*, pp. 83-85.

"Brokers and Pioneers," in *New Republic*, LXX (23 March 1932), 142-145.

"The Bronze Horseman," *New Republic*, XCIII (26 January 1938), 330-334. Reprinted as " 'The Bronze Horseman' " in *Triple Thinkers: Ten Essays*, pp. 65-82, and *Triple Thinkers: Twelve Essays*, pp. 47-59.

"Budapest," *New Yorker*, XLII, No. 15 (4 June 1966), 88, 90, 92, 94, 97-98, 100, 103-104, 106, 109-112, 115-118, 121-122, 124, 126-128, 130, 132-134, 136-139; *Europe Without Baedeker*, 1st rev. ed., pp. 418-467.

"Bureaucratic Theology: The Tax Jungle," *Cold War and the Income Tax*, pp. 32-40.

"Burlesque Shows," *Shores of Light*, pp. 274-281.

"Burton Rascoe," *New Republic*, LIX (29 May 1929), 49-50; *Shores of Light*, pp. 397-402.

["By a desperate effort in the last line"], *S4N,* Year IV, No. 26-29 (May-August 1923), p. [107].

"Byron and His Biographers." See "Two Views of Byron."

"Byron in the Twenties," *Shores of Light,* pp. 57-67;
Byron: *A Collection of Critical Essays,* ed. Paul West, No. S-TC-31 in Spectrum Books, Twentieth Century Views, ser. ed. Maynard Mack (Englewood Cliffs, New Jersey: Prentice-Hall, 1963, 1965), pp. 138-144.

"C. L. Dodgson: The Poet Logician." See "The Poet-Logician."

"The Californians," *New Republic,* CIII (16 December 1940), 839-840. Reprinted as "Facing the Pacific" in *Boys in the Back Room,* pp. 55-64; *Classics and Commercials,* pp. 45-51; and *Literary Chronicle: 1920-1950,* pp. 239-244.

"The Californians: Storm and Steinbeck," *New Republic,* CIII (9 December 1940), 784-787.

Contents
["Hans Otto Storm"]
["John Steinbeck"]

"Calvin Stowe; Francis Grierson; *The Battle Hymn of the Republic;* The Union as Religious Mysticism," *Patriotic Gore,* pp. 59-98. See also "Francis Grierson: Log House and Salon."

"Can New York Stage a Serious Play?" (printed without title in article entitled "The Doom of Lulu"), *New Republic,* XLIII (27 May 1925), 20-21. Reprinted with title in sequence entitled "On and Off Broadway" in section called "The Follies: 1923-1928" in *American Earthquake,* pp. 64-66.

"The Canons of Poetry," *Atlantic Monthly,* CLIII (April 1934), 455-462. Reprinted in revised form as "Is Verse a Dying Technique?" in *Triple Thinkers: Ten Essays,* pp. 20-41. Revised form reprinted with a 1948 postscript as "Is Verse a Dying Technique?" in *Triple Thinkers: Twelve Essays,* pp. 15-30; *Little Treasury of American Prose: The Major Writers from Colonial Times to the Present Day,* ed. George Mayberry, in The Little Treasury Series (New York: Charles Scribner's Sons, 1949), pp. 595-613; and

Criticism: the Major Texts, ed. Walter Jackson Bate (New York: Harcourt, Brace & World, 1952), pp. 588-596.

"Casanova," *New Republic,* LXXII (17 August 1932), 10-13; correction in LXXII (31 August 1932), 81. Reprinted as "Uncomfortable Casanova" in *Wound and the Bow,* pp. 182-194, and Galaxy Books reissue, pp. 148-158; and *Encore,* III (June 1943), 657-664.

"The Case of Major Eatherly," *Cold War and the Income Tax,* pp. 95-102.

"The Case of the Author," *American Jitters,* pp. 297-313.

"The Causes of the Iroquois Resurgence," *New Yorker,* XXXV, No. 38 (7 November 1959), 111-112, 114, 116, 118, 123-124, 126, 128, 130, 133-134. Reprinted as "Growth and Causes of Iroquois Resurgence" in *Apologies to the Iroquois,* pp. 270-289.

"Cavalier and Yankee," *New Yorker,* XXXVII, No. 37 (28 October 1961), 197-198, 201-202, 204-205; *Bit Between My Teeth,* pp. 282-290.

"A Censored Psychoanalysis," *New Republic,* L (11 May 1927), 334-335.

"Chaplin and His Comic Rivals." See "Some Recent Films."

"Chaplin the 'Artist' Unable to Escape Custard-Pie Taint," *Baltimore Evening Sun,* 14 November 1923, Section 2, p. 23.

"Charlotte Forten and Colonel Higginson," *New Yorker,* XXX, No. 8 (10 April 1954), 132, 135-142, 145-147. Reprinted without paragraphs on Mary Chesnut and without review of Forten's *The Journal of Charlotte L. Forten* as "Northerners in the South: Charlotte Forten and Colonel Higginson" in *Patriotic Gore,* pp. 239-257.

"The Chastening of American Prose Style; John W. De Forest," *Patriotic Gore,* pp. 635-742.

"Christian Gauss," *American Scholar,* XXI (Summer 1952), 345-355. Reprinted as "Prologue, 1952: Christian Gauss as a Teacher of Literature" in *Shores of Light,* pp. 3-26; and

Literary Chronicle: 1920-1950, pp. 9-29. Reprinted as "Christian Gauss as a Teacher of Literature" in *The American Scholar Reader,* ed. Hiram Collins Haydn and Betsy Saunders (New York: Atheneum Press, 1960), pp. 239-256.

"Christophe and Estimé," *Reporter,* II, No. 10 (9 May 1950), 21-26.
Contents
    ["King Christophe's Citadel"]
    ["Color Politics"]

"Citizen of the Union," *New Republic,* LVII (13 February 1929), 352-353;
Shores of Light, pp. 415-420;
Literary Chronicle: 1920-1950, pp. 123-128.

"The City of Our Lady the Queen of the Angels," *New Republic,* LXIX (2 December 1931), 67-68; (9 December 1931), 89-93;
American Jitters, pp. 225-244;
American Earthquake, pp. 379-396.

"Class War Exhibits," *New Masses,* VII, No. 10 (April 1932), 7.

"The Classics on the Soviet Stage," *Soviet Russia Today,* IV, No. 7 (September 1935), 22-23. Reprinted with a postscript in *Shores of Light,* pp. 610-615.

"The Cold War and the Income Tax" (essay), *Liberation: An Independent Monthly,* VIII, No. 10 (December 1963), 25. Excerpts from the essays "How Free Is the Free World?" and "The Strategy of Tax Refusal."

"Cold Water on Bakunin," *New Republic,* XCVII (7 December 1938), 137-138;
Shores of Light, pp. 716-721.

"Color Politics" (printed without title in article entitled "Christophe and Estimé"), *Reporter,* II, No. 10 (9 May 1950), 24-26. Reprinted with title and with 1956 additions in brackets in section entitled "Haiti (1949)" in *Red, Black, Blond, and Olive,* pp. 86-95.

"Comedy, Classical and American," *Theatre Arts Monthly,* IX (February 1925), 73-78, 83-84.

"Communist Criticism." See "The Literary Left."

"Communists and Cops," *New Republic,* LXV (11 February 1931), 344-347;
American Jitters, pp. 37-45;
American Earthquake, pp. 206-213.

"Complaints," *New Republic,* LXXXIX (20 January 1937), 345-348; (3 February 1937), 405-408.

   Contents
      I. "The Literary Left"
      II. "Bernard DeVoto"

   Reprinted in entirety as "American Critics, Left and Right" in *Shores of Light,* pp. 640-661.

"Comrade Prince: A Memoir of D. S. Mirsky," *Encounter,* V, No. 1 (July 1955), 10-20.

"Confession of a Non-Fighter," *Piece of My Mind,* pp. 49-50.

"Connolly's 'Unquiet Grave;' Thurber's 'White Deer,' " *New Yorker,* XXI, No. 37 (27 October 1945), 84, 86, 89. Partially reprinted without title in essay entitled "A Cry from the Unquiet Grave" in *Classics and Commercials,* pp. 280-283.

"The Conquerors by André Malraux With an Introduction by Edmund Wilson," *Modern Monthly,* VIII, No. 2 (March 1934), 69-70. EW's introduction ends on p. 70; Malraux's article continues to p. 76 and in subsequent issues of the periodical.

"A Conversation with Edmund Wilson: 'We Don't Know Where We Are' " (printed with editor's headnote), *New Republic,* CXL (30 March 1959), 13-15. Reprinted with headnote as "The Critic in Isolation: A Conversation with Edmund Wilson" in *Conversations with Henry Brandon,* by Henry Brandon *et al.* (Boston: Houghton Mifflin Company, 1968), pp. 164-181.

"Conversations with Yadin and Flusser," *New Yorker*, XLIII, No. 26 (19 August 1967), 54, 59-60, 62, 64, 66, 69; *Dead Sea Scrolls 1947-1969*, pp. 244-255.

"Conversing With Malcolm Sharp," *University of Chicago Law Review*, XXXIII, No. 2 (Winter 1966), 198-201. Pp. 191-228 of *University of Chicago Law Review*, XXXIII, No. 2 (Winter 1966), were separately reprinted by the University of Chicago in 1966 for private circulation as *Malcolm P. Sharp*; EW's essay again appears on pp. 198-201.

"The Copper Scrolls," *New Yorker*, XLV, No. 6 (29 March 1969), 51-52, 54, 57-58; *Dead Sea Scrolls 1947-1969*, pp. 170-175.

"Cotton Blossom Express," *Red, Black, Blond and Olive*, p. 71.

" 'The Country I Remember,' " *New Republic*, CIII (14 October 1940), 529-530; *Bit Between My Teeth*, pp. 107-113.

" 'Cousin Swift, You Will Never Be a Poet,' " *New Republic*, XCIII (8 December 1937), 138-139; *Shores of Light*, pp. 696-700.

"The Critic as Politician," *New Republic*, XLV (2 December 1925), 42-43.

"The Critic in Isolation: A Conversation with Edmund Wilson." See "A Conversation with Edmund Wilson: 'We Don't Know Where We Are.' "

"The Critic Who Does Not Exist." See "Literary Politics."

"Critics of the Middle Class: I, Karl Marx," *New York Herald-Tribune Books*, VIII (14 February 1932), 1, 6, 18; continued as "Critics of the Middle Class: II, Gustave Flaubert," *New York Herald-Tribune Books*, VIII (21 February 1932), 1, 6; concluded as "Critics of the Middle Class: III, Bernard Shaw," *New York Herald-Tribune Books*, VIII (28 February 1932), 1, 6. Section entitled "Critics of the Middle Class: III, Bernard Shaw" reprinted as "Bernard Shaw" in *Adelphi* (London), N.S. (3rd ser.), V, No. 1 (October 1932), 44-52.

"The Crushing of Washington Square," *New Republic,* LII
(12 October 1927), 211-212;
American Earthquake, pp. 93-94.
See also "A New York Diary" (12 October 1927).

"A Cry from the Unquiet Grave," *Classics and Commercials,*
pp. 280-285. See also "Connolly's 'Unquiet Grave;' Thurber's 'White Deer' " and "Lesser Books by Brilliant Writers."

"Current Fashions," *American Earthquake,* p. 76.

"Dahlberg, Dos Passos and Wilder," *New Republic,* LXII (26
March 1930), 156-158;
Shores of Light, pp. 442-450.
Literary Chronicle: 1920-1950, pp. 138-145.

"Dawn of the New Deal: 1932-1934." See "U. S. A., November, 1932-May, 1934."

["David Gordon, a young poet of eighteen"] (paragraph in
article by several hands entitled "The Week"), *New Republic,* LI (22 June 1927), 108-109.

"Dawn Powell: Greenwich Village in the Fifties," *New
Yorker,* XXXVIII, No. 39 (17 November 1962), 233-236,
238;
Bit Between My Teeth, pp. 526-533.

"The Dead Sea Scrolls: 1969," *New Yorker,* XLV, No. 5 (22
March 1969), 45-46, 48, 51-52, 54, 57-58, 60, 63-64, 66, 68,
73-74, 76, 78, 81-84; No. 6 (29 March 1969), 45-46, 48,
51-52, 54, 57-58, 60, 65, 68, 71-72, 74, 79-80, 82, 85-86,
88, 93-94, 96; No. 7 (5 April 1969), 45-46, 48, 51-52, 54,
56, 58, 63-64, 66, 68, 70, 75-76, 78, 80, 82, 87-88, 90,
92, 94.

Contents
    ["Introduction"]
    "Polemics"
    "The Genesis Apocryphon"
    "The Psalms"
    "John Allegro"
    "The Copper Scrolls"
    "The Texts"
    "The Testimonia"
    "The Epistle to the Hebrews"

"The Shrine of the Book"
"Masada"
"Dubious Documents
"The June War—The Temple Scroll"

See also "1955-1967."

"The Death of Elinor Wylie." See "In Memory of Elinor Wylie."

"The Decline of the Dial," *New Republic,* LII (12 October 1927), 211. See also "A New York Diary" (12 October 1927).

"Decline of the Revolutionary Tradition: Anatole France," *New Republic,* LXXX (24 October 1934), 302-307.
To the Finland Station, pp. 55-68, and Anchor Books reissues, pp. 55-68.

"Decline of the Revolutionary Tradition: Renan," *New Republic,* LXXX (19 September 1934), 150-153.
To the Finland Station, pp. 36-44, and Anchor Books reissues, pp. 35-43.

"Decline of the Revolutionary Tradition: Taine," *New Republic,* LXXX (3 October 1934), 207-210.
To the Finland Station, pp. 45-54, and Anchor Books reissues, pp. 44-54.

"Deep River and Gentlemen Prefer Blondes," *New Republic,* XLVIII (20 October 1926), 245-246.

"A Definitive Edition of Ben Jonson," *New Yorker,* XXXIV, No. 37 (6 November 1948), 123-124, 126-127. Reprinted as "Morose Ben Jonson" in *Triple Thinkers: Twelve Essays,* pp. 213-232; and *Ben Jonson: A Collection of Critical Essays,* ed. Jonas A. Barish, in Spectrum Books, Twentieth Century Views, ser. ed. Maynard Mack (Englewood Cliffs, New Jersey: Prentice-Hall, 1963), pp. 60-74.

"Deganiya," *New Yorker,* XXX, No. 42 (4 December 1954), 217-220. Reprinted as "Degániya" in *Red, Black, Blond and Olive,* pp. 483-488.

"The Delegates from Duquesne" (printed with inclusion of material later entitled "The Zero Hour"), *Modern Monthly,*

VIII (July 1934), 331-336. Reprinted in abridged form without "The Zero Hour" in *American Earthquake,* pp. 551-560.

"The Delinquent in the Hands of the IRS," *Cold War and the Income Tax,* pp. 10-19.

"Departure" (printed without title in article entitled "A Reporter in New Mexico: Shalako"), *New Yorker,* XXV, No. 8 (16 April 1949), 92-94. Reprinted with title in section entitled "Zuñi (1947)" in *Red, Black, Blond and Olive,* pp. 65-68.

"Departure" (in essay entitled " 'On the Eve' "), *New Yorker,* XLIII, No. 26 (19 August 1967), 69-70, 72, 74; *Dead Sea Scrolls 1947-1969,* pp. 256-260.

"The Despot of Dearborn" (with a headnote), *Scribner's Magazine,* XC (July 1931), 24-35.

"Detroit Motors," *New Republic,* LXVI (25 March 1931), 145-150; *American Jitters,* pp. 46-85; *American Earthquake,* pp. 214-248.

"Detroit Paradoxes," *New Republic,* LXXV (12 July 1933), 230-233.

"The Dial Award," *New Republic,* XLIX (5 January 1927), 192.

"Dickens and the Marshalsea Prison" (printed alone) *Atlantic Monthly,* CLXV (April 1940), 473-483; (May 1940), 681-691. Reprinted without title in a long essay entitled "Dickens: The Two Scrooges" in *Wound and the Bow,* pp. 3-48, 50-57, and Galaxy Books reissue, pp. 5-40, 42-47; and *Eight Essays,* pp. 13-47, 49-55.

"Dickens: The Two Scrooges" (printed alone) *New Republic,* CII (4 March 1940), 297-300; (11 March 1940), 339-342. Reprinted without title in the longer essay entitled "Dickens: The Two Scrooges" in *Wound and the Bow,* pp. 61-74, and Galaxy Books reissue, pp. 51-61; and *Eight Essays,* pp. 58-68.

"Dickens: The Two Scrooges" (longer essay), *Wound and the Bow,* pp. 1-104, and Galaxy Books reissue, pp. 3-85.

Contents

["Dickens and the Marshalsea Prison"]
["Dickens: The Two Scrooges"] (the shorter essay by this title)
["The Mystery of Edwin Drood"]

Reprinted in entirety in *Eight Essays,* pp. 11-91.

"A Dissenting Opinion on Kafka," *New Yorker,* XXIII, No. 23 (26 July 1947), 53-57;
Classics and Commercials, pp. 383-392;
Literary Chronicle: 1920-1950, pp. 389-397;
Kafka: A Collection of Critical Essays, ed. Ronald [D.] Gray, No. S-TC-17 in Spectrum Books, Twentieth Century Views, ser. ed. Maynard Mack (Englewood Cliffs, New Jersey: Prentice-Hall, 1962), pp. 91-97.

"Diversity of Opinion in the South: William J. Grayson, George Fitzhugh, Hilton [sic] R. Helper," *Patriotic Gore,* pp. 336-379.

"Doctor Life and His Guardian Angel," *New Yorker,* XXXIV, No. 39 (15 November 1958), 201-206, 209-216, 219-222, 224-226;
Bit Between My Teeth, pp. 420-446.

"The Documents on the Marquis de Sade," *New Yorker,* XLI, No. 31 (18 September 1965), 175-186, 189-192, 195-197, 201-204, 208-214, 217-224;
Bit Between My Teeth, pp. 174-227.

"Donmanship," *Nation,* CLXXXIX (26 September 1959), 174-175;
Bit Between My Teeth, pp. 473-478.

"The Doom of Lulu," *New Republic,* XLIII (27 May 1925), 20-21.

Contents

["Can New York Stage a Serious Play?"]
["American Jazz Ballet"]

"Dos Passos and the Social Revolution," *New Republic,* LVIII (17 April 1929), 256-257;
Shores of Light, pp. 429-435;
Literary Chronicle: 1920-1950, pp. 128-133.

"Dos Passos in the Pacific—Shaw's Birthday—A Note for Mr. Behrman," *New Yorker*, XXII, No. 28 (24 August 1946), 66, 69-70.

"Dostoevsky Abroad," *New Republic*, LVII (30 January 1929), 302-303;
Shores of Light, pp. 408-414;
Literary Chronicle: 1920-1950, pp. 117-122.

"Dr. Johnson," *New Yorker*, XX, No. 40 (18 November 1944), 78, 81-82. Reprinted as "Reëxamining Dr. Johnson" in *Classics and Commercials*, pp. 244-249; *Literary Chronicle: 1920-1950*, pp. 328-333; and *Samuel Johnson: A Collection of Critical Essays*, ed. Donald J. Greene, in Spectrum Books, Twentieth Century Views, ser. ed. Maynard Mack (Englewood Cliffs, New Jersey: Prentice-Hall, 1965), pp. 11-14.

"Drama, Music, Films" (by EW *et al.*), *New Republic*, LXVI (1 April 1931), 182-183.

"Drama on Macdougal Street Again," *New Republic*, LXVI (29 April 1931), 303.

"The Dream of H. C. Earwicker." See "H. C. Earwicker and Family."

"Dream Poetry," *New Yorker*, XIII, No. 24 (31 July 1937), 50-52. Reprinted with a postscript in *Shores of Light*, pp. 688-695.

"Dubious Documents," *New Yorker*, XLV, No. 7 (5 April 1969), 66, 68, 70, 75-76, 78;
Dead Sea Scrolls 1947-1969, pp. 213-220.

"Dwight Morrow in New Jersey," *New Republic*, LXVI (5 November 1930), 316-317;
American Jitters, pp. 1-5;
American Earthquake, pp. 169-173.

"E. E. Cummings's *Him*." See "Him."

"E. E. Paramore, Jr., '14," *Hill School Bulletin*, V, No. 3 (February 1926), 34-36.

"An Early Theater Guild Production" (printed without title in article entitled "The Theatre"), *Dial*, LXXIV (April

1923), 420. Reprinted with title in sequence entitled "On and Off Broadway" in section called "The Follies: 1923-1928" in *American Earthquake,* pp. 52-53.

"The Earthquake: October, 1930-October, 1931," published with inclusion of the essays "The Independent Farmer" and "The Case of the Author" as the book *American Jitters.* Reprinted without these two essays as "The Earthquake: October, 1930-October, 1931" in *American Earthquake,* pp. 167-442.

"The Economic Interpretation of Wilder," *New Republic,* LXV (26 November 1930), 31-32;
Shores of Light, pp. 500-503.

"Edith Wharton: A Memoir by an English Friend," *New Yorker,* XXIII, No. 33 (4 October 1947), 94-97;
Classics and Commercials, pp. 412-418;
Edith Wharton: A Collection of Critical Essays, ed. Irving Howe, No. S-TC-20 in Spectrum Books, Twentieth Century Views, ser. ed. Maynard Mack (Englewood Cliffs, New Jersey: Prentice-Hall, 1962), pp. 172-176.

"Editorial," *Nassau Literary Magazine,* LXXI (April 1915), 43-47.

Contents
    I. "The Fog Lifts," pp. 43-45
    II. "The Need for a Nimbus," pp. 45-47

"Editorial," *Nassau Literary Magazine,* LXXI (June 1915), 160-161.

Contents
    I. "The Question of Costume," pp. 160-161
    II. "Sacrosanct Prospect," p. 161

"Edmund Wilson: Background of a Critic," *New York Herald Tribune Book Review,* XXIX, No. 9 (12 October 1952), 10.

"Edmund Wilson Eludes the Interviewer." See Wain, John ("Literature and Life—6: Edmund Wilson Eludes the Interviewer"), in Items about Wilson.

"Edmund Wilson replies [*sic*]," *New York Review of Books,* V, No. 2 (26 August 1965), 26.

"Edna St. Vincent Millay: A Memoir," *Nation,* CLXXIV (19 April 1952), 370-383. Reprinted as "Epilogue, 1952: Edna St. Vincent Millay" in *Shores of Light,* pp. 744-793.

"Education," *Piece of My Mind,* pp. 137-168.

"Eisenstein in Hollywood," *New Republic,* LXVIII (4 November 1931), 320-322;
American Jitters, pp. 244-253;
American Earthquake, pp. 397-413.

"Election Night," *Travels in Two Democracies,* pp. 11-13;
American Earthquake, pp. 445-446.

"Emergence of Angus Wilson." See "Bankrupt Britons and Voyaging Romantics."

"Emergence of Ernest Hemingway," *Shores of Light,* pp. 115-124;
Hemingway and His Critics: An International Anthology, ed. Carlos Baker, No. AC36 in American Century Series (New York: Hill and Wang, 1961), pp. 55-60.
Reprinted with a 1953 postscript in *Literary Chronicle: 1920-1950,* pp. 41-49.

"Emil Jannings' American Film." See "Jannings' First American Film."

"The Emotional Pattern in Marx," *New Republic,* CII (19 February 1940), 239-242.

"The Enchanted Forest," *New Republic,* LXVIII (28 October 1931), 290-294;
American Jitters, pp. 193-206;
American Earthquake, pp. 348-360.

"Engaged," *New Republic,* XLIII (29 July 1925), 262-263.

"Engels to Marx, February 13, 1851." See Engels, Friedrich, in Translations by Wilson.

"An English Critic on the French Novel—Gertrude Stein as a Young Woman," *New Yorker,* XXVII, No. 31 (15 September 1951), 124-126, 129-131. Reprinted without review of Martin Turnell's *The Novel in France* and with a postscript as "Things As They Are" in *Shores of Light,* pp. 580-586.

"Enlightenment Through the Movies," *New Republic*, XLIV
(11 November 1925), 303-304. Reprinted as "Enlightenment through the Films" in *American Earthquake*, pp. 75-
76.

"Epilogue." See "The Traveler."

"Epilogue, 1952: Edna St. Vincent Millay." See "Edna St.
Vincent Millay: A Memoir."

"The Epistle to the Hebrews," *New Yorker*, XLV, No. 6 (29
March 1969), 79-80, 82, 85-86, 88;
Dead Sea Scrolls 1947-1969, pp. 189-195.

"Eretz Yisrael," *New Yorker*, XXX, No. 42 (4 December
1954), 174, 176-184, 186-222. Reprinted as "Éretz Yisraél"
in *Red, Black, Blond and Olive*, pp. 427-492.

"Eretz Yisrael" (shorter essay), *New Yorker*, XXX, No. 42
(4 December 1954), 220-222. Reprinted as "Éretz Yisraél"
in *Red, Black, Blond and Olive*, pp. 488-492.

"Eric Partridge, the Word King," *New Yorker*, XXVII, No.
25 (4 August 1951), 63-66;
Bit Between My Teeth, pp. 131-136.

"Ernest Hemingway: Bourdon Gauge of Morale," *Atlantic
Monthly*, CLXIV, No. 1 (July 1939), 36-46. Reprinted as
"Hemingway: Gauge of Morale" in *Wound and the Bow*,
pp. 214-242, and Galaxy Books reissue, pp. 174-197; *Ernest
Hemingway: The Man and His Work*, ed. John K[erwin]
M[ichael] McCaffery (Cleveland and New York: World
Publishing Company, 1950, 1951), pp. 236-257; *Eight Es-
says*, pp. 92-114; and *Literature in America: An Anthology
of Literary Criticism*, comp. Philip Rahv, No. MG 11 in
Meridian Books Giant Original Editions (New York:
Meridian Books, 1957), pp. 373-390.

"Essay with Translation: The Fabric of Paul Verlaine With
a Translation of One of his Poems By Eric Elberson Quoits"
(by EW and John Peale Bishop), *Playboy*, II, No. 1
(March 1923), 43. Includes a satiric translation of Verlaine's poem "Le ciel."

"The Essays of V. S. Pritchett—The Journals of Baudelaire," *New Yorker*, XXIII, No. 37 (1 November 1947), 93-94, 96. Reprinted without review of V. S. Pritchett's *The Living Novel* as "The Sanctity of Baudelaire" in *Classics and Commercials*, pp. 419-422.

"The Essene Order" (printed without title in article entitled "The Scrolls from the Dead Sea") *New Yorker*, XXXI, No. 13 (14 May 1955), 54-57, 59-60, 63-64, 66-68, 70. Reprinted alone with title in *Scrolls from the Dead Sea*, pp. 22-40, and Collins "amplified" ed., pp. 28-46. Reprinted with title in section entitled "The Scrolls from the Dead Sea, 1955" in *Dead Sea Scrolls 1947-1969*, pp. 22-41.

"Eugene O'Neill and the Naturalists," *Shores of Light*, pp. 99-104.

"Eugene O'Neill as Prose-Writer." See "Two Young Men and An Old One."

"Europe," *Piece of My Mind*, pp. 51-64.

"Everybody Is Under Suspicion," *Cold War and the Income Tax*, pp. 20-24.

"Every Man His Own Eckermann." See in Plays and Dialogues.

" 'Evgeni Onegin.' " See " 'Evgeni Onegin': In Honor of Pushkin, 1799-1837."

" 'Evgeni Onegin': In Honor of Pushkin, 1799-1837," *New Republic*, LXXXIX (9 December 1936), 165-171. Reprinted as " 'Evgeni Onegin' " in *Triple Thinkers: Ten Essays*, pp. 42-65, and *Triple Thinkers: Twelve Essays*, pp. 31-47. Reprinted as "In Honor of Pushkin" in *Modern Literary Criticism: An Anthology*, ed. Irving Howe (Boston: Beacon Press, 1958), pp. 404-418.

"Exchanges," *Hill School Record*, XX (June 1911), 336-337.

"Exchanges," *Hill School Record*, XXI (October 1911), 51-52. Comments on influence of O. Henry, W. W. Jacobs, Conan Doyle, and Chesterton on college writers.

"Exchanges," *Hill School Record,* XXI (December 1911), 97-98. Comments on George Crabbe and Edmund Burke.

"Exchanges," *Hill School Record,* XXI (February 1912), 150-152. General lack of quality in prep-school poetry is proved by specimens from "Exchanges."

"Exchanges," *Hill School Record,* XXI (April 1912), 216-219. A general discussion of certain magazines.

"Exchanges," *Hill School Record,* XXI (May 1912), 257-258. Not much in this except a summary of what EW had commented on in previous "Exchanges." See also "Exchanges" in Poems.

"Ezra Pound's Patchwork." See "Mr. Pound's Patchwork."

"F. Scott Fitzgerald." See "The Literary Spotlight, VI: F. Scott Fitzgerald; With a Caricature by William Gropper."

"Facing the Pacific." See "The Californians."

"Family," *New Yorker,* XLIII, No. 10 (29 April 1967), 78, 81-82, 84, 89-90, 92;
Prelude, pp. 27-38.

"The Fashion" in article entitled "Theatres, Books and Ladies' Wear"), *New Republic,* XLIV (11 November 1925), 304. Reprinted without title in essay entitled "Current Fashions" in section called "The Follies: 1923-1928" in *American Earthquake,* p. 76.

"The Ferry," *New Republic,* XLIII (22 July 1925), 236. Reprinted as "The New Jersey Ferry" in *American Earthquake,* p. 68.

"The Fettered College," *Nassau Literary Magazine,* LXX (February 1915), 513-518.

"The Fiction of S. Y. Agnon," *New Yorker,* XXX, No. 42 (4 December 1954), 186-193. Reprinted as "The Fiction of S. Y. Agnón" in *Red, Black, Blond and Olive,* pp. 443-452. Reprinted as "A Man of Unquestionable Genius" in *S. Y. Agnon: The Writer and His Work,* No. 17 in *Ariel: A Quarterly of the Arts and Sciences in Israel,* ed. Isaac Halevi-Levin (Jerusalem: Ministry of Foreign Affairs,

Cultural and Scientific Relations Division, Winter 1966-1967), pp. 31-36.

"Final Reflections" (printed without title in article entitled "Russian Paradoxes"), *New Republic*, LXXXVII (13 May 1936), 12-13. Reprinted without title in section entitled "On the Margin of Moscow" in *Discovery of Europe: The Story of American Experience in the Old World*, ed. Philip Rahv (Boston: Houghton Mifflin Company [Cambridge, Massachusetts: Riverside Press], 1947), pp. 618-621. Reprinted with title in section entitled "U.S.S.R., May-October, 1935" in *Travels in Two Democracies*, pp. 319-322. Reprinted with title and a long postscript added in brackets in section entitled "Soviet Russia (1935)" in *Red-Black, Blond and Olive*, pp. 374-384.

"The Finale at the Follies (Dress Rehearsal.)," *New Republic*, XLII (25 March 1925), 125-126. Reprinted as "The Finale at the Follies: Dress Rehearsal" in *American Earthquake*, pp. 44-47.

["The fine photographs by Cartier-Bresson"] (in section entitled "Russia"), *Piece of My Mind*, pp. 67-80.

"A Fine Picture to Hang in the Library: Brooks's Age of Irving," *New Yorker*, XX, No. 34 (7 October 1944), 69-70, 73-74. Reprinted as "A Picture to Hang in the Library: Brooks's Age of Irving" in *Classics and Commercials*, pp. 224-230; and *Literary Chronicle: 1920-1950*, pp. 317-323.

"Firbank and Beckford," *New Republic*, XLVIII (8 September 1926), 70-71;
Shores of Light, pp. 264-266.

"First Days in Moscow," *New Republic*, LXXXVI (25 March 1936), 184-186. Reprinted without title in essay entitled "On the Margin of Moscow" in section called "U.S.S.R., May-October 1935" in *Travels in Two Democracies*, pp. 181-182, 185-188, 196-197, 203-207. Reprinted without title in same essay in section entitled "Soviet Russia (1935)" in *Red, Black, Blond and Olive*, pp. 191-193, 196-200, 207-208, 215-219. Reprinted without title in the longer essay entitled "On the Margin of Moscow" in *Discovery of*

Europe: The Story of American Experience in the Old World, ed. Philip Rahv (Boston: Houghton Mifflin Company [Cambridge, Massachusetts: Riverside Press], 1947), pp. 590, 592-594.

"The First of May." See "Progress and Poverty."

"First Trip to Europe, 1908," *New Yorker,* XLIII, No. 10 (29 April 1967), 50-52, 54, 57-58, 60, 63-64, 66, 69-70, 72, 75-76; *Prelude,* pp. [vii]-26.

"Fitzgerald before the Great Gatsby." See "The Literary Spotlight, VI: F. Scott Fitzgerald; With a Caricature by William Gropper."

"Flaubert's Politics," *Partisan Review,* IV, No. 1 (December 1937), 13-24;
Triple Thinkers: Ten Essays, pp. 100-121;
The Modern Critical Spectrum, ed. Gerald Jay Goldberg and Nancy Marmer Goldberg, in Prentice-Hall English Literature Series, ser. ed. Maynard Mack (Englewood Cliffs, New Jersey: Prentice-Hall, 1962), pp. 124-134.
Reprinted as "The Politics of Flaubert" in *Triple Thinkers: Twelve Essays,* pp. 72-87; and *American Critical Essays: Twentieth Century,* comp. Harold Lowther Beaver, No. 575 in The World's Classics (London: Oxford University Press, 1959), pp. 51-70.
See also "Critics of the Middle Class," the second part of which ("Critics of the Middle Class: II, Gustave Flaubert") is an earlier statement of many of the ideas of "Flaubert's Politics."

"The Fog Lifts." See "Editorial" (April 1915).

"The Follies as an Institution" (printed without title in article entitled "The Theatre"), *Dial,* LXXIV (April 1923), 421-422. Reprinted with title in sequence entitled "On and Off Broadway" in section called "The Follies: 1923-1928" in *American Earthquake,* pp. 50-52.

"The Follies in New Quarters." See "Summer Revues."

"The Follies: 1923-1928," *American Earthquake,* pp. 13-166.

"Foreword," *The Complete Works of Kate Chopin,* by Kate Chopin, ed. Per Seyersted, in Southern Literary Studies, ser. ed. Louis D. Rubin Jr. (Baton Rouge: Louisiana State University Press, 1969), pp. 13-15.

"Foreword," *Dickens and Ellen Ternan,* by Ada Nisbet (Berkeley and Los Angeles: University of California Press, 1952), pp. vii-xii.

"Foreword," *Last Tycoon,* pp. ix-xi.

"Foreword," *Reveille* ("Published by Base Hospital No. 36 for the members of the unit and the folks back home"), No. 1 (9 November 1917), p. 2.

"Foreword," *Shock of Recognition,* pp. vii-ix.

"Foreword," *Shores of Light,* pp. ix-xii.

"Foreword" (to "A Season in the Life of Emmanuel," by Marie-Claire Blais), *Tamarack Review,* No. 39 (Spring 1966), pp. 3-6;
A Season in the Life of Emmanuel, by Marie-Claire Blais, trans. Derek Coltman (New York: Farrar, Straus and Giroux, 1966; London: Jonathan Cape, 1967), pp. v-ix.
Reprinted as "Introduction" in *A Season in the Life of Emmanuel* (paperback), by Marie-Claire Blais, trans. Derek Coltman, No. 234 in Universal Library, ser. ed. Joseph Greene (New York: Grosset & Dunlap, 1969), pp. v-ix.

"Foreword," *Triple Thinkers: Twelve Essays,* pp. vii-ix.

"Foreword by Edmund Wilson" (to *Aubrey's Brief Lives*). See "Miscellaneous Memorabilia: Oscar Wilde, James Joyce, John Aubrey."

"Foreword, 1953," *I Thought of Daisy,* Farrar, Straus and Young and Ballantine Books 1953 reissues only, pp. [v-vii].

"Foster and Fish," *New Republic,* LXV (24 December 1930), 158-162;
American Jitters, pp. 10-27;
American Earthquake, pp. 179-195.

"Fourth of July," *New Republic,* LXVIII (7 October 1931), 204. Reprinted as "The Fourth of July" in *American Jitters,* pp. 211-212. Reprinted as "Fourth of July Celebration" in *American Earthquake*, pp. 366-367.

"Francis Grierson: Log House and Salon," *New Yorker*, XXIV, No. 30 (18 September 1948), 101-102, 105-107. Segments reprinted without title as part of essay entitled "Calvin Stowe; Francis Grierson; *The Battle Hymn of the Republic*; The Union as Religious Mysticism" in *Patriotic Gore*, pp. 73-82.

"Frank Keeney's Coal Diggers" (printed with editors' endnote), *New Republic*, LXVII (8 July 1931), 195-199; (15 July 1931), 229-231. Reprinted without endnote in *American Jitters*, pp. 150-169; and *American Earthquake*, pp. 310-327.

"Friedrich Engels: The Young Man from Manchester." See "The Young Man from Manchester."

"The Freight-Car Case," *New Republic*, LXVIII (26 August 1931), 38-43; correction in LXVIII (4 November 1931), 334;
American Jitters, pp. 175-192.
Reprinted as "The Scottsboro Freight-Car Case" in *American Earthquake*, pp. 334-347.

"The Fruits of the MLA: I. 'Their Wedding Journey,' " *New York Review of Books*, XI, No. 5 (26 September 1968), 7-10; concluded as "The Fruits of the MLA: II. Mark Twain," *New York Review of Books*, XI, No. 6 (10 October 1968), 6, 8, 10, 12, 14. Reprinted without division and with a long postscript containing several letters as the book *Fruits of the MLA*.

"Fugitives." See "The Tennessee Poets" (essay).

"General Reflections," *Dead Sea Scrolls 1947-1969*, pp. 273-292.

"General Yadin" (printed without title in article entitled "The Scrolls from the Dead Sea"), *New Yorker*, XXXI, No. 13 (14 May 1955), 125-131. Reprinted alone with title in *Scrolls from the Dead Sea*, pp. 113-121, and Collins "amplified" ed., pp. 119-127. Reprinted with title in section entitled "The Scrolls from the Dead Sea, 1955" in *Dead Sea Scrolls 1947-1969*, pp. 114-122.

"The Genesis Apocryphon," *New Yorker*, XLV, No. 5 (22 March 1969), 60, 63-64, 66, 68, 73-74, 76;
Dead Sea Scrolls 1947-1969, pp. 143-146.

"The Genie of the Via Giulia," *New Yorker*, XLI, No. 1 (20 February 1965), 152-154, 157-162;
Bit Between My Teeth, pp. 653-668;
Friendship's Garland: Essays Presented to Mario Praz on His Seventieth Birthday, Vol. I, ed. Vittorio Gabrieli, No. 106 in *Storia e letteratura: Raccolta di studi e testi* (Roma: Edizioni de Storia e Letteratura, 1966), pp. 5-17.

"George Ade: The City Uncle," *New Yorker*, XXIII, No. 29 (6 September 1947), 72, 74, 77;
Bit Between My Teeth, pp. 101-106.

"George Bellows," *New Republic*, XLIV (28 October 1925), 254-255;
American Earthquake, pp. 95-97.

"George F. Kennan." See "Unscrupulous Communists and Embattled Democracies."

"George Grosz in the United States." See "Stephen Spender and George Grosz on Germany."

"George Saintsbury," *New Republic*, LXXIII (8 February 1933), 338-339.

"George Saintsbury: Gourmet and Glutton," *New Yorker*, XXIII, No. 13 (17 May 1947), 99-101;
Classics and Commercials, pp. 366-371.

"George Saintsbury's Centenary." See "Saintsbury's Centenary—Spadework on Kipling."

"A German Director in Hollywood." See "Mürger and Wilde on the Screen."

"Gertrude Stein," *Axel's Castle*, pp. 237-256.

Gertrude Stein Old and Young," *Shores of Light*, pp. 575-586.

"The Ghost of an Anglophile," *New Republic*, XCVII (29 January 1939), 347-349;
Bit Between My Teeth, pp. 117-124.

"Gilbert Seldes and the Popular Arts" (1950), *New Yorker*, XXVI, No. 36 (28 October 1950), 121-126. Reprinted as *"The Great Audience* (1950)" in *Shores of Light*, pp. 165-173; and *Literary Chronicle: 1920-1950*, pp. 57-65.

"Gilbert Seldes and the Popular Arts" (1952), *Shores of Light*, pp. 156-173;
Literary Chronicle: 1920-1950, pp. 49-65.

"Gilbert Without Sullivan," *New Yorker*, XXIII, No. 8 (12 April 1947), 110, 113-116;
Classics and Commercials, pp. 359-365.

"'Give That Beat Again,'" *New Republic*, XCI (28 July 1937), 338-340;
Shores of Light, pp. 681-687.

"Glenway Wescott's War Work." See "Greeks and Germans by Glenway Wescott."

"Gogol: the Demon in the Overgrown Garden," *Nation*, CLXXV (6 December 1952), 520-524. Reprinted as "Gogol: The Demon in the Overgrown Garden" in *One Hundred Years of The Nation: A Centennial Anthology*, ed. Henry M. Christman and Abraham Feldman (New York: Macmillan Company; London: Collier-Macmillan, 1965), pp. 295-304.

"The Great Audience (1950)." See "Gilbert Seldes and the Popular Arts" (1950).

"The Great Baldini: A Memoir and a Collaboration." See in Stories.

"'A Great Dream Come True': An Entertainment Palace That Pleased Rockfeller's [*sic*] Rivals" (printed with journalistic subheadings), *Common Sense*, III, No. 8 (August 1934), 21-22. Reprinted without subheadings as "A Great Dream Come True" in *Travels in Two Democracies*, pp. 38-43; and *American Earthquake*, pp. 473-477.

"A Great Magician," *New Republic*, LVI (17 October 1928), 248-250;
Shores of Light, pp. 286-292.

" 'The Greater Movie Season,' " *New Republic*, XLIV (23 September 1925), 124-125. Partially reprinted as "An American Caligari" in *American Earthquake*, pp. 73-75.

"The Greatest Show on Earth," *New Republic*, XLII (13 May 1925), 320;
American Earthquake, pp. 40-43.

"Greek Diary: Communists, Socialists, and Royalists," *New Yorker*, XXI, No. 36 (20 October 1945), 32-36, 40, 43;
Europe Without Baedeker, pp. 335-356, and 1st rev. ed., pp. 280-296.

"Greek Diary: A Trip to Delphi; Notes on the British," *New Yorker*, XXI, No. 34 (6 October 1945), 56, 58-62, 65-71. Reprinted as "Greek Diary: A Trip to Delphi—Notes on the British in Greece" in *Europe Without Baedeker*, pp. 311-334. Reprinted as "Greek Diary: A Trip to Delphi; Notes on the British in Greece" in *Europe Without Baedeker*, 1st rev. ed., pp. 261-279.

"Greek Diary: Notes on Liberated Athens." See "Notes on Liberated Athens."

"Greek Diary: Views of Bullheaded Crete," *New Yorker*, XXI, No. 40 (17 November 1945), 65-75. Reprinted as "Greek Diary: Views of Bull-Headed Crete" in *Europe Without Baedeker*, pp. 357-388, and 1st rev. ed., pp. 297-323.

"Greeks and Germans by Glenway Wescott," *New Yorker*, XXI, No. 3 (3 March 1945), 76-78. Reprinted as "Glenway Wescott's War Work" in *Classics and Commercials*, pp. 275-279.

"Growth and Causes of Iroquois Resurgence." See "The Causes of the Iroquois Resurgence."

"The Guardians of the City," *New Yorker*, XXX, No. 42 (4 December 1954), 180-186;
Red, Black, Blond and Olive, pp. 435-443.

"A Guide to 'Finnegan's Wake,'" *New Yorker*, XX, No. 25 (5 August 1944), 54, 57-58, 60. Reprinted as "A Guide to *Finnegans Wake*" in *Classics and Commercials*, pp. 182-189; and *Literary Chronicle: 1920-1950*, pp. 295-302.

"A Guide to Gertrude Stein: The Evolution of a Master of Fiction into a Painter of Cubist Still-Life in Prose," *Vanity Fair*, XXI, No. 1 (September 1923), 60, 80.

"Guitry without the Guitrys" (printed without title in article entitled "The Theatre"), *Dial*, LXXIV (June 1923), 635-636. Reprinted with title in sequence entitled "On and Off Broadway" in section called "The Follies: 1923-1928" in *American Earthquake*, pp. 54-55

"The Guitrys in New York," *New Republic*, XLIX (12 January 1927), 219.

"The Gulf in American Literature: A Discussion of the Irreconcilable Breach between the Illiterates and the Illuminati," *Vanity Fair*, XV, No. 1 (September 1920), 65, 96.

" 'H. C.,'" *New Republic*, LXIII (16 July 1930), 266-268; *Shores of Light*, pp. 476-484.

"H. C. Earwicker and Family," *New Republic*, XCIX (28 June 1939), 203-206; concluded as "The Dream of H. C. Earwicker," *New Republic*, XCIX (12 July 1939), 270-274. Reprinted without division as "The Dream of H. C. Earwicker" in *Wound and the Bow*, pp. 243-271; *James Joyce: Two Decades of Criticism*, by Eugene Jolas *et al.*, ed. Seon Givens (New York: Vanguard Press, 1948), pp. 319-342; and *Critiques and Essays on Modern Fiction, Representing the Achievement of Modern American and British Critics*, ed. John [Watson] Aldridge (New York: Ronald Press Company, 1952), pp. 160-175. Reprinted without division and with a 1961 postscript as "The Dream of H. C. Earwicker" in *Modern British Fiction*, ed. Mark Schorer, No. GB64 in Galaxy Books (New York: Oxford University Press, 1961; Magnolia, Massachusetts: Peter Smith, 1962), pp. 358-375, and *Modern British Fiction: Essays in Criticism*, ed. Mark Schorer, No. GB64 in Galaxy Books (New York: Oxford University Press, 1968), pp.

358-375. Reprinted without division and with a 1964 post-script as "The Dream of H. C. Earwicker" in *Wound and the Bow,* Galaxy Books reissue, pp. 198-222.

"H. L. Mencken," *Dial,* LXVIII (April 1920), 469-472.

"H. L. Mencken," *New Republic,* XXVII (1 June 1921), 10-13.

"Haiti: Landscape and Morale" (with editors' headnote), *Reporter,* II, No. 12 (6 June 1950), 29-33. Reprinted without headnote as "Port-au-Prince" in *Red, Black, Blond and Olive,* pp. 135-146.

"Haiti (1949)," *Red, Black, Blond and Olive,* pp. 69-146. See *Red, Black, Blond and Olive* in Books by Wilson for contents.

"Haiti: UNESCO at Marbial," *Reporter,* II, No. 11 (23 May 1950), 29-33. Reprinted as "Marbial" in *Red, Black, Blond and Olive,* pp. 95-109.

"Haitian Literature," *Red, Black, Blond and Olive,* pp. 109-125. See also "The Marcelins—Novelists of Haiti."

" 'Half Hours With the Best Authors,' " *Nassau Literary Magazine,* LXVIII, No. 5 (December 1912), 201-206. Comments on G. K. Chesterton and George Bernard Shaw.

"A Half-Baked Shaw Production," *New Republic,* LXVI (15 April 1931), 236-237.

"Hannah Whitall Smith." See "Stephen Crane—Hannah Whitall Smith."

"Hans Otto Storm" (printed without title in article entitled "The Californians: Storm and Steinbeck"), *New Republic,* CIII (9 December 1940), 784-785. Reprinted alone with title in *Boys in the Back Room,* pp. 33-38. Reprinted with title in section entitled "The Boys in the Back Room" in *Classics and Commercials,* pp. 32-35; and *Literary Chronicle: 1920-1950,* pp. 227-230.

"Hans Stengel," *New Republic,* LIV (22 February 1928), 17-18;
Shores of Light, pp. 363-366.

"Harriet Beecher Stowe," *New Yorker,* XXXI, No. 30 (10 September 1955), 137-138, 143-150, 153; *Patriotic Gore,* pp. 3-58.

"Harvard, Princeton, and Yale" (with headnote), *Forum,* LXX (September 1923), 1871-1879.

"Hedda Gabler," *New Republic,* XXXIX (4 June 1924), 49. Review of Henrik Ibsen's play *Hedda Gabler.*

"Hedda Gabler and Little Eyolf," *New Republic,* XLV (17 February 1926), 356-357.

"Hell As I Know It," *New Republic,* XLIX (29 December 1926), 162-164.

"Hemingway: Gauge of Morale." See "Ernest Hemingway: Bourdon Gauge of Morale."

"Henri Becque as Good-Will Ambassador." See "The Theatre" (February 1925).

"Henry James," *Nassau Literary Magazine,* LXX (November 1914), 286-295.

"Herbert Williams" (printed without title in article entitled "The Theatre"), *Dial,* LXXV (July 1923), 102. Reprinted with title in sequence entitled "On and Off Broadway" in section called "The Follies: 1923-1928" in *American Earthquake,* pp. 58-59.

"The Hero," *Liberator,* V, No. 2 (February 1922), 12.

" 'Herr Vogt,' " *New Republic,* CI (15 November 1939), 106-108.

"Herr Vogt and His Modern Successors" (same as "Appendix D"), *To the Finland Station* (except Anchor Books reissues), p. 490.

"High Discourse on the Arts: André Malraux and Arnold Schoenberg," *New Yorker,* XXVII, No. 9 (14 April 1951), 129-134. Reprinted without review of Schoenberg's *Style and Idea* and with a 1965 postscript reviewing Malraux's *Les voix du silence* in *Bit Between My Teeth,* pp. 137-150.

"Him," *New Republic,* LII (2 November 1927), 293-294. Reprinted as "E. E. Cummings's *Him*" in *Shores of Light,* pp. 282-285.

"Historical Actors: Bakúnin," *To the Finland Station,* pp. 260-287, and Anchor Books reissues, pp. 260-288. Partially reprinted without title and with editors' comments in essay entitled "Marx, Engels, and Bakunin" in *Readings for Opinion,* 2nd ed., ed. Earle [Rosco] Davis and William C[astle] Hummel, in Prentice-Hall English Composition and Introduction to Literature Series, ser. ed. Thomas Clark Pollock (Englewood Cliffs, New Jersey: Prentice-Hall, 1960), pp. 382-386 (esp. pp. 384-385).

"Historical Actors: Lassalle," *To the Finland Station,* pp. 228-259, and Anchor Books reissues, pp. 228-259.

"Historical Criticism." See "The Historical Interpretation of Literature."

"The Historical Interpretation of Literature," *The Intent of the Critic,* ed. Donald A. Stauffer (Princeton: Princeton University Press, 1941; London: Milford, 1942; Gloucester, Massachusetts: Peter Smith, 1963), pp. 39-42; reissued in Bantam Matrix Editions (New York: Bantam Books, 1966), pp. 33-52.

EW's essay was reviewed as follows:

Signed Reviews

Barzun, Jacques. *Nation,* CLIII (18 October 1941), 376-378.

Collaci, Mario. *New York Herald Tribune Books,* XVIII (28 September 1941), 18.

D[rew], E[lizabeth]. *Atlantic Monthly,* CLXVIII (November 1941), "Atlantic Bookshelf," pages not numbered.

Hellman, George S. *New York Times Book Review,* 26 October 1941, p. 16.

Jones, Howard Mumford. *Saturday Review of Literature,* XXIV, No. 25 (11 October 1941), 1, 3-4, 20.

Mercier, Louis J. A. *Commonweal,* XXXV (9 January 1942), 298-299.

Olson, Elder. See in Items about Wilson.

Unsigned Reviews

New Yorker, XVII, No. 33 (27 September 1941), 79.

Times Literary Supplement, 22 August 1942, p. 418.

Essay reprinted as "The Historical Interpretation of Literature" in *Triple Thinkers: Twelve Essays,* pp. 257-270; *American Literary Criticism 1900-1950,* ed. Charles I. Glicksberg (New York: Hendricks House, 1951), pp. 485-497; *Essays in Modern Literary Criticism,* ed. Ray B[enedict] West (New York: Rinehart & Company, 1952), pp. 278-289; *The Achievement of American Criticism: Representative Selections from Three Hundred Years of American Criticism,* comp. Clarence Arthur Brown (New York: Ronald Press, 1954), 654-664.

Reprinted as "Literary Criticism and History" in *Atlantic Monthly,* CLXVIII (November 1941), 610-617.

Reprinted as "Historical Criticism" in *Critiques and Essays in Criticism, 1920-1948, Representing the Achievement of Modern British and American Critics,* ed. Robert Wooster Stallman (New York: Ronald Press, 1949), pp. 449-459; and *An Introduction to Literary Criticism,* ed. Marlies K. Danziger and Wendell Stacy Johnson (Boston: D. C. Heath and Company, 1961; London: George H. Harrap and Company, 1962), pp. 277-287; reissued in paperback as No. 21154 in Raytheon (Boston: D. C. Heath and Company, 1968), pp. 277-287.

The essay "The Historical Interpretation of Literature" was originally a lecture delivered by EW at Princeton University, 23 October 1940.

"The Holmes-Laski Correspondence." See "Justice Holmes and Harold Laski: Their Relationship."

"Holocaust: The New Devastation" (by EW and John Peale Bishop), *Playboy,* II, No. 1 (March 1923), 42-43. Includes the poem "The Best Things from Abroad: Two Esquimaux Love Songs Translated from the Esquimaux by Maida Thompson and Nanook Kruger." Also includes a satiric translation of Paul Verlaine's poem "Le ciel" under title "Essay With Translation: The Fabric of Paul Verlaine

With a Translation of One of his Poems By Eric Elberson Quoits."

"Homecoming—Final Reflections," *Europe Without Baedeker,* pp. 399-427. Reprinted as "Homecoming; Final Reflections" in *Europe Without Baedeker,* 1st rev. ed., pp. 332-356.

"Hoover Dam," *New Republic,* LXVIII (2 September 1931), 66-69;
American Jitters, pp. 213-225;
American Earthquake, pp. 368-378.

"Hospital in Odessa." See "Scarlet Fever in Odessa."

"Houdini," *New Republic,* XLIII (24 June 1925), 125-126;
Shores of Light, pp. 174-178.

"How Can We Account for Ourselves?," *Cold War and the Income Tax,* pp. 58-73.

"How Free is the Free World?," *Cold War and the Income Tax,* pp. 90-95. Partially reprinted in article entitled "The Cold War and the Income Tax" in *Liberation: An Independent Monthly,* VIII, No. 10 (December 1963), 25.

"How They Are Voting: II." See ["I expect to vote for Norman Thomas"].

"Hull-House in 1932: I," *New Republic,* LXXIII (18 January 1933), 260-262; continued as "Hull-House in 1932: II," *New Republic,* LXXIII (25 January 1933), 287-290; concluded as "Hull-House in 1932: III," *New Republic,* LXXIII (1 February 1933), 317-322. Reprinted without divisions and without material originally appearing in "Hull-House in 1932: II" as "Hull-House in 1932" in *Travels in Two Democracies,* pp. 13-32; and *American Earthquake,* pp. 447-464. Section entitled "Hull-House in 1932: III" in essay as originally printed partially reprinted as "Hull House in 1932" in *Journal of the National Education Association,* XXII (April 1933), 126.

["I expect to vote for Norman Thomas"] (printed without title in article by several hands entitled "How They Are

Voting: II"), *New Republic*, CIII (30 September 1940), 445.

["I should like to write about Christian Gauss's influence as a teacher of literature"] (printed without title in article by several hands entitled "In Tribute to Christian Gauss— Eight Appreciations By Alumni"), *Princeton Alumni Weekly*, LII, No. 11 (7 December 1951), 14-15.

"Illinois Miners," *New Republic*, LXXV (14 June 1933), 120-122.

"An Immediate Need." See "Editorial" (May 1915).

"Impressions of Leningrad." See "As I Saw Leningrad."

"In Honor of Pushkin," *Triple Thinkers: Ten Essays*, pp. 42-82, and *Triple Thinkers: Twelve Essays*, pp. 31-59. See " 'Evgeni Onegin': In Honor of Pushkin, 1799-1837."

"In Memory of Carlo Tresca" (by EW *et al.*), *Martello*, XXVIII, No. 4 (28 March 1943), 46.

"In Memory of Elinor Wylie," *New Republic*, LVII (6 February 1929), 316-317. Reprinted as "The Death of Elinor Wylie" in *Shores of Light*, pp. 392-396; and *Literary Chronicle: 1920-1950*, pp. 109-113.

"In Memory of Octave Mirbeau," *New Yorker*, XXV, No. 6 (2 April 1949), 96-98, 101-103;
Classics and Commercials, pp. 471-485.

"In Tribute to Christian Gauss—Eight Appreciations By Alumni." See ["I should like to write about Christian Gauss's influence as a teacher of literature"].

"Inaugural Parade," *New Republic*, LXXIV (22 March 1933), 154-156;
Travels in Two Democracies, pp. 43-49.
Reprinted as "Washington: Inaugural Parade" in *American Earthquake*, pp. 478-483.

"The Independent Farmer," *American Jitters*, pp. 260-270.

"Indian Corn Dance," *New Republic*, LXVIII (7 October 1931), 202-203;

American Jitters, pp. 206-211;
American Earthquake, pp. 361-365.

"The Inevitable Literary Biography: With the Usual Apologies to Arthur Symons, Holbrook Jackson and Frank Harris," *Vanity Fair,* XIII, No. 10 [or XIV, No. 1] (March 1920), 49, 102.

"Inside Dope," *Reveille* ("Published by Base Hospital No. 36 for the members of the unit and the folks back home"), No. 1 (9 November 1917), p. 4.

"The Intelligence of Bees, Wasps, Butterflies, and Bombing Planes," *New Yorker,* XXVII, No. 22 (14 July 1951), 73-76. Reprinted without review of Alexander B. Klots's *A Field Guide to the Butterflies of North America, East of the Great Plains* as "Bees, Wasps and Bombers" in *Bit Between My Teeth,* pp. 333-338.

"An Interview with Edmund Wilson." See in Plays and Dialogues.

"Introduction," *All Men Are Mad.* See "On 'All Men are Mad.' "

"Introduction," *Collected Essays of John Peale Bishop,* pp. vii-xiii. Reprinted as "John Peale Bishop" in *Bit Between My Teeth,* pp. 6-15.

"Introduction" (printed without title in essay entitled "The Dead Sea Scrolls: 1969"), *New Yorker,* XLV, No. 5 (22 March 1969), 45. Reprinted with title in section entitled "1955-1967" in *Dead Sea Scrolls 1947-1969,* pp. 125-126.

"Introduction," *Harold Frederic's Stories of York State,* by Harold Frederic, ed. Thomas F. O'Donnell (Syracuse, New York: Syracuse University Press, 1966), pp. xi-xvi.

"Introduction," *The Novels of A. C. Swinburne.* See "Swinburne of Capheaton and Eaton."

"Introduction," *Patriotic Gore,* pp. ix-xxxii. Reprinted in slightly abridged form as "Patriotic Gore" in *Liberation: An Independent Monthly,* VII, No. 7 (September 1962), 5-10.

"Introduction," *The Pencil of God*. See "The Marcelins—Novelists of Haiti."

"Introduction" (to *A Season in the Life of Emmanuel*). See "Foreword" (to "A Season in the Life of Emmanuel," by Marie-Claire Blais).

"Introduction" (to Amy Lowell), *Shock of Recognition*, pp. 1078-1079.

"Introduction" (to Bayard Taylor), *Shock of Recognition*, pp. 296-298.

"Introduction" (to D. H. Lawrence), *Shock of Recognition*, pp. 905-906.

"Introduction" (to Emerson and Lowell on Thoreau), *Shock of Recognition*, pp. 205-207.

"Introduction" (to Emerson and Whitman), *Shock of Recognition*, pp. 244-245.

"Introduction" (to George Santayana on William James and Josiah Royce), *Shock of Recognition*, p. 866.

"Introduction" (to H. G. Wells on Stephen Crane), *Shock of Recognition*, pp. 659-660.

"Introduction" (to H. L. Mencken), *Shock of Recognition*, pp. 1155-1159.

"Introduction" (to Henry Adams on George Cabot Lodge), *Shock of Recognition*, pp. 742-746.

"Introduction" (to Henry James on Hawthorne), *Shock of Recognition*, pp. 425-426.

"Introduction" (to Henry James on Howells), *Shock of Recognition*, pp. 566-569.

"Introduction" (to Howells on Twain), *Shock of Recognition*, pp. 672-673.

"Introduction" (to John Dos Passos and E. E. Cummings), *Shock of Recognition*, p. 1246.

"Introduction" (to John Jay Chapman on Emerson), *Shock of Recognition*, pp. 595-599.

"Introduction" (to Lowell's "A Fable for Critics"), *Shock of Recognition*, pp. 21-22.

"Introduction" (to Melville on Hawthorne), *Shock of Recognition*, pp. 185-186.

"Introduction" (to Poe). See "Poe as a Literary Critic."

"Introduction" (to Sherwood Anderson), *Shock of Recognition*, pp. 1254-1255.

"Introduction" (to Lowell on Poe), *Shock of Recognition*, pp. 1-4.

"Introduction" (to T. S. Eliot on Henry James), *Shock of Recognition*, p. 853.

"Introduction" (to the Poe Memorial), *Shock of Recognition*, pp. 417-418.

"Introduction" (to Twain on Cooper), *Shock of Recognition*, pp. 580-581.

"Introduction by Edmund Wilson," *In Our Time: Stories,* by Ernest Hemingway (New York: Charles Scribner's Sons, 1931, copyrighted 1930), pp. ix-xv, and Sun Rise Ed., Vol. I (New York: Charles Scribner's Sons, 1938), pp. ix-xv.

"Introduction: Max Nomad and Waclaw Machajski." See "Max Nomad and Waclaw Machajski."

"Introduction: Philoctetes: The Wound and the Bow." See "The Wound and the Bow."

"The Invisible World of S. Y. Agnon," *Commentary*, XLII, No. 6 (December 1966), 31-32.

["The Irish Players have returned to New York"] (paragraph printed without title in article by several hands entitled "A New York Diary"), *New Republic*, LIII (4 January 1928), 191-192.

"Is It Possible to Pat Kingsley Amis?," *New Yorker*, XXXII, No. 5 (24 March 1956), 140-142, 145-147; *Bit Between My Teeth*, pp. 274-281.

"Is Politics Ruining Art?: A Debate." See "What Is Mr. Krutch Defending?"

"Is Verse a Dying Technique?" See "The Canons of Poetry."

"Israel (1954)," *Red, Black, Blond and Olive*, pp. 385-492.

" 'It's Great to Be a New Yorker!,' " *New Republic*, XLII (11 March 1925), 69-70;
American Earthquake, pp. 29-31.

"It's Terrible! It's Ghastly! It Stinks!," *New Republic*, XCI (21 July 1937), 311-312;
Shores of Light, pp. 662-668;
New Republic, CXXXI (22 November 1954), 72-74;
Literary Chronicle: 1920-1950, pp. 206-211.

"J. Dover Wilson on Falstaff," *New Yorker*, XX, No. 11 (29 April 1944), 82, 84-86;
Classics and Commercials, pp. 161-167;
Literary Chronicle: 1920-1950, pp. 278-284.

"J. P. McEvoy in the Ziegfeld Follies." See "Theatre, Concert Hall and Gallery."

"The James Branch Cabell Case Reopened," *New Yorker*, XXXII, No. 9 (21 April 1956), 140-142, 145-148, 151-158, 161-168. Reprinted with a footnote in *Bit Between My Teeth*, pp. 291-321.

"James Branch Cabell: 1879-1958," *Nation*, CLXXXVI (7 June 1958), 519-520;
Bit Between My Teeth, pp. 322-325.

"James Joyce," *New Republic*, LXI (18 December 1929), 84-93;
Axel's Castle, pp. 191-236;
Literary Opinion in America: Essays Illustrating the Status, Methods, and Problems of Criticism in the United States Since the War, ed. Morton Dauwen Zabel (New York: Harper & Brothers, 1937), pp. 145-177; Rev. Ed., published as *Literary Opinion in America: Essays Illustrating the Status, Methods, and Problems of Criticism in the United States in the Twentieth Century* (New York: Harper & Brothers, 1951), pp. 183-206; 3rd Ed. Rev., published with same title as Rev. Ed., Vol. I, No. TB3013 in Harper Torchbooks, The University Library (New

York: Harper and Row, 1962), pp. 183-206; and 3rd Ed. Rev. reprinted, Vol. I (Gloucester, Massachusetts: Peter Smith, 1968), pp. 183-206.

"James Joyce as a Poet," *New Republic*, XLIV (4 November 1925), 279-280.

"James M. Cain" (printed without title in essay entitled "The Boys in the Back Room: James M. Cain and John O'Hara"), *New Republic*, CIII (11 November 1940), 665. Reprinted alone with title in *Boys in the Back Room*, pp. 9-14. Reprinted with title in section entitled "The Boys in the Back Room" in *Classics and Commercials*, pp. 19-22; and *Literary Chronicle: 1920-1950*, pp. 216-219.

"Jannings' First American Film," *New Republic*, LI (3 August 1927), 283. Reprinted as "Emil Jannings' American Film" in *American Earthquake*, pp. 91-93.

"Japanese Cherry Blossoms," *Modern Monthly*, VIII (July 1934), 327;
Travels in Two Democracies, pp. 111-112;
American Earthquake, pp. 534-535.

"The Jazz Problem," *New Republic*, XLV (13 January 1926), 217-219. Reprinted as "The Problem of the Higher Jazz" in *American Earthquake*, pp. 112-115.

"Jean-Paul Sartre: The Novelist and the Existentialist," *New Yorker*, XXIII, No. 24 (2 August 1947), 58, 60-63;
Classics and Commercials, pp. 393-403;
Literary Chronicle: 1920-1950, pp. 398-407;
Sartre: A Collection of Critical Essays, ed. Edith Kern, No. S-TC-21 in Spectrum Books, Twentieth Century Views, ser. ed. Maynard Mack (Englewood Cliffs, New Jersey: Prentice-Hall, 1962), pp. 47-53.

"Jersey Coast," *Poets, Farewell!*, pp. 35-39;
Night Thoughts, pp. 51-54.

"The Jersey Coast—A Highball," *New Republic*, XLIV (30 September 1925), 156. Reprinted as "The Summer Hotel" in *Poets, Farewell!*, pp. 38-39; and *Night Thoughts*, pp. 53-54.

"Jerusalem the Golden," *New Yorker*, XXX, No. 42 (4 December 1954), 204-217;
Red, Black, Blond and Olive, pp. 468-483.

"The Jews," *Piece of My Mind*, pp. 83-136.

"John Allegro," *New Yorker*, XLV, No. 6 (29 March 1969), 45-46, 48, 51;
Dead Sea Scrolls 1947-1969, pp. 162-169.

"John Jay Chapman," *Atlantic Monthly*, CLX (November 1937), 581-595. Reprinted as "John Jay Chapman: The Mute and the Open Strings" in *Triple Thinkers: Ten Essays*, pp. 165-209, and *Triple Thinkers: Twelve Essays*, pp. 133-164.

"John Jay Chapman," *New Republic*, LIX (22 May 1929), "Second Spring Literary Section," 28-33; correction in (29 May 1929), 54.

"John Jay Chapman: The Mute and the Open Strings." See "John Jay Chapman," *Atlantic Monthly*.

"John Morley," *New Republic*, LXXII (14 September 1932), 119-120.

"John Mulholland and the Art of Illusion," *New Yorker*, XX, No. 4 (11 March 1944), 91-94;
Classics and Commercials, pp. 147-152.

"John O'Hara" (printed without title in the essay "The Boys in the Back Room: James M. Cain and John O'Hara"), *New Republic*, CIII (11 November 1940), 665-666. Reprinted alone with title in *Boys in the Back Room*, pp. 15-22. Reprinted with title in section entitled "The Boys in the Back Room" in *Classics and Commercials*, pp. 22-26; and *Literary Chronicle: 1920-1950*, pp. 219-222.

"John Peale Bishop," *We Moderns: Gotham Book Mart, 1920-1940* (paperback), Gotham Book Mart Catalog No. 42, comp. Frances Steloff and Kay Steele (New York: Gotham Book Mart, [1939]), p. 14. See also "Introduction," *Collected Essays of John Peale Bishop*.

"John Singleton Mosby, 'The Gray Ghost,'" *New Yorker*, XXXIV, No. 52 (14 February 1959), 117-118, 120, 123-

130, 133-136. Reprinted in rearranged form without title as part of essay entitled "Southern Soldiers: Richard Taylor, John S. Mosby, Robert E. Lee" in *Patriotic Gore*, pp. 307-327.

"John Steinbeck" (printed without title in essay entitled "The Californians: Storm and Steinbeck"), *New Republic*, CIII (9 December 1940), 785-787. Reprinted alone with title in *Boys in the Back Room*, pp. 39-54. Reprinted with title in section entitled "The Boys in the Back Room" in *Classics and Commercials*, pp. 35-45; and *Literary Chronicle: 1920-1950*, pp. 230-239.

"Joseph de Maistre," *New Republic*, LXXII (24 August 1932), 35-39;
Shores of Light, pp. 509-517.

"Judd Gray and Mrs. Snyder" (printed without title in article by several hands entitled "The Week"), *New Republic*, LIII (25 January 1928), 258. Reprinted with title in section entitled "The Follies: 1923-1928" in *American Earthquake*, pp. 161-163.

"The Jumping-Off Place," *New Republic*, LXIX (23 December 1931), 156-158;
American Jitters, pp. 253-260;
The New Republic Anthology, 1915-1935, ed. Groff Conklin (New York: Dodge Publishing Company, 1936, 1941), pp. 404-410;
American Earthquake, pp. 414-420.

"The June War—The Temple Scroll," *New Yorker*, XLV, No. 7 (5 April 1969), 78, 80, 82, 87-88, 90, 92, 94. Reprinted as "The June War and the Temple Scroll" in *Dead Sea Scrolls 1947-1969*, pp. 261-272.

"Justice Holmes and Harold Laski: Their Relationship," *New Yorker*, XXIX, No. 13 (16 May 1953), 122, 124, 127-134, 137-141. Reprinted as "The Holmes-Laski Correspondence" in *Eight Essays*, pp. 217-238. Reprinted as "The Holmes-Laski Correspondence" with a note pertaining to Kingsley Martin in *Bit Between My Teeth*, pp. 78-100.

"Justice Oliver Wendell Holmes," *Patriotic Gore*, pp. 743-796.

"Justice to Edith Wharton," *New Republic*, XCV (29 June 1938), 209-213;
> *Wound and the Bow*, pp. 195-213, and Galaxy Books reissue, pp. 159-173;
> *Criticism: The Foundations of Modern Literary Judgment*, ed. Mark Schorer, Josephine Miles, and Gordon Mackenzie (New York: Harcourt, Brace and Company, 1948), pp. 162-168;
> *Edith Wharton: A Collection of Critical Essays*, ed. Irving Howe, No. S-TC-20 in Spectrum Books, Twentieth Century Views, ser. ed. Maynard Mack (Englewood Cliffs, New Jersey: Prentice-Hall, 1962), pp. 19-31.

"Karl Marx Decides to Change the World." See "Marx Decides to Change the World."

"Karl Marx Dies at His Desk," *To the Finland Station*, pp. 329-346, and Anchor Books reissues, pp. 330-346.

"Karl Marx: Poet of Commodities," *New Republic*, CII (8 January 1940), 46-47. Reprinted in a very much expanded form as "Karl Marx: Poet of Commodities and Dictator of the Proletariat" in *To the Finland Station*, pp. 288-328, and Anchor Books reissues, pp. 289-329.

"Karl Marx: Prometheus and Lucifer," *New Republic*, XCV (6 July 1938), 244-247;
> *To the Finland Station*, pp. 112-120, and Anchor Books reissues, pp. 111-119.

"Katherine Anne Porter," *New Yorker*, XX, No. 33 (30 September 1944), 64-66;
> *Classics and Commercials*, pp. 219-223;
> *Literary Chronicle: 1920-1950*, pp. 313-317.

"Kay Boyle and the Saturday Evening Post," *New Yorker*, XIX, No. 48 (15 January 1944), 74, 76, 78. Reprinted as "Kay Boyle and the *Saturday Evening Post*" in *Classics and Commercials*, pp. 128-132.

"King Christophe's Citadel" (printed without title in essay entitled "Christophe and Estimé"), *Reporter*, II, No. 10

(9 May 1950), 21-24. Reprinted with title in section entitled "Haiti (1949)" in *Red, Black, Blond and Olive*, pp. 78-85.

"The Kipling That Nobody Read," *Atlantic Monthly*, CLXVII (February 1941), 340-354;
Kipling's Mind and Art: Selected Critical Essays, ed. Andrew Rutherford (Edinburgh and London: Oliver and Boyd; Stanford, California: Stanford University Press, 1964), pp. 17-69.
Reprinted as "The Kipling that Nobody Read" in *Wound and the Bow*, pp. 105-181, and Galaxy Books, reissue, pp. 86-147.

"Kipling's Debits and Credits," *New Republic*, XLVIII (6 October 1926), 194-195.

"Koussevitzky at Tanglewood," *New Yorker*, XXIV, No. 28 (4 September 1948), 56, 58-64.

"Landscape," *New Republic*, XXVI (23 March 1921), 96; *1916 P-Rade* [*sic*] (Princeton), Formation VII (May 1921), p. 11.

"The Last Phase of Anatole France," *New Republic*, XLI (11 February 1925), 308-310.

"The Last Phase of Bernard Shaw." See "Bernard Shaw Still Speaking."

"The Last Phase of Henry James," *Partisan Review*, IV, No. 3 (February 1938), 3-8.

"Late Pinero and Early Cornell" (printed without title in article entitled "The Theatre"), *Dial*, LXXXIV (June 1923), 636. Reprinted with title in sequence entitled "On and Off Broadway" in section called "The Follies: 1923-1928" in *American Earthquake*, pp. 55-56.

"Late Violets from the Nineties," *Dial*, LXXV (October 1923), 387-390;
Shores of Light, pp. 68-72.

"A Later Bulletin," *Piece of My Mind*, pp. 81-82.

"Lawrence, Mass.," *New Republic*, LXIX (25 November 1931), 36-39;

American Jitters, pp. 270-284.

Reprinted as "Back East: October Again: A Strike in Lawrence, Mass." in *American Earthquake,* pp. 421-431.

"Legend and Symbol in 'Doctor Zhivago'" (by EW, Barbara Deming and Evgenia Lehovich), *Nation,* CLXXXVIII (25 April 1959), 363-373;

Encounter, XII, No. 6 (June 1959), 5-16.

Reprinted with a 1965 postscript as "Legend and Symbol in *Doctor Zhivago*" in *Bit Between My Teeth,* pp. 447-472.

"Lenin at the Finland Station," *To the Finland Station,* pp. 458-476, and Anchor Books reissues, pp. 456-474.

"Lenin Identifies Himself with History," *To the Finland Station,* pp. 447-457, and Anchor Books reissues, pp. 445-455.

"Lenin: The Brothers Ulyánov," *To the Finland Station,* pp. 349-373, and Anchor Books reissues, pp. 347-371.

"Lenin: The Great Headmaster," *To the Finland Station,* pp. 374-404, and Anchor Books reissues, pp. 372-402.

"Leningrad and a Hospital in Odessa," *The Great Travelers: A Collection of Firsthand Narratives of Wayfarers, Wanderers and Explorers in All Parts of the World from 450 B. C. to the Present,* ed. Milton [Allan] Rugoff, Vol. II (New York: Simon and Schuster, 1960), pp. 649-655.

Contents
 "Impressions of Leningrad"
 "Hospital in Odessa"

"Leningrad Theaters." See "As I Saw Leningrad."

"Leonid Leonov: The Sophistication of a Formula," *New Yorker,* XX, No. 43 (9 December 1944), 100, 102, 105-106; *Classics and Commercials,* pp. 250-256; *Literary Chronicle: 1920-1950,* pp. 333-338.

"Lesser Books by Brilliant Writers," *New Yorker,* XXII, No. 22 (13 July 1945), 81-82; correction in No. 24 (27 July 1946), 66-67. Partially reprinted without title and with a postscript in essay entitled "A Cry from the Unquiet Grave" in *Classics and Commercials,* pp. 283-285. Partially reprinted without title in essay entitled "Splendors and Miseries of Evelyn Waugh" in *Classics and Commercials*, pp. 302-304; and *Literary Chronicle: 1920-1950*, pp. 357-358.

"A Letter to Elinor Wylie," *New Republic*, XLIV (7 October 1925), 176-177;
Shores of Light, pp. 259-263.

"Letter to the Russians about Hemingway," *New Republic*, LXXXV (11 December 1935), 135-136. Reprinted with introductory statement by EW and followed by EW's translation of "Ot redaktsii" in *Shores of Light*, pp. 616-629; and *Literary Chronicle: 1920-1950*, pp. 194-206. See also "Ot redaktsii" in Translations by Wilson and in Items about Wilson.

"Letters in the Soviet Union," *New Republic*, LXXVI (1 April 1936), 212-214. Reprinted without title in essay entitled "On the Margin of Moscow" in section called "U.S.S.R.: May-October, 1935" in *Travels in Two Democracies*, pp. 184-185, 210-217. Reprinted without title in essay entitled "On the Margin of Moscow" in section entitled "Soviet Russia: (1935)" in *Red, Black, Blond and Olive*, pp. 195-196, 223-231. Reprinted without title in a longer essay entitled "On the Margin of Moscow" in *Discovery of Europe: The Story of American Experience in the Old World*, ed. Philip Rahv (Boston: Houghton Mifflin Company [Cambridge, Massachusetts: Riverside Press], 1947), pp. 589-590, 595-596.

"The Lexicon of Prohibition," *New Republic*, L (9 March 1927), 71-72;
American Earthquake, pp. 89-91.

"The Library: The Alfred Raymond Memorial Prize Essay," *Hill School Record*, XXI (June 1912), 270-275. May not appear in bound Vol. XXI of *Hill School Record*.

" 'The Life and Times of John Barrymore,' " *New Yorker*, XIX, No. 49 (22 January 1944), 58, 60, 62, 65. Reprinted as "The Life and Times of John Barrymore" in *Classics and Commercials*, pp. 133-139; and *Literary Chronicle: 1920-1950*, pp. 259-265.

"Lincoln Steffens and Upton Sinclair," *New Republic*, LXXII (28 September 1932), 173-175.

"The Literary Class War: I," *New Republic*, LXX (4 May 1932), 319-323; concluded as "The Literary Class War: II," *New Republic*, LXX (11 May 1932), 347-349. Section entitled "The Literary Class War: I" partially reprinted as "The Literary Class War" in *Shores of Light*, pp. 534-539.

"The Literary Consequences of the Crash," *Shores of Light*, pp. 492-499.

"Literary Criticism and History." See "The Historical Interpretation of Literature."

"The Literary Left," *New Republic*, LXXXIX (20 January 1937), 345-348. Reprinted as "Communist Criticism" in *Shores of Light*, pp. 640-650.

"Literary Politics," *New Republic*, LIII (1 February 1928), 289-290. Reprinted as "The Critic Who Does Not Exist" in *Shores of Light*, pp. 367-372.

"The Literary Spotlight, VI: F. Scott Fitzgerald; With a Caricature by William Gropper," *Bookman*, LV (March 1922), 20-25. Reprinted as "F. Scott Fitzgerald" in *The Literary Spotlight*, in The Bookman Books (New York: George H. Doran Company, 1924), pp. 125-134; *Shores of Light*, pp. 27-35; *Literary Chronicle: 1920-1950*, pp. 30-37; and *The Great Gatsby: A Study*, ed. Frederick J. Hoffman, No. SL1 in The Scribner Library (New York: Charles Scribner's Sons, 1962), pp. 21-28. Reprinted as "Fitzgerald before The Great Gatsby" in *F. Scott Fitzgerald: The Man and His Work*, ed. Alfred Kazin (Cleveland: World Publishing Company, 1951), pp. 77-83.

"The Literary Worker's Polonius," *Atlantic Monthly*, CLV (June 1935), 674-682. Reprinted as "The Literary Worker's Polonius: A Brief Guide for Authors and Editors" in *Shores of Light*, pp. 593-609; and *Literary Chronicle: 1920-1950*, pp. 178-194.

"Literature and Life—6: Edmund Wilson Eludes the Interviewer." See Wain, John, (same title), in Items about Wilson.

"The Little Water Ceremony," *New Yorker*, XXXV, No. 38 (7 November 1959), 134, 136-140, 143-150;
Apologies to the Iroquois, pp. 290-310.

"Logan Pearsall Smith," *Bit Between My Teeth*, pp. 114-130.

"London in Midsummer," *Europe Without Baedeker*, pp. 205-234, and 1st rev. ed., pp. 176-199.

"London to Leningrad,"*New Yorker*, XII, No. 8 (4 April 1936), 36, 38, 40, 42, 47-48;
Travels in Two Democracies, pp. 150-162;
Red, Black, Blond and Olive, pp. 153-165.

"A Long Talk about Jane Austen," *New Yorker*, XX, No. 19 (24 June 1944), 70, 72-74, 77-78;
Classics and Commercials, pp. 196-203;
Literary Chronicle: 1920-1950, pp. 302-309;
Jane Austen: A Collection of Critical Essays, ed. Ian Watt, No. S-TC-26 in Spectrum Books, Twentieth Century Views, ser. ed. Maynard Mack (Englewood Cliffs, New Jersey: Prentice-Hall, 1963), pp. 35-40.

"A Lost Lady," *Dial*, LXXVI (January 1924), 79-80. Reprinted as *"A Lost Lady"* in *Shores of Light*, pp. 41-43; and *Willa Cather and Her Critics*, ed. James [Marvin] Schroeter (Ithaca, New York: Cornell University Press, 1967), pp. 27-29.

"Lucian versus Plato," *New Republic*, LXVIII (30 September 1931), 180-182.

"Lysistrata," *New Republic*, XLV (6 January 1926), 188. Reprinted as "'Lysistrata'" in *American Earthquake*, pp. 116-118.

"Lytton Strachey," *New Republic*, LXXII (21 September 1932), 146-148;
Shores of Light, pp. 551-556;
Literary Chronicle: 1920-1950, pp. 166-171.
Reprinted with editor's headnote in *Essay Annual: A Yearly Collection of Significant Essays, Personal, Critical, Controversial, and Humorous* (1933), ed. Erich Albert Walter (Chicago: Scott, Foresman and Company, 1933), pp. 140-145.

"Madam Secretary," *American Earthquake,* pp. 560-564.

"Mammonart," *New Republic,* XLII (22 April 1925), 236-237. Reprinted as "Upton Sinclair's *Mammonart*" in *Shores of Light,* pp. 212-216.

"A Man in the Street," *American Jitters,* p. 313; *American Earthquake,* p. 441.

"A Man of Unquestionable Genius." See "The Fiction of S. Y. Agnon."

"Many Marriages," *Dial,* LXXIV (April 1923), 399-400. Reprinted as "Sherwood Anderson's *Many Marriages*" in *Shores of Light,* pp. 91-93.

"Marbial." See "Haiti: UNESCO at Marbial."

"Marcel Proust." See "A Short View of Proust."

"The Marcelins—Novelists of Haiti," *Nation,* CLXXI (14 October 1950), 341-344. Reprinted alone as "Introduction" in *The Pencil of God,* by Philippe Thoby-Marcelin and Pierre Marcelin, trans. Leonard Thomas (Boston: Houghton Mifflin Company [Cambridge, Massachusetts: Riverside Press], 1951), pp. v-xvii. Partially reprinted without title in fragments as part of essay entitled "Haitian Literature" in section entitled "Haiti (1949)" in *Red, Black, Blond and Olive,* pp. 109-125 (esp. 109-113, 119-120, 123-125).

"Mario Praz: 'The Romantic Agony,' " *New Yorker,* XXVIII, No. 34 (11 October 1952), 146, 149-152. Reprinted as "Mario Praz: *The Romantic Agony*" in *Bit Between My Teeth,* pp. 151-157.

"Marx and Engels Go Back to Writing History," *To the Finland Station,* pp. 199-227, and Anchor Books reissues, pp. 199-227. See also "Marxist Humanism."

"Marx and Engels: Grinding the Lens," *New Republic,* XCVI (7 September 1938), 125-128; *To the Finland Station,* pp. 151-161, and Anchor Books reissues, pp. 151-161.

Partially reprinted without title and with editors' comments in essay entitled "Marx, Engels, and Bakunin" in *Read-*

ings for Opinion, 2nd ed., ed. Earle [Rosco] Davis and William C[astle] Hummel, in Prentice-Hall English Composition and Introduction to Literature Series, ser. ed. Thomas Clark Pollock (Englewood Cliffs, New Jersey: Prentice-Hall, 1960), pp. 382-386 (esp. pp. 382-383, 385-386).

"Marx and Engels Take a Hand at Making History," *To the Finland Station,* pp. 162-178, and Anchor Books reissues, pp. 162-178.

"Marx Decides to Change the World," *New Republic,* XCV (20 July 1938), 301-304. Reprinted as "Karl Marx Decides to Change the World" in *To the Finland Station,* pp. 121-128, and Anchor Books reissues, pp. 120-127.

"Marx, Engels, and Bakunin" (with editors' comments), *Readings for Opinion,* 2nd ed., ed. Earle [Rosco] Davis and William C[astle] Hummel, in Prentice-Hall English Composition and Introduction to Literature Series, ser. ed. Thomas Clark Pollock (Englewood Cliffs, New Jersey: Prentice-Hall, 1960), pp. 382-386.

Contents
["Marx and Engels: Grinding the Lens"]
["Historical Actors: Bakúnin"]

"Marx on the Differential Calculus" (same as "Appendix B" of *To the Finland Station*), *To the Finland Station* (except Anchor Books reissues), pp. 484-486.

"The Marx-Engels Partnership," *New Republic,* XCVI (17 August 1938), 40-43. Reprinted as "The Partnership of Marx and Engels" in *To the Finland Station,* pp. 140-150, and Anchor Books reissues, pp. 139-150.

"Marxism and Literature," *Atlantic Monthly,* CLX (December 1937), 741-750;
Triple Thinkers: Ten Essays, pp. 266-289, and *Triple Thinkers: Twelve Essays,* pp. 197-212;
Literary Opinion in America: Essays Illustrating the Status, Methods, and Problems of Criticism in the United States in the Twentieth Century, Rev. Ed., ed. Morton Dauwen Zabel, Vol. II (New York: Harper, 1951), pp. 693-705;

3rd ed. rev., ed. Morton Dauwen Zabel, Vol. II, No. TB3014 in Harper Torchbooks, The University Library (New York: Harper and Row, 1962; Gloucester Massachusetts: Peter Smith, 1968), pp. 693-705.

"Marxism at the End of the Thirties." See "What Has Happened to Marxism."

"Marxist History," *New Republic*, LXXII (12 October 1932), 226-228;
  New Statesman & Nation, IV (15 October 1932), "Autumn Books Supplement," pp. v-vi.

"Marxist Humanism," *New Republic*, XCVIII (3 May 1939), 371-372. Reprinted without title as part of the essay "Marx and Engels Go Back to Writing History" in *To the Finland Station*, pp. 212-216, and Anchor Books reissues, pp. 212-217.

"Masada," *New Yorker*, XLV, No. 7 (5 April 1969), 45-46, 48, 51-52, 54, 56, 58, 63-64, 66;
  Dead Sea Scrolls 1947-1969, pp. 196-212.

"Max Eastman in 1941," *New Republic*, CIV (10 February 1941), 173-176;
  Classics and Commercials, pp. 57-69.

"Max Nomad and Waclaw Machajski," *New Yorker*, XXXVI, No. 35 (15 October 1960), 192-198, 201-204; *Bit Between My Teeth*, pp. 485-499.
  Reprinted in revised form as "Introduction: Max Nomad and Waclaw Machajski" in *Aspects of Revolt*, by Max Nomad (New York: Noonday Press, 1961), pp. vii-xx.

"May First: The Empire State Building; Life on the Passaic River." See "Progress and Poverty."

"Meditations on Dostoyevsky: Bad Quarter-Hour of a Literary Critic," *New Republic*, LVI (24 October 1928), 274-276.

"Meetings with Max Beerbohm," *Encounter*, XXI, No. 6 (December 1963), 16-22. Reprinted with a note pertaining to a letter from Virginia Woolf and with two postscripts as "A Miscellany of Max Beerbohm" in *Bit Between My Teeth*, pp. 41-62.

"Mencken Through the Wrong End of the Telescope," *New Yorker*, XXVI, No. 11 (6 May 1950), 111-114;
Bit Between My Teeth, pp. 28-33.

"Mencken's Democratic Man," *New Republic*, XLIX (15 December 1926), 110-111;
Shores of Light, pp. 293-297;
Literary Chronicle: 1920-1950, pp. 92-96.

"The Metropolitan." See "La Boheme."

"The Metropolitan Opera House." See "La Boheme."

"The Metropolitan Samuel" (printed without title in essay entitled "The Scrolls from the Dead Sea"), *New Yorker*, XXXI, No. 13 (14 May 1955), 45-50, 52, 54. Reprinted alone with title in *Scrolls from the Dead Sea*, pp. 3-21, and Collins "amplified" ed., pp. 9-27. Reprinted with title in section entitled "The Scrolls from the Dead Sea, 1955" in *Dead Sea Scrolls 1947-1969*, pp. 3-21.

"Miami," *Red, Black, Blond and Olive*, pp. 71-74.

"Michelet," *New Republic*, LXXII (31 August 1932), 64-66.

"Michelet and the Middle Ages," *New Republic*, LXXX (29 August 1934), 65-67;
To the Finland Station, pp. 7-12, and Anchor Books reissues, pp. 5-11.

"Michelet and the Revolution," *New Republic*, LXXX (5 September 1934), 91-95;
To the Finland Station, pp. 28-35, and Anchor Books reissues, pp. 27-34.

"Michelet Discovers Vico," *New Republic*, LXXX (29 August 1934), 64-65;
To the Finland Station, pp. 3-6, and Anchor Books reissues, pp. 1-4.

"Michelet Tries to Live His History," *New Republic*, LXXX (12 September 1934), 123-124;
To the Finland Station, pp. 25-27, and Anchor Books reissues, pp. 24-26.

"The Milk Interests Write the Milk Code," *Common Sense*, II, No. 6 (December 1933), 8-11.

"The Milk Strike," *New Republic,* LXXVI (13 September 1933), 122-125. Reprinted as "The Second Battle of Oriskany" in *Travels in Two Democracies,* pp. 79-86; and *American Earthquake,* pp. 511-517.

"Miscellaneous Memorabilia: Oscar Wilde, James Joyce, John Aubrey," *New Yorker,* XXVI, No. 26 (19 August 1950), 78, 81-83. Reprinted without reviews of Stanislaus Joyce's *Recollections of James Joyce by His Brother Stanislaus Joyce* and Lucie Noel's *James Joyce and Paul L. Léon* as "Foreword by Edmund Wilson" in *Aubrey's Brief Lives,* by John Aubrey, ed. with a life of Aubrey by Oliver Lawson Dick (Ann Arbor: University of Michigan Press, 1957), pp. [v-vi].

"A Miscellany of Max Beerbohm." See "Meetings with Max Beerbohm."

"Miss Barrows and Doctor Wirt: An Inside Story of a Famous Episode," *Scribner's Magazine,* XCVI (August 1934), 102-104. Reprinted as "Miss Barrows and Doctor Wirt" in *Travels in Two Democracies,* pp. 103-111. Reprinted as "Miss Barrows and Dr. Wirt" in *American Earthquake,* pp. 538-544.

" 'Miss Buttle' and 'Mr. Eliot,' " *New Yorker,* XXXIV, No. 14 (24 May 1958), 112, 114-120, 122-124, 127-134, 137-142. Reprinted with a 1965 short postscript in *Bit Between My Teeth,* pp. 364-402.

"Modern Literature: Between the Whirlpool and the Rock," *New Republic,* XLVIII (3 November 1926), 296-297.

"A Modest Self Tribute," *Griffin,* I, No. 9 (October 1952), 6-8;
Bit Between My Teeth, pp. 1-5.

"The Monastery" (printed without title in essay entitled "The Scrolls from the Dead Sea"), *New Yorker,* XXXI, No. 13 (14 May 1955), 70-72, 74, 76-78, 81-82. Reprinted alone with title in *Scrolls from the Dead Sea,* pp. 41-53, and Collins "amplified" ed., pp. 47-59. Reprinted with title in section entitled "The Scrolls from the Dead Sea, 1955" in *Dead Sea Scrolls 1947-1969,* pp. 42-54.

"The Moon in a Dream," *Note-Books of Night,* pp. 79-81; *Night Thoughts,* pp. 143-145.

"More Notes on Current Clichés," *New Statesman,* LXVI (6 December 1963), 847; *Bit Between My Teeth,* pp. 571-575.

"More on the Dead Sea Scrolls," *Encounter,* VI, No. 5 (May 1956), 3-9.

"More Words of Ill-Omen." See "Words of Ill-Omen."

"Morley Callaghan of Toronto," *New Yorker,* XXXVI, No. 41 (26 November 1960), 224, 226, 228, 230, 233-234, 236-237. Reprinted with a long 1964 postscript in *O Canada,* pp. 7-32.

"Morose Ben Jonson." See "A Definitive Edition of Ben Jonson."

"The Moscow Art Theater" (printed without title in article entitled "The Theatre"), *Dial,* LXXIV (March 1923), 319-320. Reprinted with title in sequence entitled "On and Off Broadway" in section called "The Follies: 1923-1928" in *American Earthquake,* pp. 49-50.

"Moscow, Athens and Paris," *American Earthquake,* pp. 116-120.

" 'The Most Unhappy Man on Earth,' " *New Yorker,* XXIV, No. 48 (22 January 1949), 63-64, 67-68. Reprinted without review of *The Portable Swift* in *Classics and Commercials,* pp. 453-459.

"Movies and Burlesque," *New Republic,* XLIII (8 July 1925), 181. Reprinted in somewhat abridged form as "The National Winter Garden" in *Shores of Light,* pp. 274-277.

"Movietone and Musical Show," *New Republic,* LV (18 July 1928), 226-227.

"Mr. and Mrs. X." See "The Best People."

"Mr. Bell, Miss Cather and Others," *Vanity Fair,* XIX, No. 2 (October 1922), 26-27. Section subheaded "Willa Cather's New Novel" (review of Willa Cather's *One of Ours*) reprinted as *"One of Ours"* in section entitled "Two Novels of Willa Cather" in *Shores of Light,* pp. 39-41; and *Willa Cather and Her Critics,* ed. James [Marvin] Schroeter (Ithaca, New York: Cornell University Press, 1967), pp. 25-27.

"Mr. Brooks's Second Phase," *New Republic,* CIII (30 September 1940), 452-454. Reprinted as "Van Wyck Brooks's Second Phase" in *Classics and Commercials,* pp. 10-18.

"Mr. E. A. Robinson's Moonlight." See "Mr Robinson's Moonlight."

" 'Mr. Ed,' " *New Republic,* LV (25 July 1928), 251-254.

"MR. EDMUND WILSON IN THE NEW REPUBLIC (New York)." See "Ulysses."

"Mr Hemingway's Dry Points," *Dial,* LXXII (October 1924), 340-341. Reprinted as "Mr. Hemingway's Dry Points" in *Shores of Light,* pp. 119-124; and *Hemingway and His Critics: An International Anthology,* ed. Carlos Baker, No. AC36 in American Century Series (New York: Hill and Wang, 1961), pp. 58-59. Reprinted with a 1953 short postscript as "Mr. Hemingway's Dry Points" in *Literary Chronicle: 1920-1950,* pp. 45-49.

" 'Mr. Holmes, They Were the Footprints of a Gigantic Hound!,' " *New Yorker,* XXI, No. 1 (17 February 1945), 73-78;
Classics and Commercials, pp. 266-274;
Literary Chronicle: 1920-1950, pp. 346-353.

"Mr. Joseph E. Davies as a Master of Prose," *Partisan Review,* XI (Winter 1944), 116-119. Reprinted as "Mr. Joseph E. Davies as a Stylist" in *Classics and Commercials,* pp. 98-104; and *Literary Chronicle: 1920-1950,* pp. 254-259.

"Mr. Lardner's American Characters," *Dial,* LXXVII (July 1924), 69-72. Reprinted as "Ring Lardner's American Characters" in *Shores of Light,* pp. 94-98; and *Literary Chronicle: 1920-1950,* pp. 37-40.

"Mr. More and the Mithraic Bull," *New Republic,* XCI (26 May 1937), 64-68;
Triple Thinkers: Ten Essays, pp. 3-19, and *Triple Thinkers: Twelve Essays,* pp. 3-14.

"Mr. Pound's Patchwork," *New Republic*, XXX (19 April 1922), 232-233. Reprinted as "Ezra Pound's Patchwork" in *Shores of Light*, pp. 44-48.

"Mr Robinson's Moonlight," *Dial*, LXXIV (May 1923), 515-517. Reprinted as "Mr. E. A. Robinson's Moonlight" in *Shores of Light*, pp. 36-38.

" 'Mr. Rolfe,' " *Atlantic Monthly*, CLXXI (March 1943), 97-107;
Triple Thinkers: Twelve Essays, pp. 233-256.

"Mr. Wilder in the Middle West," *New Republic*, LXXXI (16 January 1935), 282-283;
Shores of Light, pp. 587-592.

"Mrs. Alving and Oedipus," *Literary Review* (*New York Evening Post*), IV (9 February 1924), 501-502. Review of Henrik Ibsen's play *Ghosts*.

"Mürger and Wilde on the Screen," *New Republic*, XLVI (24 March 1926), 144-145. Partially reprinted as "A German Director in Hollywood" in *American Earthquake*, pp. 78-79.

"The Muses Out of Work," *New Republic*, L (11 May 1927), 319-321. Reprinted with letters by Hart Crane and John Crowe Ransom and with a rejoinder by EW in *Shores of Light*, pp. 197-211.

"Mushrooms, Russia and the Wassons," *Nation*, CLXXXV (16 November 1957), 364-370. Reprinted as "Mycophile and Mycophobe" in *Bit Between My Teeth*, pp. 339-354.

"The Musical Glasses of Peacock," *New Yorker*, XXIII, No. 27 (23 August 1947), 65-66, 69-70;
Classics and Commercials, pp. 404-411;
Literary Chronicle: 1920-1950, pp. 407-413.

"My Fifty Years with Dictionaries and Grammars," *New Yorker*, XXXIX, No. 9 (20 April 1963), 165-176, 189-190, 193-204, 206-208. Reprinted with some additional notes in *Bit Between My Teeth*, pp. 598-652.

["My introduction to the cultural life of Canada"], *O Canada*, pp. 3-6.

"Mycophile and Mycophobe." See "Mushrooms, Russia and the Wassons."

"The Mystery of Edwin Drood," *New Republic,* CII (8 April 1940), 463-467. Reprinted without title in the long essay entitled "Dickens: The Two Scrooges" in *Wound and the Bow,* pp. 85-104, and Galaxy Books reissue, pp. 70-85; and *Eight Essays,* pp. 77-91.

"The Myth of the Marxist Dialectic," *Partisan Review,* VI, No. 1 (Fall 1938), 66-81. Reprinted as "The Myth of the Dialectic" in *To the Finland Station,* pp. 179-198, and Anchor Books reissues, pp. 179-198.

"The Myth of the Old South; Sidney Lanier; The Poetry of the Civil War; Sut Lovingood," *Patriotic Gore,* pp. 438-528. See also " 'Poisoned!' "

"The Nahum Pesher," *New Yorker,* XLV, No. 5 (22 March 1969), 76, 78, 81-84;
Dead Sea Scrolls 1947-1969, pp. 153-161.

"The Narrative of Robert Gathorne-Hardy." See "Virginia Woolf and Logan Pearsall Smith."

"Narrow Knowledge Shown in Ten Best Books Symposium," *Baltimore Evening Sun,* 6 June 1923, section 2, p. 21.

"Nathalia Crane," *New Republic,* XLIX (2 February 1927), 310-311. Reprinted as "A Water Colorist" in *Shores of Light,* pp. 191-192.

"A Nation of Foreigners," *New Republic,* LII (5 October 1927), 161-162.

"The National Winter Garden." See "Movies and Burlesque."

"Navaho Interlude," *Red, Black, Blond and Olive,* pp. 43-51.

"The Need for a Nimbus." See "Editorial" (April 1915).

"The Need for Judaic Studies," *Piece of My Mind,* pp. 151-158.

" 'Never Apologize, Never Explain': The Art of Evelyn Waugh," *New Yorker,* XX, No. 3 (4 March 1944), 75-76, 78, 81;

Classics and Commercials, pp. 140-146;
Literary Chronicle: 1920-1950, pp. 265-271.

"The New American Comedy," See "American Comedy."

"The New Byron Letters," *New York Tribune Weekly Review of the Arts* (in Vol. LXXXII of *New York Tribune*), 2 July 1922, p. 4, cols. 4-5;
Shores of Light, pp. 57-62;
Byron: A Collection of Critical Essays, ed. Paul West, No. S-TC-31 in Spectrum Books, Twentieth Century Views, ser. ed. Maynard Mack (Englewood Cliffs, New Jersey: Prentice-Hall, 1963, 1965), pp. 138-141.

"The New Chaplin Comedy," *New Republic,* LXIV (2 September 1925), 45-46;
American Earthquake, pp. 68-73.

"The New Englander Abroad: With an Account of Nathaniel Hawthorne's Infidelity to the Venus di Medici," *Vanity Fair,* XVI, No. 2 (April 1921), 44, 96, 98.

"The New Israel National Museum," *Dead Sea Scrolls, 1947-1969,* pp. 239-243.

"A New Jersey Childhood: 'These Men Must Do Their Duty!,'" *New Yorker,* XV, No. 40 (18 November 1939), 65-72. Reprinted as "At Laurelwood: 1939" in *Note-Books of Night,* pp. 93-113; and *Night Thoughts,* pp. 157-177.

"The New Jersey Ferry." See "The Ferry."

"New Jersey: The Slave of Two Cities." See "These United States—V: New Jersey: The Slave of Two Cities."

"New Mexico Notes," *New Republic,* LXVIII (7 October 1931), 202-204.

Contents
"Indian Corn Dance"
"Fourth of July"

"A New York Diary," *New Republic,* LII (12 October 1927), 211-212.

Contents
"The Decline of the Dial"
"The Crushing of Washington Square"

"A New York Diary." See ["The Irish players have returned to New York"].

"New York, 1916-1917," *New Yorker*, XLIII, No. 11 (6 May 1967), 138, 140-149;
Prelude, pp. 153-170.

"News from Illinois," *New Republic*, LXXV (21 June 1933), 148-149.

"Newton Arvin's *Longfellow*." See "Arvin's Longfellow and New York State's Geology."

"The Nietzschean Line," *New Republic*, LXIV (22 October 1930), 248-249;
Shores of Light, pp. 485-491;
Literary Chronicle: 1920-1950, pp. 161-166.

"Night Clubs," *New Republic*, XLIV (9 September 1925), 71;
American Earthquake, pp. 32-35.

"Night Thoughts in Paris: A Rhapsody," *New Republic*, XXX (15 March 1922), 75-77.

"Nikolai Gogol—Greek Paideia," *New Yorker*, XX, No. 30 (9 September 1944), 65-66, 69. Partially reprinted as "Vladimir Nabokov on Gogol" in *Classics and Commercials*, pp. 215-218.

"1955-1967," *Dead Sea Scrolls 1947-1969*, pp. 123-220. See also "The Dead Sea Scrolls: 1969."

"Noel Coward, Camille, Etc.," *New Republic*, LXVI (18 February 1931), 19-20.

"Northern Soldiers: Ulysses S. Grant," *Patriotic Gore*, pp. 131-173. See also "Tales of Soldiers and Civilians." See also Grant, Ulysses S., in Book Reviews.

"Northern Soldiers: William T. Sherman." See "Uncle Billy."

"Northerners in the South: Charlotte Forten and Colonel Higginson." See "Charlotte Forten and Colonel Higginson."

"Northerners in the South: Frederick L. Olmsted, John T. Trowbridge." See "Olmsted on the Old South."

"A Note on the Elegiac Meter," *Night Thoughts,* pp. 275-282.

"Notes for a New Piranesi," *Town & Country,* C, No. 4286 (July 1946), 76-77, 125. Reprinted in an expanded version as "Roman Diary: Sketches for a New Piranesi" in *Europe Without Baedeker,* pp. 65-88, and 1st rev. ed., pp. 56-79. See also "A Roman Summer: 1945."

"Notes from a European Diary—1963-1964," *New Yorker,* XLII, No. 13 (21 May 1966), 54-56, 58, 61-62, 64, 67-68, 70, 73-74, 76, 79-80, 82, 84, 86, 91-92, 94; No. 14 (28 May 1966), 42-46, 48, 51, 54, 57-58, 60, 63-64, 66, 69-71, 74, 76; No. 15 (4 June 1966), 88, 90, 92, 94, 97-98, 100, 103-104, 106, 109-112, 115-118, 121-122, 124, 126-128, 130, 132-134, 136-139;
Europe Without Baedeker, 1st rev. ed., pp. 357-467.

"Notes on Babbitt and More," *New Republic,* LXII (19 March 1930), 115-120;
The Critique of Humanism: A Symposium, ed. C[linton] Hartley Grattan (New York: Brewer and Warren, 1930, 1933), pp. 39-60;
Shores of Light, pp. 451-467;
Literary Chronicle: 1920-1950, pp. 146-160.

"Notes on Gentile Pro-Semitism: New England's 'Good Jews,'" *Commentary,* XXII (October 1956), 329-335. Reprinted without title and with some introductory material and a postscript in section entitled "The Jews" in *Piece of My Mind,* pp. 85-107.

"Notes on Liberated Athens," *New Yorker,* XXI, No. 31 (15 September 1945), 30-34, 36, 39-40, 42-45. Reprinted as "Greek Diary: Notes on Liberated Athens" in *Europe Without Baedeker,* pp. 279-310, and 1st rev. ed., pp. 236-260.

"Notes on Liberated Milan," *New Yorker,* XXI, No. 26 (11 August 1945), 40, 42-49;
Europe Without Baedeker, pp. 255-278, and 1st rev. ed., pp. 217-235.

"Notes on London at the End of the War," *New Yorker,* XXI, No. 16 (2 June 1945), 42, 44-48, 51-57;

Europe Without Baedeker, pp. 1-42, and 1st rev. ed., pp. 3-37.

"Notes on Modern Literature," *New Republic,* XLI (24 December 1924), 118; XLII (24 March 1925), 39-40.

"Notes on Russian Literature" (with editor's headnote), *Atlantic Monthly,* CLXXII, No. 5 (November 1943), 78-81.

"Notes on Russian Literature: Pushkin," *Atlantic Monthly,* CLXXII, No. 6 (December 1943), 79-83.

"Notes on Russian Literature: Tyutchev," *Atlantic Monthly,* CLXXIII, No. 1 (January 1944), 78-80.

"Notes on the Churches," *Piece of My Mind,* pp. 11-18.

"A Novel by Salvador Dali." See "Salvador Dali as a Novelist."

"Novelists of the Post-War South: Albion W. Tourgée, George W. Cable, Kate Chopin, Thomas Nelson Page." See "The Ordeal of George Washington Cable."

"O Canada: An American's Notes on Canadian Culture," *New Yorker,* XL, No. 39 (14 November 1964), 63-66, 68, 71-72, 74, 77-78, 80, 84, 87-88, 90, 92, 94, 99-100, 102, 104, 106, 109-110, 112, 115-116, 118, 120, 122, 127-128, 130, 132-134, 137-140; No. 40 (21 November 1964), 64-66, 68, 71-74, 77-78, 80, 82, 84, 87-88, 90, 92, 94, 99-100, 102, 104, 106, 109-110, 112, 115-116, 118, 120, 122, 127-128, 130, 132-134, 137-138, 140; No. 41 (28 November 1964), 143-144, 146, 148, 150, 153-154, 156, 159-160, 162, 164-166, 169-172, 176-178, 181-201. Reprinted with a slight amount of additional material in *O Canada,* pp. 33-245.

"Odessa: Counter-Idyll." See "Scarlet Fever in Odessa."

"Off New York: July, 1919," *New Republic,* LVII (28 November 1928), 45. Reprinted as "Off New York: July 1919" in *Types of Exposition: Form, Style, and Substance,* ed. R[obert] A[rchibald] Jelliffe (New York: Farrar & Rinehart, 1937), pp. 264-267.

"The Old Brick and Marble Shell," *American Earthquake,* pp. 535-538.

"Old England," *Travels in Two Democracies,* pp. 47-150;
Red, Black, Blond and Olive, pp. 149-152.

"An Old Friend of the Family: Thackeray," *New Yorker,*
XXII, No. 52 (8 February 1947), 80, 83-86, 89;
Classics and Commercials, pp. 348-358.

"The Old Stone House," *Scribner's Magazine,* XCIV (December 1933), 368-372;
Travels in Two Democracies, pp. 62-78;
American Earthquake, pp. 496-510.

Reprinted with editor's headnote in *The Open Form: Essays for Our Time,* ed. Alfred Kazin (New York: Harcourt, Brace & World, 1961), pp. 127-139, and 2nd ed. (New York: Harcourt, Brace & World, 1965), pp. 160-173.

Reprinted in a badly abridged version and with a letter by EW in *America's 93 Greatest Living Authors Present This Is My Best: Over 150 Self-Chosen and Complete Masterpieces, Together with Their Reasons for Their Selections,* ed. Whit Burnett (New York: Dial Press, 1942), pp. 324-332.

"Olmsted on the Old South," *New Yorker,* XXX, No. 7 (3 April 1954), 119-130. Reprinted without review of Frederick L. Olmsted's *The Cotton Kingdom* and with additional material on John T. Trowbridge as "Northerners in the South: Frederick L. Olmsted, John T. Trowbridge" in *Patriotic Gore,* pp. 219-238.

"On 'All Men Are Mad,'" *New York Review of Books,* XIV, No. 6 (26 March 1970), 12, 14. Reprinted as "Introduction" in *All Men Are Mad,* by Philippe Thoby-Marcelin and Pierre Marcelin, trans. Eva Thoby-Marcelin (New York: Farrar, Straus and Giroux, 1970), pp. vii-xii.

"On and Off Broadway," *American Earthquake,* pp. 48-94.

"On First Reading Genesis," *New Yorker,* XXX, No. 13 (15 May 1954), 130-140, 143-150, 153-160;
Red, Black, Blond and Olive, pp. 387-426.

"'On the Eve,'" *New Yorker,* XLIII, No. 26 (19 August 1967), 38-40, 42, 44, 47-48, 50, 52, 54, 59-60, 62, 64,

66, 69-70, 72, 74. Reprinted with addition of the essay "The New Israel National Museum" as " 'On the Eve,' 1967" in *Dead Sea Scrolls 1947-1969,* pp. 221-260.

"On the Margin of Moscow" (in section entitled "U.S.S.R., May-October, 1935"), *Travels in Two Democracies,* pp. 178-257. Reprinted with later additions in brackets in section entitled "Soviet Russia (1935)" in *Red, Black, Blond and Olive,* pp. 189-305. Version appearing in *Travels in Two Democracies* partially reprinted without title in longer essay entitled "On the Margin of Moscow" in *Discovery of Europe: The Story of American Experience in the Old World,* ed. Philip Rahv (Boston: Houghton Mifflin Company [Cambridge, Massachusetts: Riverside Press], 1947), pp. 588-605. See also "Russian Paradoxes."

"On the Margin of Moscow" (a longer essay prefaced by editor's headnote), *Discovery of Europe: The Story of American Experience in the Old World,* ed. Philip Rahv (Boston: Houghton Mifflin Company [Cambridge, Massachusetts: Riverside Press], 1947), pp. 588-621.

Contents
["On the Margin of Moscow"] (excerpts)
   ["First Days in Moscow"]
   ["Letters in the Soviet Union"]
   ["Stalin as Ikon"] (fragment)
   ["Russian Idyls"] (fragment)
["Odessa: Counter-Idyll"]
["Final Reflections"]

" 'On This Site Will Be Erected,' " *New Republic,* XLII (20 May 1925), 342;
American Earthquake, pp. 15-18.

"One of Ours." See "Mr. Bell, Miss Cather and Others."

"The Oneida County Fair," *New Republic,* XLIV (30 September 1925), 155. Reprinted as "Oneida County Fair: Up-State New York" in *Poets, Farewell!,* pp. 40-42; and *Night Thoughts,* pp. 55-56.

"Onondaga," *New Yorker,* XXXV, No. 35 (17 October 1959), 60, 62, 64, 66-68, 70-71;
Apologies to the Iroquois, pp. 58-71.

"Oo, Those Awful Orcs!," *Nation*, CLXXXII (14 April 1956), 312-314;
Bit Between My Teeth, pp. 326-332.

"An Open Letter to Mike Nichols," *New York Review of Books*, IX, No. 12 (4 January 1968), 5-6, 8. Reprinted as "Open Letter to Mike Nichols" in *Duke of Palermo and Other Plays*, pp. 235-250.

"An Open Letter to Walter Lippmann," *New Republic*, LXVIII (11 November 1931), 344-345.

"Opéra Comique," *New Republic*, XLV (20 January 1926), 240-241;
American Earthquake, pp. 118-120.

"The Ordeal of George Washington Cable," *New Yorker*, XXXIII, No. 37 (9 November 1957), 172, 174-184, 189-196, 199-206, 209-216. Reprinted in rearranged fashion without review of Arlin Turner's *George W. Cable: A Biography* and with very much additional material as "Novelists of the Post-War South: Albion W. Tourgée, George W. Cable, Kate Chopin, Thomas Nelson Page" in *Patriotic Gore*, pp. 529-616 (esp. pp. 548-587, 593-606).

"Origin of This Pamphlet," *Culture and the Crisis: An Open Letter to the Writers, Artists, Teachers, Physicians, Engineers, Scientists and Other Professional Workers of America* (New York: Workers Library Publishers for League of Professional Groups for Foster and Ford, 1932), pp. 31-32.

"The Original of Tolstoy's Natasha," *New Yorker*, XXIV, No. 27 (28 August 1948), 57-58, 61-62;
Classics and Commercials, pp. 442-452;
Literary Chronicle: 1920-1950, pp. 413-422.

"Origins of Socialism; I: Babeuf's Defense," *New Republic*, XCI (9 June 1937), 121-124. Reprinted as "Origins of Socialism: Babeuf's Defense" in *To the Finland Station*, pp. 71-79, and Anchor Books reissues, pp. 69-78.

"Origins of Socialism; II: Saint Simon's Hierarchy," *New Republic*, XCI (16 June 1937), 149-151. Reprinted as "Origins of Socialism: Saint Simon's Hierarchy" in *To the*

Finland Station, pp. 80-86, and Anchor Books reissues, pp. 79-85.

"Origins of Socialism; III: The Communities of Fourier and Owen," *New Republic,* XCI (30 June 1937), 213-217. Reprinted as "Origins of Socialism: The Communities of Fourier and Owen" in *To the Finland Station,* pp. 87-98, and Anchor Books reissues, pp. 86-97.

"Origins of Socialism; IV: Enfantin and the American Socialists," *New Republic,* XCI (7 July 1937),241-246. Reprinted as "Origins of Socialism: Enfantin and the American Socialists" in *To the Finland Station,* pp. 99-111, and Anchor Books reissues, pp. 98-110.

"Oscar Wilde: 'One Must Always Seek What Is Most Tragic,' " *New Yorker,* XXII, No. 20 (29 June 1946), 69-70, 73-74, 76-77. Reprinted with a postscript in *Classics and Commercials,* pp. 331-342; and *Literary Chronicle: 1920-1950,* pp. 369-380.

"The Oxford Boys Becalmed," *New Republic,* XC (24 February 1937), 77-78;
Shores of Light, pp. 669-673.

"Painting, Opera and Theatre," *New Republic,* LXV (4 February 1931), 322-323. The sections subheaded "La Boheme" and "Schnitzler and Philip Barry" were reprinted separately.

"Palestinians," *New Yorker,* XLIII, No. 26 (19 August 1967), 39-40;
Dead Sea Scrolls 1947-1969, pp. 228-230.

"Paris," *New Yorker,* XLII, No. 13 (21 May 1966), 54-56, 58, 61-62, 64, 67-68, 70, 73-74, 76, 79-80, 82, 84, 86, 91-92, 94;
Europe Without Baedeker, 1st rev. ed., pp. 359-388.

"The Partnership of Marx and Engels." See "The Marx-Engels Partnership."

"Pastor McConnell," *Red, Black, Blond and Olive,* pp. 130-134.

"Patriotic Gore." See "Introduction," *Patriotic Gore.*

"Paul Rosenfeld: Three Phases," *Paul Rosenfeld: Voyager in the Arts,* ed. Jerome Mellquist and Lucie Wiese (New York: Creative Age Press; Toronto: McClelland and Stewart, 1948), pp. 3-19;
Classics and Commercials, pp. 503-519;
The Commentary Reader: Two Decades of Articles and Stories, ed. Norman Podhoretz (New York: Atheneum Publications, 1966), pp. 545-555.
Reprinted as "Paul Rosenfeld: Three phases: Portrait of a Humanist Man of Letters" in *Commentary,* V, No. 2 (February 1948), 111-118.

"Paul Valéry," *Dial,* LXXVIII (June 1925), 491-497.

"Paul Valéry," *New Republic,* LX (9 October 1929), 191-196. Reprinted as "Paul Valery" in *Axel's Castle,* pp. 64-92.

"Paul Valéry in the Academy," *New Republic,* XLV (23 December 1925), 134-135.

"Peaches: A Humdinger," *New Republic,* XLVIII (18 August 1926), 365-366. Reprinted as "Peaches—A Humdinger" in *Shores of Light,* pp. 277-281.

"Peggy Bacon: Poet with Pictures," *New Republic,* XCIV (27 April 1938), 363;
Shores of Light, pp. 701-704.

"The People Against Dorothy Perkins," *New Republic,* XLIII (15 July 1925), 202-205;
American Earthquake, pp. 19-28.

"The Personality of Proust," *New Republic,* LXI (12 February 1930), 316-321.

"Philip Barry and Clyde Fitch" (printed without title in article entitled "The Theatre"), *Dial,* LXXV (July 1923), 100-101. Reprinted with title in sequence entitled "On and Off Broadway" in section called "The Follies: 1923-1928" in *American Earthquake,* pp. 56-57.

"Philoctetes: The Wound and the Bow." See "The Wound and the Bow."

"A Picture to Hang in the Library: Brooks's Age of Irving."
See "A Fine Picture to Hang in the Library: Brooks's Age
of Irving."

"The Pilgrimage of Henry James," *New Republic*, XLIII
(6 May 1925), 283-286. Reprinted as *"The Pilgrimage of
Henry James"* in *Shores of Light*, pp. 217-228. Reprinted
as "The Pilgrimage, II" in *Henry James: A Collection of
Critical Essays*, ed. Leon Edel, No. S-TC-34 in Spectrum
Books, Twentieth Century Views, ser. ed. Maynard Mack
(Englewood Cliffs, New Jersey: Prentice-Hall, 1963), pp.
63-71.

"The Pilgrimage, II." See "The Pilgrimage of Henry James."

"Plattsburgh, Summer of 1916," *New Yorker*, XLIII, No. 11
(6 May 1967), 137-138;
Prelude, pp. 149-152.

"The Pleasures of Literature: By a Booklover," *Nation*, CXLVI
(29 January 1938), 128-129. Reprinted as "The Pleasures
of Literature: By a Book Lover" in *Shores of Light*, pp.
711-715.

"Poe as a Literary Critic," *Nation*, CLV (31 October 1942),
452-453. Reprinted as "Introduction" (to Poe) in *Shock
of Recognition*, pp. 79-84.

"Poe at Home and Abroad," *New Republic*, XLIX (8 De-
cember 1926), 77-80;
Shores of Light, pp. 179-190;
Literary Chronicle: 1920-1950, pp. 65-76.

"The Poet of Hosiery" (in essay entitled "Theatres, Books
and Ladies' Wear"), *New Republic*, XLIV (11 November
1925), 304. Reprinted without title in essay entitled "Current Fashions" in sequence entitled "On and Off Broadway"
in section called "The Follies: 1923-1928" in *American
Earthquake*, p. 76.

"A Poet of the Pacific," *New Republic*, LVII (12 December
1928), 99-100;
Shores of Light, pp. 345-350.

"The Poet-Logician," *New Republic*, LXXI (18 May 1932), 19-21. Reprinted with a long postscript reviewing Florence Becker Lennon's *Victoria Through the Looking-Glass: The Life of Lewis Carroll* as "C. L. Dodgson: The Poet Logician" in *Shores of Light*, pp. 540-550.

"The Poetry of Angelica Balabanoff," *Nation*, CLVII (27 November 1943), 615-616, 618;
Classics and Commercials, pp. 94-97.

"The Poetry of Drouth," *Dial*, LXXIII (December 1922), 611-616.

"The Point of View of a Former Socialist," *Cold War and the Income Tax*, pp. 41-46.

" 'Poisoned!,' " *New Yorker*, XXXI, No. 12 (7 May 1955), 150-154, 157-159. Reprinted without title as part of essay entitled "The Myth of the Old South; Sidney Lanier; The Poetry of the Civil War; Sut Lovingood" in *Patriotic Gore*, pp. 507-519.

"Polemics," *New Yorker*, XLV, No. 5 (22 March 1969), 45-46, 48, 51-52, 54, 57-58, 60;
Dead Sea Scrolls 1947-1969, pp. 127-142.

"Politeness a Virtue That is Unknown to the New Yorker," *Baltimore Evening Sun*, 6 November 1923, section 2, p. 21.

"Political Headquarters," *New Republic*, LXV (19 November 1930), 15-16;
American Jitters, pp. 6-10;
American Earthquake, pp. 175-178.

"The Politics of Flaubert." See "Flaubert's Politics."

"Pope and Tennyson," *New Republic*, XLIV (16 September 1925), 96-97;
Shores of Light, pp. 254-258.

"Port-au-Prince." See "Haiti: Landscape and Morale."

"Portrait: Christian Gauss." See "Christian Gauss."

"Postscript," *Boys in the Back Room*, pp. 65-72;
Classics and Commercials, pp. 51-56;
Literary Chronicle: 1920-1950, pp. 245-249.

"Postscript," *Red, Black, Blond and Olive,* pp. 493-500.

"Postscript of 1957," *American Earthquake,* pp. 566-576.

"A Postscript to Fowler: Current Clichés and Solecisms," *New Statesman,* LXV (8 February 1963), 195, 198. Reprinted with a 1965 note and short postscript in *Bit Between My Teeth,* pp. 561-570.

"Post-War Shaw and Pre-War Bennett," *New Republic,* LXXI (8 June 1932), 92-94.

"Preface," *The Confessions of Jean-Jacques Rousseau,* Vol. I, by Jean-Jacques Rousseau, trans. from the French, in The Borzoi Classics (New York: Alfred A. Knopf, 1923, 1928), pp. v-x.

"Preface," *Five Plays,* pp. 7-8.

"Preface," *Peasants and Other Stories,* pp. vii-xi.

"Preface," *Undertaker's Garland,* pp. 13-23.

"A Preface to Modern Literature," *New Republic,* LVIII (20 March 1929), "Spring Book Section," pp. 134-139.

Signed Review

M., L. *Revue Germanique,* XXI (1930), 187-188.

The essay "A Preface to Modern Literature" was reprinted as "Symbolism" in *Axel's Castle,* pp. 1-25; *Modern American Prose,* ed. Carl Van Doren (New York: Harcourt Brace and Company, 1934), pp. 687-700; *Five Kinds of Writing: Selections from British and American Authors, Old and New,* ed. Theodore Morrison and the staff of English A. at Harvard University (Boston: Little, Brown and Company, 1939, 1941), pp. 255-269; and *Experience & Expression: An Approach to Critical Reading and Writing,* ed. Mary Alice Wyman, Lavinia Bonner Eves, and William A. S. Dollard (New York: Prentice-Hall, 1940), pp. 71-78.

"A Preface to Persius," *New Republic,* LII (19 October 1927), 237-239. Reprinted as "A Preface to Persius: Maudlin Meditations in a Speakeasy" in *Shores of Light,* pp. 267-273.

"Preface to the First Edition" (printed alone without title), *Europe Without Baedeker,* pp. vii-viii. Reprinted alone with title in *Europe Without Baedeker,* 1st rev. ed., pp. vii-viii.

"Preface to the Second Edition," *Europe Without Baedeker,* 1st. rev. ed., pp. ix-xi.

"A Prelude—I: Landscapes, Characters, and Conversations from the Earlier Years of My Life," *New Yorker,* XLIII, No. 10 (29 April 1967), 50-52, 54, 57-58, 60, 63-64, 66, 69-70, 72, 75-76, 78, 81-82, 84, 89-90, 92, 95-96, 98, 101-102, 104, 107-108, 110, 113-114, 116, 119-120, 122, 124, 126, 128-131; continued as "A Prelude—II: Landscapes, Characters, and Conversations from the Earlier Years of My Life," *New Yorker,* XLIII, No. 11 (6 May 1967), 52-54, 56, 59-60, 62, 64-66, 71-72, 74, 76-78, 81-82, 84, 86-88, 90, 95-96, 98, 100-102, 104, 107-108, 110, 112, 114, 119-120, 122, 124, 126, 129, 132-138, 140-149; concluded as "A Prelude—III: Landscapes, Characters, and Conversations from the Earlier Years of My Life," *New Yorker,* XLIII, No. 12 (13 May 1967), 54-56, 58, 61-62, 64, 67-68, 70, 73-76, 78, 80, 85-86, 88, 91-93, 95, 98, 101-102, 104, 109-114, 116, 119-122, 125-128, 131-136, 138, 140-154, 157. Reprinted with some additions as the book *Prelude.*

"The Pre-Presidential T. R.," *New Yorker,* XXVII, No. 36 (20 October 1951), 132, 135-136, 138, 140-142, 145-148; *Eight Essays,* pp. 203-216; *Bit Between My Teeth,* pp. 63-77. Reprinted alone without title in *Perspectives USA,* No. 5 (Fall, 1953), pp. 152-160, and *Perspectives* (British ed. of *Perspectives USA*), No. 5 (Autumn 1953), pp. 152-160.

"Princeton, 1912-1916," *New Yorker,* XLIII, No. 11 (6 May 1967), 52-54, 56, 59-60, 62, 64-66, 71-72, 74, 76-78, 81-82, 84, 86-88, 90, 95-96, 98, 100-102, 104, 107-108, 110, 112, 114, 119-120, 122, 124, 126, 129, 132-137; *Prelude,* pp. 71-148.

"Prize-Winning Blank Verse," *New Republic,* XCI (23 June 1937), 193-194; *Shores of Light,* pp. 674-680.

"The Problem of English," *Piece of My Mind,* pp. 159-168.

"The Problem of the Higher Jazz." See "The Jazz Problem."

"Progress and Poverty," *New Republic*, LXVII (20 May 1931), 13-16. Reprinted as "The First of May" in *American Jitters*, pp. 132-143. Reprinted as "May First: The Empire State Building; Life on the Passaic River" in *American Earthquake*, pp. 292-302.

"The Progress of Psychoanalysis: The Importance of the Discovery, by Dr. Siegmund Freud, of the Subconscious Self," *Vanity Fair*, XIV, No. 6 (August 1920), 41, 86, 88.

"Prologue, 1952: Christian Gauss as a Teacher of Literature." See "Christian Gauss."

"Prose," *Poets, Farewell!*, pp. 33-42. Reprinted as "Prose of the Twenties" in *Night Thoughts*, pp. 49-56.

"Prose of the Thirties," *Night Thoughts*, pp. 137-178.

"Prose of the Twenties." See "Prose."

"Proust and Yeats," *New Republic*, LII (5 October 1927), 176-177, 177a.

"The Psalms," *New Yorker*, XLV, No. 5 (22 March 1969), 66, 68, 73-74, 76;
Dead Sea Scrolls 1947-1969, pp. 147-152.

"A Publisher's List," *New Republic*, XLVIII (27 October 1926), 269-270.

"The Pueblo" (printed without title in essay entitled "A Reporter in New Mexico: Shalako"), *New Yorker*, XXV, No. 7 (9 April 1949), 62, 65-68. Reprinted with title in section entitled "Zuñi (1947)" in *Red, Black, Blond and Olive*, pp. 3-15.

["The question of American expansion"] (in section entitled "War"), *Piece of My Mind*, pp. 39-48.

"The Question of Costume." See "Editorial" (June 1915).

"The Rag-Bag of the Soul," *Literary Review* (*New York Post*), III, No. 12 (25 November 1922), 1-2.

"The Real Religion of the Witches: A Note on Miss Margaret Murray's Theory of the Witch Cult in Western Europe," *Vanity Fair*, XXI, No. 2 (October 1923), 63, 108.

"Red Cross and County Agent," *Scribner's Magazine*, XC
(September 1931), 249-258;
American Jitters, pp. 86-105;
American Earthquake, pp. 249-266.
　　Partially reprinted with editor's headnote as "Red Cross
　　Worker" in *A Quarto of Modern Literature*, ed. Leonard
　　Brown and Porter G[ale] Perrin, new ed. (New York:
　　Charles Scribner's Sons, 1940), pp. 348-352.

"Red Cross Worker." See "Red Cross and County Agent."

"Reëxamining Dr. Johnson." See "Dr. Johnson."

"Reflections on Leaving New York," *New Republic*, XLVI
(17 March 1926), 105. Reprinted as "Thoughts on Leaving
New York for New Orleans" in *American Earthquake*, pp.
121-123.

"Reflections on Returning to New York from Louisiana,"
New Republic, XLVI (28 April 1926), 304-305. Reprinted
as "Return from Louisiana" in *Note-Books of Night*, pp.
65-69; and *American Earthquake*, pp. 135-138.

"Reflections on the Teaching of Latin," *Archbishop* (ed. Fes-
senden Wilder [North Andover, Massachusetts: Brooks
School]), XVIII [mistakenly printed as XVIIII], No. 3
(June 1955), 5-9;
Classical Journal, LI (February 1956), 197-202;
Piece of My Mind, pp. 139-150.

"Reinstating the Red Man," *Modern Monthly*, VIII (July
1934), 327-331;
American Earthquake, pp. 544-551.

"Religion," *Piece of My Mind*, pp. 1-18.

["Religion is the cult of a god"] (in section entitled "Religion"), *Piece of My Mind*, pp. 3-10.

"A Reporter in New Mexico: Shalako," *New Yorker*, XXV,
No. 7 (9 April 1949), 62, 65-73; No. 8 (16 April 1949),
80-94. Reprinted with addition of the essay "Navaho Interlude" and other material as "Zuñi 1947)" in *Red, Black,
Blond and Olive*, pp. 1-68.

"Reports on the G. I. by Gertrude Stein and Saroyan," *New Yorker*, XXII, No. 18 (15 June 1946), 90-93. Reprinted without review of Gertrude Stein's *Brewsie and Willie* as "William Saroyan and His Darling Old Providence" in *Classics and Commercials*, pp. 327-330.

"Respectable Productions," *New Republic*, LXVI (13 May 1931), 357-358.

"Return from Louisiana." See "Reflections on Returning to New York from Louisiana."

"Reveries," *New Republic*, XLIV (30 September 1925), 155-156.

Contents
I. "The Oneida County Fair"
II. "The Jersey Coast—A Highball"

"A Revival of Ronald Firbank," *New Yorker*, XXV, No. 42 (10 December 1949), 141-146, 149-150; *Classics and Commercials*, pp. 486-502.

"Ring Lardner's American Characters." See "Mr. Lardner's American Characters."

"Roman Diary: Arrival—a Visit to Santayana." See "Santayana at the Convent of the Blue Nuns."

"Roman Diary: British Officials," *Europe Without Baedeker*, pp. 185-204, and 1st rev. ed., 159-175.

"Roman Diary: Russian Exiles," *Europe Without Baedeker*, pp. 159-184, and 1st rev. ed., pp. 138-158.

"Roman Diary: Sketches for a New Piranesi." See "Notes for a New Piranesi." See also "A Roman Summer: 1945."

"A Roman Summer: 1945," *Horizon: A Review of Literature and Art*, XVI (August 1947), 102-120. Partially reprinted without title in essay entitled "Roman Diary: Sketches for a New Piranesi" in *Europe Without Baedeker*, pp. 65-68, 72-82, and 1st rev. ed., pp. 56-58, 61-66, 70-74; and in essay entitled "Rome in Midsummer" in *Europe Without Baedeker*, pp. 235-252, and 1st rev. ed., pp. 200-214.

"Romance: Maxine Elliott's Theatre," *Nassau Literary Magazine*, LXIX (May 1913), 109-110.

"Rome," *New Yorker*, XLII, No. 14 (28 May 1966), 42-46, 48, 51, 54, 57-58, 60, 63-64, 66, 69-71, 74, 76; *Europe Without Baedeker,* 1st rev. ed., pp. 389-417.

"Rome in Midsummer" *Europe Without Baedeker,* pp. 235-254, and 1st rev. ed., pp. 200-216. See also "A Roman Summer: 1945."

"Russia," *Piece of My Mind,* pp. 65-82.

"Russian Idyls," *New Republic*, LXXXVI (29 April 1936), 339-342. Reprinted without title in essay entitled "On the Margin of Moscow" in section called "U.S.S.R., May-October, 1935" in *Travels in Two Democracies*, pp. 230-234, 239-245. Reprinted without title in same essay in section called "Soviet Russia (1935)" in *Red, Black, Blond and Olive*, pp. 251-255, 260-267. Partially reprinted without title in longer essay entitled "On the Margin of Moscow" in *Discovery of Europe: The Story of American Experience in the Old World*, ed. Philip Rahv (Boston: Houghton Mifflin Company [Cambridge, Massachusetts: Riverside Press], 1947), pp. 598-601.

"Russian Paradoxes," *New Republic*, LXXXVII (13 May 1936), 11-13.

Contents
["On the Margin of Moscow"] (fragment)
["Final Reflections"]
The fragment of "On the Margin of Moscow" is reprinted as part of essay entitled "On the Margin of Moscow" in section called "U.S.S.R., May-October, 1935" in *Travels in Two Democracies*, pp. 245-247, 252-257; and as part of same essay in section called "Soviet Russia (1935)" in *Red, Black, Blond and Olive*, pp. 267-268, 274-279. For reprintings of "Final Reflections" see "Final Reflections."

"Rutherford and Son: The West End Theatre," *Nassau Literary Magazine*, LXIX (April 1913), 44-45.

"Sacrosanct Prospect." See "Editorial" (June 1915).

"Saintsbury's Centenary—Spadework on Kipling," *New Yorker*, XXI, No. 51 (2 February 1946), 74-77. Reprinted without review of Hilton Brown's *Rudyard Kipling* as

"George Saintsbury's Centenary" in *Classics and Commercials*, pp. 306-310; and *Literary Chronicle: 1920-1950*, pp. 359-363.

"Salute to an Old Landmark: Sinclair Lewis," *New Yorker*, XXI, No. 35 (13 October 1945), 94, 96-97;
Sinclair Lewis: A Collection of Critical Essays, ed. Mark Schorer, No. S-TC-6 in Spectrum Books, Twentieth Century Views, ser. ed. Maynard Mack (Englewood Cliffs, New Jersey: Prentice-Hall, 1962), pp. 139-142.

"Salvador Dali as a Novelist," *New Yorker*, XX, No. 20 (1 July 1944), 61-62, 65. Reprinted as "A Novel by Salvador Dali" in *Classics and Commercials*, pp. 190-195.

"Samaritan Passover," *New Yorker*, XXX, No. 42 (4 December 1954), 174, 176-180;
Red, Black, Blond and Olive, pp. 427-435.

"The Sanctity of Baudelaire." See "The Essays of V. S. Pritchett—The Journals of Baudelaire."

"Santayana at the Convent of the Blue Nuns," *New Yorker*, XXII, No. 8 (6 April 1946), 55-62. Reprinted as "Roman Diary: Arrival—a Visit to Santayana" in *Europe Without Baedeker*, pp. 43-64. Reprinted as "Roman Diary: Arrival; A Visit to Santayana" in *Europe Without Baedeker*, 1st rev. ed., pp. 38-55.

"The Satire of Samuel Butler," *New Republic*, LXXV (24 May 1933), 35-37;
Triple Thinkers: Ten Essays, pp. 210-219;
Shores of Light, pp. 557-565.

"Saving the Better Classes and Their Butlers," *New Yorker*, X, No. 7 (31 March 1934), 34-40. Reprinted as "Saving the Right People and Their Butlers" in *Travels in Two Democracies*, pp. 86-95; and *American Earthquake*, pp. 518-526.

"Scarlet Fever in Odessa," *New Yorker*, XII, No. 9 (11 April 1936), 32, 34, 36, 38, 43-44, 46-47. Reprinted in expanded form containing EW's translation of S. Marshak's poem "Stripes and Whiskers" as "Odessa: Counter-Idyll" in section entitled "U.S.S.R., May-October, 1935" in *Travels in Two Democracies,* pp. 271-319 (esp. pp. 289-298, 302-303, 310-313); and in section entitled "Soviet Russia (1935)" in *Red, Black, Blond and Olive,* pp. 322-373 (esp. pp. 341-351, 354-356, 364-367). Expanded form partially reprinted without title and without EW's translation of S. Marshak's poem "Stripes and Whiskers" in the long essay entitled "On the Margin of Moscow" in *Discovery of Europe: The Story of American Experience in the Old World,* ed. Philip Rahv (Boston: Houghton Mifflin Company [Cambridge, Massachusetts: Riverside Press], 1947), pp. 605-618 (esp. pp. 612-618). Expanded form partially reprinted without EW's translation of S. Marshak's poem "Stripes and Whiskers" as "Hospital in Odessa" in a section entitled "Leningrad and a Hospital in Odessa" in *The Great Travelers: A Collection of Firsthand Narratives of Wayfarers, Wanderers and Explorers in All Parts of the World from 450 B.C. to the Present,* ed. Milton [Allan] Rugoff, Vol. II (New York: Simon and Schuster, 1960), pp. 651-655.

"Schnitzler and Philip Barry," *New Republic,* LXV (4 February 1931), 322-323;
Shores of Light, pp. 504-508.

"School and College Friends," *New Yorker,* XLIII, No. 10 (29 April 1967), 95-96, 98, 101-102, 104, 107-108, 110, 113-114, 116, 119-120, 122, 124, 126, 128-131;
Prelude, pp. 39-70.

"The Scorpion" (in essay entitled "'On the Eve'"), *New Yorker,* XLIII, No. 26 (19 August 1967), 52, 54. Reprinted without title at the end of essay entitled "The Two Jerusalems" in section called "'On the Eve,' 1967" in *Dead Sea Scrolls 1947-1969,* p. 238.

"The Scottsboro Freight-Car Case." See "The Freight-Car Case."

"The Scrolls from the Dead Sea" (printed without chapter headings), *New Yorker,* XXXI, No. 13 (14 May 1955), 45-50, 52, 54-57, 59-60, 63-64, 66-68, 70-72, 74, 76-78, 81-82, 84-86, 88, 93-94, 96-100, 103-110, 112-118, 121-131.

Reprinted with chapter headings as the book *Scrolls from the Dead Sea*. Reprinted with chapter headings as section entitled "The Scrolls from the Dead Sea, 1955" in *Dead Sea Scrolls 1947-1969*, pp. 1-122.

"The Sea," *New Republic*, XLIII (22 July 1925), 236. Reprinted as "Swimming" in *Poets, Farewell!*, pp. 36-37; and *Night Thoughts*, p. 52.

"The Second Battle of Oriskany." See "The Milk Strike."

["The second two decades of the century"] (printed without title in a special section entitled "American Writing: 1941," ed. EW), *New Republic*, CIV, No. 16 (21 April 1941), Part 2, p. 545. See also *New Republic* in Periodicals Edited by Wilson.

"A Senator and an Engineer," *New Republic*, LXVII (27 May 1931), 36-38. Reprinted as "Senator and Engineer" in *American Jitters*, pp. 105-112; and *American Earthquake*, pp. 267-273.

"Seneca New Year's Ceremonies, *New Yorker*, XXXV, No. 37 (31 October 1959), 71, 74-78, 81-83, 86-88, 93-97, 100-104, 109-116;
Apologies to the Iroquois, pp. 198-251.

"The Seneca Republic," *New Yorker*, XXXV, No. 37 (31 October 1959), 50-52, 54, 56, 59-60, 62, 65-66, 68, 71;
Apologies to the Iroquois, pp. 169-197.

"*The Seven Lively Arts* (1924)." See "The Seven Low-Brow Arts."

"The Seven Low-Brow Arts," *Dial*, LXXVII (September 1924), 244-250. Reprinted as "*The Seven Lively Arts* (1924)" in *Shores of Light*, pp. 156-164; and *Literary Chronicle: 1920-1950*, pp. 49-57.

"Sex," *Piece of My Mind*, pp. 195-208.

"Shakespeare by Arthur Hopkins" (printed without title in article entitled "The Theatre"), *Dial*, LXXIV (March 1923), 320. Reprinted with title in sequence entitled "On and Off Broadway" in section called "The Follies: 1923-1928" in *American Earthquake*, pp. 48-49.

"Shalako" (printed without title in essay entitled "A Reporter in New Mexico: Shalako"), *New Yorker,* XXV, No. 7 (9 April 1949), 69-73; No. 8 (16 April 1949), 80-86. Reprinted with title in section entitled "Zuñi (1947)" in *Red, Black, Blond and Olive,* pp. 23-43.

"Shalako Continued" (printed without title in essay entitled "A Reporter in New Mexico: Shalako"), *New Yorker,* XXV, No. 8 (16 April 1949), 86-92. Reprinted with title in section entitled "Zuñi (1947)" in *Red, Black, Blond and Olive,* pp. 51-65.

"Sharp Impression that Schoenberg Had a Headache," *Baltimore Evening Sun,* 19 June 1923, section 2, p. 19.

"Shaw in the Metropolitan," *New Republic,* LXXIV (26 April 1933), 298-299. Reprinted as "Shaw at the Metropolitan" in *Travels in Two Democracies,* pp. 49-55. Reprinted as "Bernard Shaw at the Metropolitan" in *American Earthquake,* pp. 490-495.

"Shaw Versus the Triangle Club." See "Editorial" (May 1915).

"Sheilah Graham and Scott Fitzgerald," *New Yorker,* XXXIV, No. 49 (24 January 1959), 115-118, 121-124;
Bit Between My Teeth, pp. 16-27.

"Sherwood Anderson's *Many Marriages.*" See "Many Marriages."

"A Short View of Proust," *New Republic,* LIV (21 March 1928), 140-148. Reprinted in very much revised and expanded form as "Marcel Proust" in *Axel's Castle,* pp. 132-190. Version appearing in *Axel's Castle* partially reprinted as "Axel's Castle" in *Marcel Proust: Reviews and Estimates in English,* comp. Gladys Dudley Lindner (Stanford, California: Stanford University Press, 1942), pp. 140-148.

"The Shrine of the Book," *New Yorker,* XLV, No. 6 (29 March 1969), 88, 93-94, 96. See also "The Dead Sea Scrolls: 1969."

"Shut Up That Russian Novel," *New Republic,* XCIV (6 April 1938), 264-267;
Shores of Light, pp. 722-731.

"Signs of Life," *New Republic,* LXIX (3 July 1929), 184-185. Reprinted as "Signs of Life: *Lady Chatterley's Lover*" in *Shores of Light,* pp. 403-407; and *Literary Chronicle: 1920-1950,* pp. 113-117.

"The Six Nations Reserve," *New Yorker,* XXXV, No. 38 (7 November 1959), 96, 98, 101-102, 104, 106, 108, 111; *Apologies to the Iroquois,* pp. 252-269.

"Sixty-Five Years of Realism," *New Republic,* XLIII (17 June 1925), 101.

"The Socialists Meet," *New Republic,* LXXI (8 June 1932), 95-96. Signed "Harry W. Laidler," but attributed to EW in his corrected copy of Arthur Mizener's "Edmund Wilson: A Checklist," *Princeton University Library Chronicle,* V, No. 2 (February 1944), 73, in the Yale University Library.

"The Soft Sell for CBR," *Cold War and the Income Tax,* pp. 83-90.

"Some Letters After 1848," *New Republic,* XCVIII (8 February 1939), 21-23. Contains letters by Friedrich Engels, Gustave Flaubert, and Maxime du Camp translated by EW.

"Some Recent Films," *New Republic,* XLV (16 December 1925), 109. Partially reprinted as "Chaplin and His Comic Rivals" in *American Earthquake,* pp. 77-78.

"Some Reviews of Job," *Dial,* LXVIII (April 1920), 469-472.

"Somerset Maugham and an Antidote," *New Yorker,* XXII, No. 17 (8 June 1946), 96-100. Reprinted with a postscript and without review of Newton Arvin's edition of *Hawthorne's Short Stories* as "The Apotheosis of Somerset Maugham" in *Classics and Commercials,* pp. 319-326.

"Sophocles, Babbitt and Freud," *New Republic,* LXV (3 December 1930), 68-70. Reprinted with a postscript in *Shores of Light,* pp. 468-475.

"Southern Soldiers: Richard Taylor, John S. Mosby, Robert E. Lee," *Patriotic Gore,* pp. 299-335.

"Soviet Russia (1935)." See "U.S.S.R., May-October, 1935."

"Splendors and Miseries of Evelyn Waugh," *New Yorker,* XXI, No. 47 (5 January 1946), 64-67. Reprinted with part of the essay "Lesser Books by Brilliant Writers" and with a postscript reviewing Evelyn Waugh's *Scott-King's Modern Europe* and *The Loved One* in *Classics and Commercials,* pp. 298-305 (esp. pp. 298-302); and *Literary Chronicle: 1920-1950,* pp. 353-359 (esp. pp. 353-357). See also "Lesser Books by Brilliant Writers."

"The Sportsman's Tragedy," *New Republic,* LIII (14 December 1927), 102-103;
Shores of Light, pp. 339-344;
Literary Chronicle: 1920-1950, pp. 96-101.

"Spring Comedy," *New Republic,* XLVI (19 May 1926), 404-405.

"St. Regis," *New Yorker,* XXXV, No. 35 (17 October 1959), 71-72, 77-79, 81-82, 84, 86-88, 91-92, 94-98, 103-107, 109-114;
Apologies to the Iroquois, pp. 72-125.

"Stalin as Ikon," *New Republic,* LXXXVI (15 April 1936), 271-273. Reprinted without title in essay entitled "On the Margin of Moscow" in section called "U.S.S.R., May-October, 1935" in *Travels in Two Democracies,* pp. 219-227, 229. Reprinted in same essay in section called "Soviet Russia (1935)" in *Red, Black, Blond and Olive,* pp. 238-247, 249-250. Partially reprinted without title in longer essay entitled "On the Margin of Moscow" in *Discovery of Europe: The Story of American Experience in the Old World,* ed. Philip Rahv (Boston: Houghton Mifflin Company [Cambridge, Massachusetts: Riverside Press], 1947), pp. 596-598.

"Standing Arrow," *New Yorker,* XXXV, No. 35 (17 October 1959), 49-52, 54, 57, 59-60;
Apologies to the Iroquois, pp. 39-57.

"Stendhal," *Nassau Literary Magazine,* LXXI (April 1915), 33-38.

"Stephen Crane—Hannah Whitall Smith," *New Yorker,* XXVI, No. 46 (6 January 1951), 77-78, 81-85. Reprinted without review of John Berryman's *Stephen Crane* as "Hannah Whitall Smith" in *Bit Between My Teeth*, pp. 114-117.

"Stephen Spender and George Grosz on Germany," *New Yorker*, XXII, No. 47 (4 January 1947), 64-66, 69-70. Reprinted without review of Stephen Spender's *European Witness* as "George Grosz in the United States" in *Classics and Commercials*, pp. 343-347.

"The Stieglitz Exhibition," *New Republic*, XLII (18 March 1925), 97-98;
American Earthquake, pp. 98-103.

" 'Still'—Meditations of a Progressive," *New Republic*, LXVI (8 April 1931), 198-200. Reprinted as " 'Still—': Meditations of a Progressive" in *American Jitters*, pp. 113-120; and *American Earthquake*, pp. 274-280.

"Stopover in Naples," *Europe Without Baedeker*, pp. 389-398, and 1st rev. ed., pp. 324-331.

"The Strategy of Tax Refusal," *Cold War and the Income Tax*, pp. 102-118. Partially reprinted in article entitled "The Cold War and the Income Tax" in *Liberation: An Independent Monthly*, VIII, No. 10 (December 1963), 25.

"Stravinsky," *New Republic*, XLII (1 April 1925), 156-157. Reprinted with inclusion of ["Stravinsky and Others"] and a 1957 postscript in *American Earthquake*, pp. 104-111 (esp. pp. 104-108).

"Stravinsky and Others," *New Republic*, XLVI (10 March 1926), 73-74. Reprinted without title and with a 1957 postscript as part of essay entitled "Stravinsky" in section called "The Follies: 1923-1928" in *American Earthquake*, pp. 108-111.

"Summary as of 1940." See "What Has Happened to Marxism."

"Summer," *New Republic*, XLIII (22 July 1925), 236. The subdivisions entitled "The Ferry," "The Sea," and "A Train's Whistle" were reprinted.

"The Summer Hotel." See "The Jersey Coast—A Highball."

"Summer Revues," *New Republic,* XLVII (28 July 1926), 279-280. Partially reprinted as "The Follies in New Quarters" in *American Earthquake,* pp. 79-80.

"Sunshine Charley," *New Republic,* LXXV (28 June 1933), 176-178;
Travels in Two Democracies, pp. 55-62;
American Earthquake, pp. 484-489.
Reprinted with questions about the essay in *The Essay: A Critical Anthology,* ed. John L[incoln] Stewart, in Prentice-Hall English Literature Series, ser. ed. Maynard Mack (New York: Prentice-Hall, 1952), pp. 492-498 (the questions appear on pp. 627-628).

"Swimming." See "The Sea."

"Swinburne of Capheaton and Eaton," *New Yorker,* XXXVIII, No. 33 (6 October 1962), 165-170, 173-180, 183-188, 190, 193-200;
The Novels of A. C. Swinburne: Love's Cross-Currents, Lesbia Brandon, by Algernon Charles Swinburne (New York: Farrar, Straus and Cudahy, 1962), pp. 3-37.
EW's essay was reviewed as follows:

Signed Reviews
Adams, Phoebe. *Atlantic Monthly,* CCXI (March 1963), 164.
Buchen, Irving R. *Saturday Review,* XLV, No. 51 (29 December 1962), 36.
Daiches, David. *Victorian Studies,* VII (March 1964), 314-316.
Igoe, W. J. *Critic: A Magazine of Christian Culture* (Chicago), XXI, No. 5 (April 1963), 79.
Willingham, John R. *Library Journal,* LXXXVIII (15 January 1963), 238.
Wills, G[ary]. *National Review,* XIV (26 March 1963), 247.
Yerker, P. M., and Brian Lee. *Year's Work in English Studies,* XLIV (1963), 295.

Unsigned Reviews
Newsweek, LX (17 December 1962), 95-96.

Nineteenth-Century Fiction, XVIII (June 1963), 101.

Time: The Weekly Newsmagazine, LXXXI (25 January 1963), 84-86.

Essay reprinted as "Swinburne's Letters and Novels" in *Bit Between My Teeth,* pp. 228-269.

"Swinburne's Letters and Novels." See "Swinburne of Capheaton and Eaton."

"Symbolism." See "A Preface to Modern Literature."

"T. K. Whipple: A Prefatory Memoir," *Study Out the Land: Essays,* by T. K. Whipple (Berkeley and Los Angeles: University of California Press, 1943), pp. xi-xxii. Reprinted as "T. K. Whipple" in *Classics and Commercials,* pp. 70-80.

"T. S. Eliot," *New Republic,* LX (13 November 1929), 341-349;
Axel's Castle, pp. 93-131;
Literary Opinion in America: Essays Illustrating the Status, Methods, and Problems of Criticism in the United States Since the War, ed. Morton Dauwen Zabel (New York: Harper & Brothers, 1937), pp. 145-177; Rev. Ed., published as *Literary Opinion in America: Essays Illustrating the Status, Methods, and Problems of Criticism in the United States in the Twentieth Century* (New York: Harper & Brothers, 1951), pp. 206-227; 3rd Ed. Rev., published with same title as Rev. Ed., Vol. I, No. TB3013 in Harper Torchbooks, The University Library (New York: Harper and Row, 1962), pp. 206-227; and 3rd Ed. Rev. reprinted, Vol. I (Gloucester, Massachusetts: Peter Smith, 1968), pp. 206-227;
T. S. Eliot: A Selected Critique, ed. Leonard Unger (New York: Rinehart & Company, 1948), pp. 170-194.

"T. S. Eliot and the Church of England," *New Republic,* LVIII (24 April 1929), 283-284;
Shores of Light, pp. 436-441;
Literary Chronicle: 1920-1950, pp. 133-138.

"Tales of Soldiers and Civilians," *New Yorker,* XXXII, No. 16 (9 June 1956), 132, 134, 137-141. Reprinted without title and without reviews of John T. Trowbridge's *The Desolate South, 1865-66* and Sylvanus Cadwaller's *Three Years with Grant, As Recalled by War Correspondent Sylvanus Cadwaller,* but with additional comments on Richard Taylor, as part of essay entitled "Southern Soldiers: Richard Taylor, John S. Mosby, Robert E. Lee" in *Patriotic Gore,* pp. 299-307. Paragraphs reviewing Sylvanus Cadwaller's *Three Years with Grant, As Recalled by War Correspondent Sylvanus Cadwaller* reprinted without title as part of essay entitled "Northern Soldiers: Ulysses S. Grant" in *Patriotic Gore,* pp. 138-141.

"Tales of the Marvelous and the Ridiculous," *New Yorker,* XXI, No. 41 (24 November 1945), 100, 103-104, 106. Reprinted without review of A. N. Afanas'ev's *Russian Fairy Tales* in *Classics and Commercials,* pp. 286-290.

"Talk with Edmund Wilson." See Breit, Harvey, in Items about Wilson.

"Talking United States," *New Republic,* LXXXVII (15 July 1936), 299-300. Reprinted with a postscript in *Shores of Light,* pp. 630-639.

"Tanach," *New Yorker,* XXX, No. 42 (4 December 1954), 196-204. Reprinted as "Tanách" in *Red, Black, Blond and Olive,* pp. 456-468.

"Tattoo," *New Yorker,* XLIII, No. 26 (19 August 1967), 38-39;
Dead Sea Scrolls 1947-1969, pp. 223-227.

"The Teacher of Righteousness" (printed without title in essay entitled "The Scrolls from the Dead Sea"), *New Yorker,* XXXI, No. 13 (14 May 1955), 82, 84-86, 88, 93-94, 96-100. Reprinted with title in *Scrolls from the Dead Sea,* pp. 54-76, and Collins "amplified" ed., pp. 60-82. Reprinted with title in section entitled "The Scrolls from the Dead Sea, 1955" in *Dead Sea Scrolls 1947-1969,* pp. 55-77.

"Tennessee Agrarians," *New Republic,* LXVII (29 July 1931), 279-281;
American Jitters, pp. 169-175;
American Earthquake, pp. 328-333.

"The Tennessee Poets" (essay), *New Republic,* LIV (7 March 1928), 103-104. Reprinted with inserted heading "Book Review of Fugitives, An Anthology of Verse" in *The Fugitive: Clippings and Comment about the Magazine and the Members of the Group that Published It,* comp. Merrill Moore (Boston: n.p., 1939), pp. 59-61. Reprinted without inserted heading as *"Fugitives"* in *Shores of Light,* pp. 192-196.

"The Tennessee Poets" (section), *Shores of Light,* pp. 191-196.

"The Testimonia," *New Yorker,* XLV, No. 6 (29 March 1969), 68, 71-72, 74, 79;
Dead Sea Scrolls 1947-1969, pp. 182-188.

"The Texts," *New Yorker,* XLV, No. 6 (29 March 1969), 58, 60, 65, 68;
Dead Sea Scrolls 1947-1969, pp. 176-181.

"Thackeray's Letters: A Victorian Document," *New Yorker,* XXI, No. 45 (22 December 1945), 77-78, 81;
Classics and Commercials, pp. 291-297.

"That Summer in Paris," *New Yorker,* XXXIX, No. 1 (23 February 1963), 139-142, 145-148;
Bit Between My Teeth, pp. 515-525.

"The Theatre," *Dial,* LXXIV (March 1923), 319-320.

Contents
["The Moscow Art Theater"]
["Shakespeare by Arthur Hopkins"]

"The Theatre," *Dial,* LXXIV (April 1923), 420-422.

Contents
["An Early Theater Guild Production"]
["The Follies as an Institution"]

"The Theatre," *Dial,* LXXIV (May 1923), 526-528;
A Dial Miscellany, ed. William Wasserstrom (Syracuse, New York: Syracuse University Press, 1963), pp. 121-123.
See also "A Greenwich Village Production" in Plays and Dialogues.

"The Theatre," *Dial,* LXXIV (June 1923), 635-636.

Contents
["Guitry without the Guitrys"]
["Late Pinero and Early Cornell"]

"The Theatre," *Dial*, LXXV (July 1923), 100-102.

Contents
["Philip Barry and Clyde Fitch"]
["Animals at the Circus"]
["Herbert Williams"]

"The Theatre," *Dial*, LXXV (August 1923), 204-205. Partially reprinted as "Bert Savoy and Eddie Cantor of the Follies" in *American Earthquake*, pp. 59-60.

"The Theatre," *Dial*, LXXV (September 1923), 309-310.

"The Theatre," *Dial*, LXXV (October 1923), 404-405. Partially reprinted as "Why not Restoration Comedy?" in *American Earthquake*, pp. 60-61.

"The Theatre," *Dial*, LXXV (November 1923), 512-514.

"The Theatre," *Dial*, LXXVIII (February 1925), 163-166. Partially reprinted as "Henri Becque as Good-Will Ambassador" in *American Earthquake*, pp. 61-62.

"Theatre, Concert Hall and Gallery," *New Republic*, XLII (8 April 1925), 181-182. Partially reprinted as "J. P. McEvoy in the Ziegfeld Follies" in *American Earthquake*, pp. 63-64.

"Theatres, Books, and Ladies' Wear," *New Republic*, XLIV (11 November 1925), 303-304. The subdivisions entitled "Enlightenment through the Movies," "The Poet of Hosiery," and "The Fashion" were reprinted. The review of Raymond Radiguet's *Les joues en feu* was not reprinted.

"Theocracy," *New Yorker*, XXX, No. 42 (4 December 1954), 193-196;
Red, Black, Blond and Olive, pp. 452-456.

"These United States—V: New Jersey: The Slave of Two Cities," *Nation*, CXIV (14 June 1922), 712-714. Reprinted as "New Jersey: The Slave of Two Cities" in *These United States: A Symposium*, ed. Ernest Gruening, 1st ser. [or Vol. I] (New York: Boni and Liveright, 1923), pp. 56-66.

"Things As They Are." See "An English Critic on the French Novel—Gertrude Stein as a Young Woman."

"Things I Consider Overrated: Being a Second Series of Essays in Purely Destructive Criticism," *Vanity Fair,* XV, No. 4 (December 1920), 59, 104, 106.

"Things I Consider Overrated: Some Popular Institutions Subjected to a Purely Destructive Criticism," *Vanity Fair,* XV, No. 2 (October 1920), 65, 104.

"Things I Consider Underrated: Three Little Essays in Constructive Criticism," *Vanity Fair,* XVI, No. 1 (March 1921), 38.

["This month the 'Reveille' is bigger and better than ever"], *Reveille* ("Published by Base Hospital 36 on Active Service, A. E. F."), No. 2 (February 1918), p. 2.

"Thornton Wilder," *New Republic,* LV (8 August 1928), 303-305;
Shores of Light, pp. 384-391;
Literary Chronicle: 1920-1950, pp. 102-108.

"Thoughts on Being Bibliographed," *Princeton University Library Chronicle,* V, No. 2 (February 1944), 51-61;
Classics and Commercials, pp. 105-120.

"Thoughts on Leaving New York for New Orleans." See "Reflections on Leaving New York."

"Three Confederate Ladies," *New Yorker,* XXXI, No. 38 (5 November 1955), 179-180, 185-186, 188-192, 195-202, 205-209. Reprinted without review of Katherine M. Jones's *Heroines of Dixie: Confederate Women Tell Their Story of the War* as "Three Confederate Ladies: Kate Stone, Sarah Morgan, Mary Chesnut" in *Patriotic Gore,* pp. 258-298.

"Through the Abruzzi with Mattie and Harriet," *Europe Without Baedeker,* pp. 109-158, and 1st rev. ed., pp. 97-137.

"Through the Embassy Window: Harold Nicolson," *New Yorker,* XIX, No. 46 (1 January 1944), 63-67;
Classics and Commercials, pp. 121-127.

"To the Finland Station: I" (with editor's headnote), *New Republic*, LXXX (29 August 1934), 64-67; (5 September 1934), 91-95; (12 September 1934), 123-127; (19 September 1934), 150-153; (3 October 1934), 207-210; (24 October 1934), 302-307.

Contents
1. "Michelet Discovers Vico"
2. "Michelet and the Middle Ages"
3. "Michelet and the Revolution"
4. "Michelet Tries to Live His History"
5. "Michelet Between Nationalism and Socialism"
6. "Decline of the Revolutionary Tradition: Renan"
7. "Decline of the Revolutionary Tradition: Taine"
8. "Decline of the Revolutionary Tradition: Anatole France"

These essays were reprinted without editor's headnote in the same order as the first part of *To the Finland Station*, pp. 3-68, and Anchor Books reissues, pp. 1-68.

"A Toast and a Tear for Dorothy Parker," *New Yorker*, XX, No. 14 (20 May 1944), 75-76;
Classics and Commercials, pp. 168-171;
Literary Chronicle: 1920-1950, pp. 284-287.

"A Train's Whistle," *New Republic*, XLIII (22 July 1925), 236;
Poets, Farewell!, p. 35;
Night Thoughts, p. 51.

"The Traveler" (same as "Epilogue"), *Travels in Two Democracies*, pp. 323-325 (esp. p. 325).

"A Treatise on Tales of Horror," *New Yorker*, XX, No. 15 (27 May 1944), 72, 75-78, 81-82;
Classics and Commercials, pp. 172-181;
Literary Chronicle: 1920-1950, pp. 287-295.

"Trotsky," *New Republic*, LXXIII (4 January 1933), 207-209; concluded as "Trotsky: II," *New Republic*, LXXIII (11 January 1933), 235-238;
Adelphi (London), N.S. (3rd ser.) VI, No. 3 (June 1933), 185-191; No. 4 (July 1933), 253-259.

"Trotsky Identifies History with Himself," *To the Finland Station*, pp. 430-446, and Anchor Books reissues, pp. 428-444.

"Trotsky: The Young Eagle," *To the Finland Station,* pp. 405-429, and Anchor Books reissues, pp. 403-427.

"Turgenev and the Life-Giving Drop," *New Yorker,* XXXIII, No. 35 (19 October 1957), 163-186, 189-196, 199-206, 209, 212-216;
   Literary Reminiscences and Autobiographical Fragments, by Ivan Sergeevich Turgenev, trans. David Magarshack (New York: Farrar, Straus and Cudahy, 1958), pp. 3-64; also published as *Turgenev's Literary Reminiscences and Autobiographical Fragments,* by Ivan Sergeevich Turgenev, trans. David Magarshack (London: Faber and Faber, 1958), pp. 9-59.

"The Tuscaroras," *New Yorker,* XXXV, No. 36 (24 October 1959), 48-50, 52, 54, 57, 59-60, 62, 64, 69-70, 72, 74, 76, 81-84;
   Apologies to the Iroquois, pp. 126-168.

"27 rue de Fleurus," *New Republic,* LXXVI (11 October 1933), 246-247. Reprinted as "27, rue de Fleurus" in *Shores of Light,* pp. 575-580.

"Twilight of the Expatriates," *New Republic,* XCIV (9 March 1938), 140. Reprinted with a letter by Henry Miller in *Shores of Light,* pp. 705-710; *Literary Chronicle: 1920-1950,* pp. 211-216; and *Henry Miller and the Critics,* ed. George Wickes, in Crosscurrents: Modern Critiques, ser. ed. Harry T. Moore (Carbondale: Southern Illinois University Press, 1963), pp. 25-30.

"The Two Jerusalems," *New Yorker,* XLIII, No. 26 (19 August 1967), 40, 42, 44, 47-48, 50, 52;
   Dead Sea Scrolls 1947-1969, pp. 231-238.

"Two Neglected American Novelists," *New Yorker,* XLVI, No. 14 (23 May 1970), 112-116, 120-122, 125-127, 131-132, 134, 137-139; No. 16 (6 June 1970), 112-114, 117-119, 123-126, 129-134.

"Two Novels of Willa Cather," *Shores of Light,* pp. 39-43. Reprinted as " 'Two Novels of Willa Cather' " in *Willa Cather and Her Critics,* ed. James [Marvin] Schroeter

(Ithaca, New York: Cornell University Press, 1967), pp. 25-29.

"Two Protests," *New Republic,* LXVII (22 July 1931), 251-253;
American Jitters, pp. 143-150;
American Earthquake, pp. 303-309.

"Two Soviet Households," *New Yorker,* LIII, No. 42 (9 December 1967), 231-232, 234-238, 241-242, 244.

"Two Survivors: Malraux and Silone," *New Yorker,* XXI, No. 30 (8 September 1945), 74-78, 81-86;
Horizon: A Review of Literature and Art, XII (October 1945), 245-256;
Europe Without Baedeker, pp. 89-108, and 1st rev. ed., pp. 80-96.

"Two Views of Byron," *Dial,* LXXVIII (June 1925), 511-514. Reprinted as "Byron and His Biographers" in *Shores of Light,* pp. 62-67; and *Byron: A Collection of Critical Essays,* ed. Paul West, No. S-TC-31 in Spectrum Books, Twentieth Century Views, ser. ed. Maynard Mack (Englewood Cliffs, New Jersey: Prentice-Hall, 1963, 1965), pp. 141-144.

"Two West Indian Authors," *Red, Black, Blond and Olive,* pp. 74-78.

"Two Young Men and An Old One," *Vanity Fair,* XIX, No. 3 (November 1922), 24-25 (a section by Burton Rascoe subheaded "A Literary Vaudeville Team" concludes the article on pp. 25, 108). Section subheaded "Eugene O'Neill as Prose-Writer" (review of Eugene O'Neill's *The Hairy Ape, Anna Christie, The First Man*) reprinted in *Shores of Light,* pp. 99-101; same section reprinted as "Eugene O'Neill as a Prose Writer" in *O'Neill and His Plays: Four Decades of Criticism,* ed. Oscar Cargill, N[athan] Bryllion Fagin, and William J. Fisher (New York: New York University Press, 1961), pp. 464-467. See also "All God's Chillun and Others" and "The All-Star Literary Vaudeville."

"Types of American Presidents" (printed without title and with much additional material in section entitled "The United States"), *Piece of My Mind,* pp. 21-31. Reprinted with title and with questions by the editors in *Form and Thought in Prose,* ed. Wilfred H[ealey] Stone and Robert Hoopes, 2nd ed. (New York: Ronald Press, 1960), pp. 475-477.

"U. S. A., November, 1932-May, 1934," *Travels in Two Democracies,* pp. 9-112. Reprinted in slightly rearranged form with omissions and additions as "Dawn of the New Deal: 1932-1934" in *American Earthquake,* pp. 443-576.

"U.S.S.R., May-October, 1935," *Travels in Two Democracies,* pp. 145-322. Reprinted with additional material in brackets as "Soviet Russia (1935)" in *Red, Black, Blond and Olive,* pp. 147-384.

"Ulysses," *New Republic,* XXXI (5 July 1922), 164-166. Partially reprinted as "MR. EDMUND WILSON IN THE NEW REPUBLIC (New York)" in *Extracts from Press Notices of Ulysses By James Joyce* (Harlesden: Leveridge & Company, [1923?]), p. 2.

"Uncle Billy," *New Yorker,* XXXIV, No. 16 (7 June 1958), 114, 116-124, 127-134, 137-144. Reprinted with less material reviewing William Tecumseh Sherman's *Memoirs of General William T. Sherman* and with additional paragraphs concluding the essay as "Northern Soldiers: William T. Sherman" in *Patriotic Gore,* pp. 174-218.

"Uncomfortable Casanova." See "Casanova."

"The United States," *Piece of My Mind,* pp. 19-36.

"Unscrupulous Communists and Embattled Democracies," *New Yorker,* XXXVII, No. 30 (9 September 1961), 140-146, 149-152. Reprinted as "George F. Kennan" in *Bit Between My Teeth,* pp. 500-514.

"Upton Sinclair's *Mammonart.*" See "Mammonart."

"Van Wyck Brooks on the Civil War Period," *New Yorker,* XXIII, No. 41 (29 November 1947), 116, 118, 121-122; *Classics and Commercials,* pp. 423-430.

"Van Wyck Brooks's Second Phase." See "Mr. Brooks's Second Phase."

"Vantine's in Five Floors," *New Republic,* XLIX (5 January 1927), 192;
American Earthquake, p. 86.

"Variations on a Landscape," *New Republic,* XLVIII (10 November 1926), 325-326;
Note-Books of Night, pp. 82-92;
Night Thoughts, pp. 146-156.

"Virginia Woolf and Logan Pearsall Smith," *New Yorker,* XXVI, No. 4 (27 May 1950), 99-100, 103-105. Reprinted without review of Virginia Woolf's *The Captain's Death Bed and Other Stories* as "The Narrative of Robert Gathorne-Hardy" in *Bit Between My Teeth,* pp. 124-130.

"Virginia Woolf and the American Language," *Shores of Light,* pp. 421-428.

"Vladimir Nabokov on Gogol." See "Nikolai Gogol—Greek Padeia."

"The Vogue of the Marquis de Sade," *New Yorker,* XXVIII, No. 35 (18 October 1952), 163-164, 166, 168-170, 173-176;
Eight Essays, pp. 167-180;
Bit Between My Teeth, pp. 158-173.

"Volga Idyll," *Travels in Two Democracies,* pp. 257-271;
Red, Black, Blond and Olive, pp. 306-321.

"Voodoo Converts," *Red, Black, Blond and Olive,* pp. 125-130.

"A Vortex in the Nineties," *New Republic,* XXXVII (2 January 1924), 153-154. Reprinted as "A Vortex in the Nineties: Stephen Crane" in *Shores of Light,* pp. 109-114.

"W. B. Yeats," *New Republic,* XLII, No. 541 (15 April 1925), Part 2 ("Spring Book Section"), pp. 8-10. See also "William Butler Yeats."

"W. H. Auden in America," *New Statesman and Nation,* LI (9 June 1956), 658-659;
Auden: A Collection of Critical Essays, ed. Monroe Kirklyndorf Spears, in Spectrum Books, Twentieth Century

Views, ser. ed. Maynard Mack (Englewood Cliffs, New Jersey: Prentice-Hall, 1964), pp. 54-59; *Bit Between My Teeth,* pp. 355-363.

"Wallace Stevens and E. E. Cummings," *New Republic,* XXXVIII (19 March 1924), 102-103. Reprinted with a postscript in *Shores of Light,* pp. 49-56.

"Wanted: A City of the Spirit: Reflections upon the Spiritual Problems Which Confront the Younger Generation in America," *Vanity Fair,* XXI, No. 5 (January 1924), 63, 94.

"War," *Piece of My Mind,* pp. 37-50.

"Washington: Glimpses of the New Deal," *American Earthquake,* pp. 534-565. See also "The Zero Hour in Washington."

"Washington: Inaugural Parade." See "Inaugural Parade."

"A Water-Colorist." See "Nathalia Crane."

"The Week." See ["David Gordon, a young poet of eighteen"] and "Judd Gray and Mrs. Snyder."

"A Weekend at Ellerslie," *Shores of Light,* pp. 373-382.

"What About American Literature?," *Cold War and the Income Tax,* pp. 52-58.

"What Became of Louis Bromfield," *New Yorker,* XX, No. 8 (8 April 1944), 80, 83-84, 86, 90. Reprinted with a postscript in *Classics and Commercials,* pp. 153-160; and *Literary Chronicle: 1920-1950,* pp. 271-278.

"What Do the Liberals Hope For?," *New Republic,* LXIX (10 February 1932), 345-348.

"What Has Happened to Marxism: I Marx and Engels: Background," *Call: Official Weekly Publication of the Socialist Party* (New York), 22 February 1941, p. 3; continued as "What Has Happened to Marxism: II The Russian Experiment," *Call: Official Weekly Publication of the Socialist Party* (New York), 1 March 1941, p. 3; concluded as "What Has Happened to Marxism: III A Will and a Way," *Call: Official Weekly Publication of the Socialist Party* (New York), 8 March 1941, p. 3. Reprinted without subheadings as "Marxism at the End of the Thirties" in *Shores of Light*, pp. 732-743. Reprinted without subheadings as "Summary as of 1940" in *To the Finland Station*, Anchor Books reissues, pp. 475-484.

"What I Believe," *Nation*, CXXXIV (27 January 1932), 95-98.

"What Is Mr. Krutch Defending?" (EW's part of the article "Is Politics Ruining Art?: A Debate"), *Forum*, XC (August 1933), 82-84.

"What Our Money Is Going For," *Cold War and the Income Tax*, pp. 46-52.

"What Rip Van Winkle Woke Up To," *Cold War and the Income Tax*, pp. 25-32.

"What Would Renan Have Said?" (printed without title in essay entitled "The Scrolls from the Dead Sea"), *New Yorker*, XXXI, No. 13 (14 May 1955), 100, 103-110, 112-118, 121-125. Reprinted alone with title in *Scrolls from the Dead Sea*, pp. 77-112, and Collins "amplified" ed., pp. 83-118. Reprinted with title in section entitled "The Scrolls from the Dead Sea, 1955" in *Dead Sea Scrolls 1947-1969*, pp. 78-113.

"Who Cares Who Killed Roger Ackroyd?: A Second Report on Detective Fiction," *New Yorker*, XX, No. 49 (20 January 1945), 52-54, 57-58. Reprinted as "Who Cares Who Killed Roger Ackroyd?" in *Classics and Commercials*, pp. 257-265; *Literary Chronicle: 1920-1950*, pp. 338-345; and *Mass Culture: The Popular Arts in America*, ed. Bernard Rosenberg and David Manning White (Glencoe, Illinois: Free Press and Falcon's Wing Press, 1957), pp. 149-153. Reprinted with editor's headnote and footnote in *Art of the Mystery Story: A Collection of Critical Essays*, ed. Howard Haycraft (New York: Simon and Schuster, 1946), pp. 390-397.

"Why Do People Read Detective Stories?," *New Yorker*, XX, No. 35 (14 October 1944), 73-74, 76;
Classics and Commercials, pp. 231-237;
Literary Chronicle: 1920-1950, pp. 322-328.

"Why not Restoration Comedy?" See "The Theatre" (October 1923).

"Willa Cather's New Novel." See "Mr. Bell, Miss Cather and Others."

"William Butler Yeats," *New Republic,* LX (25 September 1929), 141-148. Reprinted alone as "W. B. Yeats" in *Axel's Castle,* pp. 26-63; and *The Permanence of Yeats: Selected Criticism,* ed. James Hall and Martin Steinmann (New York: Macmillan Company, 1950), pp. 15-41. Reprinted alone without title in *The Permanence of Yeats* (paperback), ed. James Hall and Martin Steinmann (New York: Collier Books, 1961), pp. 14-37.

"William Faulkner's Reply to the Civil-Rights Program," *New Yorker,* XXIV, No. 35 (23 October 1948), 106, 109-113;
Classics and Commercials, pp. 460-470;
Literary Chronicle: 1920-1950, pp. 422-431;
Faulkner: A Collection of Critical Essays, ed. Robert Penn Warren, in Spectrum Books, Twentieth Century Views, ser. ed. Maynard Mack (Englewood Cliffs, New Jersey: Prentice-Hall, 1966), pp. 219-225.

"William Saroyan." See "The Boys in the Back Room: William Saroyan."

"William Saroyan and His Darling Old Providence." See "Reports on the G. I. by Gertrude Stein and Saroyan."

"Wilson on Lincoln" (*Perspectives USA*). See "Abraham Lincoln: The Union as Religious Mysticism."

"Wilson on Theodore Roosevelt" (*Perspectives USA*). See "The Pre-Presidential T. R."

"Woodrow Wilson at Princeton." See "Woodrow Wilson: Political Preacher."

"Woodrow Wilson: Political Preacher," *New Republic,* LIII (30 November 1927), 35-42. Reprinted with a postscript as "Woodrow Wilson at Princeton" in *Shores of Light,* pp. 298-324.

"Woollcott and Fourier," *Nation*, CLVI (6 February 1943), 194-196. Reprinted as "Alexander Woollcott of the Phalanx" in *Classics and Commercials*, pp. 87-93; and *Literary Chronicle: 1920-1950*, pp. 249-254.

"Word-Fetishism," *New Republic*, XC (17 February 1937), 43-44. Reprinted as "Word-Fetishism or Sick in Four Languages at Odessa" in *Note-Books of Night*, pp. 75-78. Reprinted as "Word-Fetishism or Sick in Four Languages in Odessa" in *Night Thoughts*, pp. 139-142.

"Words of Ill-Omen," *New Statesman*, LVI (6 September 1958), 304, 306, 308; concluded as "More Words of Ill-Omen," *New Statesman*, LVI (13 September 1958), 344, 346. Reprinted without division as "Words of Ill-Omen" in *Bit Between My Teeth*, pp. 403-419.

"The Wound and the Bow," *New Republic*, CIV (21 April 1941), 548-551, 554-555. Reprinted as "Philoctetes: The Wound and the Bow" in *Wound and the Bow*, pp. 272-295, and Galaxy Books reissue, pp. 223-242; *Literary Criticism in America*, ed. Albert D. Van Nostrand, No. 16 in The American Heritage Series, ser. ed. Oskar Priest (New York: Liberal Arts Press, 1957), pp. 293-310; and *Art and Psychoanalysis*, ed. William Phillips (New York: Criterion Books, 1957), pp. 521-537. Reprinted as "Introduction: Philoctetes: The Wound and the Bow" in *Philoctetes*, by Sophocles, trans. Kenneth Cavander, in Chandler Editions in Drama, ser. ed. Robert W. Corrigan (San Francisco: Chandler Publishing Company, 1965), pp. vii-xix.

" 'You Can't Do This to Me!' Shrilled Celia: Inquiry into a Current Best-Seller," *New Yorker*, XX, No. 28 (26 August 1944), 58, 61-62. Reprinted as " 'You Can't Do This to Me!' Shrilled Celia" in *Classics and Commercials*, pp. 204-208; and *Literary Chronicle: 1920-1950*, pp. 309-313.

"The Young Man from Manchester," *New Republic*, XCV (3 August 1938), 352-356. Reprinted as "Friedrich Engels: The Young Man from Manchester" in *To the Finland Station*, pp. 129-139, and Anchor Books reissues, pp. 128-138.

"The Zero Hour" (printed without title in essay entitled "The Delegates from Duquesne" in article called "The Zero Hour in Washington"), *Modern Monthly,* VIII (July 1934), 336. Reprinted with title and with a 1957 postscript in sequence entitled "Washington: Glimpses of the New Deal" in section called "Dawn of the New Deal: 1932-1934" in *American Earthquake,* pp. 564-565.

"The Zero Hour in Washington," *Modern Monthly,* VIII (July 1934), 327-336.

Contents
     I. "Japanese Cherry Blossoms"
    II. "Reinstating the Red Man"
   III. "The Delegates from Duquesne"
       ["The Zero Hour"]
See also "Washington: Glimpses of the New Deal."

"The Ziegfeld Theatre," *New Republic,* L (2 March 1927), 45;
American Earthquake, pp. 88-89.

"Zuñi (1947)." See "A Reporter in New Mexico: Shalako."

III / BOOK REVIEWS

Adams, Franklin P. *In Other Words,* in *Nassau Literary Magazine,* LXVIII (February 1913), 347-348.

Adams, Henry. *Democracy,* in *New Republic,* XLIV (14 October 1925), 203.

Adams, Samuel Hopkins. *A. Woollcott: His Life and His World,* in *New Yorker,* XXI, No. 17 (9 June 1945), 73-74, 77.

Ade, George. *The Permanent Ade: The Living Writings of George Ade.* See "George Ade: The City Uncle" in Essays.

Aeschylus. See MacNeice, Louis.

Afanas'ev, A. N., comp. *Russian Fairy Tales.* See "Tales of the Marvelous and the Ridiculous" in Essays.

Agnón, S. Y. *Two Tales,* trans. Walter Lever. See "The Invisible World of S. Y. Agnon" in Essays.

Aldington, Richard, ed. *The Portable Oscar Wilde.* See "Oscar Wilde: 'One Must Always Seek What Is Most Tragic'" in Essays.

Allegro, John M. *The Dead Sea Scrolls,* in *New Statesman and Nation,* LII (27 October 1956), 521-522.

Allen, James Lane. *The Heroine in Bronze,* in *Nassau Literary Magazine,* LXIX (May 1913), 118-119.

Alliluyeva, Svetlana. *Twenty Letters to a Friend.* See "Two Soviet Households" in Essays.

Amis, Kingsley. *Lucky Jim* and *That Uncertain Feeling.* See "Is It Possible to Pat Kingsley Amis?" in Essays.

Anderson, Charles R. See Lanier, Sidney.

Anderson, John Q., ed. *Brockenburn: The Journal of Kate Stone, 1861-1868.* See "Three Confederate Ladies" in Essays.

Anderson, Maxwell. *High Tor, The Masque of Kings,* and *Winterset.* See "Prize-Winning Blank Verse" in Essays.

Anderson, Melville B. See Dante.

Anderson, Sherwood. *Many Marriages.* See "Many Marriages" in Essays.

Archer, William. *Three Plays,* with foreword by Bernard Shaw, in *New Republic,* LIII (21 December 1927), 148, 149.

Arkright, Frank. *The A B C of Technocracy,* in *New Republic,* LXXIV (22 February 1933), 30-51.

Arvin, Newton. *Longfellow: His Life and Work.* See "Arvin's Longfellow and New York State's Geology" in Essays.

———, ed. *Hawthorne's Short Stories.* See "Somerset Maugham and an Antidote" in Essays.

Aubrey, John. *Aubrey's Brief Lives.* See "Miscellaneous Memorabilia: Oscar Wilde, James Joyce, John Aubrey" in Essays.

Auden, W. H. *The Ascent of F-6* and *On This Island.* See "The Oxford Boys Becalmed" in Essays.

———. *The Enchafèd Flood, or the Romantic Iconography of the Sea.* See "Bankrupt Britons and Voyaging Romantics" in Essays.

———, comp. *The Oxford Book of Light Verse,* in *New Republic,* XCVII (18 January 1939), 321.

———, ed. See James, Henry (*The American Scene*), and Tennyson, Alfred Lord.

Austen, Jane. *The Watsons,* concluded by L. Oulton, in *Dial,* LXXIV (June 1923), 621-623.

Babbitt, Irving, P. E. More, *et al. Humanism and America: Essays on the Outlook of Modern Civilization,* ed. Norman Foerster. See "Notes on Babbitt and More" in Essays.

Bacon, Peggy. *Animosities* and *Cat-Calls.* See "Peggy Bacon: Poet with Pictures" in Essays.

Baker, Ray Stannard. *Woodrow Wilson: Life and Letters.* See "Woodrow Wilson: Political Preacher" in Essays.

Balabanoff, Angelica. *Tears.* See "The Poetry of Angelica Balabanoff" in Essays.

Barmine, Alexander. *One Who Survived: The Life Story of a Russian Under the Soviets,* in *New Yorker,* XXI, No. 22 (14 July 1945), 65-66, 69-70.

Barrett, William. *What Is Existentialism?* See "Jean-Paul Sartre: The Novelist and the Existentialist" in Essays.

Barry, Philip. *Tomorrow and Tomorrow.* See "Schnitzler and Philip Barry" in Essays.

Basher, Roy P., ed. *The Collected Works of Abraham Lincoln.* See "Abraham Lincoln: The Union as Religious Mysticism" in Essays.

Basso, Hamilton. *Relics and Angels,* in *New Republic,* LX (23 October 1929), 274-275.

Baudelaire, [Pierre Charles]. *Intimate Journals,* trans. Christopher Isherwood. See "The Essays of V. S. Pritchett— The Journals of Baudelaire" in Essays.

Beal, Fred. E. *Proletarian Journey,* in *Nation,* CXLV (13 November 1937), 531-532, 534-535.

Becker, Carl C. *How New Will the Better World Be?,* in *New Yorker,* XX, No. 9 (15 April 1944), 77-78.

Beer, Thomas. *Stephen Crane: A Study in American Letters.* See "A Vortex in the Nineties" in Essays.

Beerbohm, Max. *A Christmas Garland,* in *Nassau Literary Magazine,* LXVIII (February 1913), 346-347.

———. *Mainly on the Air.* See "An Analysis of Max Beerbohm" in Essays.

———. *Rossetti and His Circle*, in *Vanity Fair*, XIX, No. 5 (January 1923), 17.

Bell, Clive. *Since Cézanne.* See "Mr. Bell, Miss Cather and Others" in Essays.

Bellow, Saul. *Dangling Man*, in *New Yorker*, XX, No. 7 (1 April 1944), 78, 81.

Benchley, Belle J. *My Friends, the Apes*, in *New Yorker*, XX, No. 31 (September 1944), 72-73.

Benchley, Robert C. *Love Conquers All*, in *Bookman*, LVI (January 1923), 636-637.

———. *Of All Things*, in *New Republic*, XXX (29 March 1922), 150.

Benét, Stephen. *The Ballad of William Sycamore*, in *Vanity Fair*, XX, No. 5 (July 1923), 19.

Bennett, Arnold. *These Twain*, in *Nassau Literary Magazine*, LXXI (February 1916), 396-399.

Benton, Thomas H., illus. *The Autobiography of Benjamin Franklin*, by Benjamin Franklin, and *Life on the Mississippi*, by Mark Twain, in *New Yorker*, XX, No. 42 (2 December 1944), 90.

Berryman, John. *Stephen Crane.* See "Stephen Crane—Hannah Whitall Smith" in Essays.

Bessie, Alvah C., trans. *Torture Garden* (*Le jardin des supplices*), by Octave Mirbeau. See "In Memory of Octave Mirbeau" in Essays.

Bierce, Ambrose. *The Collected Writings of Ambrose Bierce*, in *New Yorker*, XXII, No. 49 (18 January 1947), 82, 84-85.

Bikle, Lucy Leffingwell Cable. *George W. Cable: His Life and Letters.* See "Citizen of the Union" in Essays.

Billington, Ray Allen, ed. *The Journal of Charlotte L. Forten.* See "Charlotte Forten and Colonel Higginson" in Essays.

Bingham, Alfred M. *The Practice of Idealism*, in *New Yorker*, XX, No. 9 (15 April 1944), 77-78, 81-82.

The Black Book of Polish Jewry, in *New Yorker,* XIX, No. 50 (29 January 1944), 77.

Blake, William. *The Marriage of Heaven and Hell,* in *New Republic,* LIII (8 February 1928), 330.

―――. *The Poetry and Prose of William Blake,* ed. Geoffrey Keynes, in *New Republic,* LIII (8 February 1928), 330.

―――, illus. See Dante.

Blum, John M., ed. *The Letters of Theodore Roosevelt.* See "The Pre-Presidential T. R." in Essays.

Bogan, Louise. *Body of This Death,* in *Vanity Fair,* XXI, No. 3 (November 1923), 26.

Bolton, Isabel. *Do I Wake or Sleep,* in *New Yorker,* XXII, No. 37 (26 October 1946), 107-108.

A Book of Vassar Verse, in *Nassau Literary Magazine,* LXXII (February 1917), 342-343.

Bowen, Catherine Drinker. *Yankee from Olympus,* in *New Yorker,* XX, No. 10 (22 April 1944), 83-84.

Bowman, Peter. *Beach Red,* in *New Yorker,* XXI, No. 46 (29 December 1945), 54.

Boyd, Ernest. *Ireland's Literary Renaissance,* in *Vanity Fair,* XX, No. 1 (March 1923), 11.

―――, trans. and ed. See Maupassant, Guy de.

Boyd, Thomas, *Through the Wheat,* in *Dial,* LXXV (July 1923), 19.

Boyle, Kay. *Avalanche.* See "Kay Boyle and the Saturday Evening Post" in Essays.

Bradford, Gamaliel. *Damaged Souls,* in *Vanity Fair,* XXI, No. 1 (September 1923), 23.

Brod, Max. *Franz Kafka: A Biography.* See "A Dissenting Opinion on Kafka" in Essays.

―――, ed. *Gesammelte Schriften,* by Franz Kafka. See "A Dissenting Opinion on Kafka" in Essays.

Bromfield, Louis. *The Green Bay Tree, The Strange Case of Miss Annie Spragg,* and *What Became of Anna Bolton.* See "What Became of Louis Bromfield" in Essays.

Brontë, Charlotte. See Wilson, Edward A.

Brooks, Van Wyck. *The Flowering of New England.* See "Mr. Brooks's Second Phase" in Essays.

―――. *New England: Indian Summer.* See " 'The Country I Remember' " and "Mr. Brooks's Second Phase" in Essays.

―――. *The Pilgrimage of Henry James.* See "The Pilgrimage of Henry James" in Essays.

―――. *The Times of Melville and Whitman.* See "Van Wyck Brooks on the Civil War Period" in Essays.

―――. *The World of Washington Irving.* See "A Fine Picture to Hang in the Library: Brooks's Age of Irving" in Essays.

Brown, Abbie Farwell. *The Silver Stair,* in *New Republic,* XLVIII (17 November 1926), 383-384.

Brown, Hilton. *Rudyard Kipling.* See "Saintsbury's Centenary—Spadework on Kipling" in Essays.

Brown, Wenzell. *Dynamite on Our Doorstep,* in *New Yorker,* XXI, No. 46 (29 December 1945), 53-54.

Buckley, John J., ed. *The Letters of Theodore Roosevelt.* See "The Pre-Presidential T. R." in Essays.

Bucknell Verse for 1926, in *New Republic,* XLVIII (17 November 1926), 384.

Buitrón, Aníbal. See Collier, John, Jr.

Burns, John Horne. *The Gallery,* in *New Yorker,* XXIII, No. 25 (9 August 1947), 60-62.

Burrows, Millar. *The Dead Sea Scrolls.* See "More on the Dead Sea Scrolls" in Essays.

Buttle, Myra (pseud. for Victor Purcell?). *Cadmus: The Poet and the World* and *The Sweeniad.* See " 'Miss Buttle' and 'Mr. Eliot' " in Essays.

Byron, George Gordon Lord. *Lord Byron's Correspondence,* ed. John Murray. See "The New Byron Letters" in Essays.

Cabell, James Branch. *As I Remember It: Some Epilogues in Recollection.* See "The James Branch Cabell Case Reopened" in Essays.

Cable, George Washington. *George W. Cable: His Life and Letters.* See "Citizen of the Union" in Essays.

Cadwaller, Sylvanus. *Three Years with Grant, As Recalled by War Correspondent Sylvanus Cadwaller.* See "Tales of Soldiers and Civilians" in Essays.

Cain, James M. *Past All Dishonor,* in *New Yorker,* XXII, No. 15 (25 May 1946), 90-91.

Cairns, Huntingdon, and John Walker. *Masterpieces of Painting from the National Gallery of Art,* in *New Yorker,* XX, No. 42 (4 December 1944), 94, 96.

Cairns, Huntingdon, ed. *French Literature and Its Masters,* by George Saintsbury. See "George Saintsbury's Centenary —Spadework on Kipling" in Essays.

Caldwell, Erskine. *Tragic Ground,* in *New Yorker,* XX, No. 38 (4 November 1944), 74.

Callaghan, Morley. *The Many Colored Coat.* See "Morley Callaghan of Toronto" in Essays.

———. *That Summer in Paris.* See "That Summer in Paris" in Essays.

Campbell, Joseph, and Henry Morton Robinson. *"A Skeleton Key to Finnegan's Wake."* See "A Guide to 'Finnegan's Wake'" in Essays.

Campbell, Mrs. Patrick. *My Life and Letters,* in *Vanity Fair,* XIX, No. 6 (February 1923), 22.

Camus, Albert. *The Stranger,* in *New Yorker,* XXII, No. 9 (13 April 1946), 113-114.

Canfield, Mary Cass. *Grotesque, and Other Reflections,* in *New Republic,* LII (16 November 1927), 344.

Cantine, Holley, and Dachine Rainer, eds. *Prison Etiquette,* in *New Yorker,* XXVI, No. 12 (13 May 1950), 125-127.

Carr, E. H. *Michael Bakunin.* See "Cold Water on Bakunin" in Essays.

Carroll, Gordon, comp. *The Desolate South, 1865-66,* by John T. Trowbridge. See "Tales of Soldiers and Civilians" in Essays.

Carroll, Lewis. *The Lewis Carroll Book,* ed. Richard Herrick. See "The Poet-Logician" in Essays.

The Case of Leon Trotsky (a publication of the Preliminary Commission of Inquiry into the Charges Made against Leon Trotsky in the Moscow Trials [John Dewey *et al.*]), in *Nation,* CXLV (11 December 1937), 648-649.

Cather, Willa. *A Lost Lady.* See "A Lost Lady" in Essays.

———. *One of Ours.* See "Mr. Bell, Miss Cather and Others" in Essays.

Chambers, R. W. See Symons, Katherine E.

Chapman, John Jay. *Dante,* in *New Republic,* L (18 May 1927), 361-363.

———. *Lucian, Plato and Greek Morals.* See "Lucian versus Plato" in Essays.

———. *New Horizons in American Life,* in *New Republic,* LXXII (26 October 1932), 306.

Chase, Stuart. *Technocracy: An Interpretation,* in *New Republic,* LXXIV (22 February 1933), 50-51.

Chavchavadze, Paul. *Family Album,* in *New Yorker,* XXV, No. 46 (7 January 1950), 74, 77.

Cheney, Ralph. See Trent, Lucia.

Chesterton, G. K. *The Victorian Age in Literature,* in *Nassau Literary Magazine,* LXIX (June 1913), 168-170.

Chukovskaya, Lydia. *The Deserted House (Opustely Dom).* See "Two Soviet Households" in Essays.

Clark, Walter Van Tilburg. *The City of the Trembling Leaves,* in *New Yorker,* XXI, No. 15 (26 May 1945), 75-77.

Clemens, Samuel Langhorne. See DeVoto, Bernard (*The Portable Mark Twain*), and Benton, Thomas H.

Clutton-Brock A[rthur]. *Shakespeare's "Hamlet,"* in *Dial,* LXXIV (March 1923), 297-302.

Coats, R. H. *John Galsworthy as a Dramatic Artist,* in *New Republic,* XLIX (9 February 1927), 335-336.

Cocteau, Jean. *Le grand écarte, roman,* in *Vanity Fair,* XX, No. 6 (August 1923), 6.

Collier, John, Jr., and Aníbal Buitrón. *The Awakening Valley,* in *New Yorker,* XXV, No. 47 (14 January 1950), 83.

Colum, Mary. *Life and the Dream,* in *New Yorker,* XXII, No. 5 (22 March 1947), 99-102.

Colum, Padraic. *The Way of the Cross,* in *New Republic,* XLIX (2 February 1927), 310.

Connell, John. *W. E. Henley,* in *New Yorker,* XXV, No. 44 (24 December 1949), 57-58.

Connolly, Cyril. *The Condemned Playground.* See "Lesser Books by Brilliant Writers" in Essays.

———. *The Unquiet Grave.* See "Connolly's 'Unquiet Grave;' Thurber's 'White Deer'" in Essays.

Cossery, Albert. *Men God Forgot,* in *New Yorker,* XXII, No. 30 (7 September 1946), 97-98.

Cowley, Malcolm, ed. *The Portable Faulkner,* in *New Yorker,* XXII, No. 24 (27 July 1946), 65.

Craigie, William A. See *Dictionary of American English.*

Crane, Nathalia. *Nathalia Crane* (selections), ed. Hughes Mearns, and *The Singing Crow.* See "Nathalia Crane" in Essays.

Crane, Stephen. *An Omnibus,* ed. Robert Wooster Stallman, in *New Yorker,* XXIX, No. 11 (2 May 1953), 123-124.

———. See also Curry, John S.

Crapsey, Adelaide. *Verse.* See "Mr. Bell, Miss Cather and Others" in Essays.

Creeps by Night, with introduction by Dashiell Hammett. See "A Treatise on Tales of Horror" in Essays.

Cummings, E. E. *Him*. See "Him" in Essays.

———. *Tulips and Chimneys*. See "Wallace Stevens and E. E. Cummings" in Essays.

Curran, C. H. *Insects in Your Life*. See "The Intelligence of Bees, Wasps, Butterflies, and Bombing Planes" in Essays.

Curry, John S., illus. *The Essays of Ralph Waldo Emerson*, by Ralph Waldo Emerson, and *The Red Badge of Courage*, by Stephen Crane, in *New Yorker*, XX, No. 42 (2 December 1944), 90.

Dahlberg, Edward. *Bottom Dogs*. See "Dahlberg, Dos Passos and Wilder" in Essays.

Dali, Salvador, *Hidden Faces*. See "Salvador Dali as a Novelist" in Essays.

Dante. *The Divine Comedy*, trans. Melville B. Anderson, illus. William Blake, in *New Yorker*, XX, No. 42 (2 December 1944), 90, 92.

Davies, Joseph E. *Mission to Moscow*. See "Mr. Joseph E. Davies as a Master of Prose" in Essays.

Davis, Esmé. *Esmé of Paris* in *New Yorker*, XX, No. 18 (17 July 1944), 64-66, 69.

De Forest, John. *A Volunteer's Adventures*, in *New Yorker*, XXII, No. 26 (10 August 1946), 65-67.

Dell, Floyd. *The Briary Bush*, in *Baltimore Evening Sun*, 18 February 1922, p. 6.

Derleth, August. *H.P.L.: A Memoir*. See "Tales of the Marvelous and the Ridiculous" in Essays.

———, and H. P. Lovecraft. *The Larker at the Threshold*. See "Tales of the Marvelous and the Ridiculous" in Essays.

DeVoto, Bernard, ed. *The Portable Mark Twain*, in *New Yorker*, XXII, No. 24 (27 July 1946), 65.

———. See also Grierson, Francis.

Dewey, John. See *The Case of Leon Trotsky*.

Dickinson, Kate L. *Flesh and Spirit,* in *New Republic,* XLVIII (17 November 1920), 384.

Dictionary of American English, ed. William A. Craigie, in *New Yorker,* XX, No. 1 (19 February 1944), 81-82, 84, 86.

Dodgson, Charles Lutwidge. *The Lewis Carroll Book,* ed. Richard Herrick. See "The Poet-Logician" in Essays.

Dos Passos, John. *The 42nd Parallel.* See "Dahlberg, Dos Passos and Wilder" in Essays.

———. *Airways, Inc.* See "Dos Passos and the Social Revolution" in Essays.

———. *A Pushcart at the Curb,* in *Vanity Fair,* XIX, No. 6 (February 1923), 22.

———. *State of the Nation,* in *New Yorker,* XX, No. 24 (29 July 1944), 49-50, 53.

———. *Tour of Duty.* See "Dos Passos in the Pacific— Shaw's Birthday—A Note for Mr. Behrman" in Essays.

Dostoevsky, Anna Grigoryevna. *The Diary of Dostoevsky's Wife.* See "Dostoevsky Abroad" in Essays.

Dostoevsky, Fedor. See Reisman, Philip.

Douglas, Lloyd C. *The Robe.* See " 'You Can't Do This to Me!' Shrilled Celia: Inquiry into a Current Best-Seller" in Essays.

Douglas, Norman. *Good-bye to Western Culture: Some Footnotes on East and West* (British title: *How about Europe?*). See "The Nietzschean Line" in Essays.

Dreiser, Theodore. *The Bulwark,* in *New Yorker,* XXII, No. 6 (23 March 1946), 84, 86.

———. *Tragic America,* in *New Republic,* LXX (30 March 1932), 185-186.

Dubreuil, Henri. *Standards: Le travail américain vu par un ouvrier français,* in *New Republic,* LXIV (29 October 1930), 301-303.

Duhamel, Georges. *Scènes de la vie future,* in *New Republic,* LXIV (29 October 1930), 301-303.

Earnest, Ernest. *S. Weir Mitchell: Novelist and Physician,* in *New Yorker,* XXVI, No. 24 (5 August 1950), 63-64.

Eastman, Max. *Marxism: Is It Science?* and *Stalin's Russia and the Crisis in Socialism.* See "Max Eastman in 1941" in Essays.

Edgar, Pelham. *Henry James: Man and Author,* in *New Republic,* L (16 March 1927), 112-113.

Eichenberg, Fritz, illus. *Tales of Edgar Allen Poe,* in *New Yorker,* XX, No. 42 (2 December 1944), 90, 92.

Einstein, Albert. *Relativity,* in *Vanity Fair,* XXI, No. 2 (October 1923), 20.

Eliot, Charlotte. *Savonarola: A Dramatic Poem,* in *New Republic,* XLVIII (17 November 1926), 383.

Eliot, T. S. *Ash Wednesday,* in *New Republic,* LXIV (20 August 1930), 24-25.

————. *For Lancelot Andrewes.* See "T. S. Eliot and the Church of England" in Essays.

————. *Homage to John Dryden,* in *New Republic,* XLI (7 January 1925), 177-178.

————. *Old Possum's Book of Practical Cats,* in *New Republic,* CI (20 December 1939), 266.

————. *The Waste Land,* in *Vanity Fair,* XIX, No. 5 (January 1923), 17, 92.

Ellmann, Richard. *Yeats: The Man and the Masks,* in *New Yorker,* XXIV, No. 43 (18 December 1948), 103-104.

Emerson, Ralph Waldo. See Curry, John S.

Engels, Friedrich. See Marx, Karl, and Friedrich Engels.

English-Russian Dictionary. See Müller, V[ladimir] K[arlovich].

Farrell, James T. *A Note on Literary Criticism,* in *Nation,* CXLII (24 June 1936), 808-810.

Fatout, Paul. *Ambrose Bierce: The Devil's Lexicographer.* See "Ambrose Bierce on the Owl Creek Bridge" in Essays.

Faulkner, William. *Collected Stories of William Faulkner*, in *New Yorker*, XXVI, No. 42 (9 December 1950), 161-162.

———. *Intruder in the Dust*. See "William Faulkner's Reply to the Civil-Rights Program" in Essays.

———. *Knight's Gambit*, in *New Yorker*, XXV, No. 44 (24 December 1949), 58-59.

———. See also Cowley, Malcolm.

Feuchtwanger, Lion. *Moscow, 1937*, in *Nation*, CXLV (13 November 1937), 531-532, 534-535.

Fields, Mrs. James T. *Memoirs of a Hostess*, in *Vanity Fair*, XIX, No. 6 (February 1923), 22.

Firbank, Ronald. *Five Novels*. See "A Revival of Ronald Firbank" in Essays.

———. *The Flower Beneath the Foot*. See "Late Violets from the Nineties" in Essays.

———. *Prancing Nigger*, in *New Republic*, XXXVIII (21 May 1924), 342.

Fischer, Makoosha. *My Lives in Russia*, in *New Yorker*, XX, No. 13 (13 May 1944), 80, 83-86, 89.

Fitts, Dudley, and Robert Fitzgerald, trans. *The Antigone of Sophocles: An English Version*, in *New Republic*, XCVIII (1 March 1939), 106-107.

Fitzgerald, F. Scott. *Tales of the Jazz Age*. See "Two Young Men and An Old One" in Essays.

———. *This Side of Paradise*. See "The Literary Spotlight, VI: F. Scott Fitzgerald; With a Caricature by William Gropper" in Essays.

———. *The Vegetable*, in *Vanity Fair*, XX, No. 4 (June 1923), 18.

Fitzgerald, Robert. See Fitts, Dudley.

Flexner, Stuart Berg. See Wentworth, Harold.

Flores, Angel, ed. *The Kafka Problem*. See "A Dissenting Opinion on Kafka" in Essays.

Foerster, Norman, ed. *Humanism and America: Essays on the Outlook of Modern Civilization,* by Irving Babbitt, P. E. More, *et al.* See "Notes on Babbitt and More" in Essays.

Forbush, Gabrielle. See Roosevelt, Mrs. James.

Forster, E. M. *Aspects of the Novel,* in *New Republic,* LIV (22 February 1928), 21-22.

————. *Pharos and Pharillon,* in *Vanity Fair,* XXI, No. 2 (October 1923), 20.

Forten, Charlotte L. *The Journal of Charlotte L. Forten,* ed. Ray Allen Billington. See "Charlotte Forten and Colonel Higginson" in Essays.

Foster, Charles H. *The Rungless Ladder: Harriet Beecher Stowe and New England Puritanism.* See "Harriet Beecher Stowe" in Essays.

Foster, Stephen. *A Treasury of Stephen Foster,* in *New Yorker,* XXII, No. 44 (14 December 1946), 122, 125-126.

Fowler, Gene. *Good Night, Sweet Prince.* See " 'The Life and Times of John Barrymore' " in Essays.

France, Anatole. *La vie en fleur.* See "Two Young Men and an Old One" in Essays.

Frank, Tenney. *Virgil: A Biography,* in *Dial,* LXXV (November 1923), 492-497.

Frank, Waldo. *Holiday,* in *Vanity Fair,* XXI, No. 2 (October 1923), 20.

Franklin, Benjamin. See Benton, Thomas H.

Fraser, Phyllis, and Herbert A. Wise. *Great Tales of Terror and the Supernatural.* See "A Treatise on Tales of Horror" in Essays.

Fredborg, Arvid. *Behind the Steel Wall,* in *New Yorker,* XIX, No. 52 (12 February 1944), 82-86.

Frederick, J. George, ed. *For and Against Technocracy: A Symposium,* in *New Republic,* LXXIV (22 February 1933), 50-51.

Fry, Roger, trans. *Some Poems of Mallarmé,* with commentaries by Charles Mauron, in *New Republic,* XCIII (26 January 1938), 346.

Fuchs, James. See Shaw, George Bernard (*The Socialism of Shaw*).

Fugitives: An Anthology of Verse. See "The Tennessee Poets" in Essays.

Gale, Zona. *Faint Perfume,* in *Vanity Fair,* XXI, No. 1 (September 1923), 23.

Galsworthy, John. *The Dark Flower,* in *Nassau Literary Magazine,* LXIX (December 1913), 297-298.

————. *Plays: Sixth Series, Representative Plays,* and *Verse New and Old,* in *New Republic,* XLIX (9 February 1927), 335-336.

Gantt, W. Horsley. *A Medical Review of Soviet Russia,* in *Nation,* CXLV (13 November 1937), 531-532, 534-535.

Garnett, Louise Ayres. *Eve Walks in Her Garden,* in *New Republic,* XLVIII (17 November 1920), 383-384.

Garnett, Mrs. R. S. *Samuel Butler and His Family Relations,* in *New Republic,* L (30 March 1927), 177.

Garnett, R. A. *Lady into Fox,* in *Vanity Fair,* XX, No. 6 (August 1923), 6.

Garrod, H. W. *Wordsworth,* in *New York Tribune Magazine and Books* [in Vol. LXXXIII of *New York Tribune*], 18 November 1923, p. 18.

————, ed. *The Poetical Works of John Yeats,* in *New Republic,* C (30 August 1939), 110.

Gathorne-Hardy, Robert. *Recollections of Logan Pearsall Smith.* See "Virginia Woolf and Logan Pearsall Smith" in Essays.

————, and Logan Pearsall Smith, eds. *Philadelphia Quaker: The Letters of Hannah Whitall Smith.* See "Stephen Crane—Hannah Whitall Smith" in Essays.

Gauss, Christian. *Through College on Nothing a Year*, in *Nassau Literary Magazine*, LXXII (June 1916), 153-154.

Geismar, Maxwell. *The Last of the Provincials*, in *New Yorker*, XXIII, No. 45 (27 December 1947), 57-59.

Geologic Map of New York. See "Arvin's Longfellow and New York State's Geology" in Essays.

Gernsheim, Helmut. *Lewis Carroll, Photographer*, in *New Yorker*, XXVI, No. 12 (13 May 1950), 127-128.

Gide, André. *Imaginary Interviews*, in *New Yorker*, XX, No. 38 (4 November 1944), 74, 76.

———. *Imaginary Interviews*, in *New Yorker*, XX, No. 42 (4 December 1944), 94.

———. *Retouches à mon retour de l'U. R. S. S.*, in *Nation*, CXLV (13 November 1937), 531-532, 534-535.

Gilbert, W. S. *Plays and Poems of W. S. Gilbert*. See "Gilbert Without Sullivan" in Essays.

Goodman, Paul. *Kafka's Prayer*. See "A Dissenting Opinion on Kafka" in Essays.

Gorey, Edward. *The Doubtful Guest, The Listing Attic, The Object-Lesson*, and *The Unstrung Harp: or Mr. Earbrass Writes a Novel."* See "The Albums of Edward Gorey" in Essays.

Gorky, Maxim. *Days with Lenin*, in *New Republic*, LXXIV (15 February 1933), 23.

———. *On Guard for the Soviet Union*, in *New Republic*, LXXVII (22 November 1933), 53-54.

Gorman, Herbert S. *James Joyce: His First Forty Years*, in *Dial*, LXXVII (November 1924), 430-435.

Gosse, Edmund. *Leaves and Fruit*, in *New Republic*, LIV (22 February 1928), 21-22.

Gow, A. S. F. See Symons, Katharine E.

Grahame, Kenneth. See Rackham, Arthur.

Grant, Ulysses S. *The Personal Memoirs of U.S. Grant*, ed. E. B. Long, in *New Yorker*, XXIX, No. 7 (4 April 1953),

103-106, 109-112. See also "Northern Soldiers: Ulysses S. Grant" in Essays.

Granville, Wilfred, and Eric Partridge. *Sea Slang of the Twentieth Century.* See "Eric Partridge, the Word King" in Essays.

Greene, Graham. *The Power and the Glory,* in *New Yorker,* XXII, No. 6 (23 March 1946), 86, 89.

Grew, Joseph C. *Ten Years in Japan,* in *New Yorker,* XX, No. 16 (3 June 1944), 69-70

Grierson, Francis. *The Valley of Shadows,* with introduction by Theodore Spencer and a note by Bernard DeVoto. See "Francis Grierson: Log House and Salon" in Essays.

Grimm, Jakob, and Wilhelm Grimm. *Grimm's Fairy Tales,* in *New Yorker,* XX, No. 42 (2 December 1944), 90.

Grimm, Wilhelm. See Grimm, Jakob.

Grosz, George. *A Little Yes and a Big No: The Autobiography of George Grosz.* See "Stephen Spender and George Grosz on Germany" in Essays.

Grove, Victor. *The Language Bar.* See "Eric Partridge, the Word King" in Essays.

Gruening, Ernest, ed. *These United States: A Symposium,* in *Vanity Fair,* XX, No. 6 (August 1923), 6.

Guedalla, Philip. *The Second Empire,* in *Vanity Fair,* XIX, No. 5 (January 1923), 17.

Guerney, Bernard Gilbert, trans. *Doctor Zhivago,* by Boris Pasternak. See "Doctor Life and His Guardian Angel" in Essays.

Gutterman, Norbert, trans. *Road to the Ocean,* by Leonid Leonov. See "Leonid Leonov: The Sophistication of a Formula" in Essays.

Hagen, Paul. *Germany after Hitler,* in *New Yorker,* XIX, No. 52 (12 February 1944), 82-86.

Hamilton, David. *Pale Warriors,* in *New Republic,* LXIX, (26 June 1929), 158.

Hammett, Dashiell. See *Creeps by Night*.

Handy, W[illiam] C[hristopher], ed. *Blues: An Anthology*, in *New Republic*, XLVII (14 July 1926), 227-229.

Harari, Manya, trans. *Doctor Zhivago*, by Boris Pasternak. See "Doctor Life and His Guardian Angel" in Essays.

Harding, G. Lankester. *Judæan Desert*. See "More on the Dead Sea Scrolls" in Essays.

Harrington, Karl Pomeroy. *Catullus and His Influence*, in *Dial*, LXXVIII (February 1925), 149-152.

Harris, Abram L. *Pure Capitalism and the Disappearance of the Middle Class*, in *New Republic*, C (18 October 1939), 317-319.

Harris, George Washington. *Sut Lovingood*, ed. Brom Weber. See " 'Poisoned!' " in Essays.

Hart, B. H. Liddell. See Sherman, William Tecumseh.

Harvey, George. *Henry Clay Frick: The Man*. See "American Heroes" in Essays.

Hatton, Thomas. See *The Nonesuch Dickens*.

Hawthorne, Nathaniel. *Hawthorne's Short Stories*, ed. Newton Arvin. See "Somerset Maugham and an Antidote" in Essays.

Hayward, Max. trans. *Doctor Zhivago*, by Boris Pasternak. See "Doctor Life and His Guardian Angel" in Essays.

Heiden, Konrad. *Der Fuehrer*, in *New Yorker*, XIX, No. 52 (12 February 1944), 82-86.

Hemingway, Ernest. *The Fifth Column and the First Forty-Nine Stories* and *The Spanish War*, in *Nation*, CXLVII (10 December 1938), 628, 630.

———. *For Whom the Bell Tolls*, in *New Republic*, CIII (28 October 1940), 591-592.

———. *In Our Time* and *Three Stories and Ten Poems*. See "Mr Hemingway's Dry-Points" in Essays.

Herbart, Pierre. *En U. R. S. S., 1936*, in *Nation*, CXLV (13 November 1937), 531-532, 534-535.

Herford, Charles Harold, ed. *Ben Jonson* (collected works). See "A Definitive Edition of Ben Jonson" in Essays.

Hergesheimer, Joseph. *Cytherea,* in *Baltimore Evening Sun,* 11 March 1922, p. 6.

Herrick, Richard, ed. *The Lewis Carroll Book.* See "The Poet-Logician" in Essays.

Highet, Gilbert. *The Art of Teaching,* in *New Yorker,* XXVI, No. 47 (13 January 1951), 81-82.

―――. *The Classical Tradition,* in *New Yorker,* XXVI, No. 3 (11 March 1950), 97-98, 101.

Hingley, Robert. *Chekhov: A Biographical and Critical Study,* in *New Yorker,* XXVIII, No. 40 (22 November 1952), 180, 182-184, 187-189, 192-194, 197-198.

Hoellering, Franz. *The Defenders,* in *New Republic,* CIII (26 August 1940), 283-284.

Holden, Raymond. *Granite and Alabaster,* in *Vanity Fair,* XIX, No. 6 (February 1923), 22.

Holme, Jamie Sexton. *Star Gatherer,* in *New Republic,* XLVIII (17 November 1926), 384.

Holmes, Justice [Oliver Wendell], and Harold J. Laski. *Holmes-Laski Letters,* ed. Mark DeWolfe Howe. See "Justice Holmes and Harold Laski: Their Relationship" in Essays.

Hook, Sidney. *From Hegel to Marx: Studies in the Intellectual Development of Karl Marx* and *Toward the Understanding of Karl Marx: A Revolutionary Interpretation,* in *New Republic,* XCI (4 August 1937), 366-368.

―――, ed. *The Meaning of Marx: A Symposium,* by Bertrand Russell *et al.,* in *New Republic,* XCI (4 August 1937), 366-368.

Hooton, Earnest. *Man's Poor Relations,* in *New Yorker,* XX, No. 31 (16 September 1944), 72-73.

Housman, A. E. *Last Poems,* in *Vanity Fair,* XIX, No. 5 (January 1923), 17.

Housman, Laurence. *Echo de Paris* and *My Brother, A. E. Housman,* in *New Republic,* XCV (1 June 1938), 107-108.

————. See also Symons, Katharine E.

Howard, John. See Huysmans, [Joris Karl].

Howe, Mark DeWolfe, ed. *Holmes-Laski Letters*. See "Justice Holmes and Harold Laski: Their Relationship" in Essays.

Howells, William. *Mankind So Far,* in *New Yorker,* XX, No. 31 (16 September 1944), 71-72.

Howells, William Dean. *Their Wedding Journey,* ed. John K. Reeves. See "The Fruits of the MLA: I. 'Their Wedding Journey'" in Essays.

Hughes, Randolph, ed. *Lesbia Brandon: An Historical and Critical Commentary Being Largely a Study (and Elevation) of Swinburne as a Novelist, Lucretia Borgia: The Chronicle of Tebaldea Tebaldei; Renaissance Period,* and *Pasiphaë: A Poem,* by Algernon Charles Swinburne. See "Swinburne of Capheaton and Eaton" in Essays.

Humphries, Rolfe. *Summer Landscape,* in *New Yorker,* XX, No. 42 (4 December 1944), 94.

Huxley, Aldous. *Time Must Have a Stop.* See "Aldous Huxley in the World Beyond Time" in Essays.

Huxley, Julian. *On Living in a Revolution,* in *New Yorker,* XX, No. 31 (16 September 1944), 71-72.

Huysmans, [Joris Karl]. *Against the Grain (A rebours),* trans. John Howard (pseud. for Jacob Howard Lewis), *Vanity Fair,* XX, No. 4 (June 1923), 18.

Isherwood, Christopher. *The Condor and the Cows: A South American Travel Diary,* in *New Yorker,* XXV, No. 47 (14 January 1950), 83.

————. *Goodbye to Berlin,* in *New Republic,* XCIX (17 May 1939), 51.

————. *Prater Violet,* in *New Yorker,* XXI, No. 39 (10 November 1945), 93.

————, trans. See Baudelaire, [Pierre Charles].

Jackson, Charles. *The Lost Weekend,* in *New Yorker,* XIX, No. 51 (5 February 1944), 78, 81.

Jaeger, Werner. *Paideia: The Ideals of Greek Culture.* See "Nikolai Gogol—Greek Paideia" in Essays.

James, Henry. *The American Scene,* ed. W. H. Auden, in *New Yorker,* XXII, No. 33 (28 September 1946), 94, 97-99.

———. *The Complete Plays of Henry James,* in *New Yorker,* XXV, No. 47 (14 January 1950), 83-85.

———. *Eight Uncollected Tales of Henry James,* comp. Edna Kenton, in *New Yorker,* XXVI, No. 42 (9 December 1950), 165-166.

———. *The Great Short Novels of Henry James,* ed. Philip Rahv, and *Stories of Writers and Artists,* ed. F. O. Matthiessen, in *New Yorker,* XX, No. 41 (25 November 1944), 86.

———. See also Matthiessen, F. O., and Kenneth B. Murdock, eds.

James, M. R. *Best Ghost Stories of M. R. James.* See "A Treatise on Tales of Horror" in Essays.

Johansen, Albert. *The House of Beadle and Adams and Its Dime and Nickel Novels,* in *New Yorker,* XXVI, No. 24 (5 August 1950), 63.

Johnston, Alva. *The Great Goldwyn.* See "It's Terrible! It's Ghastly! It Stinks!" in Essays.

Jones, Katherine M. *Heroines of Dixie: Confederate Women Tell Their Story of the War.* See "Three Confederate Ladies" in Essays.

Jonson, Ben. *Ben Jonson* (collected works), ed. Charles Harold Herford, Percy Simpson, and Evelyn Mary [Spearing] Simpson, and *Selected Works,* ed. Harry Levin. See "A Definitive Edition of Ben Jonson" in Essays.

Joyce, James. *Pomes Penyeach,* in *New Republic,* LII (26 October 1927), 268.

———. *Stephen Hero,* in *New Yorker,* XX, No. 47 (6 January 1945), 63-64.

———. *Ulysses,* in *Baltimore Evening Sun,* 5 August 1922, p. 6. See also "Ulysses" in Essays.

Joyce, Stanislaus. *Recollections of James Joyce, by His Brother Stanislaus Joyce.* See "Miscellaneous Memorabilia: Oscar Wilde, James Joyce, John Aubrey" in Essays.

Kafka, Franz. *Gesammelte Schriften,* ed. Max Brod. See "A Dissenting Opinion on Kafka" in Essays.

Karloff, Boris. See *Tales of Terror.*

Karski, Jan. *Story of a Secret State,* in *New Yorker,* XX, No. 41 (25 November 1944), 84.

Kasenkina, Mrs. Oksana. *Leap to Freedom,* in *New Yorker,* XXV, No. 46 (7 January 1950), 77-79.

Kaye-Smith, Sheila, and G. B. Stern. *Speaking of Jane Austen.* See "A Long Talk about Jane Austen" in Essays.

Keats, John. See Garrod, H. W., ed.

Kellock, Harold. *Houdini: His Life Story.* See "A Great Magician" in Essays.

Kemler, Edgar. *The Irreverent Mr. Mencken.* See "Mencken Through the Wrong End of the Telescope" in Essays.

Kemp, Harry, ed. *The Bronze Treasury,* in *New Republic,* LIII (8 February 1928), 330.

Kennan, George F. *Russia and the West Under Lenin and Stalin.* See "Unscrupulous Communists and Embattled Democracies" in Essays.

Kenton, Edna. See James, Henry (*Eight Uncollected Tales of Henry James*).

Ker, Alan. See Symons, Katharine E.

Keynes, Geoffrey. See Blake, William (*The Poetry and Prose of William Blake.*)

Kipling, Rudyard. *Brazilian Sketches* and *Rudyard Kipling's Verse: Definitive Edition,* in *New Republic,* CIV (24 March 1941), 413-414.

———. *Limits and Renewals,* in *New Republic,* LXXI (25 May 1932), 50-51.

————. *Something of Myself for My Friends Known and Unknown,* in *New Republic,* XC (24 March 1937), 214-215.

Klots, Alexander B. *A Field Guide to the Butterflies of North America, East of the Great Plains.* See "The Intelligence of Bees, Wasps, Butterflies, and Bombing Planes" in Essays.

Knox, Ronald A., trans. *The New Testament in English,* in *New Yorker,* XX, No. 39 (11 November 1944), 88.

Koenig, Eleanor C. *Herb Woman,* in *New Republic,* XLVIII (17 November 1926), 384.

Koestler, Arthur. *Thieves in the Night,* in *New Yorker,* XXII, No. 40 (16 November 1946), 109-110, 113-114.

Kravchenko, Victor. *I Chose Freedom,* in *New Yorker,* XXII, No. 12 (4 May 1946), 108-110.

Krutch, Joseph Wood. *Samuel Johnson.* See "Dr. Johnson" in Essays.

Kuzminskaya, Tatyana A[ndreyevna] B[ehrs]. *Tolstoy as I Knew Him: My Life at Home and at Yasnaya Polyana.* See "The Original of Tolstoy's Natasha" in Essays.

Lakond, Wladimir. See Tchaikovsky, Petr Ilich.

Lamott, Willis. *Nippon: The Crime and Punishment of Japan,* in *New Yorker,* XX, No. 16 (3 June 1944), 70, 73.

Lang, Cecil Y., ed. *Letters,* by Algernon Charles Swinburne. See "Swinburne of Capheaton and Eaton" in Essays.

Lanier, Sidney. *The Centennial Edition of the Works of Sidney Lanier,* ed. Charles R. Anderson, in *New Yorker,* XXII, No. 44 (14 December 1946), 120, 122.

Lardner, Ring. *How to Write Short Stories.* See "Mr Lardner's American Characters" in Essays.

Laski, Harold J., and Justice Holmes. *Holmes-Laski Letters,* ed. Mark DeWolfe Howe. See "Justice Holmes and Harold Laski: Their Relationship" in Essays.

Lavrin, Janko. *Nikolai Gogol: A Centenary Survey.* See "Gogol: the Demon in the Overgrown Garden" in Essays.

Lawrence, D. H. *Lady Chatterley's Lover.* See "Signs of Life" in Essays.

Legay, Kléber. *Un mineur français chez les russes.* See "Shut Up That Russian Novel" in Essays.

Leighton, Isabel. See Roosevelt, Mrs. James.

Lely, M. Gilbert. *Le Marquis de Sade.* See "The Vogue of the Marquis de Sade" in Essays.

Lennon, Florence Becker. *Victoria Through the Looking-Glass: The Life of Lewis Carroll.* See "The Poet-Logician" in Essays.

Leonov, Leonid. *Road to the Ocean,* trans. Norbert Gutterman. See "Leonid Leonov: The Sophistication of a Formula" in Essays.

Lever, Walter. See Agnón, S. Y.

Levin, Harry, ed. *Selected Works,* by Ben Jonson. See "A Definitive Edition of Ben Jonson" in Essays.

Levy, Gilbert. *Vie du Marquis de Sade.* See "The Documents on the Marquis de Sade" in Essays.

Lewis, Jacob Howard. See Huysmans, [Joris Karl].

Lewis, Sinclair. *Babbitt,* in *Vanity Fair,* XIX, No. 4 (December 1922), 25.

————. *Cass Timberlane.* See "Salute to an Old Landmark: Sinclair Lewis" in Essays.

Ley, Willy. *Dragons in Amber: Further Adventures of a Romantic Naturalist.* See "The Intelligence of Bees, Wasps, Butterflies, and Bombing Planes" in Essays.

————. *Rockets: The Future of Travel Beyond the Stratosphere,* in *New Yorker,* XX, No. 17 (10 June 1944), 67-69.

Lincoln, Abraham. *The Collected Works of Abraham Lincoln,* ed. Roy P. Basher. See "Abraham Lincoln: The Union as Religious Mysticism" in Essays.

Lindley, Ernest K. *Franklin D. Roosevelt,* in *New Republic,* LXXV (5 April 1933), 219-220.

Lindsay, Vachel. *Collected Poems,* in *Vanity Fair,* XXI, No. 1 (September 1923), 23.

Lintz, Gertrude Davies. *Animals Are My Hobby,* in *New Yorker,* XX, No. 31 (16 September 1944), 72-73.

Lippmann, Walter. *A Preface to Morals,* in *New Republic,* LXIX (10 July 1929), 210-211.

Lockhart, R. H. *Retreat from Glory,* in *New Republic,* LXXXI (28 November 1934), 79-80.

Loeb, Harold. *Life in a Technocracy,* in *New Republic,* LXXIV (22 February 1933), 50-51.

Long, E. B. See Grant, Ulysses S.

Longfellow, Ernest W. *Random Memories,* in *Vanity Fair,* XIX, No. 1 (September 1922), 19, 86.

Looker, Earle. *This Man Roosevelt,* in *New Republic,* LXXIV (5 April 1933), 219-220.

Lovecraft, H. P. *Best Supernatural Stories, Marginalia, The Shadow Out of Time,* and *Supernatural Horror in Literature.* See "Tales of the Marvelous and the Ridiculous" in Essays.

———, and August Derleth. *The Larker at the Threshold.* See "Tales of the Marvelous and the Ridiculous" in Essays.

Lubbock, Percy: *Portrait of Edith Wharton.* See "Edith Wharton: A Memoir by an English Friend" in Essays.

Ludwig, Emil. *Talks with Mussolini,* in *New Republic,* LXXIV (15 March 1933), 136-137.

Lyons, Eugene. *Assignment in Utopia,* in *Nation,* CXLV (13 November 1937), 531-532, 534-535.

Lytle, Andrew. *A Name for Evil,* in *New Yorker,* XXIII, No. 31 (20 September 1947), 90, 92.

McCoy, Melvin H., and S. M. Mellnik. *Ten Escape from Tojo,* in *New Yorker,* XX, No. 6 (25 March 1944), 92, 94.

McCullers, Carson. *The Member of the Wedding,* in *New Yorker,* XXII, No. 7 (30 March 1946), 80.

Mack, Effie Mona. *Mark Twain in Nevada,* in *New Yorker,* XXIII, No. 16 (7 June 1947), 118.

Mackail, J[ohn] W[illiam]. *Virgil and His Meaning to the World of Today,* in *Dial,* LXXV (November 1923), 492-497.

―――. *Virgil and His Meaning to the World of Today,* in *Vanity Fair,* XX, No. 6 (August 1923), 6.

Mackenzie, Compton. *Sinister Street,* in *Nassau Literary Magazine,* LXX (February 1915), 533-534.

MacNeice, Louis, trans. *The Agamemnon of Aeschylus,* in *New Republic,* XCI (19 May 1937), 52.

McWilliams, Vera. *Lafcadio Hearn,* in *New Yorker,* XXII, No. 9 (9 April 1946), 114-115.

Magarshack, David. *Chekhov the Dramatist,* in *New Yorker,* XXVIII, No. 40 (22 November 1952), 180, 182-184, 187-189, 192-194, 197-198.

―――. *Turgenev, a Life.* See "Turgenev and the Life-Giving Drop" in Essays.

Malaquais, Jean. *War Diary,* in *New Yorker,* XIX, No. 50 (29 January 1944), 75-77.

Mallarmé, Stéphane. See Fry, Roger.

Mallea, Eduardo. *The Bay of Silence,* in *New Yorker,* XX, No. 5 (18 March 1944), 89-90, 92.

Malraux, André. *La condition humaine.* See "André Malraux" in Essays.

―――. *Psychologie de l'art, The Twilight of the Absolute,* and *Les voix du silence.* See "High Discourse on the Arts: André Malraux and Arnold Schoenberg" in Essays.

Maran, René. *Batouala,* trans. Adele Szold Seltzer. See "Mr. Bell, Miss Cather and Others" in Essays.

Marcelin, Pierre, and Phillippe Thoby-Marcelin. **Canapé-Vert,** in *New Yorker,* XX, No. 2 (26 February 1944), 76, 78, 81.

March, Joseph Moncure. *The Wild Party,* in *New Republic,* LVI (3 October 1928), 182-183.

Marquand, John P. *Repent in Haste,* in *New Yorker,* XXI, No. 39 (10 November 1945), 93.

Marx, Karl. *The Civil War in France* and *Critique of the Gotha Program,* in *New Republic,* LXXVI (16 August 1933), 26.

————. *The German Ideology,* in *New Republic,* C (18 October 1939), 317-319.

————. *Letters to Dr. Kugelmann,* in *New Republic,* LXXXI (23 January 1935), 311.

————. *The Living Thoughts of Karl Marx.* See Trotsky, Leon, comp.

————, and Friedrich Engels. *Revolution in Spain,* in *New Republic,* C (18 October 1929), 317-319.

Masefield, John. *Esther and Berenice* and *King Cole,* in *New Republic,* XXX (3 May 1922), 291.

————. *The Tragedy of Nan,* in *Nassau Literary Magazine,* LXIX (April 1913), 53-54.

Masters, Edgar Lee. *Lee: A Dramatic Poem,* in *New Republic,* XLVIII (17 November 1926), 383.

Matthiessen, F. O. *Henry James: The Major Phase,* in *New Yorker,* XX, No. 41 (25 November 1944), 86, 89.

————. *The James Family,* in *New Yorker,* XXIII, No. 43 (13 December 1947), 119-120, 123-125.

————, ed. See James, Henry (*Stories of Writers and Artists*), and Melville, Herman.

————, and Kenneth B. Murdock, eds. *The Notebooks of Henry James,* in *New Yorker,* XXIII, No. 43 (13 December 1947), 119-120, 123-125.

Maugham, W. Somerset. *Then and Now.* See "Somerset Maugham and an Antidote" in Essays.

————. See also Parker, Dorothy (*Dorothy Parker*).

Maupassant, Guy de. *The Collected Novels and Stories of Guy de Maupassant,* trans. and ed. Ernest Boyd, in *Vanity Fair,* XIX, No. 4 (December 1922), 26.

Mauron, Charles. See Fry, Roger.

Maxwell, William. *The Folded Leaf,* in *New Yorker,* XXI, No. 7 (31 March 1945), 81-82.

Mearnes, Hughes, ed. *Nathalia Crane* (selections). See "Nathalia Crane" in Essays.

Mellnik, S. M. See McCoy, Melvin H.

Melville, Herman. *Selections from Herman Melville's Poetry,* ed. F. O. Matthiessen, in *New Yorker,* XX, No. 42 (2 December 1944), 94.

Mencken, H. L. *The American Language: An Inquiry into the Development of English in the United States.* See "Talking United States" in Essays.

———. *James Branch Cabell* and *Prejudices: Sixth Series,* in *New Republic,* LIII (7 December 1927), 75.

———. *Notes on Democracy.* See "Mencken's Democratic Man" in Essays.

———. *Prejudices,* in *Vanity Fair,* XIX, No. 4 (December 1922), 25-26.

———. *Supplement to the American Language,* in *New Yorker,* XXI, No. 28 (25 August 1945), 57-58.

Menckeniana: A Schimpflexikon, in *New Republic,* LIV (14 March 1928), 131.

Michaud, Régis. *Autour d'Emerson,* in *New Republic,* XLIII (5 August 1925), 297-298.

Miles, Hamish, See Mortimer, Raymond.

Millay, Edna St. Vincent. *Conversations at Midnight.* See " 'Give That Beat Again' " in Essays.

Miller, Henry. *The Air-Conditioned Nightmare,* in *New Yorker,* XXI, No. 46 (29 December 1945), 54, 57-58.

———. *The Tropic of Cancer.* See "Twilight of the Expatriates" in Essays.

Mills, John. *Within the Atom,* in *Vanity Fair,* XXI, No. 3 (November 1923), 26.

Mirbeau, Octave. *Le Calvaire,* in *Vanity Fair,* XIX, No. 4 (December 1922), 26.

————. *Torture Garden* (*Le jardin des supplices*), trans. Alvah C. Bessie. See "In Memory of Octave Mirbeau" in Essays.

Montgomery, Elizabeth Shaw. *Scarabaeus,* in *New Republic,* XLVIII (17 November 1926), 384.

Moore, Marianne. *Nevertheless,* in *New Yorker,* XX, No. 42 (2 December 1944), 94.

Morand, Paul. *Champions du monde,* in *New Republic,* LIV (29 October 1930), 301-303.

More, Paul Elmer. *Pages from an Oxford Diary,* in *New Republic,* XCIII (19 January 1938), 319.

————, Irving Babbitt, *et al. Humanism and America: Essays on the Outlook of Modern Civilization,* ed. Norman Foerster. See "Notes on Babbitt and More" in Essays.

Morison, Elting E. See Roosevelt, Theodore.

Morris, Lloyd. *The Poetry of Edwin Arlington Robinson.* See "Mr. Robinson's Moonlight" in Essays.

Mortimer, Raymond, and Hamish Miles. *The Oxford Circus,* in *Vanity Fair,* XX, No. 4 (June 1923), 18.

Morton, David. *Ships in Harbor,* in *New Republic,* XXVI (4 May 1921), 304.

Mosby, John Singleton. *The Memoirs of Colonel John S. Mosby,* ed. Charles Wells Russell, and *Mosby's War Reminiscences* [*and*] *Stuart's Cavalry Campaigns.* See "John Singleton Mosby, 'The Gray Ghost' " in Essays.

Muchnic, Helen. *An Introduction to Russian Literature,* in *New Yorker,* XXIII, No. 18 (21 June 1947), 66, 69-71.

Müller, V[ladimir] K[arlovich], comp. *English-Russian Dictionary,* 3rd ed. rev. and enl., and *Russian-English Dictionary,* New 1944 Ed., in *New Yorker,* XX, No. 5 (18 March 1944), 92-93.

————. *Russian-English Dictionary*, New 1944 Ed., in *New Yorker*, XX, No. 5 (18 March 1944), 92-93.

Muirhead, Gilbert. *Life of Edward Moore Gresham.* See "The Inevitable Literary Biography: With the Usual Apologies to Arthur Symons, Holbrook Jackson, and Frank Harris" in Essays.

Mulholland, John. *The Art of Illusion: Magic for Men to Do.* See "John Mulholland and the Art of Illusion" in Essays.

Murdock, Kenneth B. See Matthiessen, F. O., and Kenneth B. Murdock.

Murray, Gilbert. *The Classical Tradition in Poetry,* in *New Republic,* LIV (22 February 1928), 21-22.

Murray, John, ed. *Lord Byron's Correspondence.* See "The New Byron Letters" in Essays.

Nabokov, Vladimir. *Nikolai Gogol.* See "Nikolai Gogol—Greek Paideia" in Essays.

————, trans. *Eugene Onegin: A Novel in Verse,* by Aleksandr Pushkin, in *New York Review of Books,* IV, No. 12 (15 July 1965), 3-6.

Naeve, Lowell, in collaboration with David Wieck. *A Field of Broken Stones,* in *New Yorker,* XXVI, No. 12 (13 May 1950), 125-127.

Nathan, George Jean. *The Critic and the Drama,* in *Baltimore Evening Sun,* 25 March 1922, p. 6.

Nevins, Allan. *Frémont: The West's Greatest Adventure.* See "American Heroes" in Essays.

Nicolson, Harold. *Byron: The Last Journey.* See "Two Views of Byron" in Essays.

————. *The Desire to Please* and *Some People.* See "Through the Embassy Window: Harold Nicolson" in Essays.

————. *Tennyson,* in *Vanity Fair,* XXI, No. 3 (November 1923), 26.

Nin, Anaïs. *Ladders to Fire,* in *New Yorker,* XXII, No. 40 (16 November 1946), 114.

————. *This Hunger*, in *New Yorker*, XXI, No. 39 (10 November 1945), 93-94, 96.

————. *Under a Glass Bell*, in *New Yorker*, XX, No. 7 (1 April 1944), 81, 82.

————. *Under a Glass Bell*, in *New Yorker*, XX, No. 42 (2 December 1944), 94.

Nizer, Louis. *What to Do with Germany*, in *New Yorker*, XIX, No. 52 (12 February 1944), 82-86.

Noel, Lucie. *James Joyce and Paul L. Léon: The Story of a Friendship*. See "Miscellaneous Memorabilia: Oscar Wilde, James Joyce, John Aubrey" in Essays.

Nomad, Max. *Aspects of Revolt*. See "Max Nomad and Waclaw Machajski" in Essays.

The Nonesuch Dickens, ed. Arthur Waugh, Hugh Walpole, and Thomas Hatton, in *New Republic*, C (4 October 1939), 247-248.

Oates, Whitney J., and Eugene O'Neill Jr. *The Complete Greek Drama*, in *New Republic*, XCVII (9 November 1939), 24.

O'Casey, Sean. *Red Roses for Me*, in *New Yorker*, XIX, No. 51 (5 February 1944), 81-82.

O'Hara, John. *Pal Joey*. See "John O'Hara" in Essays.

Olmsted, Frederick Law. *The Cotton Kingdom*. See "Olmsted on the Old South" in Essays.

O'Neill, Eugene. *All God's Chillun*. See "All God's Chillun and Others" in Essays.

————. *The Hairy Ape, Anna Christie, The First Man*. See "Two Young Men and An Old One" in Essays.

————. *"Thirst" and Other One-Act Plays*, in *Nassau Literary Magazine*, LXX (February 1915), 533.

O'Neill, Eugene, Jr. See Oates, Whitney J.

Orwell, George. *Animal Farm*, in *New Yorker*, XXII, No. 30 (30 September 1946), 97.

———. *Dickens, Dali & Others: Studies in Popular Culture,* in *New Yorker,* XXII, No. 15 (25 May 1946), 86, 89-90.

———. *Shooting an Elephant and Other Essays,* in *New Yorker,* XXVI, No. 47 (13 January 1951), 76.

Oulton, L. See Austen, Jane.

The Pamphlet Poets, in *New Republic,* XLVIII (17 November 1926), 383.

Parker, Dorothy. *Dorothy Parker* (selections), with an introduction by W. Somerset Maugham. See "A Toast and a Tear for Dorothy Parker" in Essays.

———. *Enough Rope,* in *New Republic,* XLIX (19 January 1927), 256.

Partridge, Eric. *A Dictionary of Slang and Unconventional English from the Fifteenth Century to the Present Day, A Dictionary of the Underworld, Here, There, and Everywhere, Name Into Word, Shakespeare's Bawdy: A Literary and Psychological Essay and a Comprehensive Glossary, Slang Today and Yesterday,* and *Usage and Abusage: A Guide to Good English.* See "Eric Partridge, the Word King" in Essays.

———, and Wilfrid Granville. *Sea Slang of the Twentieth Century.* See "Eric Partridge, the Word King" in Essays.

Pasternak, Boris. *Doctor Zhivago.* See "Doctor Life and His Guardian Angel" and "Legend and Symbol in Doctor Zhivago" in Essays.

Patch, Blanch. *Thirty Years with G.B.S.* See "Bernard Shaw Still Speaking" in Essays.

Peacock, Thomas Love. *The Pleasures of Peacock,* ed. Ben Ray Redman. See "The Musical Glasses of Peacock" in Essays.

Pearson, Hesketh. *Oscar Wilde: His Life and Wit.* See "Oscar Wilde: 'One Must Always Seek What Is Most Tragic' " in Essays.

Pei, Mario. *The Story of Language,* in *New Yorker,* XXVI, No. 3 (11 March 1950), 96-97.

Pennell, Joseph. *The Great New York,* in *Nassau Literary Magazine,* LXIX (May 1913), 119.

Pepys, Samuel. See Wheatley, Henry B.

Perényi, Eleanor. *More Was Lost,* in *New Yorker,* XXII, No. 4 (9 March 1946), 86, 88.

Phillmore, J. S. *Pastoral and Allegory: A Re-reading of the Bucolics of Virgil,* in *New Republic,* XLVII (23 June 1926), 148.

The Pocket Book of Mystery Stories. See "A Treatise on Tales of Horror" in Essays.

The Pocket Mystery Reader. See "A Treatise on Tales of Horror" in Essays.

Poe, Edgar Allan. *Tales of Edgar Allen Poe.* See Eichenberg, Fritz.

———. *Tales of Mystery and Imagination.* See Sharp, William.

Pollard, A. W. See Symons, Katharine E.

Pope-Hennessey, Una. *Charles Dickens,* in *New Yorker,* XXII, No. 9 (9 April 1946), 114-115.

Porter, Katherine Anne. *The Leaning Tower and Other Stories.* See "Katherine Anne Porter" in Essays.

Post, Emily. *Etiquette.* See "Books of Etiquette and Emily Post" in Essays.

Potter, Stephen. *Supermanship, or How to Continue to Stay Top Without Actually Falling Apart.* See "Donmanship" in Essays.

Pound, Ezra. *Patria Mia,* in *New Yorker,* XXVI, No. 24 (5 August 1950), 64-67.

———. *Poems 1918-1921.* See "Mr. Pound's Patchwork" in Essays.

Pound, Louise, ed. *American Ballads and Songs,* in *Vanity Fair,* XX, No. 1 (March 1923), 11.

Powell, Dawn. *The Golden Spur.* See "Dawn Powell: Greenwich Village in the Fifties" in Essays.

————. *My Home Is Far Away*, in *New Yorker*, XX, No. 39 (11 November 1944), 87-88.

Praz, Mario. *The House of Life* and *An Illustrated History of Furnishing from the Renaissance to the 20th Century*. See "The Genie of the Via Giulia" in Essays.

————. *The Romantic Agony* (*La carne, la Morte e il Diavolo nella letteratura romantica*). See "Mario Praz: 'The Romantic Agony'" in Essays.

Preliminary Commission of Inquiry into the Charges Made against Leon Trotsky in the Moscow Trials. See *The Case of Leon Trotsky*.

Pritchett, V. S. *The Living Novel*. See "The Essays of V. S. Pritchett—The Journals of Baudelaire" in Essays.

Prokosch, Frederic. *Age of Thunder*, in *New Yorker*, XXI, No. 7 (31 March 1945), 81.

Proust, Marcel. *A la recherche du temps perdu*. See "A Short View of Proust" in Essays.

Purcell, Victor. See Buttle, Myra.

Pushkin, Aleksandr. See Nabokov, Vladimir, trans.

Putnam, Phelps. *The Five Seasons*. See *New Republic* (18 April 1934) in Letters by Wilson.

Quinn, Arthur Hobson. See Wharton, Edith (*Edith Wharton Treasury*).

Rackham, Arthur, illus. *The Wind in the Willows*, by Kenneth Grahame, in *New Yorker*, XX, No. 42 (2 December 1944), 90, 92.

Radiguet, Raymond. *Le Diable au corps*, in *Vanity Fair*, XXI, No. 1 (September 1923), 23.

————. *Les joues en feu*. See "Theatres, Books and Ladies' Wear" in Essays.

Rahv, Philip. See James, Henry (*The Great Short Novels of Henry James*).

Rainer, Dachine. See Cantine, Holley.

Ransom, John Crowe. *Two Gentlemen In Bonds,* in *New Republic,* XLIX (2 February 1927), 310.

Rascoe, Burton. *A Bookman's Daybook.* See "Burton Rascoe" in Essays.

Ratchford, Fannie E. See Wise, Thomas J.

Ray, Gordon N., ed. *The Letters and Private Papers of William Makepeace Thackeray.* See "Thackeray's Letters: A Victorian Document" in Essays.

Raymond, Allen. *What Is Technocracy?,* in *New Republic,* LXXIV (22 February 1933), 50-51.

Raymond, Dora Neill. *The Political Career of Lord Byron.* See "Two Views of Byron" in Essays.

Redman, Ben Ray. See Peacock, Thomas Love.

Reese, Lizette Woodworth. *Little Henrietta,* in *New Republic,* LIV (14 March 1928), 129.

Reeves, John K. See Howells, William Dean.

Reisman, Philip, illus. *Crime and Punishment,* by Fedor Dostoevsky, in *New Yorker,* XX, No. 42 (2 December 1944), 90.

Rickaby, Franz Lee. *Ballads and Songs of the Shanty-Boy,* in *New Republic,* XLVII (14 July 1926), 227-229.

Riordan, John. *On the Make,* in *New Republic,* LXII (19 February 1930), 24-25.

Robinson, Boardman, illus. *Leaves of Grass,* by Walt Whitman, in *New Yorker,* XX, No. 42 (2 December 1944), 90.

Robinson, Edwin Arlington. *Roman Bartholow,* in *Vanity Fair,* XX, No. 5 (July 1923), 19. See also "Mr Robinson's Moonlight" in Essays.

Robinson, Henry Morton, and Joseph Campbell. *A Skeleton Key to Finnegans Wake.* See "A Guide to 'Finnegans Wake'" in Essays.

Rollins, Bill. *The Shadow Before.* See *New Republic* (18 April 1934) in Letters by Wilson.

Roosevelt, Franklin D. *Government—Not Politics* and *Looking Forward,* in *New Republic,* LXXIV (5 April 1933), 219-220.

Roosevelt, Mrs. James. *My Boy Franklin,* as told to Isabel Leighton and Gabrielle Forbush, in *New Republic,* LXXIV (5 April 1933), 219-220.

Roosevelt, Theodore. *The Letters of Theodore Roosevelt* (esp. Vols. I and II, *The Years of Preparation*), ed. Elting E. Morison, John M. Blum, and John J. Buckley. See "The Pre-Presidential T. R." in Essays.

Root, E. Merrill. *Frank Harris,* in *New Yorker,* XXIII, No. 16 (7 June 1947), 118, 121-122.

Rosenfeld, Paul. *Men Seen,* in *New Republic,* XLIII (3 June 1925), 48.

——. *Musical Chronicle,* in *Freeman* (New York: Freeman Corporation), VIII (27 February 1924), 594-596.

Rothenstein, William. *Since Fifty: Men and Memories, 1922-1938, Recollections of William Rothenstein,* in *New Republic,* CIII (5 August 1940), 194-195.

Roughley, T. C. *Wonders of the Great Barrier Reef,* in *New Yorker,* XXIII, No. 31 (20 September 1947), 90, 92.

Russell, Bertrand. See Hook, Sidney, ed.

Russell, Charles Wells, ed. *The Memoirs of Colonel John S. Mosby.* See "John Singleton Mosby, 'The Gray Ghost'" in Essays.

Russian-English Dictionary. See Müller, V[ladimir] K[arlovich] comp. (*Russian-English Dictionary*).

Sagarin, Edward. *The Science and Art of Perfumery,* in *New Yorker,* XXII, No. 24 (27 July 1946), 65-66.

Saintsbury, George. *French Literature and Its Masters,* ed. Huntingdon Cairns. See "Saintsbury's Centenary—Spadework on Kipling" in Essays.

——. *The Peace of the Augustans* and *A Saintsbury Miscellany.* See "George Saintsbury: Gourmet and Glutton" in Essays.

Sandoz, Maurice. *The Maze.* See "Tales of the Marvelous and the Ridiculous" in Essays.

Santayana, George. *The Middle Span* (Vol. II of *Persons and Places*), in *New Yorker*, XXI, No. 12 (5 May 1945), 83-85.

———. *Persons and Places*, in *New Yorker*, XIX, No. 47 (8 January 1944), 64-66.

Saroyan, William. *The Adventures of Wesley Jackson.* See "Reports on the G. I. by Gertrude Stein and Saroyan" in Essays.

———. *Three Plays.* See "The Boys in the Back Room: William Saroyan" in Essays.

Sartre, Jean-Paul. *The Age of Reason,* trans. Eric Sutton, and *Existentialism.* See "Jean-Paul Sartre: The Novelist and the Existentialist" in Essays.

———. *Baudelaire,* trans. Martin Turnell, in *New Yorker*, XXVI, No. 47 (13 January 1951), 76, 78, 81.

———. *The Reprieve,* trans. Eric Sutton, in *New Yorker*, XXIII, No. 40 (22 November 1947), 125-127.

Sassoon, Siegfried. *Siegfried's Journey,* in *New Yorker*, XXII, No. 7 (30 March 1946), 80-81.

Schlamm, Willi. *Diktatur der Lüge: Eine Abrechnung,* in *Nation*, CXLV (11 December 1937), 648-649, 652-653.

Schlesinger, Arthur M. *Learning How to Behave: A Historical Study of American Etiquette Books.* See "Books of Etiquette and Emily Post" in Essays.

Schnitzler, Arthur. *The Affairs of Anatole.* See "Schnitzler and Philip Barry" in Essays.

Schoenberg, Arnold. *Style and Idea.* See "High Discourse on the Arts: André Malraux and Arnold Schoenberg" in Essays.

Schultz, Sigrid. *Germany Will Try It Again,* in *New Yorker*, XIX, No. 52 (12 February 1944), 82-86.

Scott, Howard, *et al. Introduction to Technocracy,* in *New Republic*, LXXIV (22 February 1933), 50-51.

Sedgwick, William Ellery. *Herman Melville: The Tragedy of Mind*, in *New Yorker*, XX, No. 41 (25 November 1944), 89.

Seldes, Gilbert. *The Great Audience*, in *New Yorker*, XXVI, No. 36 (28 October 1950), 121-126.

————. *The Seven Lively Arts*. See "The Seven Low-Brow Arts" in Essays.

Seltzer, Adele Szold, trans. *Batouala*, by René Maran. See "Mr. Bell, Miss Cather and Others" in Essays.

Serge, Victor. *Assignment in Utopia*, in *Nation*, CXLV (13 November 1937), 531-532, 534-535.

Seton, Anya. *The Turquoise*. See "Ambushing a Best-Seller: 'The Turquoise' " in Essays.

Shakespeare, William. *The Golden Shakespeare: An Anthology*, comp. Logan Pearsall Smith. See "Virginia Woolf and Logan Pearsall Smith" in Essays.

Sharp, William, illus. *Tales of Mystery and Imagination*, by Edgar Allan Poe, in *New Yorker*, XX, No. 42 (2 December 1944), 90, 92.

Shaw, Charles MacMahon. *Bernard's Brethren*, in *New Republic*, CII (22 April 1940), 551.

Shaw, George Bernard. *Bernard Shaw's Rhyming Picture Guide to Ayot St. Lawrence* and *Buoyant Billions, Farfetched Fables, & Shakes versus Shaw*. See "Bernard Shaw Still Speaking" in Essays.

————. *Everybody's Political What's What?* See "Bernard Shaw on the Training of a Statesman" in Essays.

————. *Major Barbara, Pygmalion*, and *Saint Joan*. See "Dos Passos in the Pacific—Shaw's Birthday—A Note for Mr. Behrman" in Essays.

————. *Short Stories, Scraps and Shavings* and *Too True to be Good; Village Wooing and On the Rocks: Three Plays*, in *New Republic*, LXXIX (18 July 1934), 269-270.

———. *The Simpleton of the Unexpected Isles, The Six of Calais, The Millionairess: Three New Plays,* in *New Republic,* LXXXVII (24 June 1936), 209-210.

———. *The Socialism of Shaw,* ed. James Fuchs, in *New Republic,* LIII (23 November 1927), 24.

———. *Translations and Tomfooleries,* in *New Republic,* XLIX (9 February 1927), 337, 338.

———. *What I Really Wrote about the War,* in *New Republic,* LXX (13 April 1932), 241-242.

———. See also Archer, William.

Sheean, Vincent. *The Indigo Bunting.* See "Edna St. Vincent Millay: A Memoir" in Essays.

Sheldon, Edward. *Romance.* See "Romance: Maxine Elliott's Theatre" in Essays.

Sherman, Stuart P. *The Significance of Sinclair Lewis,* in *Vanity Fair,* XX, No. 1 (March 1923), 11.

Sherman, William Tecumseh. *Memoirs of General William T. Sherman,* with foreword by B. H. Liddell Hart. See "Uncle Billy" in Essays.

Sherrod, Robert. *Tarawa: The Story of a Battle,* in *New Yorker,* XX, No. 6 (25 March 1944), 88, 91-92, 94.

Showerman, Grant. *Horace and His Influence,* in *Dial,* LXXVIII (February 1925), 149-152.

Sieff, Mark. *Colloquial Russian,* in *New Yorker,* XX, No. 5 (18 March 1944), 92-93.

Simpson, Evelyn Mary [Spearing], ed. *Ben Jonson* (collected works). See "A Definitive Edition of Ben Jonson" in Essays.

Simpson, Percy, ed. *Ben Jonson* (collected works). See "A Definitive Edition of Ben Jonson" in Essays.

Sinclair, Upton. *Mammonart: An Essay in Economic Interpretation.* See "Mammonart" in Essays.

Smith, David Nichol, comp. *The Oxford Book of Eighteenth Century Verse,* in *New Republic,* L (30 March 1927), 175-176.

Smith, Hannah Whitall. *Philadelphia Quaker: The Letters of Hannah Whitall Smith,* ed. Logan Pearsall Smith and Robert Gathorne-Hardy. See "Stephen Crane—Hannah Whitall Smith" in Essays.

Smith, Logan Pearsall. *Trivia* and *Unforgotten Years.* See "The Ghost of an Anglophile" and "Virginia Woolf and Logan Pearsall Smith" in Essays.

———, comp. *The Golden Shakespeare: An Anthology.* See "Virginia Woolf and Logan Pearsall Smith" in Essays.

———, and Robert Gathorne-Hardy, eds. *Philadelphia Quaker: The Letters of Hannah Whitall Smith.* See "Stephen Crane—Hannah Whitall Smith" in Essays.

Sophocles. See Fitts, Dudley.

Sowerby, Githa. *Rutherford and Son.* See "Rutherford and Son: The West End Theatre" in Essays.

Sparrow, John. See Symons, Katharine E.

Spencer, Theodore. See Grierson, Francis.

Spender, Stephen. *European Witness.* See "Stephen Spender and George Grosz on Germany" in Essays.

Spingarn, Amy. *Humility and Pride,* in *New Republic,* XLVIII (17 November 1926), 383-384.

Spots by Suba, in *New Yorker,* XX, No. 42 (4 December 1944), 94.

Stallman, Robert Wooster· See Crane, Stephen (*An Omnibus*).

Stein, Gertrude. *The Autobiography of Alice B. Toklas.* See "27 rue de Fleurus" in Essays.

———. *Brewsie and Willie.* See "Reports on the G. I. by Gertrude Stein and Saroyan" in Essays.

———. *Composition as Explanation, The Making of Americans,* and *Three Lives,* in *New Republic,* L (13 April 1927), 228-229.

———. *Geography and Plays,* in *Vanity Fair,* XX, No. 4 (June 1923), 18.

———. *Portraits and Prayers,* in *New Republic,* LXXXI (26 December 1934), 198.

———. *Things As They Are (Quod erat demonstrandum).* See "An English Critic on the French Novel—Gertrude Stein as a Young Woman" in Essays.

———. *Useful Knowledge,* in *New Republic,* LVIII (20 February 1929), 21-22.

———. *Wars I Have Seen,* in *New Yorker,* XXI, No. 5 (17 March 1945), 91-92.

———. *The World Is Round,* in *New Republic,* CI (20 December 1939), 266.

Steinbeck, John. *Cannery Row,* in *New Yorker,* XX, No. 47 (6 January 1945), 62-63.

Stern, G. B., and Sheila Kaye-Smith. *Speaking of Jane Austen.* See "A Long Talk about Jane Austen" in Essays.

Stevens, Wallace. *Harmonium.* See "Wallace Stevens and E. E. Cummings" in Essays.

Stone, Kate. *Brockenburn: The Journal of Kate Stone, 1861-1868,* ed. John Q. Anderson. See "Three Confederate Ladies" in Essays.

Storm, Hans Otto. *Count Ten.* See "Hans Otto Storm" in Essays.

Stout, Rex. *The Nero Wolfe Omnibus* and *Not Quite Dead Enough.* See "Why Do People Read Detective Stories?" in Essays.

Stowe, Harriet Beecher. *Uncle Tom's Cabin,* in *New Yorker,* XXIV, No. 40 (27 November 1948), 134, 136, 138, 141. See also "Harriet Beecher Stowe" in Essays.

Strachey, Lytton. *Characters and Commentaries,* in *New Republic,* LXXVII (13 December 1933), 137.

———. *Landmarks of French Literature,* in *Vanity Fair,* XX, No. 6 (August 1923), 6.

———. *Pope: The Leslie Stephen Lecture for 1925.* See "Pope and Tennyson" in Essays.

Sukenik, E. L. *The Dead Sea Scrolls of the Hebrew University*. See "More on the Dead Sea Scrolls" in Essays.

Sullivan, J. W. N. *Aspects of Science: Second Series*, in *New Republic*, XLIX (26 January 1927), 280.

Sutton, Eric, trans. *The Age of Reason*, by Jean-Paul Sartre. See "Jean-Paul Sartre: The Novelist and the Existentialist" in Essays.

———. See also Sartre, Jean-Paul (*The Reprieve*).

Swartz, Roberta Teale. *Lilliput*, in *New Republic*, XLVIII (17 November 1926), 383-384.

Swift, Jonathan. *Journal to Stella*, ed. Harold Williams. See " 'The Most Unhappy Man on Earth' " in Essays.

———. *The Poems of Jonathan Swift*, ed. Harold Williams. See " 'Cousin Swift, You Will Never Be a Poet' " in Essays.

———. *The Portable Swift*, ed. Carl Van Doren. See " 'The Most Unhappy Man on Earth' " in Essays.

Swinburne, Algernon Charles. *Lesbia Brandon: An Historical and Critical Commentary Being Largely a Study (and Elevation) of Swinburne as a Novelist, Lucretia Borgia: The Chronicle of Tebaldeo Tebaldei; Renaissance Period*, and *Pasiphaë: A Poem*, ed. Randolph Hughes. See "Swinburne of Capheaton and Eaton" in Essays.

———. *Letters*, ed. Cecil Y. Lang. See "Swinburne of Capheaton and Eaton" in Essays.

Symons, Katharine E., A. W. Pollard, Lawrence Housman, R. W. Chambers, Alan Ker, A. S. F. Gow, and John Sparrow. *Recollections of Alfred Edward Housman*, in *New Republic*, XCV (1 June 1938), 107-108.

Taggard, Genevieve. *Traveling Standing Still*. See "A Poet of the Pacific" in Essays.

Tales of Terror, with introduction by Boris Karloff. See "A Treatise on Tales of Horror" in Essays.

Taylor, Richard. *Destruction and Reconstruction: Personal Experiences of the Late War*. See "Tales of Soldiers and Civilians" in Essays.

Taylor, William R. *Cavalier and Yankee: The Old South and American National Character.* See "Cavalier and Yankee" in Essays.

Tchaikovsky, Petr Ilich. *The Diaries of Tchaikovsky,* trans. Wladimir Lakond, in *New Yorker,* XXI, No. 49 (19 January 1946), 68-70.

Tennyson, Alfred Lord. *A Selection from the Poems of Alfred Lord Tennyson,* ed. W. H. Auden, in *New Yorker,* XX, No. 42 (4 December 1944), 94.

Terhune, Alfred McKinley. *The Life of Edward Fitzgerald, Translator of the Rubáiyát of Omar Khayyám* in *New Yorker,* XXIII, No. 16 (7 June 1947), 122-123.

Thackeray, William Makepeace. *The Letters and Private Papers of William Makepeace Thackeray,* ed. Gordon N. Ray. See "An Old Friend of the Family: Thackeray" in Essays.

These United States: A Symposium. See Gruening, Ernest.

Thoby-Marcelin, Philippe. See Marcelin, Pierre.

Thomas, Edith M. *Selected Poems,* in *New Republic,* XLVIII (17 November 1926), 383-384.

Thomas, Norman. *What Is Our Destiny?,* in *New Yorker,* XX, No. 9 (15 April 1944), 77-78, 81-82.

Thompson, Edward. *The Augustan Books of Poetry,* in *New Republic,* XLVIII (17 November 1926), 383.

Thorley, Wilfrid. *A Bouquet from France,* in *New Republic,* XLVIII (17 November 1926), 383-384.

Thorndike, Ashley H. *English Comedy,* in *New Republic,* LIX (10 July 1929), 212-213. Signed "St. John Ervine," but attributed to EW in his corrected copy of Arthur Mizener's "Edmund Wilson: A Checklist," *Princeton University Library Chronicle,* V, No. 2 (February 1944), 76, in the Yale University Library.

Thurber, James. *The White Deer.* See "Connolly's 'Unquiet Grave;' Thurber's 'White Deer'" in Essays.

Tolkien, J. R. R. *The Lord of the Rings.* See "Oo, Those Awful Orcs!" in Essays.

Trent, Lucia, and Ralph Cheney, eds. *America Arraigned,* in *New Republic,* LIII (8 February 1928), 331.

Trilling, Lionel. *Matthew Arnold,* in *New Republic,* XCVIII (22 March 1939), 199-200.

Trotsky, Leon. *Letters of an Old Bolshevik: The Key to the Moscow Trials, The Stalin School of Falsification,* and *Stalinism and Bolshevism: Concerning the Historical and Theoretical Roots of the Fourth International,* in *Nation,* CXLV (11 December 1937), 648-649, 652-653.

———. *Problems of the Chinese Revolution* and *What Next? Vital Questions for the German Proletariat,* in *New Republic,* LXXIII (28 December 1932), 195.

———. *Stalin,* in *New Yorker,* XXII, No. 12 (4 May 1946), 105-108.

———, comp. *The Living Thoughts of Karl Marx,* in *New Republic,* CII (10 June 1940), 798.

Trowbridge, John T. *The Desolate South, 1865-66,* comp. Gordon Carroll. See "Tales of Soldiers and Civilians" in Essays.

Turnell, Martin. *The Novel in France.* See "An English Critic on the French Novel—Gertrude Stein as a Young Woman" in Essays.

———. See also Sartre, Jean-Paul (*Baudelaire*).

Turner, Arlin. *George W. Cable: A Biography.* See "The Ordeal of George Washington Cable" in Essays.

Twain, Mark. See DeVoto, Bernard, ed. (*The Portable Mark Twain*), and Benton, Thomas H.

Untermeyer, Jean Starr. *Steep Ascent,* in *New Republic,* LIV (14 March 1928), 129.

Untermeyer, Louis. *A Miscellany of American Poetry,* in *New Republic,* LIII (8 February 1928), 330.

Van de Water, Frederic. *Rudyard Kipling's Vermont Feud,* in *New Republic,* XCIV (16 February 1938), 53.

Van Doren, Carl, ed. *The Portable Swift.* See " 'The Most Unhappy Man on Earth' " in Essays.

Van Vechten, Carl. *The Blind Bow-Boy,* in *Vanity Fair,* XXI, No. 3 (November 1923), 26. See also "Late Violets from the Nineties" in Essays.

Veblen, Thorstein. *The Engineers and the Price System,* in *New Republic,* LXXIV (22 February 1933), 50-51.

Vercors. *The Silence of the Sea,* in *New Yorker,* XX, No. 2 (26 February 1944), 81-82.

von Frisch, Karl. *Bees: Their Vision, Chemical Senses, and Language.* See "The Intelligence of Bees, Wasps, Butterflies, and Bombing Planes" in Essays.

Von Horvath, Odon. *The Age of the Fish,* in *New Republic,* XCVIII (8 March 1939), 140.

Walker, Charles Rumford. *Steel,* in *Vanity Fair,* XX, No. 1 (March 1923), 11.

Walker, John. See Cairns, Huntingdon, and John Walker.

Walpole, Hugh. See *The Nonesuch Dickens.*

Wasson, R. Gordon, and Valentine Pavlovna Wasson. *Mushrooms, Russia, and History.* See "Mushrooms, Russia and the Wassons" in Essays.

Wasson, Valentina Pavlovna, and R. Gordon Wasson. *Mushrooms, Russia, and History.* See "Mushrooms, Russia and the Wassons" in Essays.

Waugh, Arthur. See *The Nonesuch Dickens.*

Waugh, Evelyn. *Brideshead Revisited, The Loved One,* and *Scott-King's Modern Europe.* See "Splendors and Miseries of Evelyn Waugh" in Essays.

———. *Edmund Campion.* See "Lesser Books by Brilliant Writers" in Essays.

———. *Vile Bodies.* See " 'Never Apologize, Never Explain': The Art of Evelyn Waugh" in Essays.

Weaver, John V. A. *Finders,* in *Vanity Fair,* XX, No. 1 (March 1923), 11.

Weber, Brom, ed. *Sut Lovingood,* by George Washington Harris. See " 'Poisoned!' " in Essays.

Welch, Denton. *Maiden Voyage,* in *New Yorker,* XXI, No. 10 (21 April 1945), 83-84.

Wells, H. G. *The Autocracy of Mr. Parham,* in *New Republic,* LXIV (3 September 1930), 79.

Wentworth, Harold, and Stuart Berg Flexner, eds. *Dictionary of American Slang,* in *New Yorker,* XXXVII, No. 1 (18 February 1961), 136-138.

Wescott, Glenway. *Apartment in Athens.* See "Greeks and Germans by Glenway Wescott" in Essays.

West, Nathanael. *The Day of the Locust,* in *New Republic,* XCIX (26 July 1939), 339-340.

Wharton, Edith. *The Buccaneers,* in *New Republic,* XCVI (26 October 1938), 342-343.

———. *Edith Wharton Treasury,* ed. Arthur Hobson Quinn, in *New Yorker,* XXVI, No. 42 (9 December 1950), 162, 165.

———. *The Glimpses of the Moon,* in *Vanity Fair,* XIX, No. 1 (September 1922), 19.

———. *Old New York: False Dawn, The Old Maid, The Spark, New Year's Day,* in *New Republic,* XXXIX (11 June 1924), 77.

———. *A Son at the Front,* in *Dial,* LXXVI (March 1924), 277-279.

———. *Twilight Sleep,* in *New Republic,* LI (8 June 1927), 78.

Wheatley, Henry B., ed. *Diary of Samuel Pepys,* in *New Yorker,* XXII, No. 24 (27 July 1946), 66.

White, W. L. *Report on the Russians,* in *New Yorker,* XXI, No. 5 (17 March 1945), 92-93.

Whitehead, Alfred North. *Essays in Science and Philosophy,* in *New Yorker,* XXIII, No. 31 (20 September 1947), 90.

Whitman, Walt. See Robinson, Boardman.

Wickham, Anna. *The Little Old House,* in *New Republic,* XXVI (4 May 1921), 304.

Widdemer, Margaret. *A Tree with a Bird in It,* in *Vanity Fair,* XIX, No. 4 (December 1922), 26.

Wieck, David. See Naeve, Lowell.

Wilde, Oscar. *De profundis, Being the First Complete and Accurate Version of 'Epistola: In carcere et vinculis,' the Last Prose Work in English of Oscar Wilde,* in *New Yorker,* XXVI, No. 26 (19 August 1950), 78, 81.

——. *The Portable Oscar Wilde,* ed. Richard Aldington. See "Oscar Wilde: 'One Must Always Seek What Is Most Tragic' " in Essays.

Wilder, Thornton. *The Cabala.* See "Thornton Wilder" in Essays.

——. *Heaven's My Destination.* See "Mr. Wilder in the Middle West" in Essays.

——. *The Woman of Andros.* See "Dahlberg, Dos Passos and Wilder" in Essays.

Williams, Harold, ed. *Journal to Stella,* by Jonathan Swift. See " 'The Most Unhappy Man on Earth' " in Essays.

——. *The Poems of Jonathan Swift.* See " 'Cousin Swift, You Will Never Be a Poet' " in Essays.

Wilson, Angus. *The Wrong Set and Other Stories.* See "Bankrupt Britons and Voyaging Romantics" in Essays.

Wilson, Edward A., illus. *Jane Eyre,* by Charlotte Brontë, in *New Yorker,* XX, No. 42 (2 December 1944), 90, 92.

Wilson, J. Dover. *The Fortunes of Falstaff.* See "J. Dover Wilson on Falstaff" in Essays.

Wilson, Woodrow. *Woodrow Wilson: Life and Letters,* Vols. I and II. See "Woodrow Wilson: Political Preacher" in Essays.

Winsten, S[tephen], ed. *G. B. S. 90: Aspects of Bernard Shaw's Life and Work.* See "Dos Passos in the Pacific—Shaw's Birthday—A Note for Mr. Behrman" in Essays.

Wise, Herbert A., and Phyllis Fraser. *Great Tales of Terror and the Supernatural.* See "A Treatise on Tales of Horror" in Essays.

Wise, Thomas J. *Letters of Thomas J. Wise to John Henry Wrenn: A Further Inquiry into the Guilt of Certain Nineteenth-Century Forgers,* ed. Fannie E. Ratchford, in *New Yorker,* XX, No. 45 (23 December 1944), 54, 57-58.

Wolfe, Bertram D. *Three Who Made a Revolution: A Biographical History,* in *New Yorker,* XXIV, No. 43 (18 December 1948), 104-107.

Woolf, Virginia. *The Captain's Death Bed and Other Essays.* See "Virginia Woolf and Logan Pearsall Smith" in Essays.

Woollcott, Alexander. *The Letters of Alexander Woollcott,* in *New Yorker,* XX, No. 24 (29 July 1944), 53-54.

Wylie, Elinor. *Black Armour,* in *Vanity Fair,* XX, No. 5 (July 1923), 19.

———. *Nets to Catch the Wind,* in *Bookman,* LIV (February 1922), 579-580.

———. *The Venetian Glass Nephew.* See "A Letter to Elinor Wylie" in Essays.

Yarmolinsky, Avrahm, ed. *A Treasury of Great Russian Short Stories,* in *New Yorker,* XX, No. 5 (18 March 1944), 92-93.

Yeats, W. B. *Autobiographies,* in *New Republic,* L (23 February 1927), 22-23.

———. *Four Plays for Dancers,* in *Freeman* (New York: Freeman Corporation), V (29 March 1922), 68-69.

———. *The Herne's Egg and Other Plays,* in *New Republic,* XCV (29 June 1938), 226.

———. *A Vision* in *New Republic,* LVII (16 January 1929), 249-251.

———. *A Vision,* in *New Republic,* XCIV (20 April 1938), 339.

Yerkes, Robert M. *Chimpanzees: A Laboratory Colony,* in *New Yorker,* XX, No. 31 (16 September 1944), 72-73.

Young, Art. *On My Way.* See "Art Young" in Essays.

Young, Stark. *The Flower in Drama.* See "The Theatre" (May 1923) in Essays.

Yutang, Lin. *The Vigil of a Nation,* in *New Yorker,* XX, No. 51 (3 February 1945), 70, 73-74.

Zhitova, Varvara. *The Turgenev Family.* See "Turgenev and the Life-Giving Drop" in Essays.

IV / PLAYS AND DIALOGUES

"The Age of Pericles: An Expressionist Play." See "Fun for Old and Young: An Expressionist Play."

"Ampitheos and Elvire: A Drama," *Nassau Literary Magazine*, LXXI (March 1916), 413-418.

"Appendix A." See "Karl Marx: A Prolet-Play."

"Beautiful Old Things," *New Republic*, LXIII (30 July 1930), 313-317. Reprinted with additions in Act I of 'Osbert's Career, or the Poet's Progress" in *Duke of Palermo and Other Plays*, pp. 135-158 (esp. Scene 2, pp. 144-158). See also "Osbert's Career, or The Poet's Progress."

"Before the Wedding," *Nassau Literary Magazine*, LXIX (May 1913), 80-94.

"Beppo and Beth: Scenes from a Comedy," *Modern Monthly*, VII (May 1934), 217-224, 231. Reprinted with additions as "Beppo and Beth" in *Five Plays*, pp. 313-416; and *This Room and This Gin and These Sandwiches*, pp. 193-298.

"Broadway." See in Poems.

"A Conversation in the Galapagos: Mr. William Beebe and a Marine Iguana," *Atlantic Monthly*, CXXXVI (November 1925), 577-587. Reprinted as "In the Galapagos: Mr. William Beebe and a Marine Iguana" in *Discordant En-*

counters, pp. 89-128; and *Essays Toward Truth: Studies in Orientation,* 2nd ser., comp. Kenneth Allan Robinson, William Benfield Pressey, and James Dow McCallum (New York: Henry Holt and Company, 1929), pp. 270-291. Reprinted as "In the Galapagos" (same as "Science") in *Piece of My Mind,* pp. 169-194.

"A Conversation on Drama," *Atlantic Monthly,* CXXXVII (February 1926), 235-242. Reprinted as "Mrs. Alving and Œdipus: A Professor of Fifty and a Journalist of Twenty-five" in *Discordant Encounters,* pp. 61-88.

"The Crime in the Whistler Room: A Play in 3 Acts" (copyrighted 22 September 1924; first performed in October 1924 by Provincetown Players), *Discordant Encounters,* pp. 157-297;
This Room and This Gin and These Sandwiches, pp. 1-86;
Five Plays, pp. 129-210.

"The Critics: A Conversation," *New Republic,* XLIII (5 August 1925), 292-293;
Shores of Light, pp. 248-253.

"Cronkhite's Clocks: A Pantomime with Captions (for a score by Leo Ornstein)," *Discordant Encounters,* pp. 129-156.

"Cyprian's Prayer," *Five Plays,* pp. 9-128.

"The Delegate from Great Neck." See "Imaginary Conversations, II. Mr. Van Wyck Brooks and Mr. Scott Fitzgerald."

"Dr. McGrath: A Play," *Commentary,* XLIII, No. 5 (May 1967), 60-67. Reprinted as "Dr. McGrath" in *Duke of Palermo and Other Plays,* pp. 99-132.

"Every Man His Own Eckermann," *New York Review of Books,* I, No. 2 (Spring 1963), 1-4;
Bit Between My Teeth, pp. 576-597.

"The Evil Eye: A Comedy in Two Acts," printed as the book *Evil Eye.*

"Fun for Old and Young: An Expressionist Play," *New Republic,* XLVI (24 February 1926), 20. Reprinted as "The

Age of Pericles: An Expressionist Play" in *American Earthquake*, pp. 164-166.

"Gossip: An Eclogue," *Nassau Literary Magazine*, LXXI (June 1915), 162-164.

"A Greenwich Village Production" (printed without title in essay entitled "The Theatre"), *Dial*, LXXIV (May, 1923), 527-528;
A Dial Miscellany ed. William Wasserstrom (Syracuse, New York: Syracuse University Press, 1963), pp. 122-123. Reprinted with title in sequence entitled "On and off Broadway" in section called "The Follies: 1923-1928" in *American Earthquake*, pp. 53-54.
Reprinted with title in chapter by Charles P[aul] Frank entitled "Poems and Plays" in Frank's *Edmund Wilson*, No. 152 in Twayne's United States Authors series, ser. ed. Sylvia E. Bowman (New York: Twayne Publishers, 1970), pp. 99-100.

"Human and Hamadryad: A Masque," *Nassau Literary Magazine*, LXXI (June 1915), 111-120.

"Illinois Household," *Travels in Two Democracies*, pp. 32-38. Reprinted with a 1957 postscript in *American Earthquake*, pp. 465-472.

"An Imaginary Conversation: Mr. Paul Rosenfeld and Mr. Matthew Josephson," *New Republic*, XXXVIII (9 April 1924), 179-182. Reprinted as "The Poet's Return: Mr. Paul Rosenfeld and Mr. Matthew Josephson" in *Discordant Encounters*, pp. 7-34; and *Shores of Light*, pp. 125-140.

"Imaginary Conversations, II. Mr. Van Wyck Brooks and Mr. Scott Fitzgerald," *New Republic*, XXXVIII (30 April 1924), 249-254. Reprinted as "The Delegate from Great Neck: Mr. Van Wyck Brooks and Mr. Scott Fitzgerald" in *Discordant Encounters*, pp. 35-60; and *F. Scott Fitzgerald: The Man and His Work*, ed. Alfred Kazin (Cleveland: World Publishing Company, 1951), pp. 53-65. Reprinted with editor's headnote as "The Delegate from Great Neck" in *The Great Gatsby: A Study*, ed. Frederick J.

Hoffman, No. SL1 in The Scribner Library (New York: Charles Scribner's Sons, 1962), pp. 119-132.

"Imaginary Dialogues," *Shores of Light,* pp. 125-155.

"In the Galapagos." See "A Conversation in the Galapagos: Mr. William Beebe and a Marine Iguana."

"An Interview with Edmund Wilson," *New Yorker,* XXXVIII, No. 15 (2 June 1962), 118-128. Reprinted with a 1965 note in *Bit Between My Teeth,* pp. 534-550.

"Karl Marx: A Prolet-Play," *Partisan Review,* V, No. 1 (June 1938), 36-40. Reprinted with same title as "Appendix A" of *To the Finland Station* in *To the Finland Station* (except Anchor Books reissues), pp. 497-483.

"The Lamentable Tragedy of the Duke of Palermo by Henry Chettle and William Shakespeare Now First Discovered and Transcribed by Homer R. Winslow, M. A. Hillsdale, Ph.D. Harvard, Presented by Edmund Wilson," *New York Review of Books,* VII, No. 12 (12 January 1967), 13-23. Reprinted as "The Lamentable Tragedy of the Duke of Palermo" in *Duke of Palermo and Other Plays,* pp. 1-98.

"The Little Blue Light: A Play in Three Acts," printed as the book *Little Blue Light.* Reprinted as "The Little Blue Light" in *Five Plays,* pp. 417-541.

"The Man in the Mirror," *New Republic,* LXXXV (18 December 1935), 169-170. Reprinted with same title as "Prologue" to *Travels in Two Democracies,* pp. 1-8 (esp. pp. 3-8).

"Mrs. Alving and Œdipus: A Professor of Fifty and a Journalist of Twenty-five." See "A Conversation on Drama."

"New Year's Day, 1886—A Prologue in Heaven: A Fantastic Dissertation Upon Society, by the French Ironist Whose Centenary is Being Celebrated." See Renan, Ernest, in Translations by Wilson.

"The Novel Reader's Tragedy: An Undramatic Sketch," *Nassau Literary Magazine,* LXX (April 1914), 31-40.

"Osbert's Career, or The Poet's Progress," *Duke of Palermo and Other Plays,* pp. 133-234. Parts of Act I, pp. 135-158 (esp. Act I, Scene 2, pp. 144-158) originally appeared as "Beautiful Old Things." See also "Beautiful Old Things."

"The Poet's Return: Mr. Paul Rosenfeld and Mr. Matthew Josephson." See "An Imaginary Conversation: Mr. Paul Rosenfeld and Mr. Matthew Josephson."

"Prologue." See "The Man in the Mirror."

"A Record Board Meeting" (by EW, Bellinger, Brown, Downey, McLean and Willcox), *Hill School Record,* XXI (May 1912), 251-256.

"The Sane Tea Party," *Hill School Record,* XXI (May 1912), 226-238.

"Science." See "A Conversation in the Galapagos: Mr. William Beebe and a Marine Iguana."

"That Bright Little Play," *Hill School Record,* XXI (February 1912), 126-127. See also "An Augustan Trilogy" in General Miscellanea.

"The Theatre" (May 1923). See "A Greenwich Village Production." See also "The Theatre" (May 1923) in Essays.

"This Room and This Gin and These Sandwiches." See "A Winter in Beech Street."

"A Winter in Beech Street," *This Room and This Gin and These Sandwiches,* pp. 87-192. Reprinted as "This Room and This Gin and These Sandwiches" in *Five Plays,* pp. 211-312.

V / STORIES

"The Adventures of a Gentleman," *Hill School Record,* XX (February 1911), 132-137.

"After the Game (Princeton and Yale Ten Years Ago)," *New Republic,* XLV (25 November 1925), 16-17. Reprinted as "After the Game: Princeton and Yale Ten Years Ago" in *American Earthquake,* pp. 129-144.

"Afterwards," *Nassau Literary Magazine,* LXIX (December 1913), 239-247.

"All God's Chillun," *New Republic,* XLVI (7 April 1926), 197-198. Reprinted with a 1957 postscript in *American Earthquake,* pp. 124-128.

"As Others See Us," *Hill School Record,* XXI (April 1912), 189-191.

"Below Stairs," *Nassau Literary Magazine,* LXXI (January 1916), 267-287.

"The Conjuring Shop," *Hill School Record,* XIX (March 1910), 151-155.

"A Cotton Mill Owner," *New Republic,* XLVI (7 April 1926), 197;
American Earthquake, pp. 124-125.

"A Dandy Day," *New Republic,* XLIII (19 August 1925), 348-349.

"The Daring Flight of Addison Thinbridge," *Hill School Record*, XX (December 1910), 67-71.

"The Death of a Soldier," *Liberator*, IV, No. 9 (September 1921), 13-17;
Undertaker's Garland, pp. 99-121;
New Yorker, XLIII, No. 12 (13 May 1967), 62, 64, 67-68, 70, 73-76, 78, 80, 85;
Prelude, pp. 184-200.

"Dobell's 'Pure and Unfermented,' " *Hill School Record*, XXI (March 1912), 164-169.

"Edward Moore Gresham: Poet and Prose-Master," *Nassau Literary Magazine*, LXXI (May 1915), 68-74.

"Ellen Terhune," *Partisan Review*, IX, No. 6 (November-December 1942), 466-475, 507-528;
Memoirs of Hecate County, pp. 14-54, and New Ed., pp. 19-72.

"Emily in Hades," *Undertaker's Garland*, pp. 129-163.

"The Fable of the Three Limperary Cripples" (with headnote by EW), *New Republic*, LXII (12 March 1930), 100-101. Reprinted with a different headnote and with editor's cartoons, commentary, and endnote as "Gorgonzola: or the Future of Literary Criticism" in *Whither, Whither, or After Sex, What? A Symposium to End Symposiums*, ed. Walter S. Hankel (New York: Macaulay Company, 1930), pp. 80-91. Reprinted without headnote, commentary, cartoons, or endnote as "The Three Limperary Cripples: Musings between sleeping and waking, and immediately after reading Joyce, by the literary editor of a liberal weekly" in *Note-Books of Night*, pp. 70-74.

"15 Beech Street," *New Republic*, LI (29 June 1927), 150-151;
Shores of Light, pp. 357-362.

" 'Fire-Alarm,' " *New Republic*, L (20 April 1927), 250-252. Reprinted as "*Fire-Alarm*" in *Shores of Light*, pp. 81-90.

"Flashback: Lieutenant Franklin." See "Lieutenant Franklin."

"Galahad," *The American Caravan: A Yearbook of American Literature*, ed. Van Wyck Brooks, Lewis Mumford, Alfred Kreymborg, and Paul Rosenfeld (New York: Literary Guild of America, Macauley Company, 1927), pp. 222-261; *Galahad* [*and*] *I Thought of Daisy*, pp. 1-50.

"Glimpses of Wilbur Flick," *Town and Country*, C, No. 4281 (February 1946), 106-107, 144, 146, 148-150, 152, 154, 156;
Memoirs of Hecate County, pp. 55-81, and New Ed., pp. 73-108.

"Gorgonzola: or the Future of Literary Criticism." See "The Fable of the Three Limperary Cripples."

"Gossip," *Nassau Literary Magazine*, LXX (December 1914), 374-376.

"Gossip," *Nassau Literary Magazine*, LXX (January 1915), 457-459.

"Gossip," *Nassau Literary Magazine*, LXX (March 1915), 613-616.

"Gossip," *Nassau Literary Magazine*, LXXI (May 1915), 104-105.

"Gossip," *Nassau Literary Magazine*, LXXI (November 1915), 200-202.

"Gossip," *Nassau Literary Magazine*, LXXI (December 1915), 260-263.

"Gossip," *Nassau Literary Magazine*, LXXI (January 1916), 317-321.

"The Great Baldini: A Memoir and a Collaboration" (by EW and Edwin O'Connor), *Atlantic*, CCXXIV, No. 4 (October 1969), 64-75.

"Greenwich Village in the Early Twenties," *Shores of Light*, pp. 73-90.

"Growing Up," *Nassau Literary Magazine*, LXIX (April 1913), 17-24.

["He consulted a typical timing guide"] (printed alone without title), *Christmas Delirium*, pp. 30-32. Reprinted without title in section entitled "A Christmas Delirium: 1955" in *Night Thoughts,* pp. 248-249.

"How Akmen Amused the Princess: A Wonder Tale in Rhythmic Prose by Lord D-ns-ny," *Vanity Fair,* XIV, No. 2 (April 1920), 33.

"Into the Church," *Nassau Literary Magazine,* LXX (June 1914), 174-186.

"Lieutenant Franklin" (same as "Flashback: Lieutenant Franklin"), *Travels in Two Democracies,* pp. 113-144. Reprinted as "Lieutenant Franklin" in *New Yorker,* XLIII, No. 12 (13 May 1967), 121, 125-128, 131-136, 138, 140-147; and *Prelude,* pp. 235-265.

"Lobsters for Supper," *New Republic,* LII (28 September 1927), 145-148. Reprinted as "The Men from Rumpelmayer's" in *American Earthquake,* pp. 152-160.

["Looking out on the high chalkbound cliffs"] (printed alone without title), *Christmas Delirium,* pp. 32-33. Reprinted without title in section entitled "A Christmas Delirium: 1955" in *Night Thoughts,* pp. 250-251.

"The Man Who Shot Snapping Turtles," *Atlantic Monthly,* CLXXII, No. 2 (August 1943), 99-104;
 Memoirs of Hecate County, pp. 1-13, and New Ed., pp. 1-18;
 Contemporary Short Stories: Representative Selections, Vol. III, ed. Maurice [Charles] Baudin Jr., No. 14 in American Heritage Series, ser. ed. Oskar Priest (New York: Liberal Arts Press, 1954), pp. 83-97.

"The Men from Rumpelmayer's." See "Lobsters for Supper."

"The Messiah at the Seder: A Story," *Encounter,* VII, No. 3 (Summer 1956), 20-32. Reprinted as "The Messiah at the Seder" in *Piece of My Mind,* pp. 108-136.

"The Milhollands and Their Damned Soul," *Memoirs of Hecate County,* pp. 240-297, and New Ed., pp. 315-392.

"Mr. and Mrs. Blackburn at Home," *Memoirs of Hecate County,"* pp. 298-338, and New Ed., pp. 393-447.

"Mr. Halcrest and the Burglar," *Hill School Record,* XX, (May 1911), 241-246.

"A New Orleanian," *New Republic,* XLVI (7 April 1926), 198;
American Earthquake, pp. 126-127.

"Nightmare," *Nassau Literary Magazine,* LXX (May 1914), 122-127.

"The Old Conviviality and the New (New Orleans)," *New Republic,* XLVI (12 May 1926), 362-364. Reprinted as "The Old Conviviality and the New: New Orleans" in *American Earthquake,* pp. 129-134.

"The Oppressor: A Story," *Liberator,* IV, No. 5 (May 1921), 25-26, 28.

"Portrait of a Sage," *New Republic,* LCIII (1 May 1929), 300-305.

"The Princess with the Golden Hair," *Memoirs of Hecate County,* pp. 82-239, and New Ed., pp. 109-314.

"Reunion," *New Republic,* L (27 April 1927), 275-276; *American Earthquake,* pp. 145-151.

"The Road to Greenwich Village," *New Republic,* XLIII (15 April 1925), 215-216; *Shores of Light,* pp. 73-81.

"The Spirit of New Jersey: A Study in Drab," *Nassau Literary Magazine,* LXVIII (February 1913), 291-304.

"A Steamboat Captain," *New Republic,* XLVI (7 April 1926), 197-198;
American Earthquake, pp. 125-126.

"Still Life," *New Republic,* XLVIII (10 November 1926), 322-323.

"The Successful Mr. Sterne: 'Lives of Great Men All Remind Us,'" *Hill School Record,* XX (April 1911), 214-219.

"The Thankless Job," *Nassau Literary Magazine,* LXX (January 1915), 416-440.

"That Long Entertaining Narrative," *Hill School Record,* XXI (February 1912), 124-125. A short prose narrative. See also "An Augustan Trilogy" in General Miscellanea.

"That Readable and Interesting Work of Fiction," *Hill School Record*, XXI (February 1912), 128-130. A satiric prose narrative. See also "An Augustan Trilogy" in General Miscellanea.

"The Three Limperary Cripples: Musings between sleeping and waking, and immediately after reading Joyce, by the literary editor of a liberal weekly." See "The Fable of the Three Limperary Cripples."

"What to Do Till the Doctor Comes," *New Republic*, LXXIX (11 July 1934), 230-232. Reprinted as "What to Do Till the Doctor Comes: From the Diary of a Drinker-Out" in *Travels in Two Democracies*, pp. 95-103; and *American Earthquake*, pp. 527-533.

"The Will," *Hill School Record*, XX (March 1911), 150-159.

"The Works of Mrs. Behn," *Hill School Record*, XIX (April 1910), 193-196.

VI / POEMS

["After writing"]. See "Past Midnight."

"American Masterpieces: To Stark Young," *Poets, Farewell!*,
pp. 16-17;
Night Thoughts, pp. 44-45.

"American Officers and Men Who Killed Themselves," *A
Book of Princeton Verse II, 1919,* ed. Henry Van Dyke,
Morris William Croll, Maxwell Struthers Burt, and James
Creese Jr. (Princeton: Princeton University Press, 1919),
p. 169. Reprinted as "American Officers and Soldiers Who
Committed Suicide" in *Poets, Farewell!*, p. 64; and *Night
Thoughts*, p. 4. See also "A New Simonides."

"American Soldiers," *A Book of Princeton Verse II, 1919,* ed.
Henry Van Dyke, Morris William Croll, Maxwell Struth-
ers Burt, and James Creese Jr. (Princeton: Princeton Uni-
versity Press, 1919), p. 169;
Poets, Farewell!, p. 64;
Night Thoughts, p. 4.
See also "A New Simonides."

"Americanization," *Poets, Farewell!*, p. 25.

"Anagrams on Eminent Authors," *Wilson's Christmas Stocking*, pp. 6-7;
Night Thoughts, pp. 198-199.

["—And you who faint at either's hard expense"] (printed without title in section entitled "Poets Farewell!: 1929"),
Poets, Farewell!, p. 77;
Night Thoughts, p. 71.

"Army," *Prelude*, p. 274.

"The Art of Education," *Wilson's Christmas Stocking*, p. 3;
Night Thoughts, p. 195.

"At the Algonquin," *Christmas Delirium*, p. 11;
Night Thoughts, p. 228.

"Author to Reader," *Nassau Literary Magazine*, LXIX (December 1913), 269.

"The Best Things from Abroad: Two Esquimaux Love Songs Translated from the Esquimaux by Maida Thompson and Nanook Kruger" (by EW and John Peale Bishop), *Playboy*, II, No. 1 (March 1923), 43.

"Birth and Death of Summer," *New Yorker*, XVI, No. 32 (21 September 1940), 27;
Note-Books of Night, pp. 29-30;
Night Thoughts, pp. 127-128.

"Bishop Praxed's Apology, or the Art of Thinking in Poetry, or A Gospel of Falsity for an Age of Doubt," *New Yorker*, X, No. 5 (17 March 1934), 21. Reprinted as "Bishop Praxed's Apology or the Art of Thinking in Poetry or A Gospel of Falsity for an Age of Doubt" in *Note-Books of Night*, pp. 6-7. Reprinted as "Bishop Praxed's Apology: or The Art of Thinking in Poetry or A Gospel of Falsity for an Age of Doubt" in *Night Thoughts*, p. 89.

"Le Bluff," *New Yorker*, XXV, No. 36 (29 October 1949), 34;
Wilson's Christmas Stocking, p. 13;
Night Thoughts, p. 206.

"Boboli Gardens." See "The Olympians."

"Brief Comments on Mistaken Meanings," *New Yorker*, XXV, No. 36 (29 October 1949), 34;
Wilson's Christmas Stocking, pp. 12-13;
Night Thoughts, pp. 205-206.

"Broadway," *Hill School Record*, XXI (April 1912), 209-210. In a six-line stanza, EW records scraps of conversation overheard on Broadway—a poetic practising of a suggestion made by Charles Lamb.

"Bulletin No. 7: The Mass in the Parking Lot," *Furioso*, IV, No. 3 (Summer 1949), 49-51. Reprinted as "The Mass in the Parking Lot" in *Three Reliques of Ancient Western Poetry*, pp. 3-6; and *Night Thoughts*, pp. 181-184.

"By Dark Cocytus' Shore," *New Yorker*, XL, No. 45 (26 December 1964), 70. Reprinted with an illustration by Mary Meigs on a sheet of paper 13 1/2 by 18 inches (Harvard Yard, Cambridge, Massachusetts: Lowell-Adams House Printers, October 1965); only 85 copies were printed.

"Cape Cod" (printed without title as ["Here where your blue bay's hook is half begun"] in section entitled "Poets, Farewell!: 1929"), *Poets, Farewell!*, p. 76; *Night Thoughts*, p. 70.
    Reprinted alone with title in *East of America: A Selection of Cape Cod Poems*, ed. John V. Hinshaw (Chatham, Massachusetts: Chatham Press, 1969), p. 29.

"Cardinal Merry Del Val," *Three Reliques of Ancient Western Poetry*, pp. 9-13; *Night Thoughts*, pp. 187-191.

"Chaumont." See "G. H. Q., January, 1919."

"The Children's Hour," *Christmas Delirium*, pp. 3-5; *Night Thoughts*, pp. 221-223.

"Chorus of Stalin's Yes-Men," *Note-Books of Night*, pp. 33-34.

"A Christmas Delirium," printed as the book *Christmas Delirium*. Reprinted as "A Christmas Delirium, 1955" in *Night Thoughts*, pp. 220-262.

"A Christmas Stocking: Fun for Young and Old," printed as the book *Wilson's Christmas Stocking: Fun for Young and Old*. Reprinted as "A Christmas Stocking: Fun for Young and Old, 1953" in *Night Thoughts*, pp. 193-218.

"Club Caprice," *Poets, Farewell!*, pp. 14-15.

"Colloquial [berry (jewel)]," *New Yorker*, XLIII, No. 11 (6 May 1967), 146-147;
Prelude, p. 165.

"Colloquial [off him, it, etc.]," *New Yorker*, XLIII, No. 11 (6 May 1967), 108;
Prelude, p. 125.

"Colloquial [Oftentimes: most of the doctors]," *Prelude*, p. 274.

"Colloquy between Oneida and Lewis Counties, New York," *Wilson's Christmas Stocking*, p. 16;
Night Thoughts, p. 209.

"Conning Tower." See "The Present State of American Poetry" and "The Tables Turned, or Revenge at Last."

"Copper and White," *Poets, Farewell!*, pp. 26-29;
Night Thoughts, pp. 46-48.

["The crows of March are barking in the wood"] (printed without title in sequence entitled "Sleeping and Waking"), *Poetry*, XLVII (February 1936), 245. Reprinted alone without title in *Note-Books of Night*, p. 27. Reprinted without title in section entitled "Elegies and Wakeful Nights" in *Night Thoughts*, p. 110.

"The Dark Hour," *Nassau Literary Magazine*, LXXI (November 1915), 182;
A Book of Princeton Verse, 1916, ed. Alfred Noyes (Princeton: Princeton University Press, 1916), p. 182;
Nassau Lit, C, No. 3 [1842-1942 centennial issue] (1942), 76;
New Yorker, XLIII, No. 11 (6 May 1967), 114;
Prelude, p. 130.
See also "Swift."

"The Dark Room," *New Republic*, LXXXI (5 December 1934), 101;
Anthology of Magazine Verse for 1935 and Yearbook of American Poetry, ed. Alan F. Pater (New York: Poetry Digest Association, 1936), p. 187;

Note-Books of Night, p. 18;
Night Thoughts, p. 33.

["Dawns, dawns, that split with light"]. See "Morning."

["The days and nights—pressure and relief"] (printed alone without title), *Note-Books of Night,* p. 28. Reprinted without title in section entitled "Stamford" in *Night Thoughts,* p. 126.

"The Death of an Efficiency Expert," *Undertaker's Garland,* pp. 68-89.

"The Death of the Last Centaur," *Undertaker's Garland,* pp. 27-38.

"Death Warrant," *Poets, Farewell!,* pp. 45-46;
Night Thoughts, pp. 59-60.

"The Decadence of Modern Literature, by Brainard Spargo," *New York Evening Mail,* 18 September 1911, p. 8, "FPA's Column."

"Dedication" (of *Crack-Up*). See "On Editing Scott Fitzgerald's Papers."

"Dedication for a Book." See Housman, A. E., in Translations by Wilson.

"Dedication to a Book." See Housman, A. E., in Translations by Wilson.

["Dim screens obscure the dawn"] (printed without title in section entitled "Poets, Farewell!: 1929"), *Poets, Farewell!,* p. 78;
Night Thoughts, p. 72.

"Disloyal Lines to an Alumnus," *New Yorker,* X, No. 5 (17 March 1934), 21;
Note-Books of Night, pp. 11-12;
Night Thoughts, pp. 90-91.

"Drafts for a Quatrain," *Wilson's Christmas Stocking,* p. 15;
Night Thoughts, p. 208.

"A Dream for Daniel Updike," *New Yorker,* XXV, No. 36 (29 October 1949), 34;

Wilson's Christmas Stocking, p. 12;
Night Thoughts, p. 205.

"e. e. cummings, esquirrel," *Wilson's Christmas Stocking*, p. 4;
Night Thoughts, p. 196.

"Easy Exercises in the Use of Difficult Words," *Saturday Review of Literature*, XXXI, No. 41 (9 October 1948), 64. Reprinted with addition of "Scène de Boudoir" in *Wilson's Christmas Stocking*, pp. 10-11; and *Night Thoughts*, pp. 202-204.

"Elegies and Wakeful Nights," *Night Thoughts*, pp. 97-122.

"Elegies for a Passing World," *New Yorker*, X, No. 50 (26 January 1935), 19.

> *Contents*
>   I. "Riverton"
>   II. "A House of the Eighties"
>   III. "The Voice (On a Friend in a Sanitarium)"

See "A House of the Eighties," "Riverton," and "The Voice (On a Friend in a Sanitarium)" for subsequent publication.

"Enemies of Promise," *Wilson's Christmas Stocking*, p. 3;
Night Thoughts, p. 195.

"Epilogue," *Undertaker's Garland*, pp. 191-192.

"Epitaph for a Hospital Nurse," *May Days: An Anthology of Verse from Masses-Liberator,* comp. and ed. Genevieve Taggard (New York: Boni and Liveright, 1925), p. 248. Reprinted as "A Hospital Nurse" in *Poets, Farewell!*, p. 65; *Night Thoughts*, p. 5; and *Edmund Wilson*, by Charles P[aul] Frank, No. 152 in Twayne's United States Authors Series, ser. ed. Sylvia E. Bowman (New York: Twayne Publishers, 1970), p. 81.

"Epitaph for a Young German," *Liberator*, III, No. 2 (February 1920), 46;

> *May Days: An Anthology of Verse from Masses-Liberator,* comp. and ed. Genevieve Taggard (New York: Boni and Liveright, 1925), p. 247.

> Reprinted as "A Young German" in *Poets, Farewell!*, p. 65; and *Night Thoughts*, p. 4.

"Epitaphs," *Poets, Farewell!*, pp. 64-65;
Night Thoughts, pp. 4-5.

"Europe," *Night Thoughts*, pp. 11-18.

"Exchanges," *Hill School Record*, XXI (March 1912), 182-
185. Contains four eight-line stanzas satirizing "Silly tales."
See also "Exchanges" in Essays.

"The Extravert [*sic*] of Walden Pond," *New Yorker*, X, No.
5 (17 March 1934), 21;
Night Thoughts, pp. 79-80.
Reprinted as "The Extrovert of Walden Pond" in *Note-Books of Night*, pp. 9-10.

"FPA's Column." See "The Decadence of Modern Literature,
by Brainard Spargo."

"Fabulous Word Squares," *Holiday Greetings 1966*, pp.
[19-28]. Includes "A Short Sketch of Western Civilization"
and "Key to the Word Squares."

"First Highball," *Poetry*, LV (January 1940), 182;
Note-Books of Night, p. 22;
Night Thoughts, p. 111.
See also "Three Women."

"From the Geckese," *Christmas Delirium*, pp. 6-9;
Night Thoughts, pp. 224-227.

"From the Window." See "Sonnets."

"Fun in the Balkans," *Wilson's Christmas Stocking*, p. 17;
Night Thoughts, p. 210.

"The Funeral of a Romantic Poet," *Undertaker's Garland*,
pp. 54-58.

"G. H. Q., January, 1919," *Poetry*, XVII (November 1920),
78. Reprinted as "Chaumont" in *Poets, Farewell!*, p. 66;
and *Night Thoughts*, p. 7.

"A Ghost of Old Baltimore," *Christmas Delirium*, p. 11;
Night Thoughts, p. 229.

["Gimme the gimmick, Gustave!"] (printed alone without
title), *Christmas Delirium*, pp. 28-29. Reprinted without

title in section entitled "A Christmas Delirium, 1955" in *Night Thoughts*, pp. 246-247.

"Gluck in New York," *New Republic*, XXII (31 March 1920), 150.

"The Good Neighbor," *New Republic*, XCII (27 October 1937), 337-338;
Note-Books of Night, pp. 45-50;
Night Thoughts, pp. 129-133.

["The grass brown, the bushes dry"] (printed alone without title), *Note-Books of Night*, p. 37. Reprinted without title in section entitled "Stamford" in *Night Thoughts*, p. 136.

"Heraldic Battle," *Saturday Review of Literature*, XXXI, No. 41 (9 October 1948), 64;
Wilson's Christmas Stocking, p. 11;
Night Thoughts, p. 203.

["Here where your blue bay's hook is half begun"]. See "Cape Cod."

"Highballs: To J. H. A.," *Poets, Farewell!*, pp. 11-12. Reprinted as "Highballs: To John Amen" in *Night Thoughts*, pp. 39-40.

"History as a Crystalline Sea-Anemone" (printed alone without title as ["—Or else to imagine History as a crystalline sea-anemone"]), *Christmas Delirium*, pp. 14-15. Reprinted (title being given in table of contents) in section entitled "A Christmas Delirium, 1955" in *Night Thoughts*, pp. 230-232.

"Home to Town: Two Highballs," *Poetry*, LV (January 1940), 182-183;
Note-Books of Night, pp. 22-23;
Night Thoughts, pp. 111-112.
See also "Three Women."

"Homecoming," *Holiday Greetings 1966*, pp. [29-31].

"A Hospital Nurse." See "Epitaph for a Hospital Nurse."

"The House of a Man of Genius," *Poets, Farewell!*, p. 30.

"A House of the Eighties," *New Yorker*, X, No. 50 (26 January 1935), 19;
> *Note-Books of Night*, p. 8;
> *A Comprehensive Anthology of American Poetry*, ed. Conrad Aiken (New York: Modern Library, 1944), p. 422;
> *Twentieth-Century American Poetry*, ed. Conrad Aiken, in The Modern Library (New York: Modern Library, 1944), pp. 293-294;
> *An Anthology of Famous English and American Poetry*, ed. William Rose Benét and Conrad Aiken (New York: Modern Library, 1945), p. 874;
> *Night Thoughts*, p. 103.
> See also "Elegies for a Passing World."

"Huysmans at Chartres," *New Yorker*, XLIII, No. 11 (6 May 1967), 108, 110;
> *Prelude*, p. 126.

"Imaginary Dialogues," *Christmas Delirium*, pp. 10-13;
> *Night Thoughts*, pp. 228-229.

"An Incident of the Occupation," *Wilson's Christmas Stocking*, p. 17;
> *Night Thoughts*, p. 210.

"Infection," *Poets, Farewell!*, pp. 7-8;
> *Modern American Poetry: A Critical Anthology*, ed. Louis Untermeyer (New York: Harcourt, Brace and Company, 1930), pp. 719-720;
> *Night Thoughts*, pp. 29-30.

"John Dos Passos, Esq[re]," *Wilson's Christmas Stocking*, p. 4;
> *Night Thoughts*, p. 196.

"Junk," *New Yorker*, XXV, No. 36 (29 October 1949), 34;
> *Wilson's Christmas Stocking*, p. 12;
> *Night Thoughts*, p. 205.

"Key to the Word Squares." See "Fabulous Word Squares."

"Lakeside," *Saturday Review of Literature*, XXXI, No. 41 (9 October 1948), 64;
> *Wilson's Christmas Stocking*, p. 11;
> *Night Thoughts*, p. 203.

"Land's Edge," *Poetry*, L (July 1937), 186-187.

> *Contents*
>   I. "Provincetown, 1936"
>   II. "Past Midnight"
>   III. "Morning"

"The Lay of St. Valentine: An Ingoldsly Legend." See "Valentine Echoes."

"Lesbia," *Night Thoughts*, pp. 19-36.

"Lesbia in Hell," *Note-Books of Night*, pp. 56-61;
> *Night Thoughts*, pp. 21-26.

"Letters," *A Book of Princeton Verse II, 1919*, ed. Henry Van Dyke, Morris William Croll, Maxwell Struthers Burt, and James Creese Jr. (Princeton: Princeton University Press, 1919), p. 137.

"The Lido," *Poets, Farewell!*, pp. 3-4;
> *Night Thoughts*, p. 16;
> *Erotic Poetry: The Lyrics, Ballads, Idyls, and Epics of Love—Classical to Contemporary*, ed. William Cole (New York: Random House, 1963), p. 240.

"Lines," *Hill School Record*, XXIII (June 1914), 315-317. Nine stanzas of eight lines each, written for a literary banquet.

"Love Me; Love My Dog," *Hill School Record*, XXI (January 1912), 106-107. A complete poem of six stanzas, based on Martial, Book I, Epigram 109.

"The Mass in the Parking Lot." See "Bulletin No. 7: The Mass in the Parking Lot."

"Memories of the Poetry of the Nineties, Written Down While Waiting for Long-Distance Calls," *Wilson's Christmas Stocking*, pp. 14-15;
> *Night Thoughts*, pp. 207-208.

"Memories of Stedman's 'American Anthology,' 1890-1910 Division," *Furioso*, V, No. 3 (Summer 1950), 36.

"Merry Monsters," *Holiday Greetings 1966*, pp. [3-10].

["A message you'll expect, my friends"] (printed alone without title), *Wilson's Christmas Stocking*, pp. 20-24. Reprinted without title in section entitled "A Christmas Stocking: Fun for Young and Old, 1953" in *Night Thoughts*, pp. 213-217.

"Metternich's Great Admirer," *Wilson's Christmas Stocking*, p. 5;
Night Thoughts, p. 197.

"Miniature Dialogues," *Wilson's Christmas Stocking*, p. 16;
Night Thoughts, p. 209.

"[More Lament for the World Left Behind]," *New Yorker*, XLIII, No. 12 (13 May 1967), 86. Reprinted as "[More lament for the world left behind.]" in *Prelude*, 203-204.

"Morning" (in sequence entitled "Land's Edge"), *Poetry*, L (July 1937), 187. Reprinted without title as ["Dawns, dawns, that split with light"] in section entitled "Elegies and Wakeful Nights" in *Night Thoughts*, p. 108.

["My dear, you burn with bright green eyes"] (printed without title in sequence entitled "Three Women"), *Poetry*, LV (January 1940), 184-185. Reprinted alone without title in *Note-Books of Night*, p. 36. Reprinted without title in section entitled "Elegies and Wakeful Nights" in *Night Thoughts*, p. 118.

"New Jersey and New York," *Night Thoughts*, pp. 37-48.

"New Ode to a Nightingale: France: June 8, 1918," *A Book of Princeton Verse II, 1919*, ed. Henry Van Dyke, Morris William Croll, Maxwell Struthers Burt, and James Creese Jr. (Princeton: Princeton University Press, 1919), p. 170. Reprinted as "New Ode to a Nightingale" in *Night Thoughts*, p. 6.

"The New Patriotism," *Liberator*, III, No. 6 (June 1920), 26-27;
May Days: An Anthology of Verse from Masses-Liberator, comp. and ed. Genevieve Taggard (New York: Boni and Liveright, 1925), p. 215;

Poets, Farewell!, pp. 67-70;
Night Thoughts, pp. 8-10.

"A New Simonides," *A Book of Princeton Verse II, 1919*, ed. Henry Van Dyke, Morris William Croll, Maxwell Struthers Burt, and James Creese Jr. (Princeton: Princeton University Press, 1919), p. 169.

Contents
    1. "American Soldiers"
    2. "American Officers and Men Who Killed Themselves"

"The Night Attack," *Poets, Farewell!*, pp. 49-50;
Night Thoughts, p. 63.

"Night in May," *New Republic*, LXXXII (10 April 1935), 234;
Note-Books of Night, pp. 3-5;
Night Thoughts, pp. 99-101.

"Nightmare," *Poetry*, XLVII (February 1936), 243-244;
Note-Books of Night, p. 19;
Night Thoughts, p. 34.
See also "Sleeping and Waking."

"1917-19," *Poets, Farewell!*, pp. 61-70. Reprinted with addition of the poem "New Ode to a Nightingale" in *Night Thoughts*, pp. 1-10.

"Nocturne: Lines Inspired by the Verses of a Lady," *Playboy: A Portfolio of Art and Satire*, No. 9 (July 1924), 6. Reprinted as "Nocturne: Impromptu to a Lady" in *Poets, Farewell!*, pp. 58-60; and *Night Thoughts*, pp. 75-76.

"Nonsense," *Poets, Farewell!*, pp. 51-60.

"Not Here," *Poetry*, XVII (November 1920), 78.

"November Ride," *Poetry*, LV (January 1940), 183-184;
Note-Books of Night, pp. 31-32;
Night Thoughts, pp. 134-135.
See also "Three Women."

"Nursery Vignette," *Saturday Review of Literature*, XXXI, No. 41 (9 October 1948), 64;
Wilson's Christmas Stocking, p. 10;
Night Thoughts, p. 202.

"Old Correspondence," *A Book of Princeton Verse II, 1919,*
    ed. Henry Van Dyke, Morris William Croll, Maxwell
    Struthers Burt, and James Creese Jr. (Princeton: Prince-
    ton University Press, 1919), p. 138.

"An Old Faith for New Needs," *Christmas Delirium,* p. 11;
    Night Thoughts, p. 229.

"The Olympians," *Scribner's Magazine,* LXXIII (January
    1923), 62. Reprinted as "Boboli Gardens" in *Poets, Fare-
    well!,* pp. 23-24; and *Night Thoughts,* pp. 17-18.

"The Omelet of A. MacLeish," *New Yorker,* XIV, No. 48
    (14 January 1939), 23-24;
    Note-Books of Night, pp. 41-44;
    *Parodies: An Anthology from Chaucer to Beerbohm—ard
        After,* ed. Dwight Macdonald, in The Random House
        Lifetime Library (New York: Random House, 1960),
        pp. 224-226;
    Night Thoughts, pp. 84-88.

"On a Rose Found in a Greek Dictionary." See "A Rose
    Found in a Greek Dictionary."

"On Editing Scott Fitzgerald's Papers," *New Yorker,* XVIII,
    No. 13 (16 May 1942), 17;
    The Criterion Book of Modern American Verse, ed. W. H.
        Auden (New York: Criterion Books, 1956), pp. 166-168;
    Night Thoughts, pp. 119-122.
    Reprinted as "Dedication" in *Crack-Up,* pp. 7-9.

["One thing I know that saves me much remorse"] (printed
    without title in essay entitled "The Army, 1917-1919"),
    New Yorker, XLIII, No. 12 (13 May 1967), 86;
    Prelude, p. 204.

["—Or else to imagine History as a crystalline sea-anemone"].
    See "History as a Crystalline Sea-Anemone."

"Palace Dusk," *Saturday Review of Literature,* XXXI, No.
    41 (9 October 1948), 64;
    Wilson's Christmas Stocking, p. 11;
    Night Thoughts, pp. 203-204.

"The Paradox of Thornton Wilder," *Wilson's Christmas Stocking*, p. 3;
Night Thoughts, p. 195.

"Parnassus." See "Sonnets."

"Parody, Satire, and Nonsense," *Night Thoughts*, pp. 73-96.

"Past Midnight" (in sequence entitled "Land's Edge"), *Poetry*, L (July 1937), 187. Reprinted alone without title as ["After writing"] in *Note-Books of Night*, p. 21. Reprinted without title as ["After writing"] in section entitled "Elegies and Wakeful Nights" in *Night Thoughts*, p. 109.

"Peter Florescent, Peter Marcescent; Peter Dehiscent, Peter Resipiscent." See "Philip Florescent, Philip Marcescent; Philip Dehiscent, Philip Resipiscent."

"Peterhof," *Christmas Delirium*, p. 10;
Night Thoughts, p. 228;
The Golden Journey: Poems for Young People, comp. Louise Bogan and William Jay Smith (Chicago: Reilly and Lee, 1965), p. 153.

"Philip Florescent, Philip Marcescent; Philip Dehiscent, Philip Resipiscent," *Saturday Review of Literature*, XXXI, No. 41 (9 October 1948), 64. Reprinted as "Peter Florescent, Peter Marcescent; Peter Dehiscent, Peter Resipiscent" in *Wilson's Christmas Stocking*, p. 10; and *Night Thoughts*, p. 202.

"The Pickerel Pond: A Double Pastoral," *Furioso*, IV, No. 1 (Winter 1949), 7-14;
Christmas Delirium, pp. 16-27;
Night Thoughts, pp. 233-245.

"The Playwright in Paradise: A Legend of the Beverly Hills," *New Republic*, XCVIII (26 April 1939), 332;
Boys in the Back Room, pp. 5-8;
Night Thoughts, pp. 92-95.

"Poets, Farewell!" (printed without title as ["Poets, farewell! —farewell, gay pastorals!"] in section entitled "Poets, Farewell!: 1929"), *Poets, Farewell!*, p. 75;
Night Thoughts, p. 69.

Reprinted alone with title in *Modern American Poetry: A Critical Anthology,* ed. Louis Untermeyer (New York: Harcourt, Brace and Company, 1930), pp. 718-719.

"Poets, Farewell!: 1929," *Poets, Farewell!,* pp. 71-78;
Night Thoughts, pp. 65-72.

["Poured full of thin gold sun, September—houses white and bare"] (printed without title in sequence entitled "Sleeping and Waking"), *Poetry,* XLVII (February 1936), 244-245. Reprinted alone without title in *Note-Books of Night,* p. 16. Reprinted without title in section entitled "Elegies and Wakeful Nights" in *Night Thoughts,* p. 106.

"The Prelude," *Nassau Literary Magazine,* LXXI (April 1915), 11;
A Book of Princeton Verse, 1916, ed. Alfred Noyes (Princeton: Princeton University Press, 1916), pp. 184-185.

"The Present State of American Poetry," *New York Tribune,* 21 April 1914, p. 8, in col. headed "Conning Tower."

"Princeton" (printed without title and starting ["Well, so this is Paris!"] in essay entitled "New York, 1916-1917"), *New Yorker,* XLIII, No. 11 (6 May 1967), 146-147. Reprinted with title in same essay in *Prelude,* pp. 165-166.

"Princeton—April, 1917," *A Book of Princeton Verse II, 1919,* ed. Henry Van Dyke, Morris William Croll, Maxwell Struthers Burt, and James Creese Jr. (Princeton: Princeton University Press, 1919), pp. 16-18;
New Yorker, XLIII, No. 12 (13 May 1967), 56, 58;
Prelude, pp. 178-180.

"Princeton: February, 1916," *A Book of Princeton Verse, 1916,* ed. Alfred Noyes (Princeton: Princeton University Press, 1916), pp. 179-180.

"Princeton, 1917," *New Yorker,* XLIII, No. 11 (6 May 1967), 147;
Prelude, p. 166.

"The Professor." See "Sonnets."

"Provincetown" (printed alone with title) *Bookman,* LXIX April 1929), 166;
Poets, Farewell!, pp. 31-32;

Anthology of Magazine Verse for 1929 and Yearbook of American Poetry, ed. W. S. Braithewaite (New York: George Sully and Company, 1929), p. 395;

East of America: A Selection of Cape Cod Poems, ed. John V. Hinshaw (Chatham, Massachusetts: Chatham Press, 1969), p. 27.

Reprinted without title in essay entitled "Edna St. Vincent Millay: A Memoir" in *Nation*, CLXXIV (19 April 1952), 375.

Reprinted with title in essay entitled "Epilogue, 1952: Edna St. Vincent Millay" in *Shores of Light*, pp. 765-766.

Reprinted with title in section entitled "Lesbia" in *Night Thoughts*, p. 35.

"Provincetown, 1936," *Poetry*, L (July 1937), 186;

Note-Books of Night, p. 17;

Night Thoughts, p. 107;

East of America: A Selection of Cape Cod Poems, ed. John V. Hinshaw (Chatham, Massachusetts: Chatham Press, 1969), p. 28.

See also "Land's Edge."

"The Purist's Complaint," *New Yorker*, XXV, No. 36 (29 October 1949), 34;

Wilson's Christmas Stocking, p. 13;

Night Thoughts, p. 206.

"Quintilian: A Ballad," *Double-Dealer*, III, No. 17 (May 1922), 233. Reprinted as "Quintilian" in *Poets, Farewell!*, pp. 53-54; and *Night Thoughts*, pp. 77-78.

"The Rabbi Turned Away in Disdain," *Christmas Delirium*, p. 12;

Night Thoughts, p. 229.

"The Rats of Rutland Grange," *Christmas Delirium*, pp. 34-41;

Esquire, LVI, No. 6 (December 1961), 123-125;

Night Thoughts, pp. 252-260.

"Relaxed Crossword Puzzles," *Wilson's Christmas Stocking*, pp. 8-9;
Night Thoughts, pp. 200-201.

"Response of the Gentle Scholars," *New Republic*, LXXXII (27 March 1935), 178;
Note-Books of Night, pp. 24-25.

"Return," *Nassau Literary Magazine*, LXX (February 1915), 504.

"Reversals, or *Plus ça change*," *Three Reliques of Ancient Western Poetry*, pp. 7-8;
Night Thoughts, pp. 185-186.

"Riverton," *New Yorker*, X, No. 50 (26 January 1935), 19;
Note-Books of Night, p. 13;
    A Comprehensive Anthology of American Poetry, ed. Conrad Aiken (New York: Modern Library, 1944), pp. 422-423;
    Twentieth-Century American Poetry, ed. Conrad Aiken, in Modern Library (New York: Modern Library, 1944), p. 293;
    An Anthology of Famous English and American Poetry, ed. William Rose Benét and Conrad Aiken (New York: Modern Library, 1945), p. 873;
Night Thoughts, p. 102.
See also "Elegies for a Passing World."

"A Rose Found in a Greek Dictionary," *Nassau Literary Magazine*, LXXII (June 1916), 109;
    A Book of Princeton Verse, 1916, ed. Alfred Noyes (Princeton: Princeton University Press, 1916), p. 183;
    Cap and Gown: Some College Verse, 4th ser., comp. R. L. Paget [pseud. for Frederic Lawrence Knowles] (Boston: L. C. Page & Company, 1931), p. 307.
Reprinted as "On a Rose Found in a Greek Dictionary" in *New Yorker*, XXXIX, No. 9 (20 April 1963), 166; and *Bit Between My Teeth*, p. 600.

["Said Gayelord Hauser to Gathorne-Hardy"] (printed without title in sequence entitled "Miniature Dialogues"), *Wil-*

son's *Christmas Stocking*, p. 16. Reprinted without title in same sequence in section called "A Christmas Stocking: Fun for Young and Old, 1953" in *Night Thoughts*, p. 209.

["Said Mario Praz to Mario Pei"] (printed without title in sequence entitled "Miniature Dialogues"), *Wilson's Christmas Stocking*, p. 160. Reprinted without title in same sequence in section called "A Christmas Stocking: Fun for Young and Old, 1953" in *Night Thoughts*, p. 209.

"Scène de Boudoir," *Wilson's Christmas Stocking*, p. 10;
Night Thoughts, p. 203.

"Scurrilous Clerihews," *Wilson's Christmas Stocking*, pp. 3-5;
Night Thoughts, pp. 195-197.

"Second Highball," *Poetry*, LV (January 1940), p. 183;
Note-Books of Night, p. 23;
Night Thoughts, p. 112.
See also "Three Women."

"September Landscape," *Saturday Review of Literature*, XXXI, No. 41 (9 October 1948), 64;
Wilson's Christmas Stocking, p. 10;
Night Thoughts, p. 202.

"September, 1917," *New Yorker*, XLIII, No. 12 (13 May 1967), 54-55;
Prelude, pp. 173-176.

"A Short Sketch of Western Civilization" (Section V of "Fabulous Word Squares"), *Holiday Greetings 1966*, p. [23].

[Shut out the Square!"] (printed without title in section entitled "Three Women Remembered in Absence"), *Poets, Farewell!*, pp. 5-6. Reprinted without title in essay entitled "Edna St. Vincent Millay: A Memoir" in *Nation*, CLXXIV (19 April 1952), 376. Reprinted without title in essay entitled "Epilogue, 1952: Edna St. Vincent Millay" in *Shores of Light*, p. 770. Reprinted without title as ["Shut out the square!"] in section entitled "Lesbia" in *Night Thoughts*, pp. 27-28.

"The Shy Egoist," *Nassau Literary Magazine*, LXX (May 1914), 114.

"Sleeping and Waking," *Poetry,* XLVII (February 1936), 243-245.

Contents
    I. ["This blue world with its wide high sky of islands"]
    II. "Nightmare"
    III. ["Poured full of thin gold sun, September—houses white and bare"]
    IV. ["The crows of March are barking in the wood"]

"The Sleeping College," *Nassau Literary Magazine,* LXXI (February 1916), 381.

"Some Americans Still in Spain to Some Stalinists Still in America" (by EW and M[ary] McC[arthy], Mrs. Wilson), *Partisan Review,* VI, No. 5 (Fall 1939), 102;
Note-Books of Night, p. 35.

"Something about the Author," *Wilson's Christmas Stocking,* p. 19;
Night Thoughts, p. 212.

"Something for My Hungarian Friends," *Holiday Greetings 1966,* pp. [17-18].

"Something for My Italian Friends, *Holiday Greetings 1966,* pp. [11-16].

"Something for my Jewish Friends," *Wilson's Christmas Stocking,* p. 18;
Night Thoughts, p. 211.

"Something for my Russian Friends," *Wilson's Christmas Stocking,* p. 17;
Night Thoughts, pp. 210-211.

"Sonnet," *Wilson's Christmas Stocking,* p. 14;
Night Thoughts, p. 207.

"Sonnets," *Hill School Record,* XXII (May 1913), 234-237.

Contents
    I. "The Professor," p. 234
    II. "From the Window, p. 235
    III. "Parnassus," p. 236
    IV. "Vale," p. 237

"Southampton: November, 1917," *A Book of Princeton Verse II, 1919,* ed. Henry Van Dyke, Morris William Croll, Max-

well Struthers Burt, and James Creese Jr. (Princeton: Princeton University Press, 1919), pp. 18-19;
Poets, Farewell!, p. 63;
Night Thoughts, p. 3.

"Stamford," Night Thoughts, pp. 123-136.

"Stella," Nassau Literary Magazine, LXXI (November 1915), 181;
A Book of Princeton Verse, 1916, ed. Alfred Noyes (Princeton: Princeton University Press, 1916), p. 181;
Nassau Lit, C, No. 3 [1842-1942 centennial issue] (1942), 76.
See also "Swift."

"Stucco and Stone: To J.P.B.," Double-Dealer, IV, No. 21 (September 1922), 123-124. Reprinted as "Stucco and Stone (To J. P. B.)" in Literary Digest, LXXIV, No. 14 (30 September 1922), 30. Reprinted as "Stucco and Stone: To John Peale Bishop" in Poets, Farewell!, pp. 20-22; and Night Thoughts, pp. 14-15.

"Suburban November," A Book of Princeton Verse II, 1919, ed. Henry Van Dyke, Morris William Croll, Maxwell Struthers Burt, and James Creese Jr. (Princeton: Princeton University Press, 1919), p. 138.

"Swift," Nassau Literary Magazine, LXXI (November 1915), 181-182.

Contents
    I. "Stella"
    II. "The Dark Hour"
Reprinted in entirety in A Book of Princeton Verse, 1916, ed. Alfred Noyes (Princeton: Princeton University Press, 1916), pp. 181-182; and Nassau Lit, C, No. 3 [1842-1942 centennial issue] (1942), 76.

"The Tables Turned, or Revenge at Last," New York Tribune, 21 April 1914, p. 8, in col. headed "Conning Tower."

"Tannhäuser, A Poem to Follow Lancelot and Merlin" (by Edw-n Arl-ngt-n R-b-ns-n and EW), Playboy, II, No. 1 (March 1923), 33. Reprinted as "Tannhäuser" in Poets, Farewell!, pp. 55-57; and Night Thoughts, pp. 81-83.

"The Tates," *Wilson's Christmas Stocking,* p. 4;
Night Thoughts, p. 196.

["These funny muffled woods, the rusted stream"] (printed
alone without title), *Note-Books of Night,* p. 26. Reprinted
without title in section entitled "Stamford" in *Night
Thoughts,* p. 125.

["This blue world with its wide high sky of islands"] (printed
without title in sequence entitled "Sleeping and Waking"),
Poetry, XLVII (February 1936), 243. Reprinted alone
without title in *Note-Books of Night,* p. 15; and *Twentieth-
Century American Poetry,* ed. Conrad Aiken, in The Mod-
ern Library (New York: Modern Library, 1944), p. 295.
Reprinted without title in section entitled "Elegies and
Wakeful Nights" in *Night Thoughts,* p. 105.

"Three Reliques of Ancient Western Poetry," printed as the
book *Three Reliques of Ancient Western Poetry.* Reprinted as "Three Reliques of Ancient Western Poetry
Collected from the Ruins of the Twentieth Century, 1951"
in *Night Thoughts,* pp. 179-192.

"Three Women," *Poetry,* LV (January 1940), 182-185.

    Contents
      I. "Home to Town: Two Highballs"
          "First Highball"
          "Second Highball"
      II. "November Ride"
      III. ["My dear, you burn with bright green eyes"]

"Three Women Remembered in Absence," *Poets, Farewell!,*
pp. 1-6.

"To a Friend Going Abroad," *Scribner's Magazine,* LXXIX
(March 1926), 274. Reprinted as "To a Painter Going
Abroad" in *Poets, Farewell!,* pp. 1-2; and *Night Thoughts,*
p. 13.

"To a Painter Going Abroad." See "To a Friend Going
Abroad."

"To a Young Girl (Indicted for Murder)," *Saturday Review
of Literature,* II (20 March 1926), 647. Reprinted as "A
Young Girl Indicted for Murder" in *Poets, Farewell!,* pp.

9-10; *Night Thoughts,* pp. 31-32; and *Edmund Wilson,* by Charles P[aul] Frank, No. 152 in Twayne's United States Authors Series, ser. ed. Sylvia E. Bowman (New York: Twayne Publishers, 1970), pp. 78-79.

"To an Actress," *Poets, Farewell!,* pp. 18-19;
Night Thoughts, pp. 42-43.

"A Train Out of the Terminal," *Poets, Farewell!,* p. 13;
Night Thoughts, p. 41.

"The Trains," *New Yorker,* XLIII, No. 12 (13 May 1967), 55-56;
Prelude, pp. 176-178.

"Translations," *Poets, Farewell!,* pp. 43-50;
Night Thoughts, pp. 57-64.

"Trèves, December, 1918," *New Yorker,* XLIII, No. 12 (13 May 1967), 120;
Prelude, pp. 234-235.

"27, rue de Fleurus," *Christmas Delirium,* p. 12;
Night Thoughts, p. 229.

"Two New England Girls," *Christmas Delirium,* p. 10;
Night Thoughts, p. 228.

"Vale." See "Sonnets."

"Valentine Echoes," *Hill School Record,* XXI (February 1912), 143-149. An explanation on p. 143 reads: "While communing (as we frequently do) with the shades, the other night, we were accosted by the souls of Messrs. Robert Browning and Richard Barham who dictated to us a couple of seasonable and characteristic poems . . . on the old legend of St. Valentine. Dr. Barham composed a lay of St. Valentine, quite in his old style, and Mr. Browning communicated a Dramatic Monologue. We are much indebted to these two distinguished contributors to The Record."

Contents
I. "The Lay of St. Valentine: An Ingoldsly Legend," pp. 143-147
II. "Valentine's Apology, Rome, 270 A.D.," pp. 148-149

"Valentine's Apology, Rome, 270 A.D." See "Valentine Echoes."

"Le Violon d'Ingres de Sirine," *Wilson's Christmas Stocking,*
p. 17;
Night Thoughts, p. 210.

"The Voice (On a Friend in a Sanitarium)," *New Yorker,* X,
No. 50 (26 January 1935), 19. Reprinted as "The Voice:
On a Friend in a Sanitarium" in *Note-Books of Night,*
p. 14; *Twentieth-Century American Poetry,* ed. Conrad
Aiken, in The Modern Library (New York: Modern Library, 1944), pp. 294-295; and *Night Thoughts,* p. 104.
See also "Elegies for a Passing World."

"The Walkers," *Wilson's Christmas Stocking,* p. 5;
Night Thoughts, p. 197.

["Well, so this is Paris!"]. See "Princeton."

"When All the Young Were Dying" (printed without title as
["When all the young were dying"] in section entitled
"Poets, Farewell!: 1929"), *Poets, Farewell!,* pp. 73-74;
Night Thoughts, pp. 67-68.

Reprinted alone with title in *An Anthology of American
Poetry: Lyric America, 1630-1930,* ed. Alfred Kreymborg
(New York: Tudor Publishing Company, 1930), pp.
562-563, and New and Rev. Ed. with supplement 1930-
1935 (New York: Tudor Publishing Company, 1935),
pp. 562-563; and 2nd and rev. ed., entitled *An Anthology
of American Poetry: Lyric America, 1630-1941* (New
York: Tudor Publishing Company, 1941), pp. 562-563;
and *Lyric America: An Anthology of American Poetry*
(*1630-1930*), ed. Alfred Kreymborg, 1st ed. (New York:
Coward McCann, 1930), pp. 562-563, and 2nd rev. ed.,
entitled *An Anthology of American Poetry: Lyric America, 1630-1941* (New York: Tudor Publishing Company,
1941), pp. 562-563.

"Whistler at Battersea," *Nassau Literary Magazine,* LXX
(April 1914), 18-19.

"The White Sand," printed as the book *White Sand.* Reprinted as "The White Sand: 1950" in *Night Thoughts*, pp. 263-274. Reprinted with editor's headnote in *New Poems by American Poets*, ed. Rolfe Humphries (New York: Ballantine Books, 1953), pp. 168-174.

"The Whites," *Wilson's Christmas Stocking*, p. 5; *Night Thoughts*, p. 197.

"Wilson's Night Thoughts," *New Yorker*, X , No. 5 (17 March 1934), 21.

> *Contents*
>   I. "The Extravert [*sic*] of Walden Pond"
> II. "Bishop Praxed's Apology, or the Art of Thinking in Poetry, or A Gospel of Falsity for an Age of Doubt"
> III. "Disloyal Lines to an Alumnus"

" 'Within the Rim,' " *Christmas Delirium*, p. 10; *Night Thoughts*, p. 228.

"The Woman, the War Veteran and the Bear," *Note-Books of Night*, pp. 51-55; *Night Thoughts*, pp. 113-117.

"Words across the Channel," *New Yorker*, XXV, No. 36 (29 October 1949), 34; *Wilson's Christmas Stocking*, p. 12; *Night Thoughts*, pp. 205-206.

"A Young German." See "Epitaph for a Young German."

"A Young Girl Indicted for Murder." See "To a Young Girl (Indicted for Murder)."

"The Young Lady Reads," *Hill School Record*," XXI (December 1911), 80-81. An able adaptation of a stanzaic pattern from Hood in which EW in the person of a young lass raps Scott as a novelist.

A. Translations of Wilson's Works

1. Translations of Wilson's Books

DANISH

Skriftrullerne fra Det døde Hav (Scrolls from the Dead Sea),
trans. H. C. Huus. København: Rosenkilde og Bagger,
1956.

Erindringer fra Hecate County (Memoirs of Hecate County),
trans. Mogens Boisen. København: Glydenhal, 1967.

DUTCH

De Boekrollen van de Dode Zee (Scrolls from the Dead Sea),
trans. I. S. Herschberg, with forward by M[artinus] A[dri-
anus] Beek. Amsterdam: De Bezige Bij, 1956.

Reis naar de Revolutie (To the Finland Station), trans. P. H.
W. C. Rommers, No. 11 in Sterrenserrie. Hilversum, The
Netherlands: C. Deboer jr., Paul Brand, 1963.

De Vrouw met het gouden Haar (Memoirs of Hecate
County), trans. Else Hoog. Amsterdam: Arbeiderspers,
1966.

FRENCH

La gare de Finlande: Etude sur la manière d'écire et de vivre
l'histoire (To the Finland Station), trans. with notes by
Georgette Camille. Paris: Stock, 1965.

Mémoires du Comté d'Hecate (*Memoirs of Hecate County*), trans. Bruno Vercier. Paris: Julliard, 1966.

GERMAN

"Die Handschriften vom Toten Meer: Neue Quellen des Bibeltextes" (*Scrolls from the Dead Sea*), trans. Hermann Stresan, *Monat: Internationale Zeitschrift für Politik und geistiges Leben* (Frankfurt), VII, No. 86 (November 1955), 13-27; No. 87 (December 1955), 46-55; concluded as "Der Fund am Toten Meer: Neue Handschriften des Alten Testamento; Schuss," trans. Hermann Stresan, *Monat: Internationale Zeitschrift für Politik und geistiges Leben* (Frankfurt), VIII, No. 88 (January 1956), 46-62.

Die Schriftrollen vom Toten Meer (*Scrolls from the Dead Sea*), trans. Josephine Ewers. München: M. Winkler, 1956.

Der Weg nach Petersburg (*Europas Revolutionäre Tradition und die Enstehung des Sozialismus*) (*To the Finland Station*), trans. Ehrenfried Klauer and Hans Stern. München: Rütten & Loening Verlag, 1963.

Erinnerungen an Hekates Land (*Memoirs of Hecate County*), trans. Susanna Rademacher. Reinbeck bei Hamburg: R. Rowohlt, 1965.

HEBREW

El ha-Tahanah ha-Finlandit (*To the Finland Station*), trans. M. Atar. Tel-Aviv: Am Oved, 1955.

Megilot yam ha-Melah (*Scrolls from the Dead Sea* abridged), trans. Nahman Ben-Ami. Tel-Aviv: Al ha-mishmar, 1956.

ICELANDIC

Handritin frá Dauðahafi (*Scrolls from the Dead Sea*), trans. Haraldur Jóhannsson. Akranes, Iceland: Morkinskinna (printed in Reykjavík), 1957.

ITALIAN

Biographia di un'idea (*To the Finland Station*), trans. Alberto Tedeschi. Milano: Rizzoli, 1949.

Fino alla stazione di Finlandia: Interpreti e arteficia della storia (*Biografia di un'idea*), 2nd Ed. of *Biografia di un'idea* (*To the Finland Station*), trans. Alberto Tedeschi, No. 16 in Cultura e società. Roma: Opere Nuove (Spoleto: Panetto e Petrelli), 1960. New edition.

La ferita e l'arco: Sette studi di letteratura (*Wound and the Bow*), trans. Nemi d'Agostino. Milano: A. Garzanti, 1956.

I manoscritti del Mar Morto (*Scrolls from the Dead Sea*), trans. Bruno Tasso. Torino: Giulio Einaudi (L. Demaestri), 1958.

Signed Reviews

Donini, Abrogio. *Rinascita: Rassegna di politica e di cultura italiana* (Roma), XV (April 1958), 285-286.

Subilia, Vittorio. *Protestantesimo: Rivista trimestrale pubblicata sotto gli auspici della Facoltà valdese di teologia* (Roma), XIII, No. 4 (1958), 210-212.

Tansini, Giorgio. *Humanitas: Rivista mensile di cultura* (Brescia, Italy), XIII (Aprile 1958), 317-318.

Gli ultimi fuochi (*Last Tycoon*), trans. Bruno Oddera, with a preface by Fernando Pivano. Milano-Verona: A. Mondadori, 1959.

Fino alla stazione di Finlandia: Interpreti e arteficia della storia (*Biografia di un'idea*) (1960). See *Biographia di un'idea* (1949).

L'Età del Jazz e altri scritti (*Crack-Up*), trans. Domenico Tarizzo, with a preface by Elémire Zolla, No. 29 in La cultura: Storia, critica, testi. Milano: Il Saggiatore (Verona: A. Mondadori), 1960.

L'Età del Jazz e altri scritti (*Crack-Up*), trans. Domenico Tarizzo, with a preface by Elémire Zolla, No. 46 in I gabbiani. Milano: Il Saggiatore (Verona: A. Mondadori), 1966. Reissue.

Dovuto agli Irochesi, con un saggio di Joseph Mitchell (*Apologies to the Iroquois*), trans. Marisa Bulgheroni and Luciana Bulgheroni, Vol. LIX in La cultura. Milano: Il Saggiatore (Verona: A. Mondadori), 1962.

Il castello di Axel: Studio sugli sviluppi del simbolismo tra il 1870 e il 1930 (*Axel's Castle*), trans. Marisa Bulgheroni and Luciana Bulgheroni, Vol. C in La cultura. Milano: Il Saggiatore (Bologna: S.T.E.B.), 1965.

JAPANESE

Axel no shiro (*Axel's Castle*), trans. Saburô Ônuki. Tokyo: Kadokawa Shoten, 1953.

Kimpatsu no purinsesu (*Memoirs of Hecate County*), trans. Yasuo Ôkubo and Minora Hashiguchi. Tokyo: Rokkô Shuppan-bu, 1961.

A. P. Chekhov [title in Russian characters] (*Peasants and Other Stories*), no translator given. N.p., n.d. (1966?).

KOREAN

Geundaehyeogmyeongsasangsa (*To the Finland Station*), trans. Bong-sig Gang. Seoul: Eulyumunhwasa, 1962.

NORWEGIAN

Skriftene fra Dodehavet (*Scrolls from the Dead Sea*), trans. Louise Jor and Finn Jor. Oslo: Dreyers Forlag, 1957.

POLISH

Odkrycia nad Morzem Martwym (*Scrolls from the Dead Sea*), trans. Teresa Świécka. Warsawa: Ksiaźka i Wiedza, 1963.

PORTUGUESE

Raizes da criacão literária (*Wound and the Bow*), trans. Edilson Alkmim Cunha, in Colecão mimesis. Rio de Janeiro: Lidador, 1965.

O castelo de Axel (*Axel's Castle*), trans. José Paulo Paes. São Paulo: Editôra Cultrix L.T.D.A., 1967.

SERBO-CROATIAN

Akeselov zamak: Ili o simbolizmu (*Axel's Castle*), trans. Olga Humo, in Biblioteka éseji i studije. Novi Sad: Kultura Beograd, 1964.

SPANISH

Los rollos del Mar Muerto: El descubrimiento de los manuscritos biblicos (Scrolls from the Dead Sea), trans. Emma S. Speratti Piñero, No. 124 in Breviarios. México [City] and Buenos Aires: Fondo de Cultura Económica, 1956.

Los rollos del Mar Muerto: El descubrimiento de los manuscritos biblicos (Scrolls from the Dead Sea), trans. Emma S. Speratti Piñero, No. 124 in Breviarios. México [City] and Buenos Aires: Fondo de Cultura Económica, 1966. Reissue.

Literatura y sociedad (Triple Thinkers: Twelve Essays), trans. Héctor Vaccaro. Buenos Aires: Sur, 1957.

SWEDISH

Skriftrullarna vid Döda havet (Scrolls from the Dead Sea), trans. Kajsa Rootzén and Lily Vallqvist. Stockholm: Strömberg, 1956.

Minnen från Hecate County (Memoirs of Hecate County), trans. Thorsten Jonsson. Stockholm: PAN/Norstedt (Ny utg.), 1967.

TURKIC

Lenin Petrogivad'da (To the Finland Station), trans. Can Yücel. İstanbul: Agaoglu Yayınevï, 1967.

2. Foreign Collections

HUNGARIAN

Muvészvilág: Drámák (plays), trans. Péter Nagy, No. 27 in Modern Könyvtár. Budapest: Európa Könyvkiadó, 1959.

Contents

"A szoba, az ital meg a szendvicsek" ("This Room and This Gin and These Sandwiches"), pp. [5-135]
"Beppo és Betty" ("Beppo and Beth"), pp. [137-273]

Az élet jelei tanulmányok, cikkek (essays), trans. Szilágyi Tibor and Zubreczky György, with notes in Hungarian by Szegedi-Maszák Mihály ("Jegyzetek," pp. 313-329), No. 167 in Modern Könyvtár. Budapest: Európa Könyvkiadó (Debrecen: Alfoldi Nyomda), [1969]. Paperback.

Contents (by EW)

"Philoktétész: A seb és az íj" ("Philoctetes: The Wound and the Bow"), trans. Szilágyi Tibor, pp. 5-26

"Dokumentumok Marquis de Sade-ról" ("The Documents on the Marquis de Sade"), trans. Zubreczky György, pp. 27-78

"Hommage à Pushkin Jevgenyij Anyegin" ("Evgeni Onegin"), trans. Szilágyi Tibor, pp. 79-102

"Flaubert és a politika" ("The Politics of Flaubert"), trans. Szilágyi Tibor, pp. 103-124

"Ambrose Bierce a Bagoly-folyó hídjan" ("Ambrose Bierce on the Owl Creek Bridge"), trans. Szilágyi Tibor, pp. 125-144

"Henry James kettös értelmezhetösége" ("The Ambiguity of Henry James"), trans. Szilágyi Tibor, pp. 145-204

"H. C. Earwicker álma" ("The Dream of H. C. Earwicker," version appearing in Galaxy Books reissue of *Wound and the Bow*), trans. Szilágyi Tibor, pp. 205-232

"Haldoklik-e a vers mint technika" ("Is Verse a Dying Technique?"), trans. Szilágyi Tibor, pp. 233-254

"Az élet jelei: Lady Chatterley szeretöje" (Signs of Life: *Lady Chatterley's Lover*"), trans. Zubreczky György, pp. 255-260

"Thornton Wilder" ("Thornton Wilder"), trans. Zubreczky György, pp. 261-268

"Dahlberg, Dos Passos és Wilder" ("Dahlberg, Dos Passos and Wilder"), trans. Zubreczky György, pp. 269-278

"'Sohase szabadkozz, sohase magyarázkodj!' Evelyn Waugh müveszete" ("'Never Apologize, Never Explain': The Art of Evelyn Waugh"), trans. Zubreczky György, pp. 279-286

"Somerset Maugham apoteózisa" ("The Apotheosis of Somerset Maugham"), trans. Zubreczky György, pp. 287-296

"William Faulkner válasza a polgarjogi programra" ("William Faulkner's Reply to the Civil-Rights Program"), trans. Zubrecky [sic, Zubreczky] György, pp. 297-308

ITALIAN

Saggi letterari 1920-1950 (essays trans. from *Shores of Light* and *Classics and Commercials*), trans. Giovanni Giudici and Giovanni Galtieri, in Collezione saggi. Milano: Garzanti, 1967.

Contents

"F. Scott Fitzgerald" ("F. Scott Fitzgerald"), trans. Giovanni Galtieri, pp. 5-12

"Il mosaico di Ezra Pound" ("Ezra Pound's Patchwork"), trans. Giovanni Galtieri, pp. 13-16

"«Many Marriages»" di Sherwood Anderson" ("Sherwood Anderson's *Many Marriages*"), trans. Giovanni Galtieri, pp. 17-19

"John Steinbeck" ("John Steinbeck"), pp. 171-180

"Davanti al Pacifico" ("Facing the Pacific"), pp. 180-185

"Poscritto" ("Postscript"), pp. 185-189

"Una guida a «Finnegans Wake»" ("A Guide to *Finnegans Wake*"), trans. Giovanni Giudici, pp. 190-196

"Un lungo discorso su Jane Austen" ("A Long Talk about Jane Austen"), trans. Giovanni Giudici, pp. 197-203

"Aldous Huxley nel mondo al di là del tempo" ("Aldous Huxley in the World Beyond Time"), trans Giovanni Galtieri, pp. 204-208

"Perchè si leggono i romanzi polizieschi?" ("Why Do People Read Detective Stories?"), trans. Giovanni Galtieri, pp. 209-214

"Ancora sui romanzi polizieschi" ("Who Cares Who Killed Roger Ackroyd?"), trans. Giovanni Galtieri, pp. 215-221

"Splendori e miserie di Evelyn Waugh" ("Splendors and Miseries of Evelyn Waugh"), trans. Giovanni Galtieri, pp. 222-227

"Imboscata a un best-seller" ("Ambushing a Best-Seller"), trans. Giovanni Galtieri, pp. 228-234

"Oscar Wilde: la ricerca del tragico" ("Oscar Wilde: 'One Must Always Seek What Is Most Tragic' "), trans. Giovanni Giudici, pp. 235-245

"Un vecchio amico di famiglia: Thackeray" ("An Old Friend of the Family: Thackeray"), trans. Giovanni Giudici, pp. 246-255

"Gilbert senza Sullivan" ("Gilbert Without Sullivan"), trans. Giovanni Galtieri, pp. 256-261

"Emily Post e i libri di galateo" ("Books of Etiquette and Emily Post"), trans. Giovanni Galtieri, pp. 262-271

"Un patere contrario su Kafka" ("A Dissenting Opinion on Kafka"), trans. Giovanni Galtieri, pp. 272-279

"I cristalli musicali di Peacock" ("The Musical Glasses of Peacock"), trans. Giovanni Galtieri, pp. 280-286

"Il modello di Nataša" ("The Original of Tolstoy's Natasha"), trans. Giovanni Giudici, pp. 287-295

"In memoria di Octave Mirbeau" ("In Memory of Octave Mirbeau"), trans. Giovanni Giudici, pp. 296-308

"Rileggendo Ronald Firbank" ("A Revival of Ronald Firbank"), trans. Giovanni Galtieri, pp. 309-323

3. Translations of Wilson's Essays
(See also the titles listed in Foreign Collections.)

FRENCH

"Wilson: Abraham Lincoln" ("Abraham Lincoln: The Union as Religious Mysticism"), trans. François Vignier, *Profils*

(French ed. of *Perspectives USA*), Numéro 4 (juillet 1953), pp. 171-189.

"The Letters of Theodore Roosevelt" ("The Pre-Presidential T. R."), trans. C. B., *Profils* (French ed. of *Perspectives USA*), Numéro 5 (octobre 1953), pp. 164-175.

"Poe critique littéraire" ("Poe as a Literary Critic"), trans. [Annette Richard], *Configuration critique de Edgar Allan Poe*, ed. Claude Richard, No. 193-198 in *La revue des lettres modernes*, ser. ed. Michel J. Minard (Paris: Minard, 1969), pp. 15-21.

GERMAN

"Abraham Lincoln: Die Union als religiöser Mystizismus" ("Abraham Lincoln: The Union as Religious Mysticism"), trans. Walter Hasenclever, *Perspektiven: Musiik, Literatur, Kunst* (German ed. of *Perspectives USA*), Heft 4 (August 1953), pp. 167-184.

"Theodore Roosevelts Briefe" ("The Pre-Presidential T. R."), trans. Joachim G. Leithaüsen, *Perspektiven: Musik, Literatur, Kunst* (German ed. of *Perspectives USA*), Heft 5 (November 1953), pp. 151-161.

"Die Handschriften Vom Toten Meer: Neye Quellen des Bibeltextes" ("The Scrolls from the Dead Sea"). See in Translations of Wilson's Books, German.

ITALIAN

"T.L. Peacock" ("The Musical Glasses of Peacock"), trans. Attilio Bertolucci, *L'abbazia degli incubi* (*Nightmare Abbey*), by Thomas Love Peacock, trans. Attilio Bertolucci, No. 3 in Biblioteca Palatina (Parma: Ugo Guanda Editore, 1951), pp. v-x.

"Giustizia per Edith Wharton" ("Justice to Edith Wharton"), translator not given, *Paragone: Mensile di arte figurativa e letteratura* (Firenze), II, No. 22 (Ottobre 1951), 15-26.

"Abraham Lincoln" ("Abraham Lincoln: The Union as Religious Mysticism"), trans. Giacomo Vertova, *Prospetti:*

Arte, letteratura, musica (Italian ed. of *Perspectives USA*), Quarto Numero (Estate 1953), pp. 194-214.

"The Letters of Theodore Roosevelt Vol. I + II, *The Years of Preparation, 1868-1898*" ("The Pre-Presidential T. R."), trans. Anna Maria Gadda-Conti, *Prospetti: Arte, letteratura, musica* (Italian ed. of *Perspectives USA*), Quinto Numero (Autunno 1953), pp. 182-192.

"James Joyce" ("James Joyce"), trans. Antonio Amato, *Antologia della critica Americana del Novecento*, ed. Morton Dauwen Zabel, Vol. II, trans. Amato *et al.*, in Nuovo Mondo (Roma: Ediz. di Storia e Letteratura, 1961), pp. 13-49.

"T. S. Eliot" ("T. S. Eliot"), trans. Antonio Amato, *Antologia della critica Americana del Novecento*, ed. Morton Dauwen Zabel, Vol. II, trans. Amato *et al.*, in Nuovo Mondo (Roma: Ediz. di Storia e Letteratura, 1961), pp. 50-82.

"Leggenda e simbolo nel 'Dottor Zivago'" ("Legend and Symbol in *Doctor Zhivago*"), trans. Adele Biagi, *Tempo presente* (Roma), V (February-March 1960), 129-142.

Ivan Turgheniev ("Turgenev and the Life-Giving Drop"), trans. Nina Ruffini, No. 68 in *Biblioteca delle Silerchie* (Milano: Il Saggiatore [E. Milli], agosto 1961).

"Introduzione" ("Foreword" [to "A Season in the Life of Emmanuel," by Marie-Claire Blais]), *Una stagione nella vita di Emmanuele (Une saison dans la vie d'Emmanuel: Roman)*, by Marie-Claire Blais, trans. Ginevra Bompiani (Milano: Bompiani, 1967), pp. 7-10.

"Il sogno di H. C. Earwicker" ("The Dream of H. C. Earwicker" [long essay]), trans. Nemi D'agostino, *Introduzione a Joyce*, Vol. I in *Tutte le opere di James Joyce*, ed. Giacomo Debenedetti (Milano: A. Mondadori [Verona: A. Mondadori], 1967), pp. 1187-1219.

"Il Kipling che nessuno ha letto" ("The Kipling That Nobody Read"), *Kim, Capitani coraggiosi, Racconti: La porta dei cento dolori, La storia di Muhammed Din, Lispeth,*

Oltre i limiti, Sulla montagna di Greenhow, Una notizia sensazionale, Il dongiovanni del Tyrone regiment, I figli dello zodiaco, La più bella storia del mondo, by Rudyard Kipling, trans. Claudio Egidio Mattei, Anna M[aria] Speckel, and Paulo Petroni, No. 5 in I grandi secoli (Roma: G. Casini [Torino: Pozzo-Salvati-Gros Monti], 1967), pp. ix-xxxvi.

NORWEGIAN

"Etterord" ("Foreword" [to "A Season in the Life of Emmanuel," by Marie-Claire Blais]), *Et halvt år av Emmanuels liv (Une saison dans la vie d'Emmanuel: Roman),* by Marie-Claire Blais, trans. Tryggve Norum (Oslo: J.W. Cappelens forlag [printed by Reistad & sønn], 1967), no page numbers for "Etterord," which appears in position of a postscript.

POLISH

"Polityka u Flauberta" ("Flaubert's Politics"), trans. Halina Carroll-Najder, *Tematy* (Nowy Jork [Wilton, Connecticut]: Perspectives in Culture), Rok V, Nr. 18 (Summer 1965), pp. 22-38.

RUSSIAN

"Pis'mo sovetskim chitateliam o Kheminguee" ("Letter to the Russians about Hemingway"), translator not given, *Internatsional'naia literatura,* IX, No. 2 (1936), 151-153. See also "Ot redaktsii" in Items about Wilson.

SPANISH

"El rol de Trotsky in la historia" ("Trotsky Identifies History with Himself" in part), translator not given, *Babel: Revista de arte y critica* (ed. Enrique Espinoza; Editora Universitaria de Santiago de Chile), Año XX, Vol. II (enero-abril 1941), 171-175.

"Prologo" ("Foreword" [to "A Season in the Life of Emmanuel," by Marie-Claire Blais]), *Una estacion en la vida de Emmanuel (Une saison dans la vie d'Emmanuel: Roman),* by Marie-Claire Blais, trans. Adolfo A. de Alba (México [City]: Editorial Diana S.A., 1967), pp. 5-9.

4. Translation of a Wilson Dialogue

SPANISH

"Una entrevista con Edmund Wilson" ("An Interview with Edmund Wilson"), trans. Hernanda Valenzia Goelkel, *Eco: Revista de la cultura de occidente* (Bogotá, Colombia), VI (marzo 1963), 454-471.

5. Translation of a Wilson Story

HEBREW

"Mashich Be'lel Haseder" ("The Messiah at the Seder: A Story"), trans. Shmuel Schnitzer, *Ma'ariv* (Tel-Aviv evening newspaper), 15 April 1957, Passover literary supplement, pp. 3-4.

B.   *Translations by Wilson*

Chekhov, Anton Pavlovich. "Three Years" (story, partially trans. EW), *Peasants and Other Stories*, comp. EW, pp. 249-288.

Du Camp, Maxime. Letter (Croisset, [July 1852]) to Gustave Flaubert, trans. EW in essay entitled "Some Letters After 1848," *New Republic*, XCVIII (8 February 1939), 22-23.

["Ekh, sharaban, da, sharaban"] (Russian popular song, trans. EW without title as [" 'Ah, charabanc, yes, charabanc"] in essay entitled "Russian Idyls"), *New Republic*, LXXXVI (29 April 1936), 340. Reprinted without title as [" 'Ah, charabanc, yes, charabanc"] in essay entitled "On the Margin of Moscow" in section called "U.S.S.R., May-October,

1935" in *Travels in Two Democracies,* p. 233. Reprinted without title as ["Ah, charabanc, yes, charabanc"] in same essay in section called "Soviet Russia (1935)" in *Red, Black, Blond and Olive,* p. 254. Reprinted without title as [" 'Ah, charabanc, yes, charabanc"] in longer essay entitled "On the Margin of Moscow" in *Discovery of Europe: The Story of American Experience in the Old World,* ed. Philip Rahv (Boston: Houghton Mifflin Company [Cambridge, Massachusetts: Riverside Press], 1947), p. 600.

Engels, Friedrich. Letter (13 February 1951) to Karl Marx, trans. EW in essay entitled "Some Letters After 1848," *New Republic,* XCVIII (8 February 1939), 21-22. Reprinted as "Engels to Marx, February 13, 1851" (same as "Appendix C") in "Appendices" in *To the Finland Station* (except Anchor Books reissues), pp. 487-489.

Flaubert, Gustave. Letter (Croisset, [26 June] 1852) to Maxime du Camp, trans. EW in essay entitled "Some Letters After 1848," *New Republic,* XCVIII (8 February 1939), 22.

Housman, A. E. "Meo sodali, M. I. Jackson, harum literarum contemptori" (poem, trans. EW as "Dedication to a Book: A. E. Housman: Signa pruinosae variantia luce cavernas"), *Bookman,* LXVI (October 1927), 162. Reprinted as "Dedication for a Book" in *Poets, Farewell!,"* pp. 47-48; *Housman: 1897-1936,* by Grant Richards (Oxford, England: Oxford University Press, Humphrey Milford, 1941, 1942), pp. 442-443; and *Night Thoughts,* pp. 61-62.

Marshák, Samuil Yakovlevich. "Stripes and Whiskers" (poem, trans. EW), *Travels in Two Democracies,* pp. 306-310. Trans. as "Whiskers and Stripes" in *Red, Black, Blond and Olive,* pp. 359-363.

"Ot redaktsii" (editorial rejoinder, trans. EW without title as part of essay entitled "Letter to the Russians about Hemingway"), *Shores of Light,* pp. 626-629;
Literary Chronicle: 1920-1950, pp. 203-206.
See also "Pis'mo sovetskim chitateliam o Kheminguee" in Translations of Wilson's Works, Part 3 (Translations of

Wilson's Essays), Russian, and "Ot redaktsii" in Items about Wilson.

Pushkin, Aleksandr. "The Bronze Horseman: A Petersburg Tale" (story, trans. EW), *New Republic*, XCIII (26 January 1938), 332-334;
Triple Thinkers: Ten Essays, pp. 72-82, and *Triple Thinkers: Twelve Essays*, pp. 52-59.

Renan, Ernest. "Le jour de l'an 1886," *Drames philosophiques* (trans. EW as "New Year's Day, 1886—A Prologue in Heaven: A Fantastic Dissertation Upon Society, by the French Ironist Whose Centenary is Being Celebrated"), *Vanity Fair*, XXI, No. 3 (November 1923), 64, 112, 114.

Tzara, Tristan. "Memoirs of Dadaism by Tristan Tzara" (same as "Appendix II"), trans. EW, *Axel's Castle*, pp. 304-312.

Verlaine, Paul. ["Le ciel"] (poem, trans. EW without title and with some prose comment as "Essay with Translation: The Fabric of Paul Verlaine With a Translation of One of his Poems by Eric Elberson Quoits" in essay entitled "Holocaust: The New Devastation" [by EW and John Peale Bishop]), *Playboy*, II, No. 1 (March 1923), 43. The translation is satirical rather than exact.

A. General Miscellanea

"Appendices," *To the Finland Station* (except Anchor Books reissues), pp. 476-490.

"Appendix I." See "Three Versions of a Passage from James Joyce's New Novel."

"An Augustan Trilogy," *Hill School Record*, XXI (February 1912), 124-130.

Contents
    I. "That Long Entertaining Narrative" (story)
    II. "That Bright Little Play" (dialogue)
    III. "That Readable and Interesting Work of Fiction" (story)

"Correspondence with Fitzgerald and Wilson," ed. EW, *The Papers of Christian Gauss*, book ed. Katherine Gauss Jackson and Hiram Haydn (New York: Random House, 1957), pp. 224-352. EW edited his letters to Gauss and those of Gauss to EW. F. Scott Fitzgerald's correspondence with Gauss, pp. 211-223, was not edited by EW.

"Greenwich Village at the End of the Twenties," *Shores of Light*, pp. 357-366.

"The Jews," *Piece of My Mind*, pp. 83-136.

"Obscurity: Observations and Aphorisms," by John Peale Bishop, ed. EW, *Western Review*, XII (Winter 1948), 72-79. Reprinted as "Obscurity" in *Collected Essays of John Peale Bishop*, pp. 369-379.

"Three Versions of a Passage from James Joyce's New Novel" (same as "Appendix I"), comp. EW, *Axel's Castle*, pp. 301-303.

B.   *Editorial Comment by Wilson*

New Republic, LI (22 June 1927), 126;
  Shores of Light, pp. 210-211.

New Republic, LXII (16 April 1930), 247.

New Republic (by EW and Malcolm Cowley), LXII (16 April 1930), 248.

New Republic, LXVII (3 June 1931), 75.

New Republic, XCVIII (8 March 1939), 130-131.

New Republic, CIII (11 November 1940), 664.

C.   *Periodicals Edited by Wilson*

Hill School Record. EW was an Editor (not Editor-in-Chief) of Vol. XX, No. 2 (December 1910), through No. 7 (May 1911); and Exchange Editor of Vol. XX, No. 8 (June 1911), through Vol. XXI, No. 8 (May 1912).

Nassau Literary Magazine. EW served on the editorial staff for Vols. LXIX and LXX (April 1913 through March 1915) and was Managing Editor of Vols. LXXI and LXXII (April 1915 through March 1917).

Evening Sun (New York). EW served as a staff reporter for this newspaper from about June 1916 to about August 1917.

Vanity Fair. EW was Managing Editor of Vol. XIX, No. 1 (September 1922), through Vol. XX, No. 4 (June 1923).

Playboy. EW served on the Advisory Board for Vol. II, No. 1 (March 1923), and on the Advisory Board for *Playboy: A Portfolio of Art and Satire,* old ser. No. 9 (July 1924).

New Republic. EW was a Contributing Editor of Vol. XLV, No. 573 (25 November 1925), through Vol. XLVIII, No. 622 (3 November 1926); an Editor of Vol. XLVIII, No. 623 (10 November 1926), through Vol. LXVIII, No. 874 (2 September 1931); and the Editor of Vol. CIV, No. 16 (21 April 1941), Part 2 ("American Writing: 1941"), pp. 545-580 (see also ["The second two decades of the century"] in Essays).

New Yorker. EW was the regular book reviewer for Vol. XIX, No. 46 (1 January 1944), until about Vol. XXIII, No. 45 (27 December 1947). The highest concentration of EW's reviews in *New Yorker* was during 1944; his contributions to this periodical tapered off after 1947, although he contributed more or less irregularly to the magazine for the next 24 years.

D.   Drawings by Wilson

Christmas Delirium, p. 7 (with poem "From the Geckese");
Night Thoughts, p. 225.

Christmas Delirium, p. 9 (with poem "From the Geckese");
Night Thoughts, p. 227.

Christmas Delirium, p. 15 (opposite poem ["History as a
Crystalline Sea-Anemone"]);
Night Thoughts, p. 231.

Christmas Delirium, p. 29 (opposite poem ["Gimme the gimmick, Gustave!"]);
Night Thoughts, p. 247.

Christmas Delirium, p. 31 (opposite story ["He consulted a
typical timing guide"]);
Night Thoughts, p. 249.

Christmas Delirium, p. 33 (opposite story ["Looking out on
the high chalkbound cliffs"]);
Night Thoughts, p. 251.

Christmas Delirium, p. 42 (with caption "Superrat");
Night Thoughts, p. 261.

Holiday Greetings 1966, p. [5] (with poem "Merry Monsters").

Holiday Greetings 1966, p. [7] (with poem "Merry Monsters").

Holiday Greetings 1966, p. [9] (with poem "Merry Monsters").

Holiday Greetings 1966, p. [13] (with poem "Something for
My Italian Friends").

Holiday Greetings 1966, p. [15] (with poem "Something for
My Italian Friends").

Chicago, University of, Library
The *Poetry Magazine* Collection contains 1 telegram and several poems, letters, and postcards. The M.D. Zabel Collection includes at least two poems plus several letters and postcards. The J.U. Neff Collection contains 3 letters about EW, but none by him.

Cornell University Library, Ithaca, New York
The Department of Rare Books holds 1 letter to Margaret Bishop, 1 copy of a letter to Theodore Dreiser, 3 letters to Robert Elias, and 1 letter to Wyndham Lewis. The library also holds letters by Theodore Dreiser, Robert Elias, and Wyndham Lewis to EW.

Harvard University Houghton Library
The Houghton Reading Room holds 2 letters to William Stanley Braithewaite, 2 letters to Mark Antony DeWolfe Howe, 3 letters to Alexander Woollcott, 2 letters to M.A.D. Howe, and 1 letter from M.A.D. Howe to EW.

Haverford College Library, Haverford, Pennsylvania
The Quaker Collection contains 1 letter to John A. Lester Jr.

Indiana University Lilly Library, Bloomington
The papers of Mrs. Mary Craig Kimbrough Sinclair con-

tain one letter by EW. The papers of Upton Beall Sinclair include 1 telegram and at least 11 letters by EW.

New York Public Library Manuscript Division
The Edmund Wilson Folder in Miscellaneous Papers contains 1 letter to Richard Braun and 1 letter to Gustavus Swift Paine. The Ralph Thompson Papers contain 1 letter to John Chamberlain.

New York, State University of, Libraries, Buffalo
The Poetry Collection contains a letter to James Joyce and a manuscript of the poem "The White Sand."

Newberry Library, Chicago
This large collection contains 15 letters to Sherwood Anderson, 8 letters to Floyd Dell, at least 79 items to Malcolm Cowley, and 34 manuscripts sent to *New Republic*.

Princeton University Library, Princeton, New Jersey
The Rare Books & Special Collections Manuscript Division holds a large number of uncatalogued, significant, long correspondences. Many of these will be found in the papers of John Peale Bishop, F. Scott Fitzgerald, Christian Gauss, and Allen Tate.

Yale University Library, New Haven, Connecticut
The Beinecke Rare Book and Manuscript Library is the main depository of EW's manuscripts. Besides at least 40 documents handwritten for publication and some published but rare items, the library has a minimum of 18 letters by EW.

A. Letters by Wilson

To Burnett, Whit, *America's 93 Greatest Living Authors Present This Is My Best: Over 150 Self-Chosen and Complete Masterpieces, Together with Their Reasons for Their Selections,* ed. Burnett (New York: Dial Press, 1942), p. 324.

To *Encounter,* XII, No. 6 (June 1959), 90.

To Epstein, Jason, *New York Review of Books,* XI, No. 5 (26 September 1968), 7-10;
Fruits of the MLA, pp. 4-6.

To Frank, Waldo, *Cuba: Prophetic Island,* by Waldo Frank (New York: Marzani & Munsell, 1961), dust jacket.

To *Furioso,* V, No. 2 (Spring 1950), 88.

To Gauss, Christian, *Axel's Castle,* dedicatory epistle.

To Gauss, Christian, *The Papers of Christian Gauss,* ed. Katherine Gauss Jackson and Hiram Haydn (New York: Random House, 1957), pp. 245-250, 252-254, 256-257, 259-261, 263-265, 269-272, 274-277, 279-281, 284-285, 287, 289-291, 296-297, 299, 302-314, 317-318, 324-331, 333-336, 338-343, 346-351.

To *Internatsional'naia literatura.* See "Letter to the Russians about Hemingway" in Essays. See also "Pis'mo sovetskim chitateliam o Kheminguee" in Translations of Wilson's Works, Part 3 (Translations of Wilson's Essays), Russian.

To Lippman, Walter. See "An Open Letter to Walter Lippmann" in Essays.

To *Listener*, LVI (18 October 1956), 619-620;
Dead Sea Scrolls 1947-1969, pp. 295-299.

To *Listener*, LVI (29 November 1956), 885;
Dead Sea Scrolls 1947-1969, pp. 303-304.

To *Listener* (never published in the periodical), *Dead Sea Scrolls 1947-1969*, pp. 306-308.

To Millay, Edna St. Vincent, *Nation*, CLXXIV (19 April 1952), 380;
Shores of Light, p. 783.

To *New Republic*, LVIII (24 April 1929), 281-282;
Shores of Light, pp. 423-425.

To *New Republic*, LVIII (15 May 1929), 361-362.

To *New Republic*, LIX (29 May 1929), 47.

To *New Republic*, LIX (26 June 1929), 155.

To *New Republic*, LXII (26 March 1930), 153.

To *New Republic*, LXXVI (16 August 1933), 23.

To *New Republic*, LXXVIII (18 April 1934), 282 (quoted in article by M[alcolm] C[owley] entitled "Good Books That Almost Nobody Has Read").

To *New Republic*, LXXXIX (6 January 1937), 304.

To *New Republic*, XC (21 April 1937), 324.

To *New Republic*, XCVIII (8 March 1939), 130-131.

To *New Republic*, XCIX (12 June 1939), 283.

To *New Republic* (with editorial rejoinder), CII (22 January 1940), 118-119.

To *New Republic*, CIII (28 October 1940), 595.

To *New York Review of Books*, V, No. 4 (30 September 1965), 26.

To *New York Review of Books*, VI, No. 2 (17 February 1966), 29.

To *New York Review of Books*, VI, No. 6 (14 April 1966), 37.

To *New York Review of Books,* VII, No. 10 (15 December 1966), 42.

To *New York Review of Books,* X, No. 5 (14 March 1968), 35.

To *New York Review of Books,* XII, No. 11 (5 June 1969), 36.

To *New York Times* (by EW *et al.*), 3 August 1952, p. 8, col. 7.

To *New York Times* (by EW *et al.*), 30 August 1959, Section 4, p. 10, col· 5.

To *New York Times Book Review,* 29 November 1942, p. 40.

To Nichols, Mike. See "Open Letter to Mike Nichols" in Essays.

To *1916 P-rade* [*sic*] (Princeton), Formation III (January 1918), p. 57.

To *Princeton Alumni Weekly,* XX (25 February 1920), 460.

To *Princeton Alumni Weekly,* XX (17 March 1920), 540-541.

To *S4N.* See ["By a desperate effort in the last line"] in Essays.

To *Spectator* (with editorial rejoinder), CXCVI (22 June 1956), 854.

B. Letters *to* Wilson

By Bell, Marjorie. *Shores of Light,* by EW, pp. 694-695.

By Cross, Frank M., Jr. *Piece of My Mind,* by EW, pp. 13-14.

By Fitzgerald, F. Scott. *Crack-Up,* ed. EW, pp. 245-257, 259-265, 270-271, 273-274, 276-279, 281, 285.

———. *The Letters of F. Scott Fitzgerald,* ed. Andrew Turnbull (New York: Charles Scribner's Sons, 1963), pp. 317-349.

———. "Love to All of You, of All Generations," *Esquire,* LX, No. 1 (July 1963), 87-88.

———. *Shores of Light,* by EW, pp. 373-374.

By Gauss, Christian. *The Papers of Christian Gauss,* ed. Katherine Gauss Jackson and Hiram Haydn (New York: Random House, 1957), pp. 224-244, 247-286, 288-289, 291-302, 304-312, 314-323, 325-330, 334-339, 342-352.

By Gerber, John C. *Professional Standards and American Editions: A Response to Edmund Wilson* (New York: Modern Language Association of America, 1969), pp. 14-16.

By Hanks, W. *Europe Without Baedeker,* by EW, pp. 421-423, and 1st rev. ed., pp. 350-352. See also "Appendix A" in Essays.

By Hemingway, Ernest. *Shores of Light,* by EW, pp. 115-118, 122-124;
Literary Chronicle: 1920-1950, by EW, pp. 41-44, 47-49;
Hemingway and His Critics: An International Anthology, ed. Carlos Baker, No. AC 36 in American Century Series (New York: Hill and Wang, 1961), pp. 55-57, 59-60.

By Lyon, George W. *Shores of Light,* by EW, p. 694.

By Malraux, André. *Shores of Light,* by EW, pp. 573-574; *Literary Chronicle: 1920-1950,* by EW, pp. 177-178. Reprinted with a translation of Malraux's letter in *Malraux: A Collection of Critical Essays,* ed. R. W. B. Lewis, in Spectrum Books, Twentieth Century Views, ser. ed. Maynard Mack (Englewood Cliffs, New Jersey: Prentice-Hall), 1964, pp. 29-30.

By Millay, Edna St. Vincent. *Letters of Edna St. Vincent Millay,* ed. Allan Ross Macdougall (New York: Harper and Brothers, 1952), pp. 98-99, 115, 153-155, 159-160, 173-174, 179, 208, 230-232, 333-335.

————. *Nation,* CLXXIV (19 April 1952), 379-380;
  Shores of Light, by EW, pp. 781-783.

By Young, Stark. See in Items about Wilson.

C. *Letters about Wilson*

By Alexander, George B. *New York Review of Books,* XI,
  No. 11 (19 December 1968), 36.

By Anderson, Frederick (to *New York Review of Books,* but
  never published in the periodical). *Professional Standards
  and American Editions: A Response to Edmund Wilson*
  (New York: Modern Language Association of America,
  1969), p. 13.

By Baender, Paul. *New York Review of Books,* XI, No. 11
  (19 December 1968), 38;
  *Professional Standards and American Editions: A Response
  to Edmund Wilson* (New York: Modern Language Association of America, 1969), pp. 10-12.
  Partially reprinted in *Fruits of the MLA,* by EW, pp. 41-42.

By Barlow, Mason. *New Republic,* LXVI (11 March 1931),
  101.

By Behrman, S. N. *New Yorker,* XXII, No. 24 (27 July
  1946), 63-65.

By Behrstock, Arthur. *New Republic,* LXXXVII (3 June
  1936), 103-104.

By Bell, J. *New Statesman,* LXV (22 February 1963), 271.

By Benet, W. R. *New Republic,* CIII (11 November 1940),
  664.

By Besterman, Theodore. *New York Review of Books*, XI, No. 11 (19 December 1968), 36;
Fruits of the MLA, by EW, pp. 46-47.

By Bewley, Marius. *Scrutiny*, XVII (Autumn 1950), 255-263. See also Bewley, Marius, and Leavis, F.R., in Items about Wilson.

By Blumenthal, Joseph. *New Republic*, XC (28 April 1937), 361.

By Brewer, James L. *New Republic*, LXIX (2 December 1931), 74.

By Brown, Stuart Gerry. *New Republic*, XC (10 February 1937), 22.

By Brown, William Thurston. *New Republic*, LXX (23 March 1932), 156.

By Buechner, Frederick. *New York Review of Books*, XI, No. 11 (19 December 1968), 37.

By Cadodal, N. C. *New Republic*, LXVI (11 March 1931), 101-102.

By Cantwell, Robert. *New Republic*, LXXXVI (6 May 1936), 371.

By Cargill, Oscar (to *New York Review of Books*, but never published in the periodical). *Professional Standards and American Editions: A Response to Edmund Wilson* (New York: Modern Language Association of America, 1969), pp. 17-19.

By Catlin, George E. G. *New Republic*, LVIII (8 May 1929), 335;
Shores of Light, by EW, pp. 425-427.

By Cerf, Bennett A. *New Republic*, XC (21 April 1937), 326.

By Chase, Stuart. *New Republic*, LXIX (10 February 1932), 348-349.

By Chomsky, Noam, Frederick Crews, Florence Howe, Richard Ohmann, Paul Lauter, and Louis Kampf. *New York Review of Books*, XI, No. 11 (19 December 1968), 34.

By Clark, Roy B. *New York Times Book Review,* 6 November 1955, p. 60.

By Cooke, Harriot T. *New Republic,* LIX (17 July 1929), 236.

By Crane, Hart (to Ivor Winters). *Hart Crane: The Life of an American Poet,* by Philip Horton (New York: W. W. Norton & Company, 1937), pp. 225-226; *Shores of Light,* by EW, p. 207.

By Crawford, Bruce. *New Republic,* LXVI (25 February 1931), 47-48.

By Crews, Frederick. See Chomsky, Noam.

By Dale, R. C. *New York Review of Books,* V, No. 2 (26 August 1965), 27.

By Davis, J. Lionberger. *Princeton Alumni Weekly,* XX (17 March 1920), 539-540.

By Dennen, Leon. *New York Review of Books,* V, No. 2 (26 August 1965), 26.

By Donner, Frank J. *New York Review of Books,* XI, No. 11 (19 December 1968), 37.

By Doonping, R. *New Republic,* LXXIV (1 March 1933), 77.

By Edises, Conrad. *New Republic,* LXVI (4 March 1931), 76.

By Engel, Morris. *New Republic,* LXXXVII (13 May 1936), 20.

By Feibleman, James K. *New Republic,* XCII (1 September 1937), 105.

By Field, Herman. *New Republic,* LXXXVII (13 May 1936), 20.

By Firkins, O. W. *New Republic,* LXII (16 April 1930), 247.

By Fitzgerald, F. Scott (to Zelda, Maxwell Perkins, *et al.*). *The Letters of F. Scott Fitzgerald,* ed. Andrew Turnbull (New York: Charles Scribner's Sons, 1963), pp. 132, 153, 171, 179, 184, 215, 230, 262, 305, 385, 471, 480, 571.

———. *Princeton Alumni Weekly,* XX (10 March 1920) 514.

By Frances, Rosalind. *Times Literary Supplement,* 14 March 1952, p. 189.

By Freeman, John H. *New Republic,* LXV (11 February 1931), 355.

———. *New Republic,* LXX (9 March 1932), 103.

By Freeman, Joseph. *New Republic,* XC (21 April 1937), 324.

By Glick, M. B. (with editor's headnote). *New Republic,* XC (28 April 1937), 361.

By Godwin, Murray. *New Republic,* LXV (24 December 1930), 167-168.

By Goodman, Robert Walter. *New Republic,* XCII (1 September 1937), 104.

By Gottesman, Ronald. *New York Review of Books,* XI, No. 11 (19 December 1969), 37-38;
Professional Standards and American Editions: A Response to Edmund Wilson (New York: Modern Language Association of America, 1969), pp. 7-9.

By Goulden, Mark. *Times Literary Supplement,* 28 March 1952, p. 221.

By Gray, Mary Kramer. *New Republic,* LXXXIX (6 January 1937), 304.

By Green, Abner. *New Republic,* XC (10 February 1937), 22.

By Greene, Theodore M. *New Republic,* XCI (7 July 1937), 254.

By Gustafson, E. T. *New Republic,* LXXXVI (6 May 1936), 371.

By Hackett, William H. Y., Jr. *New York Review of Books,* XI, No. 11 (19 December 1968), 36-37. Partially reprinted in *Fruits of the MLA,* by EW, pp. 43-44.

By Hall, Bolton. *New Republic,* LXX (20 April 1932), 276.

By Hamilton, J. S. *New Republic,* XCII (11 August 1937), 21.

By Hayes, Howard. *New Republic*, LXXXVII (3 June 1936), 104.

By Hemingway, Mary. *New Yorker*, XXXIX, No. 4 (16 March 1963), 160, 162-163.

By Hinds, A. E. *New Republic*, XCII (11 August 1937), 21.

By Hitchcock, G. P. *New Republic*, XCII (1 September 1937), 105.

By Howe, Florence. See Chomsky, Noam.

By Howe, Quincey. *New Republic*, LXVI (15 April 1931), 236-237.

By Hunter, Clyde O. *New Republic*, XC (10 February 1937), 22.

By Illsley, Graydon F. *New Republic*, LXVI (25 February 1931), 47.

By Jameson, Barbara. *New York Review of Books*, V, No. 2 (26 August 1965), 26.

By Jamieson, John. *New Republic*, CII (17 June 1940), 828.

By Jones, Stephen P. *New York Review of Books*, V, No. 2 (26 August 1965), 27.

By Josephy, Robert. *New Republic*, XC (28 April 1937), 361.

By Kampf, Louis. See Chomsky, Noam.

By Kaufman, George S. *New Republic*, XCI (4 August 1937), 365;
New Republic, CXXXI (22 November 1954), 74.

By Lauter, Paul. See Chomsky, Noam.

By Leighton, J. A. *New Republic*, XCIV (4 May 1938), 398.

By Lowry, Thomas C. *New York Times Book Review*, 6 November 1955, p. 60.

By Macdonald, Dwight. *New Republic*, XCII (8 September 1937), 133.

By Magarshack, David. *New York Review of Books*, V, No. 2 (26 August 1965), 26.

By Manheim, Frank J. *New Republic*, XCII (6 October 1937), 246.

By Marini, Myra. *New Republic*, XLIX (2 February 1927), 305.

By Mather, Frank Jewett. *New Republic*, LXII (16 April 1930), 247-248.

By Michelson, E. B. *New Republic*, XC (10 February 1937), 22.

By Millard, Walter J. *New Republic*, LXV (11 February 1931), 355.

By Miller, Henry. *New Republic*, XCV (18 May 1938), 49. Reprinted in adapted form in *Shores of Light*, by EW, pp. 708-710; *Literary Chronicle: 1920-1950*, by EW, pp. 215-216; and *Henry Miller and the Critics*, ed. George Wickes, in Crosscurrents Modern Critiques, ser. ed. Harry T. Moore (Carbondale: Southern Illinois University Press, 1963), pp. 28-30.

By Milner, I. F. G. *New Republic*, XCIV (4 May 1938), 398.

By Mizener, R. P. *New Republic*, LXXXVII (3 June 1936), 104.

By Molloy, J. *New Republic*, LIX (26 June 1929), 155.

By Montefiore, Hugh. *Spectator*, CXCVI (22 June 1956), 854.

By Moskowitz, Mrs. Henry. *New Republic*, LXVII (3 June 1931), 75.

By Nabokov, Vladimir. *New York Review of Books*, V, No. 2 (26 August 1965), 25-26.

————. *New York Review of Books*, V, No. 12 (20 January 1966), 30.

By Nicholson, Watson. *New Republic*, XC (10 February 1937), 22.

By "An Observer." *New Republic*, XLVII (28 July 1926), 283.

By Ohmann, Richard. See Chomsky, Noam.

By Oppenheim, H. *New Republic,* LXXXVI (6 May 1936), 371.

By Parsons, Alice. *Nation,* CXIV (28 June 1922), 777.

By Paul, Louis. *New Republic,* XCII (11 August 1937), 21.

By Perluck, Herbert A. *New Republic,* CLV, No. 6-7 (13 August 1966), 35-37.

By Porter, Robert C. *New Republic,* LXIV (27 August 1930), 50.

By Powers, D. *New Republic,* LXIX (16 December 1931), 138.

By Priest, George M. *Princeton Alumni Weekly,* XX (3 March 1920), 482.

By R., H. C. *New Republic,* LXX (9 March 1932), 103.

By Randolph, James R. *New York Times Book Review,* 6 November 1955, p. 60.

By Ransom, John Crowe. *New Republic,* LI (22 June 1927), 125-126;
Shores of Light, by EW, pp. 207-210.

By Redmond, Stuart. *New Republic,* LXX (9 March 1932), 103.

By Reichl, Ernst. *New Republic,* XC (28 April 1937), 361.

By Rivera, Diego. *New Republic,* LXXVI (27 September 1933), 187-188.

By Rochester, Anna. *New Republic,* LXX (20 April 1932), 275.

By Sackin, L. H. *New Republic,* LXX (9 March 1932), 103.

By Saroyan, William. *New Republic,* CIII (16 December 1940), 837.

By Schachner, Joel. *New Republic,* XCII (1 September 1937), 104-105.

By Seligmann, Herbert J. *New Republic,* LIV (22 February 1928), 19.

By Sessions, Roger Huntington. *New Republic,* XLIII (3 June 1925), 49.

By "[Signature undecipherable]" [*sic*]. *Atlantic,* CCXXIV, No. 4 (October 1969), 74-75.

By Simmons, Ernest J. *New York Review of Books,* V, No. 2 (26 August 1965), 26-27.

By Sinclair, David. *New Republic,* LXXII (12 October 1932), 236-237.

By Sinclair, Upton. *New Republic,* LXV (11 February 1931), 354-355.

———— (with editorial comment). *New Republic,* XLIII (22 July 1925), 239.

By Slochower, Harry. *New Republic,* XCII (1 September 1937), 105.

By Smith, Franklin P. *New York Times Book Review,* 13 November 1955, p. 43.

By Spitzer, S. Charles. *New Republic,* LXVI (4 March 1931), 76.

By Steegmuller, Francis. *New Republic,* XCVIII (8 March 1939), 130.

By Steffens, Lincoln (2 letters to Upton Sinclair). *New Republic,* XCVI (19 October 1938), 301.

By Stern, Philip Van Doren. *New Republic,* XC (28 April 1937), 361.

By Strobel, Lee K. *New Republic,* LXXXVII (13 May 1936), 20.

By Symons, Julian. *Times Literary Supplement,* 4 April 1952, p. 237.

By Tarsaidze, Alexander. *New York Times,* 25 April 1936, p. 16, col. 6.

By Thomas, Elisabeth. *New Republic,* XLII (22 April 1925), 240.

By Thomas, Harvey. *Nation,* CXIV (28 June 1922), 776-777.

By Thomas, Norman. *New Republic*, LXV (11 February 1931), 354.

By Trueblood, Louise N. *New Republic*, LXVI (8 April 1931), 209-210.

By Untermeyer, Louis. *New Republic*, XLV (16 December 1925), 113.

By Urich, R. W. *New York Times Book Review*, 6 November 1955, p . 60.

By van Loon, Hendrik Willem. *New Republic*, LXIX (2 December 1931), 73-74.

By Vogel, Jo. *New Republic*, LXX (9 March 1932), 103.

By Wagner, C. Roland. *New York Times Book Review*, 6 November 1955, p. 60.

By Walker, Adelaide. *New Republic*, XC (10 February 1937), 22.

By Werner, M. R. *New Republic*, LXX (9 March 1932), 103.

By West, Geoffrey. *Times Literary Supplement*, 30 May 1942, p. 271.

By Wilson, A. *New Republic*, LXXIV (15 February 1933), 21.

By Wilson, Earl. *New Republic*, XCII (11 August 1937), 21.

By Winter, Ella. *New Republic*, LXXI (8 June 1932), 102.

——. *New Republic*, C (16 August 1939), 49.

By Wright, Cuthbert. *New Republic*, LVIII (15 May 1929), 361.

——. *New Republic*, LIX (29 May 1929), 47.

By Wylie, Elinor. *New Republic*, LIV (7 March 1928), 101.

By "Your Reviewer." *Listener*, LVI (25 October 1956), 665; *Dead Sea Scrolls 1947-1969*, by EW, pp. 299-303. See also "Appendix" in *Essays*.

——. *Listener*, LVI (13 December 1956), 1001; *Dead Sea Scrolls 1947-1969*, by EW, pp. 304-306. See also "Appendix" in *Essays*.

By "Your Reviewer." *Times Literary Supplement,* 6 June 1942, p. 283.

By Zeitlin, Solomon. *New York Times Book Review,* 6 November 1955, p. 60.

By Zinkin, Arthur. *New Republic,* LXXXVI (6 May 1936), 371.

Aaron, Daniel. "Edmund Wilson's War," *Massachusetts Review*, III (Spring 1962), 555-570. A review-essay on *Patriotic Gore*.

————. "Go Left Young Writers," in Aaron's *Writers on the Left: Episodes in American Literary Communism*, Vol. I in Communism in American Life, ser. ed. Clinton Rossiter (New York: Harcourt, Brace & World, 1961), pp. 161-198, 417n-423n. A carefully documented study of the relationship of EW and other writers to the Communist Party in 1932.

"About Edmund Wilson," *I Thought of Daisy*, by EW, in Ballantine Books (New York: Farrar, Straus and Young, 1953 printing only), pp. [217-218]. A resumé of EW's life and work.

Adams, J. Donald. "Speaking of Books," *New York Times Book Review*, 4 June 1944, p. 2; 11 June 1944, p. 2. Attacks EW's contention that the twenties provided an atmosphere more favorable for writers than the early forties provided, with special reference to EW's essay "A Toast and a Tear for Dorothy Parker."

Adams, Robert M. "Masks and Delays: Edmund Wilson as Critic," *Sewanee Review*, LVI (Spring 1948), 272-286. Partially reprinted without title in Dorothy Nyren's "Wilson, Edmund (1895-   )" in *A Library of Literary Criticism: Modern American Literature,* comp. Nyren (New York: Frederick Ungar Publishing Company, 1960, 1962), pp. 539-540. A discussion of EW's uniqueness as a critic, with attention to his attitudes on socialism and humanism. Attacks EW for having "no coherent point of view."

Agel, Jerome. "The Cocktail Party," *Books* (New York: Agel Publishing Company), II, No. 4 (May, 1965), 5. EW's childhood ambition was to be a magician.

Aldridge, John W. "The Village In the 20's," *New York Times Book Review,* 17 May 1953, pp. 4, 28. Reprinted as "I Thought of Daisy" in Aldridge's *Time to Murder and Create: The Contemporary Novel in Crisis* (New York: David McKay Company, 1966), pp. 222-225. Discusses *I Thought of Daisy.*

"An American Honors List," *New York Times Magazine,* 14 July 1963, pp. 16-17. EW's portrait given among those who received the Presidential Medal of Freedom on 4 July 1963.

Atkinson, Brooks. "At the Theater," *New York Times,* 30 April 1951, p. 17, cols. 2-3. An unfavorable review of *Little Blue Light,* performed by Broadway's ANTA Playhouse, 29 April 1951.

Bacon, Peggy. "Edmund Wilson" (in Bacon's "Peggy Bacon's Guillotine"), *New Republic,* LXXXI (12 December 1934), 133. A drawing, with caption, depicting EW as the man in the moon.

Bate, Walter Jackson. "Edmund Wilson (1895-   )," *Criticism: The Major Texts,* ed. Bate (New York: Harcourt, Brace & World, 1952), pp. 587-588, and Enl. Ed. (New York: Harcourt Brace Jovanovich, 1970), pp. 587-588. Reprinted in slightly revised form as "Edmund Wilson" in Bate's *Prefaces To Criticism,* No. A 165 in Anchor Books (Garden City, New York: Doubleday & Company, 1959), pp. 217-218.

Beach, Joseph Warren. "Introduction: 1954," in Beach's *The Method of Henry James,* enl. ed. with corrections (Phila-

delphia: Albert Saifer, 1954), pp. [vii]-cxiv. On pp. lii-lv
Beach comments appreciatively on EW's essay "The Ambiguity of Henry James."

Beek, M[artinus] A[drianus]. "Voorwoord," *De boekrollen van
de Dode Zee* (*Scrolls from the Dead Sea*), by EW, trans.
I. S. Herschberg (Amsterdam: De Bezige Bij, 1956), pp.
5-7. An abstract of *Scrolls from the Dead Sea*.

[Bellow, Saul]. "Arias: White House and Artists," *The Noble
Savage*, No. 5, ed. Bellow *et al.*, in Meridian Books (Cleve-
land and New York: World Publishing Company, October
1962), pp. 4-7. Bellow gives his account of EW at a White
House dinner given by President Kennedy in honor of
André Malraux.

Benét, Stephen Vincent. "Is the Costume Drama Dead?,"
Bookman, LX (December 1924), 481-484 (esp. p. 484).
This article is notable for its somewhat favorable review
of EW's early play "The Crime in the Whistler Room."

Berthoff, Warner. *Edmund Wilson*, No. 67 in University of
Minnesota Pamphlets on American Writers (Minneapolis:
University of Minnesota Press, 1968). This 47-page essay
contains some biography, but is primarily concerned with
evaluating EW's criticism.

Bewley, Marius. "Appearance and Reality in Henry James,"
Scrutiny, XVII (Summer 1950), 90-114. Supports EW's
Freudian interpretation of James's *The Turn of the Screw*
as stated in EW's essay "The Ambiguity of Henry James."
See also Leavis, F. R., in Items about Wilson and Bewley,
Marius, in Letters about Wilson.

―――. "Northern Saints and Southern Knights," *Hudson
Review*, XV (Autumn 1962), 431-439. Reprinted as "PA-
TRIOTIC GORE by Edmund Wilson" in Bewley's *Masks
& Mirrors: Essays in Criticism* (New York: Atheneum;
Toronto: McClelland and Stewart, 1970), pp. 198-210.
Discusses *Patriotic Gore*.

Bishop, John Peale. "The Discipline of Poetry," *Virginia Quarterly Review*, XIV (Summer, 1938), 343-356. Comments
concerning *Axel's Castle*.

Bonwit, Marianne. "Babel in Modern Fiction," *Comparative Literature*, II (Summer 1950), 236-247. Provides a comparative study of five works by different authors who present the decay of contemporary life through their use of language: C. S. Lewis, *That Hideous Strength;* Thomas Mann, *Doktor Faustus;* Joseph Roth, *Antichrist;* Denis de Rougement, *La part du Diable;* and EW, *Memoirs of Hecate County.*

"Book Action Is Shifted: Case Against Doubleday Goes to Special Sessions," *New York Times*, 18 July 1946, p. 23, col. 4. Mid-Manhattan summons court transfers *Memoirs of Hecate County* case to Special Sessions.

Botsford, Keith. "O Plutarco Americano, ou último Romano, ou simplesmente Edmund Wilson" (in Portuguese), *Cadernos Brasileiros* (Rio de Janeiro), V, No. 4 (Julho-Agosto 1963), 35-44. Reprinted in English as "The American Plutarch, the Last Roman, or Plain Mr. Wilson" in *Texas Quarterly*, VI, No. 3 (Autumn 1963), 129-140. A favorable critique of *Patriotic Gore.*

Braem, Helmut M. "Wildenten oder Schildkröten: Edmund Wilson, der große alte Mann der amerikanischen Literatur," *Zeit: Wochenzeitung für Politik, Wirtschaft, Handel und Kultur* (Hamburg), XXI, No. 35 (26 August 1966), 15.

Brandon, Henry. See "A Conversation with Edmund Wilson: 'We Don't Know Where We Are'" in Essays.

Breit, Harvey. "Talk With Edmund Wilson," *New York Times Book Review*, 2 November 1952, p. 18. Reprinted as "Edmund Wilson" in Breit's *The Writer Observed* (New York: World Publishing Company, 1956), pp. 267-269. Quotes EW as saying that his function as a critic " 'is to bring together a number of fields that haven't been brought together.' "

"Brief Filed in Book Suit: Edmund Wilson Story Is Obscene, Prosecutor Argues," *New York Times*, 14 November 1946, p. 27, col. 5. Assistant District Attorney files brief in Special Sessions Court against Doubleday for publishing *Memoirs of Hecate County*.

Broderick, John. "Cultural Drift," *Commonweal*, XLVI (2 May 1947), 60-61. Discusses EW's phrase "People of taste" and its good influence on the literary public; EW had used this phrase in the essay "Somerset Maugham and an Antidote."

Brown, E. K. "The Method of Edmund Wilson," *University of Toronto Quarterly*, XI (October 1941), 105-111. Partially reprinted without title in Dorothy Nyren's "Wilson, Edmund (1895-   )" in *A Library of Literary Criticism: Modern American Literature*, comp. Nyren (New York: Frederick Ungar Publishing Company, 1960, 1962), p. 539. Reviews *Axel's Castle, Boys in the Back Room, To the Finland Station, Triple Thinkers: Ten Essays*, and *Wound and the Bow*.

Burke, Kenneth. "Boring from Within" (in "The Position of the Progressive"), *New Republic*, LXV (4 February 1931), 326-329. A reply to EW's essay "An Appeal to Progressives."

Calta, Louis. "Wilson Discusses Script" (in "Lindsay, Crouse to Sponsor Play: Sign Contracts for Production of 'One Bright Day,' Miller's Story of Drug Tycoon"), *New York Times*, 3 May 1951, p. 35, cols. 7-8. EW admits differences with Quintus Productions over unauthorized cuts in script of *Little Blue Light*.

Cantwell, Robert. "Wilson as Journalist," *Nation*, CLXXXVI (22 February 1958), 166-170. Discusses EW's use of journalistic methods. Cantwell finds that during the three decades after 1925 "the concrete instance has given way to the general case, the explicit injustice to the social theory." Dwells at some length on EW's essay "The People Against Dorothy Perkins."

Chamberlain, John. "Books of the Times," *New York Times*, 1 January 1944, p. 11, cols. 5-7. EW replaces Clifton Fadiman as reviewer for *New Yorker*.

Chase, Richard. "Wilson as Critic," *Nation*, CLXXXVI (22 February 1958), 161, 164, 166. Calls EW "America's foremost critic" and exalts his socio-historical approach. However, "Wilson is rather weak on literary theory" and "the 'great' American books—*The Scarlet Letter, Moby Dick,* and the rest."

Chase, Stuart. "Mr. Chase Replies," *New Republic,* LXIX (10 February 1932), 348-349. Chase's defense against attacks made by EW in the essay "What Do the Liberals Hope For?"

"City Defends Its Ban on 'Hecate' in Minute," *New York Times,* 22 October 1948, p. 23, col. 4. Lawyer for New York City takes only one minute to defend City's ban on *Memoirs of Hecate County* before United States Supreme Court.

Clark, J. A. "The Sad Case of Edmund Wilson," *Commonweal,* XXVIII (8 July 1938), 292-295. "Wilson's career has been blighted by his unwillingness (or inability) to take a definite critical position and hold it long enough for everybody concerned to get his second wind."

Clurman, Harold. "Theatre: From Booth to Shakespeare," *New Republic,* CXXIV, No. 20 (14 May 1951), 20-22 (esp. pp. 20-21). A review and brief analysis of *Little Blue Light* as performed on stage.

Collins, Seward. "Criticism in America: III. The End of the Anti-humanist Myth," *Bookman,* LXXII (October 1930), 145-164, 209-228 (esp. pp. 162-164, 209-217). A reply to the hostile reviewers of the humanist symposium *Humanism and America;* the "most disgraceful" of all the anti-humanist exhibitions was EW's "Notes on Babbitt and More."

Corbett, Edward P. J. "America's Sainte-Beuve," *Commonweal,* LXXII (13 May 1960), 173-175. Discusses some of the influences on EW's work and points out some of EW's strengths and weaknesses as a critic.

"A Correction." See "Casanova" and "John Jay Chapman" (*New Republic*) in Essays.

Cowley, Malcolm. "Edmund Wilson's Specimen Days," *New Republic,* CXXVII, No. 19 (10 November 1952), 17-18.

Partially reprinted without title in Dorothy Nyren's "Wilson, Edmund (1895-   )" in *A Library of Literary Criticism: Modern American Literature,* comp. Nyren (New York: Frederick Ungar Publishing Company, 1960, 1962), p. 541. Believes that in some ways *Shores of Light* does not come off so well as *Classics and Commercials.* Praises EW's early ability to point out promising writers such as Hemingway and Malraux.

————. "Flight from the Masses," *New Republic,* LXXXVII (3 June 1936), 106, 108. Reprinted as "Edmund Wilson in Russia" in Cowley's *Think Back on Us: A Contemporary Chronicle of the 1930's,* ed. Henry Dan Piper (Carbondale and Edwardsville: Southern Illinois University Press; London and Amsterdam: Feffer & Simons, 1967), pp. 115-118. Discusses *Travels in Two Democracies.* See also Cowley's "Postscript to a Paragraph," below.

————. "From the Finland Station," *New Republic,* CIII (7 October 1940), 478-480. Reprinted in Cowley's *Think Back on Us: A Contemporary Chronicle of the 1930's,* ed. Henry Dan Piper (Carbondale and Edwardsville: Southern Illinois University Press; London and Amsterdam: Feffer & Simons, 1967), pp. 178-184. Attempts to point out weaknesses in *To the Finland Station.*

C[owley], M[alcolm]. "Good Books That Almost Nobody Has Read," *New Republic,* LXXVIII (18 April 1934), 281-283. Contains comments by EW on current books. A note from F. Scott Fitzgerald lists *I Thought of Daisy* as a book of unrecognized "intrinsic worth."

Cowley, Malcolm. "Postscript to a Paragraph," *New Republic,* LXXXVII (16 June 1936), 134-135. Reprinted in Cowley's *Think Back on Us: A Contemporary Chronicle of the 1930's,* ed. Henry Dan Piper (Carbondale and Edwardsville: Southern Illinois University Press; London and Amsterdam: Feffer & Simons, 1967), pp. 118-122. Concludes "Flight from the Masses," above, as an afterthought.

————. "The Religion of Art II: A Discourse over the Grave of Dada," *New Republic,* LXXVII (10 January 1934),

246-249. Reprinted as "A Brief History of Dada" in Cowley's *Exile's Return: A Narrative of Ideas* (New York: W. W. Norton & Company, 1934), pp. 146-156; reprinted as *Exile's Return: A Literary Odyssey of the 1920's* (New York: Viking Press; Toronto: Macmillan, 1951), pp. 138-147; *Exile's Return: A Literary Odyssey of the 1920's* reissued in Compass Books Ed. (New York: Viking Press, 1956; Gloucester, Massachusetts: Peter Smith [clothbound only; Viking Press appears as publisher on title page], 1967),pp. 138-147. Discusses the escapist theme in *Axel's Castle* and in the Dada movement of the 1920s.

―――. "Stalin or Satan," *New Republic*, LXXXIX (20 January 1937), 348-350. A reply to EW's essay "The Literary Left."

Co[xe], L[ouis]. "Wilson," *Chambers's Encyclopædia*, New Ed., 1950, XIV, 597; New Rev. Ed., 1967, 1968, XIV, 574.

"Criticism by Theory," *New York Times*, 25 August 1933, p. 14, col. 3. Agrees with EW's position as opposed to that of Joseph Wood Krutch in "Is Politics Ruining Art?: A Debate" (see also "What Is Mr. Krutch Defending?" in *Essays*).

Cross, Frank M., Jr. "From Manuscripts Found in a Cave: The Dead Sea Scrolls Bare New Clues to Our Historical and Religious Past," *New York Times Book Review*, 16 October 1955, pp. 1, 31. Partially reprinted without title in EW's essay entitled "Notes on the Churches" in section called "Religion" in *Piece of My Mind*, pp. 11-12.

Cruise O'Brien, Conor. "Critic into Prophet," *New Statesman*, LXVII (15 May 1964), 765-766. Reprinted in Cruise O'Brien's *Writers and Politics* (London: Chatto and Windus; New York: Pantheon Books, 1965), pp. 163-168. Discusses *Cold War and the Income Tax*.

―――― (under pseud. Donat O'Donnell). "Serpents," *Spectator*, CCIV (27 May 1960), 773. Reprinted without pseud. in Cruise O'Brien's *Writers and Politics* (New York: Pantheon Books; London: Chatto and Windus, 1965), pp. 13-16. Discusses *Apologies to the Iroquois*.

Dabney, Lewis M. "Edmund Wilson and *Patriotic Gore*," *Columbia University Forum*, V, No. 4 (Fall 1962), 20-26. Treats *Patriotic Gore* as a sort of "American epic."

"Dead Sea Scrolls Held Overvalued: 3 U.S. Theologians Deplore Hasty Interpretations, Say Long Study Is Essential," *New York Times*, 6 February 1956, p. 25, col. 6. Three theologians criticize EW for accepting thesis of André Dupont-Sommer that Dead Sea scrolls show anticipation of Christianity in Essene sect.

"Decision on 'Hecate County' Due in N. Y. November 7," *Publishers' Weekly*, CL (2 November 1946), 2608.

DeVoto, Bernard. "The Easy Chair," *Harper's Magazine*, CXC (December 1944), 34-37 (esp. pp. 36-37). Defends the detective story against EW's attacks.

————. "My Dear Edmund Wilson," *Saturday Review of Literature*, XV, No. 16 (13 February 1937), 8, 20. Reprinted with a "Preface Continued" as "Autobiography: Or, as Some Call It, Literary Criticism" in DeVoto's *Minority Report* (Boston: Little, Brown and Company, 1940), pp. 163-189. DeVoto defends his editorship of *Saturday Review of Literature* and chides EW for his Marxist views. The "Preface Continued," pp. 169-189 of the reprinted version, is more complimentary to EW.

Dolmatch, Theodore B. "Edmund Wilson as Literary Critic," *University of Kansas City Review*, XVII (Spring 1951), 213-219. Recommends EW as an introductory critic, but cites his tendency to biographical-psychological criticism while excluding examination of literary forms.

"Doubleday Fine Upheld: Appellate Court Rules Against Publishers of 'Hecate,'" *New York Times*, 17 May 1947, p. 13, col. 2. Appellate upholds conviction of Doubleday for publishing *Memoirs of Hecate County*.

"Doubleday's Appeal Heard in 'Hecate County' Case," *Publishers' Weekly*, CLI (17 May 1947), 2499.

Dupee, F. W. "Gertrude Stein," *Commentary*, XXXIII (June 1962), 519-523 (esp. p. 522). Comments on EW's contribution to Stein's reputation.

Edel, Leon. "Prefatory Note," *Nineteenth-Century Fiction*, XII (June, 1957), 1-3. Introductory explanation concerning Harold C. Goddard's essay "A Pre-Freudian Reading of *The Turn of the Screw*," *Nineteenth-Century Fiction*, XII (June 1957), 4-36, from a manuscript written by the late Professor Goddard during the 1920's and antedating the Freudian ideas which EW expressed in the essay "The Ambiguity of Henry James."

Edelstein, J. M. "Collector's Item," *Fitzgerald Newsletter*, No. 28 (Winter 1965), 8. In junk shop author finds copy of *Poets, Farewell!* inscribed to the F. Scott Fitzgeralds.

"Edmund Wilson," *Bibliography Supplement*, ed. Richard M. Ludwig, supplement to Vol. III in *Literary History of the United States*, ed. Robert E. Spiller *et al*. (New York: Macmillan Company, 1959, 1960), pp. 238-239.

"Edmund Wilson," *Bookman*, LXX (November 1929), 302. EW photographed in his *New Republic* office.

"Edmund Wilson," *Living Authors: A Book of Biographies*, ed. Dilly Tante (pseud. for Stanley Jasspon Kunitz) (New York: H. W. Wilson Company, 1931), pp. 439-440. Reprinted with slight omissions in final paragraph in *Wilson Bulletin for Librarians*, V (April 1931), 484.

"Edmund Wilson," *Nation*, CCII (20 June 1966), 733. EW receives National Medal for Literature.

"Edmund Wilson," *Saturday Review of Literature*, X (3 February 1934), 446. A picture of EW. Appears as part of an article entitled "Literature and Individualism," by J. Donald Adams.

"Edmund Wilson," *Time: The Weekly Newsmagazine*, XXXIV, No. 20 (13 November 1939), 22. A picture of EW. Appears as part of an article entitled "Public Opinion."

"Edmund Wilson: Background of a Critic." See in Essays.

"Edmund Wilson Fined: Pleads Guilty in Tax Case—Judge Blames a Lawyer," *New York Times* (15 November 1960), p. 42, col. 8. EW fined $7500 after pleading guilty of federal income tax evasion, with three of four counts dismissed. Judge blames delinquency on attorney who conducted EW's tax affairs.

"Edmund Wilson Gets Aspen Prize: $30,000 Award Granted for Work for the Humanities," *New York Times,* 1 June 1968, p. 25, cols. 4-5.

"Edmund Wilson to Receive Edward MacDowell Medal," *New York Times,* 2 August 1964, p. 53, col. 2.

"Edmund Wilson Wins National Literature Medal," *Publishers' Weekly,* CLXXXIX, No. 23 (6 June 1966), 188-189. On 3 June 1966 EW becomes second recipient of National Book Committee's National Medal for Literature.

"An Eminent Critic: Edmund Wilson," *New York Times,* 4 June 1966, p. 27, cols. 1-2. EW receives National Medal for Literature.

Farrell, James T. "James Farrell on James Farrell," *New Republic,* CIII (28 October 1940), 595-596. Farrell's reply to an EW letter concerning *Father and Son.*

Farrelly, John. "Edmund Wilson of The 'New Yorker,' " *Scrutiny,* XVIII (Winter 1951-1952), 229-233. Reprinted as "Edmund Wilson of 'The New Yorker' " in *A Selection from Scrutiny,* Vol. I, ed. F. R. Leavis, No. CAM 508 in Literature (Cambridge, England: Cambridge University Press, 1968), pp. 299-304. Discusses *Classics and Commercials* and applies to EW the term " 'cultural historian.' "

Fiess, Edward. "Edmund Wilson: Art and Ideas," *Antioch Review,* I (September 1941), 356-367. Treats EW's liberalism during the 1930s and the balance between aesthetic and sociological considerations in his criticism.

Finney, John W. "24 Writers Urge New Steps for Vietnam Peace: Call for End to Bombing in North—Group also Voices Criticism of Humphrey," *New York Times,* 27 April 1966, p. 6, col. 3. EW joins writers opposing bombing of North Vietnam.

Fisher, John H. "The MLA Editions of Major American Authors," *Professional Standards and American Editions: A Response to Edmund Wilson* (New York: Modern Language Association of America, 1969), pp. 20-26.

Fowle, Farnsworth. "Princeton Gives 2 Women Honors: Helen Hayes, India's Health Minister Get Doctorates— 653 Seniors Graduated," *New York Times*, 13 June 1956, p. 41, cols. 3-8. EW receives Doctor of Letters degree from Princeton.

Fraiberg, Louis Benjamin. "Edmund Wilson and Psychoanalysis in Historical Criticism," in Fraiberg's *Psychoanalysis & American Literary Criticism* (Detroit: Wayne State University Press, 1960), pp. 161-182. Raises some objections to EW's use of psychoanalysis in criticism, but notes that "Wilson's deficiencies are, so to speak, honorable ones." See also Fraiberg, Louis Benjamin, in Theses and Dissertations.

Frank, Charles P[aul]. *Edmund Wilson,* No. 152 in Twayne's United States Authors Series, ser. ed. Sylvia E. Bowman (New York: Twayne Publishers, 1970). A systematic analysis of EW's major and minor work, showing that his fiction has been long neglected by critics. See also Frank, Charles Paul, in Theses and Dissertations.

Unsigned Review
Choice, VII (September 1970), 842.

"Freedom Medal Citations," *New York Times,* 7 December 1963, p. 14, cols. 3-4. EW receives Presidential Medal of Freedom.

"Freedom Medal Honors Kennedy: Posthumous Award Is Also Made to Pope John XXIII—31 Others Are Cited," *New York Times,* 7 December 1963, p. 1, col. 4; p. 14, col. 2. EW in Europe during awarding of Presidential Medal of Freedom.

Freeman, Joseph. "Edmund Wilson's Globe of Glass," *New Masses,* XXVII (12 April 1938), "Literary Section," pp. 73-79. Compares *Triple Thinkers: Ten Essays* with *Axel's Castle.*

Garis, Robert. *The Dickens Theatre: A Reassessment of the Novels* (Oxford: Clarendon, 1965), pp. 4, 29, 31-32, 35-36, 61, 103. Believes EW's evaluation of Dickens misdirected.

Gauss, Christian. "Edmund Wilson, the Campus and the Nassau 'Lit.'" *Princeton University Library Chronicle,* V, No. 2 (February 1944), 41-50.

Gibbs, Wolcott. "The Odd Case of Mr. Wilson," *New Yorker,* XXVII, No. 13 (12 May 1951), 49-50. A review of *Little Blue Light* as performed at the ANTA Playhouse.

Gibson, Mary. ["Poor Edmund Wilson—Hasn't He Any Nice Friends?"], *New York Times Book Review,* 28 April 1946, p. 2. Cartoon.

Gibson, William M. "The Center for Editions of American Authors," *Scholarly Books in America* (American University Press Services), X, No. 3 (January 1969), 7-11. Reprinted in *Professional Standards and American Editions: A Response to Edmund Wilson* (New York: Modern Language Association of America, 1969), pp. 1-6. This essay does not mention EW by name, but does defend the Center for Editions of American Authors against "One misinformed critic."

Gilman, Richard. "Edmund Wilson: Then and Now," *New Republic,* CLV, No. 1 (2 July 1966), 23-28. A survey of EW's criticism with some original insights. Begins as a review of *Bit Between My Teeth.*

Gilroy, Harry. "Edmund Wilson Honored in Utica: Writer Receives 2d National Medal for Literature," *New York Times,* 4 June 1966, p. 27, col. 3. EW receives National Medal for Literature and comments on the $5000 award in relation to longtime tax problems and the war in Vietnam.

Ginzberg, Benjamin. "Against Messianism" (in "The Position of the Progressive"), *New Republic,* LXVI (18 February 1931), 15-17. A reply to EW's essay "An Appeal to Progressives."

Glicksberg, Charles I. "Edmund Wilson (1895-   )," in Glicksberg's *American Literary Criticism 1900-1950,* ed. Glicksberg (New York: Hendricks House, 1951), pp. 482-485.

————. "Edmund Wilson: Radicalism at the Crossroads," *South Atlantic Quarterly,* XXXVI (October 1937), 466-477. Discusses EW's refusal to go all the way with Marxism, but cites his "ingrained rationalism" as accounting "in part for the limited scope of his influence." Concludes that EW "must achieve some organic synthesis, some law of life, that will unify his work and his critical ideas."

Goldhurst, William. "Edmund Wilson," in Goldhurst's *F. Scott Fitzgerald and His Contemporaries* (Cleveland and New York: World Publishing Company, 1963), pp. 43-73. An analysis of EW's contributions to Fitzgerald's achievement. See also Goldhurst, William, in Theses and Dissertations.

Graves, Robert. "Edmund Wilson, a Protestant Abroad," *New Republic,* CXXXIV, No. 18 (30 April 1956), 13-16. Reprinted as "Religion: None; Conditioning: Protestant" in Graves's *5 Pens in Hand* (Garden City, New York: Doubleday and Company, 1958), pp. 129-136. Discusses *Red, Black, Blond and Olive.*

Gray, Simon. "Edmund Wilson and the Larger Subject," *Delta: The Cambridge Literary Magazine* (Cambridge, England), No. 27 (Autumn 1962), pp. 7-13. Comments that EW can make seemingly any subject interesting, although at times "we no longer believe him." Unfavorably reviews *Patriotic Gore.*

Hallowell, Robert. "Americanize America!" (in "The Position of the Progressive"), *New Republic,* LXV (4 February 1931), 324-326. A reply to EW's essay "An Appeal to Progressives."

Harari, Manya. "On Translating 'Zhivago' " *Encounter,* XII, No. 5 (May 1959), 51-53. Harari defends her translation of Pasternak's *Doctor Zhivago* in responding to EW's essay "Doctor Life and His Guardian Angel."

Hardman, J. B. S. "Drift or Mastery" (in "The Position of the Progressive"), *New Republic*, LXVI (11 March 1931), 97-99. A reply to EW's essay "An Appeal to Progressives."

Haverstick, John. "The Year's Religious Books: The Battle of the Dead Sea Scrolls," *Saturday Review*, XXXIX, No. 9 (3 March 1956), 28-29. EW in relation to André Dupont-Sommer and the controversy over the Dead Sea scrolls.

" 'Hecate' Conviction Stands as Supreme Court Splits," *Publishers' Weekly*, CLIV (6 November 1948), 1974-1975.

" 'Hecate County' Conviction Upheld in New York Appeal," *Publishers' Weekly*, CLII (22 November 1947), 2414.

" 'Hecate County' Ruled Obscene In 2-1 Decision By New York Court," *Publishers' Weekly*, CL (7 December 1946), 3104.

" 'Hecate' Obscene; Publisher Is Fined: Doubleday & Co. Pays $1,000 in Book Case—Court Splits 2 to 1—Appeal Is Planned," *New York Times*, 28 November 1946, p. 1, col. 7; p. 25, cols. 2-6. Special Sessions Court finds *Memoirs of Hecate County* obscene.

" 'Hecate' Ruling Upheld: Appeals Court Backs $1,000 Fine for Doubleday, Bars Sales," *New York Times*, 14 November 1947, p. 20, col. 6. Appeals Court upholds conviction of Doubleday for publishing *Memoirs of Hecate County*.

" 'Hecate' Sale in Court: Womrath's Held for Trial on a Vice Society Complaint," *New York Times*, 5 December 1946, p. 39, col. 2.

Heilman, Robert B[echtold]. "The Freudian Reading of *The Turn of the Screw*," *Modern Language Notes*, LXII (November 1947), 433-445. Strong disagreement with EW's essay "The Ambiguity of Henry James."

———. " 'The Turn of the Screw' as Poem," *University of Kansas City Review*, XIV (Summer 1948), 277-289. Reprinted as "*The Turn of the Screw* as Poem" in *Forms of Modern Fiction: Essays Collected in Honor of Joseph Warren Beach*, ed. William Van O'Connor (Minneapolis: University of Minnesota Press, 1948), pp. 211-228. Heilman offers his interpretation of Henry James's *The Turn of the Screw* as opposed to EW's ideas stated in his essay "The Ambiguity of Henry James."

Hess, John L. "Moses Denies Bilking Indians; Calls Tuscarora Story 'Fiction,'" *New York Times,* 26 June 1960, p. 76, cols. 2-3. See also Moses, Robert.

Hicks, Granville. "The Failure of Left Criticism," *New Republic,* CIII (9 September 1940), 345-347 (esp. pp. 346-347).

————. "The Intransigence of Edmund Wilson," *Antioch Review,* VI (Winter 1946-1947), 550-562. Discusses EW's political and social views.

'High Court Backs New York Book Ban: State Ruling Is Upheld in Tie Vote on the Obscenity of 'Memoirs of Hecate County,'" *New York Times,* 26 October 1948, p. 33, col. 2. United States Supreme Court upholds ban on *Memoirs of Hecate County.*

"High Court to Judge 'Hecate,'" *New York Times,* 16 March 1948, p. 32, col. 4. United States Supreme Court to review case against Doubleday involving *Memoirs of Hecate County.*

Highet, Gilbert. "The Criticism of Edmund Wilson," in Highet's *People, Places and Books* (New York: Oxford University Press, 1953), pp. 29-36. Partially reprinted without title in Dorothy Nyren's "Wilson, Edmund (1895-   )" in *A Library of Literary Criticism: Modern American Literature,* comp. Nyren (New York: Frederick Ungar Publishing Company, 1960, 1962), p. 541. An appreciative statement of EW's critical attitudes.

Honig, Edwin. "Edmund Wilson's Chronicles," *New Mexico Quarterly,* XXIV (Spring 1954), 99-105. Discusses *Classics and Commercials* and *Shores of Light* with particular attention to style.

Howe, Irving. "Edmund Wilson: A Reexamination," *Nation,* CLXVII (16 October 1948), 430-433. Cites EW's "sense of life" as nullifying the attacks made by Robert M. Adams (*q.v.*), Leslie Fiedler (see review of *Wound and the Bow*), and Stanley Edgar Hyman (*q.v.*).

————. "Edmund Wilson and the Sea Slugs," *Dissent: A Quarterly of Socialist Opinion*, X (Winter 1963), 70-74. Reprinted in Howe's *A World More Attractive: A View of Modern Literature and Politics* (New York: Horizon Press, 1963), pp. 300-307. This purports to be "not a review but a note about" the "Introduction" to *Patriotic Gore*. Howe discusses the idea of the sea slugs and whether EW actually carried through the idea that " 'wars fought by human beings are stimulated as a rule primarily by the same instincts as the voracity of the sea slug.' " Howe feels that this statement means only trivial roles in history for ideology and morality. In Howe's opinion, EW did not carry through this idea, but became "embroiled with the ideological disputes of his protagonists."

Howlett, Duncan. "Faith and History," *Atlantic Monthly*, CXCVII (April 1956), 64-76. A commentary on *Scrolls from the Dead Sea*.

Hunter, Marjorie. "President Names 31 For Freedom Medal," *New York Times*, 5 July 1963, p. 1, col. 1; concluded as "President Picks 31 for Top Medal," p. 10, col. 1. EW receives Presidential Medal of Freedom.

[Hutchens, John K.]. "On an Author," *New York Herald Tribune Book Review*, XXIX, No. 12 (2 November 1952), 2.

Hutchens, John K. "People Who Read and Write," *New York Times Book Review*, 21 April 1946, p. 18. The paragraph beginning "HINTERLAND FLASHES" notes the availability of *Memoirs of Hecate County* in Boston book stores.

————. "People Who Read and Write," *New York Times Book Review*, 21 July 1946, p. 14. Cites claim of a Manila newspaper that a favorable review of *Memoirs of Hecate County* would sell one billion copies in the Orient.

————. "People Who Read and Write," *New York Times Book Review*, 15 September 1946, p. 12. The section entitled "Publishers' Row" notes the removal of *Memoirs of Hecate County* from the New York Public Library.

———. "People Who Read and Write," *New York Times Book Review,* 29 September 1946, p. 37. First two paragraphs cite purchase of *Memoirs of Hecate County* by a San Francisco police officer.

Hutcherson, Dudley D. "Wilson, Edmund," *Collier's Encyclopedia,* 1962, 1963, 1964, 1965, 1966, 1967, 1968, 1969, 1970, XXIII, 506.

Hyman, Stanley Edgar. "Edmund Wilson and Translation in Criticism," in Hyman's *The Armed Vision: A Study in the Methods of Modern Literary Criticism,* in Borzoi Books (New York: Alfred A. Knopf, 1948), pp. 19-48. Treats EW as a "popularizer" of literature. Claims that EW tries to avoid explication of poetry. Believes that EW "specializes in plot-synopsis and summary."

Isaksson, Folke. "Edmund Wilson: Konversation vid Harvard Square" (in Swedish), *Dagens nyheter* (Stockholm), 27 December 1962, p. 4. An appreciative survey of EW's works and significance.

Jerome, V. J. "Edmund Wilson: To the Munich Station," *New Masses,* XXXI (4 April 1939), 23-26. Jerome's "article is in reply to one of Edmund Wilson's *New Republic* essays, which are being collected . . . [and] entitled *To the Finland Station.*"

Johnson, Gerald W. "Who Listened?," *New Republic,* CXLVII, No. 8-9 (27 August 1962), 16. EW's analysis of dissension prior to the War between the States related to problems of the early 1960s.

Jones, Howard Mumford. "The Limits of Contemporary Criticism," *Saturday Review of Literature,* XXIV, No. 20 (6 September 1941), 3-4, 17. American literary criticism, including EW's, is "of the second order of attainment rather than of the first."

Josephson, Matthew. "Essays on Modern Masters," *Saturday Review of Literature,* VII (7 March 1931), 642-643. Partially reprinted without title in Dorothy Nyren's "Wilson, Edmund (1895-)" in *A Library of Literary Criticism: Modern American Literature,* comp. Nyren (New York: Frederick Ungar Publishing Company, 1960, 1962), p. 538. Discusses *Axel's Castle.*

————. "The Road of Indignation" (in "The Position of the Progressive"), *New Republic,* LXVI (18 February 1931), 13-15. A reply to EW's essay "An Appeal to Progressives."

"Joyceiana," *New York Times,* 14 December 1929, p. 20, col. 4. A favorable comment on EW's *New Republic* discussions of James Joyce's works indicating that Joyce was influenced by Lewis Carroll.

Kaufmann, R. J. "The Critic as Custodian of Sanity: Edmund Wilson," *Critical Quarterly,* I, No. 2 (Summer 1959), 85-98. "Edmund Wilson alone has in recent times managed the balanced critical rôle required in America. How he has done this and why, seemingly, he can do so no longer is the subject of this essay."

Kazin, Alfred. "The Critic and the Age," *New Yorker,* XXVIII, No. 39 (15 November 1952), 181-182, 185. Reprinted as "Edmund Wilson: The Critic and the Age" in Kazin's *The Inmost Leaf: A Selection of Essays* (New York: Harcourt, Brace and Company, 1955), pp. 93-97. Discusses *Shores of Light.*

————. "Edmund Wilson: His Life and Books," *Atlantic Monthly,* CCXX, No. 1 (July 1967), 80-83. Discusses *Prelude* as the volume in which "one sees the mighty effort ... [EW] trained himself to, by words."

————. "The Historian as Reporter: Edmund Wilson and the 1930's," *Reporter,* XVIII, No. 6 (20 March 1958), 43-46. Reprinted as "Edmund Wilson on the Thirties" in Kazin's *Contemporaries,* in Atlantic Monthly Press Books (New York: Little, Brown and Company, 1962), pp. 405-411. Partially reprinted without title in Dorothy Nyren's "Wilson, Edmund (1895-)" in *A Library of Literary Criticism: Modern American Literature,* comp. Nyren (New York: Frederick Ungar Publishing Company, 1960,

1962), p. 542. Reviews *American Earthquake* and emphasizes the personal and artistic elements in its composition.

————. "The Imagination of a Man of Letters," *American Scholar*, XXXIV (Winter 1964-1965), 19-27. A discussion of the art of intellectual prose. Discusses EW's independent imagination in comparison with Samuel Johnson and other critics. The article was originally the main address at MacDowell Colony, Peterborough, New Hampshire, 16 August 1964, on the occasion of EW's receiving the Edward MacDowell Medal.

————. "Le Misanthrope," *Partisan Review*, XIII (Summer 1946), 375-380. This purports to be merely a review of *Memoirs of Hecate County*, but is furthermore an attempt to analyze some of the symbolism and social significance of the book.

————. *On Native Grounds: An Interpretation of Modern American Prose Literature* (New York: Reynal and Hitchcock, 1942), pp. 446-452. Discusses EW and Marxist Criticism.

Kempton, Murray. "The Social Muse," in Kempton's *Part of Our Time: Some Ruins and Monuments of the Thirties* (New York: Simon and Schuster, 1955), pp. 110-149. Discusses the affinity of EW and several other writers to the socialist and Communist movements of the early thirties.

Kermode, Frank. "Edmund Wilson and Mario Praz," *Encounter*, XVI, No. 5 (May 1961), 69-73. Reprinted in Kermode's *Puzzles and Epiphanies: Essays and Reviews 1958-1961* (London: Routledge & Kegan Paul; New York: Chilmark Press, 1962), pp. 55-63. Reviews recent editions of *Axel's Castle* in comparison with Praz's *Romantic Agony* as enduring works.

————. "Edmund Wilson's Achievement," *Encounter*, XXVI, No. 5 (May 1966), 61-66, 68, 70. A survey of EW's work, particularly with reference to Sherman Paul's *Edmund Wilson: A Study of Literary Vocation in Our Time.*

Kerr, Walter. "The Little Blue Light," *Commonweal*, LIV (18 May 1951), 141-142. An unfavorable review of *Little Blue Light* as performed on stage.

Kostelanetz, Richard. "The Other Mr. Wilson," *Twentieth Century*, CLXXIV, No. 1028 (Winter 1966), 71-72. Reprinted in revised form as " 'Our Greatest Living Man of Letters' " in *Reporter*, XXXIV, No. 2 (27 January 1966), 53-54. Lauds EW's work, with the exception of "his passion for simplicity."

Krim, Seymour. "A Trademark of Quality," *Hudson Review*, IV (Spring 1951), 150-155. Partially reprinted without title in Dorothy Nyren's "Wilson, Edmund (1895-   )" in *A Library of Literary Criticism: Modern American Literature*, comp. Nyren (New York: Frederick Ungar Publishing Company, 1960, 1962), p. 540. Takes a few jabs at the *New Yorker* and certain critics while praising EW for his ability to appeal to readers who are not necessarily professors of literature. Reviews *Classics and Commercials*.

Kronhausen, Eberhard [Wilhelm], and Phyllis Kronhausen. "Memoirs of Hecate County, by Edmund Wilson," *Pornography and the Law: The Psychology of Erotic Realism and Pornography*, No. S346K in Ballantine Books (New York: Ballantine Books, 1959), pp. 245-249. Argues that *Memoirs of Hecate County* is not obscene.

Krutch, Joseph Wood. "Drama: Two Experiments," *Nation*, CXIX (29 October 1924), 474-475. An unfavorable evaluation of the Freudian overtones of EW's play "The Murder [*sic*, Crime] in the Whistler Room."

———. "Mr. Krutch's Reply," *Forum*, XC (August 1933), 84. A reply to EW's views expressed in the essay "What Is Mr. Krutch Defending?"

"Laureate," *Newsweek*, LXVII (6 June 1966), 103. Commentary on occasion of EW's receiving the National Medal for Literature.

Leavis, F. R. "James's 'What Maisie Knew': A Disagreement," *Scrutiny*, XVII (Summer 1950), 115-127; rejoinder by Leavis in XVII (Autumn 1950), 255. Attacks Marius Bewley's approving use of EW's Freudian view of Henry James's *The Turn of the Screw*. See also Bewley, Marius, in Items about Wilson and in Letters about Wilson.

Lemon, Richard. "The Author," *Saturday Review*, XXXIX, No. 12 (24 March 1956), 17. A brief appraisal of EW as a critic.

Lewis, Anthony. "State's Ban on 'Hecate County' Facing New Test in U.S. Court," *New York Times*, 21 December 1959, p. 29, cols. 6-7. Written in anticipation of legal battles over obscenity in the L. C. Page 1959 New Ed. of *Memoirs of Hecate County*.

Lewis, William J. "Edmund Wilson: A Bibliography," *Bulletin of Bibliography*, XXV (May 1968), 145-149, 151. A nearly complete checklist of EW's books and of his articles listed in *Reader's Guide to Periodical Literature*.

Liddell, Robert. "Apology," in Liddell's *The Novels of Jane Austen* (London: Longman's; New York: Barnes and Noble, 1963), pp. xi-[xiv] (esp. pp. xii-xiii). Attacks EW's conclusions about the composition and Freudian interpretation of Austen's novels.

————. "The 'Hallucination' Theory of *The Turn of the Screw*," in Liddell's *A Treatise on the Novel* (London: Jonathan Cape, 1947), pp. 138-145. An attack on EW's Freudian interpretation of Henry James's *The Turn of the Screw*.

"Literary Broadside against the American Image," *Times* (London), 24 May 1962, p. 13, cols. 4-5. A discussion of U.S. foreign policy and EW's "Introduction" to *Patriotic Gore*.

"Literature: Mr. Wilson's War," *Time: The Weekly Newsmagazine*, XCII, No. 18 (1 November 1968), 73-74. The article is somewhat favorable to the Modern Language Association of America in regard to EW's attacks on the Center for Editions of American Authors.

Littlejohn, David. "To the Wilson Station: Edmund Wilson's Crusade Against Cant," *Commonweal*, LXXVI (7 September 1962), 492-494. A review of EW's work, with special attention to *Patriotic Gore.*

Lydenberg, John. "The Governess Turns the Screws," *Nineteenth Century Fiction*, XII (June 1957), 37-58. Some disagreement with EW's essay "The Ambiguity of Henry James."

Lyons, Eugene. "Reporting Russia: Twenty Years of Books on the Soviet Regime," *Saturday Review of Literature*, XVII, No. 9 (25 December 1937), 3-4, 15-16 (esp. p. 15). An evaluation of *Travels in Two Democracies.*

McCarty, Norma. "Edmund Wilson," *North American Review*, CCXLVI (Autumn 1938), 192-197. Treats *Triple Thinkers: Ten Essays* from the standpoint of EW's development as a critic.

Mangenelli, Giorgio. "La critica di Edmund Wilson" (in Italian), *Studi Americani: Rivista annuale dedicata alle lettere e alle arti negli Stati Uniti d'America*, IV (1958), 363-398. The essay is unexceptional, being a review of EW's rearing, educational and literary influences, publications, and interests. The use by EW of Marxist and Freudian notions is pointed out.

"Many Book Shops Halt Seized Book Sale: All Doubleday Stores Offer 'Memoirs of Hecate County' Despite Vice Society," *New York Times*, 10 July 1946, p. 21, col. 1.

Marks, Emerson R. "Poe as Literary Theorist: A Reappraisal," *American Literature*, XXXIII (November 1961), 296-306. An endorsement of EW's views expressed in the essay "Poe as a Literary Critic."

Marshall, Margaret. "Drama," *Nation*, CLXXII (12 May 1951), 450. An unfavorable review of *Little Blue Light* as performed at the ANTA Playhouse.

Matthiessen, F. O. "A Critic of Importance," *Yale Review*, XX (June 1931), 854-856. Reprinted as "Axel's Castle" in Matthiessen's *The Responsibilities of the Critic: Essays and*

Reviews, comp. John Rackliffe (New York: Oxford University Press, 1952), pp. 159-161. Favorably reviews *Axel's Castle.*

"Medal of Institute for Edmund Wilson," *New York Times,* 24 January 1955, p. 21, col. 4. EW wins National Arts and Letters Institute medal.

Metz, Robert. "Taxes on High Income: Question of Inequity Raised by Those Who Earn Too Much in a Single Year," *New York Times,* 12 November 1963, p. 57, cols. 5-6; continued as "High-Income Tax: An Examination," p. 62, col. 7. EW's income-tax plight and its relationship to tax-reform legislation.

Meyer, Howard N. "Israelites With Egyptian Principles," *Midwest Quarterly,* VI, No. 1 (October 1964), 11-42. This is an attack on *Patriotic Gore.* "Edmund Wilson was not able to transcend the 'spirit of the age' in which he had lived and in which our culture structure was erected." Frequently accuses EW of neglecting or avoiding figures which according to Meyer controvert EW's argument.

Miller, Karl. "Left of the Frontier," *New Statesman: The Week-end Review,* LXIV (2 November 1962), 627-628. Relates the pacifist attitude of *Patriotic Gore* to pacifist sentiment in the United States during the Massachusetts 1962 senatorial campaign.

Miller, Perry. "Essays and Asides: 'A Passion for Literature,'" *Nation,* CLXXII (27 January 1951), 87-88. Partially reprinted without title in Dorothy Nyren's "Wilson, Edmund (1895-   )" in *A Library of Literary Criticism: Modern American Literature,* comp. Nyren (New York: Frederick Ungar Publishing Company, 1960, 1962), p. 540. Reviews *Classics and Commercials.* Cites EW's rationality and emphasizes his "passion for literature."

Millet, Fred B. "Edmund Wilson, 1895-," in Millet's *Contemporary American Authors: A Critical Survey and 219 Bio-Bibliographies* (New York: Harcourt, Brace and Company, 1940), pp. 649-651 (see also pp. 197-198). Succinct statements about EW's critical attitudes and his social and literary milieu. Includes a selected bibliography.

Mizener, Arthur. "Edmund Wilson's New Republic," *New Republic,* CLXII, No. 19 (9 May 1970), 28-30. Observations on EW in the period 1921-1941.

————. "Edmund Wilson: A Checklist," *Princeton University Library Chronicle,* V, No. 2 (February 1944), 62-78. A bibliography almost complete through February 1944.

Montefiore, Hugh. "Mr. Wilson and the Scrolls," *Spectator,* CXCVI (18 May 1956), 681. Hopes that "Wilson, if he writes further on the Dead Sea Scrolls, will himself conform to those canons of sound learning and good judgement which he seems to think unattainable in these matters by those whom he calls 'clergymen scholars.' "

"More Confiscations of 'Memoirs of Hecate County,' " *Publishers' Weekly,* CL (20 July 1946), 287-288.

Moses, Robert, *Tuscarora Fiction and Fact: A Reply to the Author of Memoirs of Hecate County and to His Reviewers* (New York: Robert Moses, Chairman, Power Authority of the State of New York, 20 June 1960). An 8-page pamphlet written in response to *Apologies to the Iroquois.* See also Hess, John L.

"Mr. Nabokov Replies," *Times* (London), 7 February 1966, p. 11, cols. 3-4. Summarizes the contention between EW and Vladimir Nabokov over Nabokov's translation of Pushkin's *Eugene Onegin.*

"Mrs. Edmund Wilson Dies. Wife of Writer Fractured Her Skull in Fall at Santa Barbara, Cal.," *New York Times,* 1 October 1932, p. 15, col. 5. The accident resulting in the death of EW's second wife.

Mugridge, Donald H., Blanche P. McCrum, and Roy P. Basler. *A Guide to the Study of the United States of America: Representative Books Reflecting the Development of American Life and Thought* (Washington: Library of Congress, 1960), pp. 88, 105, 206, 215, 218; or items 1016, 1226, 2443, 2512, 2535-2543.

Nabokov, Vladimir. "Nabokov's Reply," *Encounter,* XXVI, No. 2 (February 1966), 80-90. Nabokov defends his translation of Pushkin's *Eugene Onegin* against EW's review.

Nagy, Péter. "Utószó" (in Hungarian), *Müvészvilág: Drámák,* by EW, trans. Nagy, No. 27 in Modern Könyvtár (Budapest: Európa Könyvkiadó, 1959), pp. [275-277]. An epilogue by the translator.

Nathan, George Jean. "The Little Blue Light," in Nathan's *Theater Book of the Year, 1950-1951: A Record and an Interpretation* (New York: Alfred A. Knopf, 1951), pp. 289-292. Discusses *Little Blue Light.*

"New York: A Pound of Waltzing Mice," *Time: The Weekly Newsmagazine,* XLVIII, No. 24 (9 December 1946), 24-25. A treatment, favorable to EW, of the *Memoirs of Hecate County* scandal through conviction of Doubleday in New York Special Sessions Court.

1916 Parade (Princeton), Formation I (December 1916), through Formation VIII (May 1922), plus 15th Reunion Number (June 1931). Contains scattered references to EW as in "Some of the '16ers at Plattsburg," *1916 Parade,* Formation I (December 1916), pp. 16-17.

Nyren, Dorothy, comp. "Wilson, Edmund (1895-   )," in *A Library of Literary Criticism: Modern American Literature,* comp. Nyren (New York: Frederick Ungar Publishing Company, 1960, 1962), pp. 538-542. Contains partial reprints of the following, *q.v.*:

> Josephson, Matthew. "Essays on Modern Masters"
> Zabel, Morton Dauwen. "The Turn of the Screw"
> Brown, E. K. "The Method of Edmund Wilson"
> Adams, Robert. "Masks and Delays: Edmund Wilson"
> Rolo, Charles J. "Read Any Good Books Lately?"
> Miller, Perry. "Essays and Asides: 'A Passion for Literature' "
> Krim, Seymour. "A Trademark of Quality"
> Cowley, Malcolm. "Edmund Wilson's Specimen Days"
> Phillips, William. "The Wholeness of Literature: Edmund Wilsons' Essays"
> Highet, Gilbert. "The Criticism of Edmund Wilson"
> Spiller, Robert. "The Influence of Edmund Wilson: The Dual Tradition"

Kazin, Alfred. "The Historian as Reporter: Edmund Wilson and the 1930's"

Olson, Elder. "Discussion: Recent Literary Criticism," *Modern Philology,* XL (February 1943), 275-283 (esp. pp. 275-280). Points out similarities between EW and the other essayists represented in *The Intent of the Critic;* EW's essay in this book is "The Historical Interpretation of Literature."

"On an Author." See [Hutchens, John K.].

"Ot redaktsii" (in Russian), *Internatsional'naia literatura,* IX, No. 2 (1936), 153-154. An editorial rejoinder to EW's essay "Letter to the Russians about Hemingway." See also "Letter to the Russians about Hemingway" in Essays; "Pis'mo sovetskim chitateliam o Kheminguee" in Translations of Wilson's Works, Part 3 (Translations of Wilson's Essays), Russian; and "Ot redaktsii" in Translations by Wilson.

Paul, Sherman. *Edmund Wilson: A Study of Literary Vocation in Our Time* (Urbana: University of Illinois Press, 1965).

Signed Reviews

Bottorff, William K. *Library Journal,* XC (1 November 1965), 4783.

Crews, Frederick C. *New York Review of Books,* V, No. 8 (25 November 1965), 4-5.

Green, Martin. *Modern Language Review,* LXIII (January 1968), 233-234.

Hicks, Granville. *Saturday Review,* XLVIII, No. 47 (20 November 1965), 35-36.

Hoffmann, Frederick J. *JEGP: Journal of English and Germanic Philology,* LXV (July 1961), 632-635.

———. *Nation,* CCII (17 January 1966), 74-75.

Jacobson, Dan. *Commentary,* XLI (May 1966), 92, 94-95.

Kermode, Frank. See same author, "Edmund Wilson's Achievement."

Lang, Hans-Joachim. *Erasmus: Speculum Scientiarvm,* XVIII, No. 11-12 (25 June 1966), cols. 361-364.

Lewis, R. W. B. *New York Times Book Review,* 12 December 1965, pp. 1, 43-45.

Lovell, Ernest J., Jr. *New England Quarterly,* XXXIX (September 1966), 424-426.

MacKenzie, Nancy K. *New York Times,* 3 February 1966, p. 29, cols. 5-6.

Poirier, Richard. *Book Week,* III, No. 15 (19 December 1965), 2-3, 11.

Rodway, Allan. *Notes and Queries,* N.S. XIII [continuous ser. CCXI] (December 1966), 480.

Rovit, Earl. *American Scholar,* XXXV (Summer 1966), 550, 552.

Sklar, Robert. *Progressive,* XXX (May 1966), 47-48.

Thorp, Willard. *American Literature,* XXXVIII (November 1966), 419-420.

Unsigned Reviews

Choice, III (March 1966), 34-35.

Christian Century, LXXXII (10 November 1965), 1385.

Times Literary Supplement, 17 February 1966, p. 124.

Virginia Kirkus' Service, Inc., XXXIII (15 August 1965), 878.

Yale Review, LV (March 1966), vi, xii.

―――. *Edmund Wilson: A Study of Literary Vocation in Our Time,* No. IB-45 in Illini Books (Urbana: University of Illinois Press, 1967). Paperback reissue.

Pellegrini, Alessandro. "L'Opera critica di Edmund Wilson" (in Italian), *Osservatore politico letterario,* XI, No. 4 (April 1965), 69-96. Traces the evolution of EW's critical thought from the beginning of his career to 1965 and discusses specific writings about major authors and works. Emphasizes EW's analysis of history, men, and events and his position in the United States contribution to civilization. Seems to regard EW as chief interpreter of the United States national culture.

"People Are Talking About . . . Edmund Wilson," *Vogue,* CXLII (1 September 1963), 199 (portrait, p. 198). A brief appraisal of EW.

Perényi, Eleanor. "Wilson," *Esquire,* LX (July 1963), 80-85. This article contains biographical information not available elsewhere, but perhaps not completely reliable.

"Philadelphia Seizes Book: 'Memoirs of Hecate County' Is Called 'Lewd and Licentious,' " *New York Times,* 11 July 1946, p. 25, col. 7. Philadelphia vice squad seizes 200 copies of *Memoirs of Hecate County.*

Phillips, William. "The Devil Theory of the Dialectic (A Reply to Edmund Wilson)," *Partisan Review,* VI, No. 1 (Fall 1938), 82-90. Replies to EW's essay "The Myth of the Marxist Dialectic."

————. "The Wholeness of Literature: Edmund Wilson's Essays," *American Mercury,* LXXV, No. 347 (November 1952), 103-107. Partially reprinted without title in Dorothy Nyren's "Wilson, Edmund (1895-   )" in *A Library of Literary Criticism: Modern American Literature,* comp. Nyren (New York: Frederick Ungar Publishing Company, 1960, 1962), p. 541. Lauds EW's awareness of the social and intellectual movements which many critics have neglected in an age of specialization.

Pivano, Fernando. "Prefazione" (in Italian), *Gli ultimi fuochi (Last Tycoon),* by F. Scott Fitzgerald, ed. EW, trans. Bruno Oddera (Milano-Verona: A. Mondadori, 1959), pp. 3-23. A summary of Fitzgerald's life followed by an analysis of this novel edited by EW.

Podhoretz, Norman. "Edmund Wilson, The Last Patrician," *Reporter,* XIX, No. 11 (25 December 1958), 25-28; XX, No. 1 (8 January 1959), 32-35. Reprinted as "The Last Patrician" in Podhoretz's *Doings and Undoings: The Fifties and After in American Writing* (New York: Farrar, Straus & Company, 1964), pp. 30-50. Traces EW's development to 1958, particularly in relation to his attitudes toward Marxism and Americanism.

————. "Edmund Wilson: Then and Now," in Podhoretz's *Doings and Undoings: The Fifties and After in American Writing* (New York: Farrar, Straus & Company, 1964), pp. 30-58.

Contents
    I. "The Last Patrician"
    II. "Mr. Wilson and the Kingdom of Heaven"

―――. "Mr. Wilson and the Kingdom of Heaven," *Show: The Magazine of the Arts*, II, No. 2 (June 1962), 102-104. Reprinted in Podhoretz's *Doings and Undoings: The Fifties and After in American Writing* (New York: Farrar, Straus & Company, 1964), pp. 50-58. Discusses *Patriotic Gore*.

"Police Here Seize Book as Obscene: 4 Doubleday Shops Entered in Vice Society's Action Against 'Memoirs of Hecate County,'" *New York Times*, 9 July 1946, p. 19, col. 5.

Pritchard, John Paul. "Edmund Wilson," in Pritchard's *Criticism in America: An Account of the Development of Critical Techniques from the Early Period of the Republic to the Middle Years of the Twentieth Century* (Norman: University of Oklahoma Press, 1956), pp. 269-276. EW in his critical milieu.

―――. *Literary Wise Men of Gotham: Criticism in New York, 1815-1860* (Baton Rouge: Louisiana State University Press, 1963), pp. 3, 12, 159. The book is based on EW's remark in the essay "Van Wyck Brooks on the Civil War Period" to the effect "that the New York writers of the nineteenth century were more representatively American than their New England contemporaries."

Pritchett, V. S. "A Commitment to Letters and Life" (printed with a photograph of EW), *New York Times Book Review*, 2 October 1966, p. 1; concluded as "To Letters and Life," *New York Times Book Review*, 2 October 1966, p. 36. Reprinted without photograph of EW as "Finding affluence in a second visit" in *Books Today*, 2 (Sunday) October 1966, [Section 9 in *Chicago Tribune*], p. 5. A discussion of *Europe Without Baedeker*, 1st rev. ed.

Professional Standards and American Editions: A Response to Edmund Wilson (New York: Modern Language Association of America, 1969).

Contents
    Gibson, William M. "The Center for Editions of American Authors"

Letters to *New York Review of Books* from Ronald Gottesman, Paul Baender, Frederick Anderson, and Oscar Cargill

A letter to EW from John C. Gerber

Fisher, John H. "The MLA Editions of Major American Authors"

Rahv, Philip. "The Turn of the Screw," in *The Great Short Novels of Henry James,* ed. Rahv, in Permanent Library (New York: Dial Press, 1944), pp. 623-625 (esp. 624-625). Cites EW's interpretation of the ghosts in *The Turn of the Screw* as "a fallacy of rationalism."

Rascoe, Burton. "Sunday, October 14," (in Rascoe's "Bookman's Day Book"), *New York Tribune Magazine and Books,* 21 October 1923, p. 26. The third paragraph describes a visit which Rascoe made to EW on 14 October 1923. EW recounts the incident in the first paragraphs of the essay "Emergence of Ernest Hemingway."

Robinson, Donald. "Edmund Wilson," in Robinson's *The 100 Most Important People in the World Today* (New York: G. P. Putnam's Sons; Toronto: Longmans Canada, 1970), pp. 323-325. Biography.

Rolo, Charles J. "Read Any Good Books Lately?," *Atlantic Monthly,* CLXXXVI, No. 5 (November 1950), 98. Partially reprinted without title in Dorothy Nyren's "Wilson, Edmund (1895-   )" in *A Library of Literary Criticism: Modern American Literature,* comp. Nyren (New York: Frederick Ungar Publishing Company, 1960, 1962), p. 540. Discusses *Classics and Commercials;* the general excellence of the volume "outweighs Wilson's crotchets."

Rosenzweig, Saul. See Trilling, Lionel.

Rubin, Louis D., Jr. "Edmund Wilson and the Despot's Heel," *Sewanee Review,* LXXI (Winter 1963), 109-115. Reprinted in Rubin's *The Curious Death of the Novel: Essays in American Literature* (Baton Rouge: Louisiana State University, 1967), pp. 120-127. Finds *Patriotic Gore* to be entertaining and educational. Disagrees with EW's attitude toward economic forces in the Civil War.

[Ruffini, Nina]. "Nota" (in Italian), *Ivan Turgheniev* (originally the essay "Turgenev and the Life-Giving Drop"), by

EW, trans. Ruffini, No. 68 in Biblioteca delle Silerchie (Milano: Il saggiatore [E. Milli], agosto 1961), pp. 7-10. An introduction to EW's essay "Turgenev and the Life-Giving Drop."

"San Francisco Jury Absolves 'Hecate,'" *New York Times,* 12 December 1946, p. 27, col. 6.

Schorer, Mark. "Foreword," *Spokesmen,* by T. K. Whipple (Berkeley: University of California Press, 1963), pp. v-xii. Compares Thomas King Whipple and EW.

Schwartz, Delmore. "The Writing of Edmund Wilson," *Accent,* II (Spring 1942), 177-186. Reprinted as "Criticism of Edmund Wilson" in *Accent Anthology: Selections from Accent, A Quarterly of New Literature, 1940-1945,* ed. Kerker Quinn and Charles Shattuck (New York: Harcourt, Brace and Company, 1946), pp. 641-655. A survey of EW's criticism from 1929 to 1942.

Scott, W. T. "The Literary Summing-Up: A Personal Winnowing of 1950's Books," *Saturday Review of Literature,* XXXIII, No. 52 (30 December 1950), 6-8, 28-29 (esp. pp. 7, 28). *Classics and Commercials* placed among the most important books of 1950.

Segal, David I. "Nerve of Edmund Wilson," *Commonweal,* LXXXVII (27 October 1967), 117-118, 120. Claims that *Prelude* is of too low quality to merit publication. Includes a review of *I Thought of Daisy* (pp. 118, 120).

Seldes, Gilbert. "The Artist at Home," *New Republic,* XLII (20 May 1925), 341. Raises objection to EW's attitude toward exile of the artist from his national culture as expressed in the essay "The Pilgrimage of Henry James."

Sheed, Wilfrid. "Mr. Wilson and the Cold War," *Commonweal,* LXXIX (10 January 1964), 434-435. Disagrees with EW's opinions on taxation as stated in *Cold War and the Income Tax.*

"600 Hear Edmund Wilson Read His 'Somewhat Fanciful' Poems," *New York Times,* 1 February 1966, p. 27, cols. 5-6. EW reads to a gathering at the Poetry Center of the

Young Men's and Young Women's Hebrew Association in New York, 31 January 1966.

[Slater, Michael]. "Announcement," *Dickensian*, LXV (January 1969), 11. A comment on EW in relation to the cover of *Dickensian*.

Snell, George. "Edmund Wilson: The Historical Critic" (Section 2 in "An Examination of Modern Critics") *Rocky Mountain Review*, VIII, No. 2 (Winter 1944), 36-44. A survey of EW's criticism with emphasis on his objectivity, though "Wilson seems to have some affinities" with Van Wyck Brooks.

Soby, James Thrall. "Writer vs. Artist," *Saturday Review of Literature*, XXIX, No. 33 (17 August 1946), 24-26.

Spiller, Robert E. "The Influence of Edmund Wilson: The Dual Tradition," *Nation*, CLXXXVI (22 February 1958), 159-161. Reprinted as "Edmund Wilson: The Dual Role of Criticism" in Spiller's *Oblique Light* (New York: Macmillan, 1968), pp. 215-220. Partially reprinted without title in Dorothy Nyren's "Wilson, Edmund (1895-   )" in *A Library of Literary Criticism: Modern American Literature*, comp. Nyren (New York: Frederick Ungar Publishing Company, 1960, 1962), p. 542. Sketches "in the outlines of the modern movement in American literary criticism." Discusses EW's contribution to socio-historical critcism as contrasted to esthetic criticism.

Steffens, Lincoln. "Bankrupt Liberalism," *New Republic*, LXX (17 February 1932), 15-16. A reply to EW's essay "What Do the Liberals Hope For?"

Stoll, Elmer Edgar. "Psychoanalysis in Criticism: Dickens, Kipling, Joyce," in Stoll's *From Shakespeare to Joyce: Authors and Critics; Literature and Life* (Garden City, New York: Frederick Ungar Company, 1965), pp. 339-388. Disapprovingly discusses EW's Freudian criticism with particular reference to *Wound and the Bow*.

"Sumner Charges 'Memoirs of Hecate County' Is Obscene," *Publishers' Weekly*, CL (13 July 1946), 179-180. Initial seizure of *Memoirs of Hecate County* described.

Tate, Allen. "Edmund Wilson," *We Moderns: Gotham Book Mart, 1920-1940* (paperback), Gotham Book Mart Catalog No. 42, comp. Frances Steloff and Kay Steele (New York: Gotham Book Mart, [1939]), p. 71. EW's contribution to public esteem of modern writers.

————. "Three Types of Poetry: II," *New Republic*, LXXVIII (28 March 1934), 180-182. Disagrees with certain aspects of *Axel's Castle*, "a book written on the assumption that all poetry is only an inferior kind of social will."

"33 Receive Highest Award in U.S. Honours List," *Times* (London), 7 December 1963, p. 8, cols. 4-5. EW and 32 others receive National Medal of Freedom.

"To Coin a Phrase," *Newsweek*, LXI, No. 8 (25 February 1963), 88. A commentary on EW's essay "A Postscript to Fowler: Current Clichés and Solecisms."

"To Rule on Wilson's Book: Court Hears Parts of 'Hecate County,' Will Read It All," *New York Times*, 30 October 1946, p. 24, col. 6. New York Special Sessions Court promises to make known decision concerning *Memoirs of Hecate County* on 27 November 1946. Lionel Trilling testifies in favor of the book.

"Topics of the Times," *New York Times*, 17 April 1936, p. 20, col. 4. Believes that EW's essay "Scarlet Fever in Odessa" attempts to praise Russian Communism without objectivity.

Trilling, Lionel. "A Note on Art and Neurosis," *Partisan Review*, XII (Winter 1945), 41-48. Disagrees with the theory of artistic creation developed by EW in *Wound and the Bow* and cited by Saul Rosenzweig in "The Ghost of Henry James," *Partisan Review*, XI (Fall 1944), 436-455.

"Trotsky Data Asked of Nuremburg Tribunal; Check-Up on Moscow Is Sought in Nazi Files," *New York Times*, 27 March 1946, p. 12, cols. 5-6. EW signs petition asking use of Nazi files to disprove that Trotsky conspired with Adolf Hitler.

Turnell, Martin. "Flaubert," *Scrutiny*, XIII (Autumn-Winter 1945), 200-218; (Spring 1946), 272-291. Views opposed to those of EW in the essay "Flaubert's Politics."

"U.S. Supreme Court to Hear 'Hecate' Appeal October 20 or 21," *Publishers' Weekly*, CLIV (16 October 1948), 1751.

"U.S. Supreme Court Will Hear 'Hecate County' Appeal," *Publishers' Weekly*, CLIII (27 March 1948), 1457-1458.

"Utószó" (in Hungarian), *Az élet jelei tanulmányok cikkek* (paperback), by EW, trans. Szilágyi Tibor and Zubreczky György, No. 167 in Modern Könyvtár (Budapest: Európa Könyvkiadó [Debrecen: Alfoldi Nyomda], [1969]), pp. 309-312. A survey of EW's life and work.

Wagenknecht, Edward [Charles]. "Edmund Wilson on Dickens," in Wagenknecht's *Dickens and the Scandalmongers: Essays in Criticism* (Norman: University of Oklahoma Press, 1965), pp. 114-120. This is an amplification of ideas which Wagenknecht had stated in "Dickens and the Scandalmongers," *College English*, XI (April 1950), 373-382. Wagenknecht attacks the biographical and Freudian arguments in EW's long essay "Dickens: The Two Scrooges."

Wain, John. "Edmund Wilson: The Critic as Novelist," *New Republic*, CXLII, No. 3 (18 January 1960), 15-17. Partially reprinted as "Edmund Wilson" in Wain's *Essays on Literature and Ideas* (London: Macmillan and Company; New York: St. Martin's Press, 1963), pp. 141-145. Explains EW's uniqueness as a critic on the basis of his love of reading.

————. "Literature and Life—6: Edmund Wilson Eludes the Interviewer," *Observer*, 3 (Sunday) November 1957, p. 3, cols. 1-8. Wain finds EW's concreteness a barrier in trying to extract from EW some general ideas about literature.

Waldock, A. J. A. "Mr. Edmund Wilson and *The Turn of the Screw*," *Modern Language Notes*, LXII (May 1947), 331-334. Reprinted as "Mr. Wilson and *The Turn of the Screw*" in *A Casebook on Henry James's "The Turn of the*

Screw," ed. Gerald Willen, in Crowell Literary Casebooks, ser. ed. William Van O'Connor (New York: Thomas Y. Crowell Company, 1959, 1960), pp. 171-173. Contends that details in *The Turn of the Screw* negate EW's views in "The Ambiguity of Henry James."

"War Among the Literati," *New York Times,* 30 April 1932, p. 14, col. 5. Treats the reaction to EW's essay "The Economic Interpretation of Wilder."

"War and the New Generation," *New Republic,* CIII (1 July 1940), 7-8. A reply to EW's essay "Archibald Macleish and 'the Word.' "

Wasserstrom, William. *The Time of the Dial* (Syracuse, New York: Syracuse University Press, 1963), pp. 29, 65, 83, 89, 96-97, 104-105, 108, 112, 141-142, 164n, 169n, 173n, 177n-178n.

West, Anthony. "Literary Letter from America: The Last Puritan: Edmund Wilson versus T. S. Eliot," *Sunday Times* (London), No. 7055 (3 August 1958), p. 7, cols. 4-6. Some slightly disapproving insights into EW's essay " 'Miss Buttle and Mr. Eliot.' "

"What We Hope For," *New Republic,* LXIX (10 February 1932), 336-337. A defense of certain *New Republic* positions with respect to EW's essay "What Do the Liberals Hope For?"

Whitman, Alden. "Edmund Wilson Criticizes War As He Accepts the Aspen Prize," *New York Times,* 13 June 1968, p. 44, cols. 1-2. EW receives the $30,000 Aspen Award for contributions to American culture.

Wicklein, John. "Scrolls Doubted as Link to Jesus: Biblical Scholar Says They Represent Exaggeration," *New York Times,* 31 December 1961, p. 17, cols. 1-5. Professor Samuel Sandmel sees no evidence linking Christianity to Dead Sea scrolls and holds EW's *Scrolls from the Dead Sea* responsible for deluding the public. EW's response via telephone is quoted.

Willingham, John. "Wilson, Edmund," *Collier's Encyclopedia,* 1971, volume and pagination uncertain.

Wilson, T[ed] C. "The Muse and Edmund Wilson," *Poetry*, LII (June 1938), 144-152. A highly unfavorable review-essay on *Triple Thinkers: Ten Essays*.

"Wilson, Edmund," *Current Biography*, VI (April 1945), 59-62. Reprinted in *Current Biography Yearbook: Who's News and Why, 1945*, Annual Cumulation, ed. Anna Rothe and Helen Demarest (New York: H. W. Wilson Company, 1946), pp. 684-687. Reprinted in revised form in *Current Biography*, XXV (January 1964), 45-48. Revised form reprinted in *Current Biography Yearbook 1964*, 25th Annual Cumulation, ed. Charles Moritz (New York: H. W. Wilson Company, 1965), pp. 464-466.

"Wilson, Edmund," *The Encyclopedia Americana*, 1957, XXIX, 357; revised in 1960, XXIX, 357; 2nd revision in 1962, 1968, XXIX, 2.

"Wilson, Edmund," *The International Who's Who* (London: Europa Publications, [EW is listed in 1st ed. {1935} through 34th ed. {1970-71}]).

"Wilson, Edmund," *Merit Students Encyclopedia*, 1967, 1968, 1969, 1970, XIX, 481.

"Wilson, Edmund," *The Standard International Encyclopedia* (New York: Standard International Library), 1953, 1955, 1957, XX, 5525-5526.

"Wilson, Edmund," *Twentieth Century Authors: A Biographical Dictionary of Modern Literature*, ed. Stanley J. Kunitz and Howard Haycraft (New York: H. W. Wilson Company, 1942), pp. 1529-1530. Reprinted in revised form in *Twentieth Century Authors, First Supplement: A Biographical Dictionary of Modern Literature*, ed. Stanley J. Kunitz and Vineta Colby (New York: H. W. Wilson Company, 1955), pp. 1095-1096. Biography and bibliography.

"Wilson, Edmund," *Who's Who: An Annual Biographical Dictionary* (London: Adam and Charles Black, annually; New York: Macmillan Company, eds. before 1962; New York: St. Martin's Press, 1962 to present, [EW is listed in 99th Year {1947} through 121st Annual Ed. {1969-1970}]).

"Wilson, Edmund," *Who's Who in America: A Biographical Dictionary of Notable Living Men and Women of the United States* (Chicago: A. N. Marquis Company, [EW is listed in Vol. XVII {1932-1933} through Vol. XXXVI {1970-1971}]).

"Wilson, Edmund," *Who's Who in the East [and Eastern Canada]* (Chicago: Marquis—Who's Who, [EW is listed in 10th ed. {1966-1967} and 11th ed. {1968-1969}]).

"Wilson, Edmund 1895-," *Contemporary Authors*, III (1963), 222-223. Reprinted in revised form with much additional material in *Contemporary Authors*, ed. James M. Ethridge and Barbara Kopala, Vols. I-IV (Detroit: Gale Research Company, 1967), pp. 1011-1013; and 200 *Contemporary Authors*, ed. Barbara Harte and Carolyn Riley (Detroit: Gale Research Company, 1969), pp. 303-305.

"Wilson, Edmund (1895-   )," *The New Funk & Wagnalls Encyclopedia* (New York: Unicorn Publishers), 1950, 1951, 1952, 1954, XXXVI, 13,205-13,206. Reprinted in revised form in *Funk & Wagnalls Standard Reference Encyclopedia*, 1969, XXV, 9223.

"Wilson Gets Harvard Post," *New York Times*, 29 April 1959, p. 25, col. 5. EW named Abbott Lawrence Lowell Professor of English for academic year effective 1 July 1959.

"Womrath 'Hecate County' Case To Be Heard December 4," *Publishers' Weekly*, CL (9 November 1946), 2726.

"Womrath Reports Prize-Winners in 'Hecate County' Contest," *Publishers' Weekly*, CL (7 December 1946), 3106.

"Womrath's Fined $500: Concern Pleaded Guilty in Sale of 'Memoirs of Hecate County,'" *New York Times*, 26 November 1947, p. 21, col. 6. Special Sessions Court fines Womrath's Book Shops $500 for selling *Memoirs of Hecate County*.

"Womrath's Guilty: To Be Sentenced Next Tuesday for Selling Banned Book," *New York Times*, 19 November 1947, p. 24, col. 6. Womrath's Book Shops pleads guilty to selling *Memoirs of Hecate County*.

"You Meet Such Interesting People," *Publishers' Weekly,* CXLIV (4 December 1943), 2102. EW appointed book reviewer for *New Yorker.*

Young, Stark. "Dear Mr. Wilson," *New Republic,* XCI (9 June 1937, 130-131. Young writes in appreciation of EW's essay "Mr. More and the Mithraic Bull" and recites some memories of Paul Elmer More.

Zabel, Morton Dauwen. "The Turn of the Screw," *Nation,* CLIII (11 October 1941), 348-350. Partially reprinted without title in Dorothy Nyren's "Wilson, Edmund (1895-   )" in *A Library of Literary Criticism: Modern American Literature,* comp. Nyren (New York: Frederick Ungar Publishing Company, 1960, 1962), p. 539. Discusses *Wound and the Bow.*

Zolla, Elémire. "Prefazione" (in Italian), *L'età del Jazz e altri scritti* (originally *Crack-Up*), by Francis Scott Fitzgerald *et al.,* ed. EW, trans. Domenico Tarizzo, No. 29 in La cultura: Storia, critica, testi (Milano: Il Saggiatore [Verona: A. Mondadori], 1960), pp. ix-xvi; reprinted as No. 46 in I Gabbiani (Milano: Il Saggiatore [Verona: A. Mondadori], 1966), pp. ix-xvi. Tells how closely one's impression of *Crack-Up* parallels the truth about Fitzgerald's life.

XII / THESES AND DISSERTATIONS

Dabney, Lewis Meriwhether, III. "Edmund Wilson: The Early Years." Ph.D. dissertation, Columbia University, 1965. Abstracted in *Dissertation Abstracts,* XXVIII (June 1968), 5048A-5049A. An intellectual biography of EW through the publication of *Axel's Castle* in 1930.

Fraiberg, Louis Benjamin. "The Use of Psychoanalytic Ideas by Literary Critics." Ph.D. dissertation, University of Michigan (Ann Arbor), 1957. Abstracted in *Dissertation Abstracts,* XVII (June 1957), 1336-1337. Published as *Psychoanalysis & American Literary Criticism.* See same author in Items about Wilson.

Frank, Charles Paul. "The Fiction of Edmund Wilson." Ph.D. dissertation, The University of Michigan, 1964. Abstracted in *Dissertation Abstracts,* XXV (December 1964), 3569. Uses EW's stated and implied critical standards as an approach to his fiction. See also Frank, Charles P[aul] in Items about Wilson.

Goldhurst, William. "Scott Fitzgerald and His Contemporaries." Ph.D. thesis, Tulane University of Louisiana, 1962. Abstracted in *Dissertation Abstracts,* XIII (January 1963), 2525-2526. Published as *F. Scott Fitzgerald and His Contemporaries.* See also Goldhurst, William, in Items about Wilson.

Kluge, Paul Frederick, "Wanderers: Three American Writers of the Twenties." Ph.D. thesis, The University of Chicago, June 1967. A treatment of the work of Carl Van Vechten, Harold Edmund Stearns, and EW during the 1920s.

Kriegel, Leonard. "The Politics of Edmund Wilson." Ph.D. dissertation, New York University, 1960. Abstracted in *Dissertation Abstracts*, XXI (1961), 2296.

Rodgers, Jane Morris. "Dynamics of Creation: The Literary Criticism of Edmund Wilson." Ph.D. dissertation, The University of Rochester, 1967. Abstracted in *Dissertation Abstracts*, XXVIII (November 1967), 1826A-1827A. Emphasizes EW's interest in the personality of the artist as the key to a literary work and relates EW to the *philosophes* of the eighteenth century; *Patriotic Gore* is the culminating achievement of EW's criticism.

Rosenthal, Melvyn. "The American Writer and His Society: The Response to Estrangement in the Works of Nathaniel Hawthorne, Randolph Bourne, Edmund Wilson, Norman Mailer, Saul Bellow." Ph.D. dissertation, University of Connecticut, 1968. Abstracted in *Dissertation Abstracts*, XXIX (March 1969), 3018A. The increasing sense of estrangement from society in five American authors.

Schlesinger, Lorraine Anne. "Edmund Wilson on American Literature." Ph.D. dissertation, University of Maryland, 1968. Abstracted in *Dissertation Abstracts*, XXIX (December 1968), 1878A-1879A. An analysis of EW's attitudes toward various types of American authors.